A SHORT HISTORY OF
ENGLISH POETRY

A Short History of English Poetry

G. S. Fraser

Open Books

First published in 1981 by Open Books Publishing Ltd
West Compton House, Near Shepton Mallet, Somerset, England.

© Mrs Paddy Fraser 1981

Hardback ISBN: 0 7291 0077 4
Paperback ISBN: 0 7291 0072 3

821·009
FRA

Text set in 11/12 pt Linotron 202 Times, printed and bound
in Great Britain at The Pitman Press, Bath

Contents

Publishers' Note

G. S. Fraser died during the final stages of the completion of this book. The Publishers are extremely grateful for the help of the following in the preparation of the manuscript:
Mrs Paddy Fraser, Michael Alexander, Professor Bernard Bergonzi, Dennis Burden, Professor Philip Collins, Professor Ian Fletcher, Professor S. S. Hussey, Professor John Lucas, Harry Ricketts and Professor J. P. W. Rogers.

Acknowledgements

The publishers gratefully acknowledge permission to reprint copyright material to the following:

For 'This Lunar Beauty' and 'In Memory of W. B. Yeats' by W. H. Auden (from *Collected Poems*), Faber & Faber Ltd. and Random House Inc., for lines from *Briggflats* by Basil Bunting (from Basil Bunting's *Collected Poems*, © Basil Bunting 1978), Oxford University Press; for lines from 'Tristan du Cunha' by Roy Campbell, Curtis Brown Ltd on behalf of the Roy Campbell Estate; for lines from 'Vergiss-meinicht' by Keith Douglas (from *The Complete Poems of Keith Douglas* edited by Desmond Graham, © Oxford University Press 1978), Oxford University Press; for 'Not Wrongly Moved' by William Empson (from *Collected Poems*), the author and Chatto and Windus Ltd., for 'And they were Richt' by Robert Garioch, the author and Southside (Publishers) Ltd; for 'The Survivor' and lines from 'Full Moon' By Robert Graves, the author and A. P. Watt & Son; for 'The Feel of Hands', © 1961, 1971 and 1973 by Thom Gunn (from *My Sad Captains*), Faber & Faber Ltd and Farrar, Straus & Giroux Inc., for 'Requiem for Croppies' by Seamus Heaney (from *Door into the Dark*), Faber & Faber Ltd; for 'In Memory of Jane Fraser' by Geoffrey Hill, Andre Deutsch Ltd; for 'Snowdrop' by Ted Hughes (from *Lupercal*), Faber & Faber Ltd and Harper & Row Inc; for 'Ecce Puer' by James Joyce, the Society of Authors as the literary representatives of the Estate of James Joyce and the Viking Press Inc.; for 'Byre' by Norman MacCaig (from *A Round of Applause*), the author and The Hogarth Press Ltd; for lines from 'Autumn Journal' by Louis MacNeice (from *The Collected Poems of Louis MacNeice*), Faber & Faber Ltd, for 'Scotland's Winter' by Edwin Muir (from *The Collected Poems of Edwin Muir*), Faber & Faber Ltd and Oxford University Press Inc; for 'In The Beck' by Kathleen Raine, George Allen & Unwin Ltd; for 'Talking to Himself' and 'Ecclesiastical Polity' by I. A. Richards (from *New and Selected Poems*), Carcanet Press Ltd; for 'The Dug-out' by Seigfried Sassoon, George Sassoon; for lines from 'My Life and Times' by C. H. Sisson (from *In the Trojan Ditch*) Carcanet Press Ltd; for 'Was he married' and 'Not Waving but Drowning' by Stevie Smith (from *The Collected Poems by Stevie Smith*), James MacGibbon and Allen Lane; for lines from 'Two Armies' by Stephen Spender (from *Collected Poems*), Faber & Faber Ltd and Random House Inc; for lines from 'Before I Knocked' by Dylan Thomas (from *Collected Poems 1934–1952*), The Trustees for the Copyrights of the late Dylan Thomas and New Directions Publishing Corp.; for 'Out In The Dark' by Edward Thomas (from *Collected Poems*), Mrs Myfanwy Thomas and Faber & Faber Ltd; for 'They', 'Looking At Sheep' and 'The Welsh Hill Country' by R. S. Thomas from *Selected Poems 1946–1968*, Granada Publishing Ltd; for 'Paring the Apple' by Charles Tomlinson, Oxford University Press; for 'A True Picture Restored' and 'Wordsworth' by Vernon Watkins, G. M. Watkins and Enitharmion Press; for lines from 'Since Our Concern', 'Adam's Curse' and 'meditations in time of Civil War' (from *Collected Poems*), M. B. Yeats, Anne Yeats and Macmillan London Ltd and Macmillan Publishing Inc.

1

Old English Poetry

I Epic Poetry

English is not of course the only language in which poetry
has been written or orally composed in Great Britain and
Ireland, nor is it the earliest. The Irish, for instance, were
composing epic stories dealing with a past several centuries
remote from them in the first century A.D. There was a
class of Irish learned men, the *file*, who made it their task in
life to preserve ancient stories; the most distinguished kind
of *file*, the *ollamh*, was master of 250 major narratives and
100 minor ones. Ireland also developed very early lyrical
nature poems of great beauty. The Welsh also developed
heroic poems early, of which one of the most striking is the
sixth century Aneirin's *Y Gododdin*, about a Welsh expedition from Edinburgh to Catterick to do battle with the
Saxons. The Welsh are defeated. There is another celebration of heroic defeat in the much later Old English *Battle of
Maldon* (which can be dated by the battle itself, recorded in
the Anglo-Saxon Chronicle as taking place in 991 A.D.) it is
the good, the English defending themselves against Viking
raiders, who are defeated.

The whole period of European history between the fall of
the Western Roman Empire and the beginnings of medieval
civilization is sometimes called the age of migrations or
folk-wanderings, sometimes the heroic age. It has, among
the Germanic peoples, of whom we are one, two main
characteristics: a loyalty of the retainer to his lord, which
outweighs loyalty to kindred, to what we would call country
(the loyalty was rather to the King's great hall, like Hroth-

1

gar's Heorot in *Beowulf*, and to the gifts and feasts with which it was associated); and a stoical acceptance of final defeat and death, as the lot of all men. The Old English poetry that survives is (except, sometimes, in matters like the blood feud) Christian in spirit. But it is nevertheless profoundly melancholy, and that note of melancholy, but with defiant bravery, has been a feature of English poetry ever since.

From Michael Alexander's splendid translation of *The Battle of Maldon*, I quote two short passages. One expresses that desire to avenge blood with blood which Christianity, at that early stage, was unable to eradicate:

> 'A man cannot linger when his lord lies
> unavenged among Vikings, cannot value breath'.

The second passage, adapted effectively by Auden in one of the odes at the end of his early work, *The Orators*, expresses the spirit of stoicism I have spoken of and also the passionate devotion of the retainer to his lord:

> 'Courage shall grow keener, clearer the will,
> the heart fiercer, as our force faileth.
> Here our lord lies levelled in the dust,
> the man all marred: he shall mourn to the end
> who thinks to wend off from this war-play now.
> Though I am white with winters I shall not away,
> for I think to lodge me alongside my dear one,
> lay me down by my lord's right hand.'

Alfred the Great, King of Wessex 871–99, called the language in which he wrote *Englisc* and the country which he was striving to unite *Englaland*, or the land of the Angles. The term *lingua Saxonica* was also used and the language of our oldest poetry is sometimes called Old English, sometimes Anglo-Saxon. I prefer the first term, because it emphasises continuity. For instance, the metre of Michael Alexander's rendering is likely to strike most readers as easy and pleasant to read but not the metre they are most accustomed to, the metre of the five-foot stress syllable line, say, of one of Shakespeare's most famous sonnets:

> Shall Í/compare/thee tó/a súm/mer's dáy?
> Thou art/more love/ly and/more temp/erate

These lines have five two-syllable feet each, of which the second syllable has a stronger stress than the first. An Old English line has four main stresses, and a necessary very sharp division in the middle (it consists, that is, of two two-stress half-lines). The half-lines are linked by alliteration. Either one or both of the syllables in the first half-line that have the strongest sense-stress must alliterate with the first (but *never* with the second) syllable of main stress in the second half-line: to illustrate:

> Coúrage shall grow kéener : cleárer the will . . .
>
> Lay me down by my : lord's right hand . . .

This seems alien to our own way of writing verse (though a number of modern poets, like Auden in *The Age of Anxiety*, have attempted to revive stress metre; and Eliot uses isolated half-lines very beautifully in *Ash Wednesday*) and yet it can still be felt to underlie the stress-syllable foot measure which we borrowed from the Italians and French. Thus, if I read aloud the two famous lines of Shakespeare's I have quoted, nobody will feel anything odd about it:

> Shall I compáre thée: to a súmmer's dáy?
> Thou art móre lóve: ly and móre témperate

People may feel, even, that this reading is nearer to what one might call the rhythm of the sense. Certainly, when Shakespeare is well acted on the stage we tend, at least with our conscious ears, to be aware of four strong sense-stresses rather than five metrical stresses of varying strength: not

> I cóme/ to búr/ y Caés/ ar, nót to praíse (him)

but

> I come to búry Cáesar: nót to práise him

It is perhaps the play of the Old English stress-metre, so close to the natural rhythm of our speech, against the exquisite but artificial patterning of the stress-syllable foot metre (natural to Romance languages, like Italian, one of Chaucer's sources for perfecting it in English) that gives

English verse at its best its peculiar combination of grace and strength, harsh impact and supple, sweet or smooth flexibility. There is, certainly, a surprising sense in which, unless we are familiar with Old English alliterative stress verse and its survival into the later Middle Ages (into Langland's *Piers Plowman*, for instance), we cannot appreciate fully verse divided into metrical feet. (Michael Alexander points out, what is not always noticed, that the stress pattern in Old English verse is much more important for the total effect than for the alliteration.)

Old English was the language of the Germanic peoples of this island for about 700 years. They came originally in small groups, independently, settling here and there where the ground was convenient, often in fertile river valleys, and only began to establish themselves into kingdoms and to drive the Welsh to the west after defeating them at the great battle of *Mons Badonicus* (c. 500) (the Romano-British leader may have been one of the sources of King Arthur). They were West Germans, to be distinguished both from the fierce Vikings of the North and the East Germans who turned their ambitions towards Italy, Spain, France, and North Africa. Though the different groups of these invading Germans (Angles, Saxons and Jutes) differed in dialects and customs, they understood each other as well as Yorkshiremen and Londoners do today.

One king sent home a Frankish bishop because he found it tiresome to converse with him in his Frankish dialect (a variant of German, not an ancestral form of modern French) but at least they could understand each other. After Alfred the dialect of the West Saxons became the one accepted for literary purposes, just as Tuscan is accepted in Italy, Castilian in Spain, or the dialect of educated people in London and the home counties today.

The treasures of the Sutton Hoo burial ship show that even the comparatively obscure kingdom of East Anglia had a rich trade with continental Europe, a splendid tradition of craftsmanship, and carried into the mid-seventh century the heathen custom of the burial of a king in a treasure ship with his riches around him, which is also described at the beginning of *Beowulf*. There survives, however, no mention of human or animal sacrifices.

The old pagan religion of the north lingered on quite long in England but in a manner at once unconfident and tolerant.

There were no Christian martyrs. *Beowulf* is a poem basically Christian in its spirit (the two monsters in the first part of the poem, Grendel and his mother, are accursed because they are descendants of Cain) but giving sometimes almost equal weight to the heathen idea of Wyrd or Weird (as in the Scots phrase 'to dree your weird,' to endure your fate) as to that of God.

The hero, Beowulf the Geat, has a name which means Bear (Bee-Wolf, a Bear is a wolf which likes honey) and in his original folk tale version may have been partly an animal figure. His adventures, triumph over the monster Grendel and Grendel's mother, and a battle with a dragon offended by invasion of its treasure hoard (the simple-minded dragon, with its duty of guarding an ancient hoard in which it takes no pleasure, has a certain pathos lacking to some at least in Grendel and his mother) in which he and the dragon are slain – if his twelve followers and not only the loyal Wiglaf had been brave enough he might have been saved – seem to belong to the wonders of folk tale. Yet Beowulf has the qualities of an epic hero in his dignity in hall, his shrewd reflections on how politic marriages to heal feuds never work, his loyalty to his royal wards, his courtesy, courage, and self-sacrificial readiness to accept a lonely death, he is a no doubt simply outlined but utterly noble and human figure like the great epic hero Hector in the *Iliad*. The story ends nobly with his funeral and burial, with the piling of the dead dragon's treasures round him, and the sad knowledge that (perhaps as God's punishment for the failure of courage in his retainers at the crucial moment) his Geatish Kingdom will come to an end, swept away by the Swedes.

Beowulf is, indeed, a strangely moving poem. Under the outer splendours of courtesy in the hall and Beowulf's strength and courage in single combat, of the giving and graceful acceptance of great gifts, there is the constant warning of the possibility of the degeneration of the noblest and of the treachery that can underlie the warmest professions of loyalty. Hrothgar, the friend of Beowulf's father, a dignified Nestor-like figure, knows that he cannot live for ever. His gracious wife, Wealhtheow, who is presented as essentially an ideal hostess, a bringer of peace and harmony, flatters Hrothgar's nephew, the powerful Hrothulf. When Wealhtheow says

For may I not count on my gracious Hrothulf to guard
   honourably
our young ones here, if you, my lord,
should give over this world earlier than he? I am sure
   that he will show to our children
answerable kindness, if he keeps in remembrance all
   that we have done to indulge and advance him,
the honours we bestowed on him when he was still a
   child!

we know in our bones that Hrothgar's children are doomed.
Similarly, after Finn, the East Frisian King, has slain the
brother of his half-Dane wife, Hildeburgh, and her son has
also been killed in the combat (Hildeburgh burns her
brother Hnaef, and her son on the same funeral pyre)
Hnaef's successor, Hengest, swears an unwilling truce with
Finn:

                                 But Hengest still,
      as he was constrained to do, stayed with Finn
      a death-darkened winter in dreams of his homeland.

But there are oaths that it is impossible to keep:

   So he did not decline the accustomed remedy
   when the son of Hunlaf set across his knees
   that best of blades, his battle-gleaming sword;
   the Giants were acquainted with the edges of that steel . . .

We are not, in fact, reading a fairy tale. I am not so sure
about the dragon, who perhaps belongs there (the sole
business of dragons is to guard treasure hoards, and the
slave who stole a piece of the dragon's treasure, to placate
his master and avoid a flogging, is a cowardly and thoughtless wretch). But Grendel the lonely cannibal and his vile
mother – rather like Caliban's mother, the witch Sycorax,
'with age and envy bent into a hoop' – are both real and
terrifying in their own right and, as children of Cain,
symbols of the treachery of such men as Hrothulf and Finn,
of the oath-breaking into which good men like Hengest are
led by the need for revenge.
   Full of exciting episodes as it is, the three main monster
episodes, and the historical episodes brought in by way of

allusive parenthesis, *Beowulf* moves nevertheless with sad deliberate dignity. Its strength is a slow and struggling strength: there is something symbolic of the poem's own grip in the fact that Beowulf is so strong that swords break in his hands (except a giant's sword with which he slays Grendel's mother): he must attack his enemies – as in Hygelac's raid on the Franks, an historical episode – with his bare hands. And in the end all triumph ends in gloomy but resigned meditation, the sense that at least duty has been done: as Wiglaf, the only companion to be worthy of Beowulf, giving orders for logs for the pyre, says:

> 'Now the flames shall grow dark
> and the fire destroy the sustainer of the warriors
> who often endured the iron shower
> when, string-driven, the storm of arrows
> sand over shield-wall, and the shaft did its work
> urged on by its feathers, furthered the arrow-head.'

A poem like *Beowulf* is, like Homer's poetry, made out of formulaic phrases; but where Homer tends to stick to one formula, so that Achilles is always swift-footed, Hector the tamer of horses, and so on, the variation of phrases (*kennings*) in Old English poetry is remarkable. The sea (which haunted these West German people, island dwellers remembering the North Sea and the Baltic) is now the 'swan's path,' now the 'whale's road,' now the 'gannet's bath': phrases aiming perhaps less at vividness than, like the descriptions of armour, helmets, weapons and, above all, golden gifts, at a sense of lavishness. Compared to the swiftness of Homer *Beowulf* moves, perhaps because of the use of alternative descriptions in parallel, interspersed with cryptic allusions to myth and history unfamiliar to us, very slowly indeed; and the purely meditative passages are among the most memorable and most full of slow *gravitas*, which may explain why some critics have found in *Beowulf* strange remembrances of the tone of Virgil's *Aeneid*:

> But to elude death
> is not easy: attempt it who will,
> he shall go to the place prepared for each
> of the sons of men, the soul-bearers
> dwelling on earth, ordained them by fate:

laid fast in that bed, the body shall sleep
when the feast is done.

It is, of course, like all epics, an aristocratic poem: it is an
objective representation of the true values of life as the
retainer loyal to his lord or as the good king understands
them, and those values *are* aristocratic: gaiety, courtesy,
courage, self-sacrifice. The poem's outlook is also canny and
fierce. Michael Alexander drily remarks of the meaning of
these lines,

'Bear your grief, wise one! It is better for a man
to avenge his friend than to refresh his sorrow'

that this is 'not a Christian sentiment'. These epic poems
were sung or chanted in hall with an appropriate pride and
clangour. In *Beowulf* there is talk of a 'harp' but the
instrument discovered at Sutton Hoo was a kind of round
lute. It may well have been twanged at the half-line break,
to make a kind of echo, a thrilling noise, rather than a tune.
The poem has the two qualities which some great English
poetry is always to have: triumph and sadness.

II Elegies and Riddles

There seems to have been in the West German peoples,
from whom our language and ourselves are largely descended, a constitutional streak of melancholy. The fullest
surviving Germanic literature, the only one that can be
called a classic one, is that of Iceland. And though the tales
of the sagas are grim and bloody, they are told with a certain
dry realistic relish, and though the Gods in the poems of the
Elder Edda are always quarrelling with each other and are
going to be destroyed in the end by the powers of evil, these
Icelandic poems, in W. H. Auden's excellent version, have
an odd jauntiness about them.

The North Germans, the Vikings, had something of that
tough elation that goes with a conquering habit. The East
Germans had a long tradition of contact with the Romans,
and were all – the Longobards in Italy, the Goths in Spain
and North Africa, the Franks in Gaul – very ready to drop
their ancient traditions (we have no East German docu-

ments equivalent to *Beowulf*) and to adopt Romance languages, derived from popular Latin. The West Germans, from the records they have left in Old English literature, had not the jauntiness of the always ruthless and nearly always successful sea raider nor, though when they became Christian they adopted Latin for religious services and for learned writing, did they feel at home with the Roman roads, Hadrian's wall, a city like Bath, when they first saw them.

These seemed to them, to use a phrase from *The Ruin, enta geweorc,* the work of giants. The early, often quite small groups of settlers, built their byres and stockades and halls of wood, amid their fields and cattle, as they had done in north-west or mid-north-west, coastal Europe. Of the three main Germanic groups, in spite of the great future that lay ahead of those who had settled in England, the West Germans seem the most provincial: brave, but defensively rather than aggressively so: not a ruthless conquering people like the North Germans, the Scandinavians: not a receptive people, ready to plunge themselves into and dominate the older Roman civilization, like the East Germans, Goths, Longobards, Franks. Their lyrical poetry expresses their staunchness, but also their habitual sadness and uneasiness.

Here, again from Michael Alexander's *The Earliest English Poems,* is a poem about a deserted Roman city, Aquae Sulis, or Bath. Lovers of Bath will know that it contains, in the Roman baths, the strange round bearded head of Sul-Minerva, a kind of male gorgon, which is the one work of art in which the Roman and the Celtic geniuses fuse to produce a masterpiece. In the poem from which I quote a few lines, and which Michael Alexander thinks of as 'the first of many English meditations on old stones' and in no way inferior to Gray's *Elegy Written in a Country Churchyard,* perhaps Roman and West Germanic genius fuse, at a greater distance, in the same way:

> Well-wrought the wall: Wierds broke it.
> The stronghold burst. . . .
>
> Snapped rooftrees, towers fallen,
> the work of the Giants, the stonesmiths,
> mouldereth.

Rime scoureth gatetowers
rime on mortar.

Shattered the showershields, roofs ruined,
age under-ate them.

And the wielders and wrights?
Earthgrip holds them – gone, long gone,
fast in gravesgrasp while fifty fathers
and sons have passed. . . .

What puzzles me a little about this poem is how, when Roman traditions lingered among the more wealthy, powerful, and cultivated Britons (like the legendary Arthur, in real life perhaps a cavalry chieftain holding a watching brief on behalf of the departed Romans in case they should ever return, a kind of plenipotentiary proconsul, with full rights of independent personal decision), Roman cities, which have been so lasting elsewhere, should have been allowed so soon to decay. It was certainly not fifty generations ('while fifty fathers/and sons have passed') between the departure of the last Roman legions and the main arrival of the West Germans, but more like fifty years.

Outside *Beowulf*, the two Old English poems best known to the ordinary reader are *The Seafarer* (through Pound's translation, a very beautiful English poem, though full, like nearly all Pound's translations, of impatient failures to grasp the sense of his original) and the rather similar *The Wanderer*. To understand either of these poems we must remember the very close relationship between the retainer and his lord, between the *hlaford,* or originally *hlaf-weard* (loafguardian), and his *heorthwerod* (hearth-companions). Most hearth-companions would have blood ties with the lord, but there were some, like Beowulf with Hrothgar, who were willing to serve as voluntary retainers because of some debt of gratitude.

No lord, however, could hand on to his successor his kin, either in the sense of those who followed him because of closeness in blood or who were voluntary retainers because of gratitude or admiration. The new lord would already have his own group of followers. In middle life the retainer became an exile, a *wraecca* (from which comes our word 'wretch'). He had to seek in new places, for a new master. To many men of our own time freedom, in the sense of being their own masters, is something they seek vainly all their lives: it is wholesome to reflect that to our Old English ancestors being a masterless man, having to wander, was the most wretched of all fates. We long, often, for solitude. Endless eating and beer-drinking and gift-giving in the crowded, smoky hall was to our ancestors as much bliss as life on earth affords.

Michael Alexander has pointed out that the theme of the misery of exile is also a favourite one in classical Chinese poetry: those who had done well in the examinations were sent to govern remote provinces and could rarely take home leave or see old friends. Here is a good short poem by Ts'en Shen (715–70 A.D., T'ang Dynasty), from Koterwall and Smith's *Penguin Book of Chinese Verse*:

> The water of the Wei River flows eastward –
> When will it reach Yungchow?
> I use it to add a double stream of tears,
> And send them flowing down to my old home.

There are subtle differences, however. The Chinese mandarin is not a wanderer, but stuck in one place far from home: and, in his position of authority, he is more like a *hlaford* without his *cynn* than like a *wraecca* who has lost his *hlaford*.

The tone of *The Wanderer*, again in Alexander's fine version of the poem, is very different. Where there are many Chinese poems about the sadness and joy of the exiled mandarin in briefly meeting but then having to say farewell to one particular friend, it is the whole throng, the drinking, the fighting, even the final heroic death, that 'the wanderer' longs for:

> A man who on these walls wisely looked
> who sounded deeply this dark life
> would think back to the blood spilt here,
> weigh it in his wit. His word would be this:
> 'Where is that horse now? Where are those men? Where
>   is the hoard-sharer?
> Where is the house of the feast? Where is the
>   hall's uproar?

Alas, bright cup! Alas, burnished fighter!
Alas, proud prince! How that time has passed,
dark under night's helm, as though it never had
    been!

There stands in the stead of staunch thanes
a towering wall wrought with worm-shapes;
the earls are off-taken by the ash-spear's point,
– that thirsty weapon. Their Wierd is glorious.'

The flashing images of the misery, beauty, and fascination of the sea – a recurrent theme in later English literature – make *The Seafarer* perhaps a more beautiful poem, but both are deeply moving.

Two poems, *Widsith* the oldest surviving English poem and *Deor* a poem with a recurrent refrain, 'That was overcome: so may this be' contain much traditional Germanic folklore and history, but need to be read with a learned commentary. Michael Alexander translates the refrain of *Deor* as 'That went by; this may too', the shorter words perhaps suggesting the drily fatalistic stoicism better. Surviving Old English poems are very thin, indeed, in what has become a central theme of later English poetry, the love between men and women. *The Wife's Complaint* is a poem of reproach to an unjust husband rather than of love. *The Husband's Message* is a set of commands rather than a love poem. The woman speaker in *Wulf and Eadwacer is* in love with Wulf, but he is an outlaw, and she apparently despises, or has ceased to love, Eadwacer, probably her husband:

Do you hear, Eadwacer? Our whelp
    Wulf shall take to the wood.
What was never bound is broken easily,
    our song together.

There are gnomic poems and riddles. The latter are clever and one is unsolved:

I saw a woman sit alone.

Might the answer be 'Nobody' and the idea that women are always gossiping or flirting?

III Religious Poetry

A considerable bulk of what survives of Old English poetry is religious, and most of it, as poetry, is disappointing. We have seen – from the brief account given of *Beowulf* and of the loyalty to lords and comrades, and misery of being a masterless man, presented in the great elegies, *The Seafarer* and *The Wanderer* – that the German peoples had much charity (a spirit of self-sacrifice and a deep love for comrades and love and reverence for lord), but were somewhat weaker in faith and hope. Things tend to end badly and in practice Wyrd, or Fate, seems stronger often than the Christian God.

The constant sea invasions from Danes and Vikings and Scottish and Irish Scots which the old English endured gave them, as in *The Battle of Maldon*, almost a pride and relish in brave defeat. Though they did not preserve their pagan memories as vividly as the Icelanders, *Widsith* and *Deor* show that they preserved some of them. The conquest of England by the Christian faith was peaceful, with no martyrs on either side, and in the occasional comparatively peaceful times (as in the flowering of the Northumbrian kingdom and later, after Alfred of Wessex had made his heroic attempt to unite England against the Danes and his Christian effort to come to a peaceful agreement with the Danish settlers) there was a fine flowering of the religious life, monastic communities, efforts at widespread religious education, the building of crosses and churches. But despite this violence and insecurity prevailed.

Those passages, particularly in the Old Testament, which attracted Old English poets (often for fairly free adaptation, rather than paraphrase) were naturally enough passages about war, vengeance, violence. Thus, one of the most powerful of the Old English religious poems, known as the *Later Genesis* or *Genesis B*, and based on an earlier continental German original of which a few passages were discovered in 1894 in the Vatican library, has a touch of Milton in it, who, as Blake said, 'was a true Poet and of the Devil's party without knowing it'.

I versify R. K. Gordon's prose version in his Everyman *Anglo-Saxon Poetry*, of Satan's speech:

He said, 'Why must I work? I want no master.
With my hands I can work wonders as many.

I have power to prepare   for myself a proper
Throne in heaven   and higher than he is.
Why with false fawning   his favour must I beg?
I dare be a God   as grand as He is.
Strong henchmen   bold-hearted heroes
Flank me and in fight   will not fail their Master.
With such peers   good plan can a man lay,
Carry it out   with companions in war.
They are hot in their hope for me   in heart most loyal:
I can rule over them   reign in this kingdom.
Right wrong it seems to me   His rule still to flatter,
Since my words win me nothing   I worship no longer.'

Rough and ready as that version is, it shows how this anonymous German poet and his Old English adapter anticipated Milton's Satan. A poem on Christ, on the other hand, is very weak, as are some versified saints' lives. The fierce world of the Old Testament had something in common with the German heroic world. The New Testament, with its ethic of love, the forgiveness of injuries, Christ's self-sacrifice for us and our duty to take up His Cross, was a strange idea in these cruel times.

But there is one shining exception, the poem called in modern English *The Dream of the Rood*, which is one of the most profoundly moving and beautiful properly Christian poems of any age. I shall try to give the reader a variety of versions, to illustrate the quality of this poem by my own version of a key passage, from the edition edited by Bruce Dickins and Alan S. C. Ross. With its excellent introduction, notes, and glossary, and because the poem is a comparatively short one, this is the text I would recommend to any reader of mine who wants to teach himself a little Old English. I was deeply struck by the poem when I studied it at St Andrews, more than forty years ago (Scots undergraduates went to university, in those days, very young, and I had completed my four-year M.A. course in July, 1936, before my twenty-first birthday). The poem struck me then so deeply that I attempted to put it into verse, according to the Old English metrical rules. I have of course lost that manuscript long ago but, in tackling it again, perhaps old memories of these first struggles have come unconsciously back to me.

The poem, as Michael Alexander points out, though so truly Christian in feeling, has an ancient German pagan form, the double riddle: the poet *sees* the Tree on which Christ was crucified, strangely illuminated, surrounded by angels. The Tree then *speaks* and describes how Christ, the young hero, climbs upon it, how it can hardly hold up against his weight (one almost thinks of Beowulf's wrestling matches) but knows that if it bowed to the ground it would surrender everything to the fiends unless it stood fast. It shares Christ's sweat and weariness, the shafts of the dark nails hurt it too. Finally, Christ's battle-companions lift him down from the Cross and to them it willingly and humbly bows at last.

This great poem or fragments of it exist in three places: in runic lettering (originally used for magical purposes, but more phonetically accurate than the Latin script of which the old English borrowed a version from the ·much more learned Irish), on the Ruthwell Cross in Dumfriesshire, this was written in the North Northumbrian dialect (this is the oldest text, probably dating from the first half of the eighth century); in the Vercelli book in the Cathedral library at Vercelli, on the pilgrims' way to Rome, in West Saxon dialect, though with a few Anglian forms, the manuscript probably dating from the second half of the tenth century; and (a very few lines) in the silverwork of the Brussels Cross reliquary at the Cathedral of St Michel and Ste Gudule in Brussels, a reliquary containing the largest fragment of the True Cross in the world, once belonging to Alfred the Great. The language is late West Saxon, the date perhaps as late as the eleventh century. If the Ruthwell Cross version is shortened, the Vercelli version has perhaps been a little over-expanded, and its last sixty lines are thought weak. Michael Alexander notes the strangeness of the fact that none of the versions of this most awesome and lovely of Old English poems survives in England itself. (One should add, alas, that in Scotland the Ruthwell Cross inscription was badly damaged by the ignorant and fanatical Covenanters.)

Here is my own version of the passage that seems to me most intensely and poignantly dramatic. It should be noted that the half lines have sometimes three stresses. This sometimes marks very solemn verse. I have used here a space, instead of obliques, for the line break:

> Then I saw the Lord of Mankind
> hasten with much might   since on me he would climb.

There and then I durst not   against the Doomster's
    word
bow down or burst   though breaking I saw
earth's floors. All I might
of man's foes fell   if fast I stood there.
Ungirded him the young hero (that was Almighty God)
strong and of stithy mood.   So he would on the
    gallows hang,
Mood-strong in many's sight.   Then he would
    Man's kin leese,
I quaked then when the Bairn clipped me;   nor
    durst I thence bow to earth,
Fall to earth's flats.   But stand fast I must.
As a Rood I was reared: I heaved up the strong
    King,
Heaven's Baron: bow down I durst not.
They throughdrove me with dark nails;   on me were
    the wounds seeable,
Open hate-hurts.   Nor durst I them anywise scathe,
They bemocked us both together.   I was all with
    blood bedewed,
Begotten of that Man's side.   When he had sent
    forth his Spirit . . .

                            Wept all created things,
Cried on the King's fall: Christ was on Cross.
Then hastily there   from afar came
To them Athelings.   I that all beheld.
Sore was I with sorrow bedriven.   Bent I thither to
    these men's hands,
Humbly yet with strength.   They took hold of Al-
    mighty God,
Heaved him from that heavy pain.   Left me these
    Commanders,
To stand with sweat weakened.   Wounded all
    through with streals I was . . .

Much of the mood of Old English verse continues in later
verse, even if the form dies. Much seems strange and
distant. It is good to end with something strange, distant, yet
universally intimate.

2

Early Middle English Poetry

I Linguistic Changes

We have seen that the tone of old English poetry was aristocratic. The lord and his retainers are the only characters who are prominent, the aristocratic virtues of loyalty, courage, and readiness for self-sacrifice are the virtues specially praised. The tone, as in much aristocratic poetry, is fundamentally gloomy, ultimate defeat is envisaged as inevitable: the word for courage is *mood*, and, even more significantly, the word for courageous *moody*. The word *mood* did not lack our modern connotations for, in *The Wanderer* for instance, *modcearig*, or in modern English *mood-chary*, means 'troubled in thought'.

The Normans were accustomed to winning all the time and in the considerable body of Anglo-Norman poetry that survives (Marie de France, the first woman to write metrical romances, may have lived and worked in England) this noble acceptance of defeat is not found. The Norman Conquest did not, of course, reduce all magnates of English or Danish blood to servitude. The Stricklands, in the north, who had come over earlier with Canute, remain a great family to this day. But it could be said that early Middle English poetry, compared to old English poetry, lacks what Matthew Arnold called 'high seriousness'.

The ordinary reader used to get his idea of the lowering of status, after the Norman Conquest, from the dialogue at the beginning of Sir Walter Scott's *Ivanhoe* between Wamba the jester and Gurth the swineheard. Gurth's pigs are served on the Normans' tables as *pork*, his oxen as *beef*, his calves as

17

veal, his sheep as *mutton* (oddly lamb does not seem to have produced a pair word, *anyo*). If you work on it, the word is English: if you consume it, the word is Norman-French. Much more abundant, in fact, than these few concrete nouns were a great many abstract ones having to do with law, administration, etiquette, the natural preoccupations of a ruling class. But, in fact, a language can absorb a great many new words into its vocabulary (as English, throughout its history, always has done) without changing its fundamental nature. A language's fundamental nature is its syntactical structure, and this changes, as it changed between Old English and Middle English (and changed between late popular Latin and the Romance languages) far more because of a drift in the speakers of a language towards an easier and more convenient way of expressing themselves than because of any outward pressures. The change both from spoken Latin to the Romance languages and from Old English to the many varieties of Middle English (there had, of course, been many varieties of Old English too) is a change from a synthetic language (one which expresses its syntactic structure, and semantic implications, by the case endings of nouns) and an analytic language (one which expresses its syntactic structure, and semantic implications, by a more or less fixed word order and by a lavish use of prepositions and auxiliary verbs).

A good example of how a synthetic language works can be found in the possible variants of order of the three words of this Latin sentence: Regina nautam amat, Nautam regina amat, Regina amat nautam, Nautam amat regina, Amat nautam regina, Amat regina nautam. No doubt in different settings these six variants would have different rhetorical emphases (The queen *loves* a sailor, The queen loves *a sailor*, *The queen* loves a sailor) but the core of sense is the same. In a modern Romance language, like French, one has to say in one order only: La reine aime un matelot (*or* le matelot, for Latin pays for its concision by a lack of preciseness about this sort of indication). *Matelot*, of course, has no connection with *nauta*, and comes from a Dutch word of rather undignified connotation, *mattegenoot*, bunk-mate: it fits perfectly well and is long established in this Romance language, French, suggesting again that structure not vocabulary is what gives a language its character. It should be noticed, however, that French is still a less analytic language than English in that it retains the perfectly pointless device of grammatical gender for nouns: we know that queens are feminine, sailors masculine, without having this underlined by 'la' and 'un' or 'le': and in such instances as 'le crayon' (the pencil) or 'la plume' (the pen) it gives the foreigner, and must give French children, a great deal of useless trouble to memorise indications of non-existent sexual differences between two non-biological objects.

Even in the old English period, the phonetic differences between case endings, nominative, vocative, accusative, genitive, dative, ablative, were not so phonetically clear as in Latin; and the learner of old English, unlike the learner of Latin, has to find the case, often, by the sense rather than the sense by the case. The Danish invasion, the variety of old English vernaculars, and the greater convenience of an analytic (fixed word-order) structure were all having their effect at least in Canute's time. Cases tended to be dropped, in all Indo-European languages, not so much because they had become phonetically blurred and hard to distinguish as because they did, at least in the spoken version of the language, the same job twice. Correct written Latin is: 'Romam ire' (to go to Rome). Spoken Latin, even among educated people, was: 'Ad Romam ire'. One can see how it would soon seem easier, and would be just as clear, to say 'Ad Roma' ire' or 'Ad Rom' ire'.

The Conquest therefore did not destroy Old English and create Middle English. Middle English is simply one of a group of vernaculars each deriving ultimately from the Old English vernacular of its region. This does not make things simple. The manuscripts that survive may have been copied by a scribe from a region far from the poet's. The poet did not read merely the poetry of his own region (the Scotsmen Dunbar and Henryson were well aware of Chaucer) and might borrow phrases and devices not traditional in his own part of the world. So, for instance, Robert Burns much later wrote in broad Scots, very difficult for English readers; in English 'with a sprinkling of Scots', as in his songs of personal emotion and adaptations of popular folk-songs; and occasionally, when he wanted to be refined and dignified (as in the 'But pleasures are like poppies spread . . .' passage in *Tam O'Shanter*) in a Scotsman's idea of correct literary English. If there are, in fact, sharp divisions between various groups of Middle English poems written in various parts of the country (the various parts including, of course, for the divisions are not political, the Lowlands of Scotland), there is also a network of unexpected resemblances and connections.

The medieval period in English poetry is generally taken to have lasted from about 1100 to 1450 A.D., or from shortly after the Conquest till about the time of the fall of Constantinople to the Turks, the revival of learning, and the invention of printing, one of whose main effects, of course, was to standardise, gradually, the language of at least literary English (though as late as the end of the sixteenth and beginning of the seventeenth century the great poet Sir Walter Raleigh was said to have spoken and written in broad Devonshire). I have spent considerable space here on linguistic matters because most scholars feel that, apart from one witty and charming poem, *The Owl and the Nightingale*, a debate poem, and apart from some fresh and delightful lyrics (the early medieval poets were aware of the beauty of spring and the greenwoods, the old English poets, seeking the shelter of the Great Hall, only of bad weather and the threatening sea), the earlier medieval period is more remarkable for its linguistic than its poetic interest: or, to put it more kindly, more remarkable for promise in various new sorts of poem than for triumph in performance.

II *The Owl and the Nightingale:* The Debate between the Poet and the Moralist

The Owl and the Nightingale is a long poem of close on two thousand lines in remarkably regular four-stress rhyming couplets on the French model. It consists of a debate between a nightingale and an owl. The nightingale is aware that he can sing beautifully and express the joy of life, but that he is not very good at argument. He is good, however, at gibing; and at the beginning of the poem, from a safe distance, from a fair blossomy bough, he reproaches the owl for his loathsome ugliness,

> 'Me luste bet speten thane singe
> Of thine fule gogelinge'

> ('It pleases me better to spit than to sing
> Of your foul goggling')

and its inability to sing. Oddly enough (or perhaps not), it is
the justest of the nightingale's reproaches, against the owl's
lack of musical ear, that incenses the owl most:

> 'Hu thincthe nu bi mine songe?
> Wenst thu that Iche ne cunne singe,
> Thegh Ich ne cunne of writelinge?
> Ilome thu dest me grame
> An seist me bothe tone an schame.
> Gif Ich the holde on mine vote
> (So hit bitide that Ich mote!)
> An thu were ut of thine rise,
> Thu sholdest singe another wise.'

('What do you think of my song? Do you think that I do not
know how to sing, even though I am no expert in trilling?
Often you do me harm and speak teen and shame to me. If I
held you in my foot (just wait till I can!) and you were away
from your branch you would be singing another tune!')

Ponderously, the owl explains himself. He is by nature a
'hawk', a bird of prey, and is no more to be blamed for
eating little birds and mice than the nightingale for eating
worms. He goes to church and keeps the church clean by
eating the mice. Is the nightingale ever near church? By his
note at night the owl comforts the weak and the wandering
and the distressed. The nightingale's song merely inspires
young folk to lechery. The owl reminds men to take life
seriously: what good has the nightingale's song ever done?
The nightingale is in a quandary but will never give in. He
tells the owl that he could be so preternaturally wise only
through witchcraft, and has been therefore excommunicated. Rather illogically, he adds that in his pretence to
knowledge of the stars the owl is a humbug: he cannot know
anything more about them than anyone else. The quarrel is
quieted down by the arrival of the wren, the king of the
birds, and owl and nightingale depart together, in a friendly
enough mood, to hear the verdict on the debate of Master
Nicholas of Guilford, a learned and good priest, who,
typically of the times, lacks promotion. (Master Nicholas
may be the author of the poem, or a friend of his may. The
earliest manuscripts are of around 1250 but the poem, which
towards the end laments the great Henry II as if recently

dead, is probably written in the reign of Richard Coeur de Lion, some thirty years earlier.)

This work has a peculiar interest among English poems in that it is the first to display that good-natured sense of humour which has been considered a central mark of the English character since, and in that its main interest is in a clash of personalities, rather than of ideas (and again it has traditionally been considered a typically English trait to be bored by abstract ideas as such). We expect, at first, a straight debate between, say, the claims of Pure Poetry, of Lyric Delight, and of Preaching and Practical Example: if the owl himself is a kind of poet he is a committed one, his poetry is merely a means.

It does not turn out that way. The owl is oddly human and touchy, very quick to defend himself, very easily hurt: and the nightingale is not just a pure lyrical poet but an obstinate and quick little creature, sly, mischievous, a little envious of the owl's solid logic and learning (as the owl perhaps is of the nightingale's singing) but knowing, when apparently utterly defeated, how to rouse the owl by throwing logic to the winds: 'You are so wise, you must be wicked – you are an astrologer, you have been excommunicated for witchcraft, and what do you know about astrology, anyway?' And yet one has a liking for both the comical creatures, feels that in a way they need each other as complements, and is glad when they fly off to Master Nicholas as friends. But for the fact that the language is more difficult, this poem, mingling the comic touches of serious argument and vivid little glimpses of nature, might be as popular as Chaucer.

III Romances, a Mythic History, an Exegesis: Fabliaux, a Beast-epic, an Interlude, a Parody

It has already been suggested that the early Middle Ages, in England the period from the beginning of the twelfth to the beginning of the fourteenth century, are more notable for what they start than for what they bring to perfection. These two centuries are notable especially for strenuous variety of effort and for adopting, particularly from France, foreign modes. In English medieval poetry, even in Chaucer, we do not look, as in post-Renaissance poetry, for the striking single line (though Chaucer sometimes throws it in, almost as if by accident): we look for vivacity and for subtle modulation of tone from the vivacious to the grave in a long passage: we learn to accept that even in the greatest poets, again, say, in Chaucer, the most exciting or amusing story may be in some degree a text for a sermon, that narrative serves homiletics, and that the homiletics can be trite. But, making all these general allowances, it must be admitted that early Middle English poetry offers us fewer strikingly pleasurable passages, and many fewer compulsively memorable ones, than does the more mature poetry we associate with Chaucer, Langland, and the poets of *The Pearl* and *Sir Gawain and the Green Knight*.

It seems best then to deal briefly with the various new kinds (some of which like the Biblical exegesis, *Ormulum* or Layamon's largely legendary history of ancient Britain, in a roughened version of old English verse, *The Brut*, rather fortunately had no progeny: for Barbour's *The Bruce* is much nearer straight history). The romances are interestingly various. One of the longest of these, *Kyng Alisaunder*, turns classical history into a romance of chivalry and, as J. A. W. Bennett and G. V. Smithers note in *Early Middle English Verse and Prose*, moves in a 'forceful and lively verse . . . much superior to the toneless alexandrines of [its] Anglo-Norman source'. I choose an example of this vigorous rhythm almost at random: a passage so clear that it requires, I think, no translation:

> 'Alisaunder, riche caysere,
> Thou ne hast on erthe no pere!
> Many is the riche londe
> Thou hast ywonne to thine honde.
> On thee hii ben well bysett,
> For thou art ful of thewes pett.
> Thou batest wrong, thou hauntest rightes,
> Thou art fader of alle knichtes.
> Thou lovest alle gentil manne
> And abatest alle tyranne.
> Thou art caiser of this londe –
> Ich me yelde to thine honde,
> And amendying I bidde thee to
> Or unrichth that is me do.'

This passage is an excuse, also, for a few notes on the

unsolved problem, or unagreed problem, of the scansion of this type of stress-syllable rhymed Middle English verse. The problem is the final -e, or sometimes final -es. This is a four-stress line sometimes of as few as seven, sometimes of as many as nine syllables. It is not in regular feet in the modern sense, for, though the general movement is iambic, in a line like this:

And ab/ átest/ áll(e) týr/anne . . .

we get a regular trochaic movement *if* we regard the -e of 'alle' as extra-metrical but pronounce the final -e of 'tyranne' as metrical. But one cannot prove that the writer's intention is not

And ab/ átest/ állě/ týrann(e),

with an iambic foot after the three trochees, for he probably has no concept equivalent to our concept of the foot. In the second scansion there, by the way, the -e of 'tyranne' could still be pronounced but it would be extra-metrical. Sometimes the final -e was stressed, and sometimes it was unstressed, but we cannot be sure. It is enough for us to be aware of this problem and to think of it less as a stumbling-block than as something that gives us a greater freedom of choice than we have had since the Renaissance in the inner or outer performance of English medieval stress-syllable rhymed verse.

The tale of Havelok has a rough northern feeling and a north-eastern setting (Grimsby, Humber, Lincoln) but attracted French writers Geoffrey Gaimer, in his *Estoire des Engleis*, and the author of the *Lai d'Haveloc*, both works earlier than the Middle English poem but, perhaps for that reason, more lacking in vigour and detail. *Havelok's* dash and almost complete lack of love-interest contrasts with the languor of *Floris and Blancheflour*, the story of a boy and a girl brought up together by a royal father of the boy. Feeling that Blancheflour is beneath Floris in birth, Floris's father sells her as a slave and pretends to Floris she is dead. But Floris's father repents and Floris tracks Blancheflour down to the Emir of Babylon's Tower of Maidens, where the Emir keeps the virtuous beauties he hopes by and by to enjoy. Floris is found in bed with Blancheflour, both are threatened with death, but in the end the magnanimous Emir pardons them. The tale has Eastern Origins, and the contrast with *Havelok*, in mood and setting, suggests in how many different directions English poetry was setting out.

Layamon's *Brut* is more interesting to the student of legendary history (as Rome was founded by Aeneas, so Britain was founded by Brutus, a Trojan prince escaping from the ruins of his fatherland to found a new Troy) than to the lover of poetry. Wace has covered much of the same ground in his Anglo-Norman verse translation of Geoffrey of Monmouth's prose account. The priest Orm's *Ormulum* is famous mainly for its mechanical regularity of metre, its avoidance of new words from the French vocabulary, and, however edifying its purpose (the exegesis of the Bible either for his fellow clerics or his congregation) for its extraordinary dullness. *Cursor Mundi* is an enormous poem of 30,000 lines (but mercifully in very short lines of three stresses and sometimes merely six syllables) running over the history of the world from the Creation to the Day of Judgment. *The Fox and the Wolf*, a beast fable too expansive to be very funny, *Dame Sirith*, apparently an Indian story which had mysteriously reached England, and *Saint Kenelm*, the legend of a martyred King's son, killed while a boy, though written in rhymed couplets very loosely reminiscent of the old English line (there are four main sense stresses) contains a fossilised couplet surviving from the late old English period:

> In Clent Cubeche   Kenelm cunebearn,
> lith under hayethorn,   haudes bereafed.

> In Clent Cubeck,   Kenelm the prince,
> lies under hawthorn,   of head bereft.

Kenelm had a considerable cult. To this day, J. A. W. Bennett and G. V. Smithers tell us, there is in the parish church of Winchcombe a large leaden coffin connected by tradition to the name of the boy saint. I do not know whether the thrill of the past, for its own sake, is a properly poetic thrill: it is certainly one which the study of our older poetry often arouses in us.

The most original longer poem, or extract from a longer poem, contained in Bennett and Smithers's *Early Middle English Verse and Prose*, apart from *The Owl and the Nightingale*, is *The Land of Cockaigne*. This is partly a satire on monkish sloth and sensuality. It is a picture of an earthly paradise of sensual not spiritual delights, in which all the virtues officially required of monks are reversed:

Whan the abbot him iseeth
That is monkes fram him fleeth,   *is:* his
He taketh maidin of the route
And turnith up her white toute,   *toute:* buttocks
And betith the taburs with his hond
To make is monkes licht to lond.
Whan is monkes that iseeth
To the maid dun hi fleeth   *hi:* they
And goth the wench all abute,
And thakketh all hir white toute,   *thakketh:* pat
And sith aftir her swinke   *her swinke:* their toil
Wendith meklich hom to drink,   *meklich hom:* meekly home
And goth to har collacione
A well fair processione.

This is too funny to be intended as savage satire and too absurd to be intended to be erotically arousing. It was written in Ireland, should that throw any light on its tone. Of the other extracts from longer poems, or fragments, included by Bennett and Smithers, *Interludium de Clerico et Puella* is the oldest secular play in our language. A clergyman wishes to seduce a young woman, is made to feel a fool as well as a rogue, and repents. One feels that it would have made a lively sketch. Bennett and Smithers also include a fragment from a versified bestiary, on the nature and allegorical meaning of the eagle, the ant, the stag, and the whale, interestingly various in metre, and reflecting the universal belief that in all natural things divine things have a symbol. The verse chronicle, on the other hand, attributed to Robert of Gloucester would be more readable in prose. One feels that our early medieval ancestors, unlike their Old English predecessors, had very largely lost the sense that there are certain moods and certain ranges of subject matter suitable to poetry, and others not. But a lyric, if it gets off the ground, cannot fail to be poetical: and perhaps in this groping time of our early poetry it was in the lyric or *carole* (song for dancing to) that the best poets of that early time, all anonymous, found themselves.

III The Early Medieval Lyric

In the early medieval English lyrics, those with a secular theme, there is a new sense of the weather, and of how it affects one's whole mood: and a direct expression, not found at all in old English poetry, of love, also echoing the weather or thwarted by it, as the expression of direct physical desire. In these early lyrics, there is nothing of the artifice of courtly love: but their passion, also, is pure, direct, sometimes agonising: it has nothing in it lingeringly sensual or gloatingly lascivious:

> Mirie it is while sumer ilast
>   With fugheles song;
> Oc nu necheth windes blast
>   And weder strong.
> Ei, ei! What this nicht is long!
> And Ich with wel michel wrong
>   Soregh and murne and fast.

The sorrow and mourning and fasting, we feel, are not just for harsh winter weather but for lost summer love.

Even the northern wind, associated with bleakness, can blow our loves to us:

> Blow, northerne wynd,
> Sent thou me my suetying!
> Blow, northerne wynd,
> Blou, blou, blou!

Ichot a burde in bourne bryht	*Ichot:* I know
That sully semly is on syht –	*sully semly:* innocently beautiful
Menskful maiden of myht,	
Feir ant fre to fonde.	*Menskful:* noble
In wurhliche won,	*wurhliche:* honourable
A burde of blod ant of bon	
Never yet Y nuste non	*nuste:* knew
Lussomore in londe . . .	*Lussomore:* lovelier

There is occasionally a lovely and confident use of the long lyrical line:

> When the nyhtegale singes the wodes waxen grene.
> Lef ant gras ant blosme springes in Aueryl, Y wene.
> Ant loue is to myn herte gon with one spere so kene
> Nyht ant day my blod hit drynkes; myn heart deth me tene . . .

The same simplicity and directness seems to me to belong to the early medieval religious lyrics, which are in a sense love songs too. Nothing could be less ornate than this short poem, but nothing could be more honest:

> No more ne willi wiked be;
> Forsake Ich wille this worldis fe,   *fe:* good
> This wildis wedis, this folen gle;   *gle:* entertainment
> Ich wul be mild of chere;
> Of cnottis scal mi girdil be,
> Becomen Ich will frere.   *frere:* friar

> Frer menur I will me make,   *Frer menur:* Franciscan
> And lecherie I wille asake;   friar
> To Iesu Crist Ich will me take
> And serve in holi churche,
> All in mi ouris forto wake,
> Goddis wille to wurche.

> Wurche I will this workes gode
> For him that boyht us in the rode;
> Fram his side ran the blode,
> So dere he gan vs bie.
> Forsothe I tel him more than wode   *tel him more than wode:*
> That hantit licherie.   think he's absolutely mad

In dealing with old English poetry we seemed to see an old culture, with obscure memories stretching into the very distant past, memories of a 'heroic age', rounding itself off: adapting itself to a Christianity which in a way was a very new and strange religion to it. Some of the actions demanded by Christianity, like self-sacrifice for one's Lord, courage, acceptance of suffering, were very much in the German heroic tradition: others, like renunciation of the blood feud, were not.

In the early Middle Ages, we come on no single poem in English that even begins to compare in impressiveness with *Beowulf*, *The Seafarer*, *The Wanderer*, or *The Dream of the Rood*. We come on some poems, like *Ormulum*, which should not have been written in verse at all and would probably, to be honest, have been fairly dull even in prose. There are stories and romances of some quality, but they fail to grip us as the greatest stories and romances do. Yet something new is happening. In *The Owl and the Nightingale* we have, for the first time in English poetry, something characteristic of our subsequent literature: a humour which is sympathetic rather than satirical, a sense of the humorous clash of personalities, both of whom we laugh at and like (we do not take sides for or against either owl or nightingale), and a feeling that there really is an important subject being debated but that the poet (whose personality can itself be felt pervading the poem) feels the subject too important to be defined too closely. It is a subject perhaps connected with the fact that the true Christian is at once a man who, like the owl, takes on himself the role of the suffering servant and who, like the nightingale, sings praise to God's creation in what seems thoughtless delight. *The Land of Cockaigne* is broader and coarser: but it looks forward to a future world of humorous fantasy, that will be very important in English poetry. Finally, in the lyrics, the language learns, unselfconsciously, how to sing. There is more in this most neglected of all periods of English poetry than we had at first thought.

3

The High Middle Ages: I

I The Theory and Practice of Medieval Poetry

We have seen in the last chapter that, outside romances, songs, and a comic allegory like *The Land of Cockaigne* or an elaborate and subtly humorous poem like *The Owl and the Nightingale*, a poem of debate between the carefree and the solemn view of life, many early English poems, like the *Ormulum*, *Cursor Mundi*, or Layamon's long historical-mythical poem seem to deal with material that we would think today more suitable for prose. And indeed a theory of poetry, in the sense of a theory of the nature and purpose of poetry, is something not really to be found in the Middle Ages. What we find instead is a series of practical rules for the poet. The trivium, the three early stages of a medieval education, consisted of grammar, rhetoric, and logic. Grammar taught you how to express yourself correctly, rhetoric how to express yourself effectively, logic (which we shall not be touching on here) how to be sure that you are not correctly and effectively talking self-contradictory nonsense. The textbooks like Geoffroi de Vinsauf's famous *Poetria Nova* would be written in Latin and use Latin examples. But they were purely manuals of technical instruction: they described and gave examples of various devices used by poets, but were not interested in the difference between a good and a bad poet.

There is a useful, condensed but clear, account of Geoffroi de Vinsauf in A. C. Spearing's *Criticism and Medieval Poetry* (Edwin Arnold, London, 1972). Spearing is also very useful on certain peculiarities of medieval poetry as compared with modern. There are few metaphors in medieval poems and the similes are brief or conventional: passages of description and passages of straightforward narrative tend to alternate in blocks rather than to coincide. On the other hand the popularity of the dream or vision form and, as in Langland, of personified abstractions, could make it possible for us to consider some medieval poems as prolonged metaphors or similes, which in a sense is what the favourite medieval form of allegory is. For Dante, for instance, *The Divine Comedy* is an allegory, as he explains in a famous letter to his patron Can Grande de la Scala: Dante's journey through hell, purgatory, and heaven is merely the literal groundwork for a long metaphor which explains how the help of wisdom and love leads the soul beyond the temptations that might land it in endless misery to the acceptance of a necessary purification through suffering and finally to a realisation that love and wisdom, in Beatrice, are one and that in the true fulfilment of the quest for pure bliss the needs of bodily affection are catered for as well as those of the soaring spirit. The 'literal' level of Dante's allegory follows in fact an orthodox Christian pattern (though no Christian is under any duty to believe that the after-life bears any physical resemblance to Dante's picture of it – in the torments of *The Inferno*, for instance, he is speaking merely of 'objective correlatives', physical metaphors, for various states of mind) but it might as well for his purposes, as in Spenser's *Faerie Queene*, have been a world of romance.

   Still, Dante is unique. There is much medieval poetry which a modern reader is likely to find tedious, or lacking in concentration and depth, simply because it follows medieval rules of rhetoric. It needs, for instance, a rather specialised training to begin properly to enjoy the device of amplification, in which a very simple idea is, by way of elegant variation, spread out into thirty or forty lines. The simple alternation of very elaborate description, as of the castle, the three hunts, and the wild northern scenery, in *Sir Gawain and the Green Knight* with the more straightforward and summary narrative may a little disconcert the modern reader. (Though in *Gawain* these possibly indigestible descriptions are counterbalanced by the very skilful use of dialogue which gives life and reality to Sir Gawain's three temptations and to his final encounter with the Green Knight in the Green Chapel.) In an even more famous poem, the General Prologue to *The Canterbury Tales*, a number of critics have felt that the descriptions of the pilgrims, who at that stage do and say nothing, has a static effect, or is only saved from a static effect by contrasting juxtapositions. Other aspects of medieval poetry which readers may find disconcerting are the moral and homiletic digressions which may seem, often, both to be trite in themselves and to interrupt an exciting story at its most exciting point. Another habit of medieval poets which modern readers may find it hard to get used to is the *sententia*, the 'wise saw' or piece of conventional wisdom, which may appear to us today trite and perhaps not wholly true. As A. C. Spearing points out, however, a sufficiently sophisticated poet like Chaucer can use, according to the rules, a *sententia* to open *The Legend of Good Women*:

> A thousand sithes have I herd men telle   *sithes:* times
> That there ys joy in hevene and payne in
>   helle,
> And I accorde wel that it ys so . . .

His authority for this *sententia* is the Church itself; it would be heresy to deny it, despite his occasional sceptical questionings of the Church's authority. For the Age of Faith was not, for men like Chaucer, to be taken with naivety. He was aware of the simpering gentility of the Prioress, the worldly accommodating temper of the Monk, the scoundreliness of the Pardoner and the Summoner: but there remained the poor Parson and his brother the Ploughman to remind this great artist and successful and accomplished civil servant of what true Christianity is. Similarly, one way of looking at Langland's *Piers Ploughman* is as one long, and often bitterly satirical grumble against Christianity in Langland's time, leading, in the end, to a complete surrender, a loving search for Christ himself. And in the elaborately beautiful northern poem, *The Pearl*, the poet is taught by the two-year-old girl he is mourning for, now across the waters and on the banks of heaven, and arrayed beautifully in a white gown embroidered with pearls and a pearly crown, the meaning of the parable of the vineyard – she has had no time to acquire any merits but has been made a queen in heaven, like the late arrivals in the vineyard getting the same wage as those who have toiled all day – to trust to God's grace and not to puff himself up with his own merits and sufferings. It is in terms of love, grace, humility (not in terms of building up a treasury of merits) that Christianity tends to express itself in the best religious poetry and devotional prose of medieval England.

Compared to the poetry of Provence, Italy, and North France, English medieval poetry developed rather slowly. It reaches its height in the fourteenth century. One possibly late thirteenth-century masterpiece (but it may be early four-teenth-century) is *Sir Orfeo* which is the myth of Orpheus and Eurydice as transformed into a happy story by the medieval imagination. Persephone is no longer the queen of Hades but the queen of Fair Elfland. Sir Ofeo comes to the palace of Persephone's king, which is not at all like the abode of gloomy Dis, and by his harping frees Heurodis, as Eurydice has become, from the enchantment that makes her wish to linger there. Both go back safely and happily to a real England, where Sir Orfeo is a king. The evocation of fairyland shows the power of pure *descriptio* interspersing narrative passages:

> He come into a fair cuntray,
> As bright so sonne on somers day,
> Smoothe and plain and all greene;
> Hille no dale was there non yseene.
> Amidde the lond a castel he seighe,
> Riche and real and wonder heighe:
> All the utmast wall
> Was clere and shine as cristal;
> An hundred towrs ther were about
> Degiselich and bataild stout: *wonderful*
> The buttrass com out of the diche
> Of rede gold y-arched riche;
> The vousour was avowed all   *vaulting, adorned*
> Of ich manner divers aumal,   *enamel*
> Within ther wer wide wones   *wide dwellings*
> All of precious stones;
> The werst pillar on to biholde
> Was all of burnist golde.

We can visualise easily the brightness and glitter, and so of course could those who listened to this poem. Medieval poems ask to be read aloud: this is particularly true of the two great northern poems combining (in different ways) the techniques of alliterative and rhymed verse, *The Pearl* and *Sir Gawain and the Green Knight.* A clang and clash, which is yet musical, was part of their expressiveness.

This flowering of English medieval poetry took place in a century marked by disasters: the battle of Bannockburn in 1314; the murder of Edward II; the ascension and long fifty years' reign of his son Edward III, which saw the start of the Hundred Years War and many hollow victories, the Black Death, the Peasants' Revolt, the Merciless Parliament, the deposition of Richard and the ascension to the throne, in Henry IV, of the House of Lancaster. Henry IV's ascension was to bring about, in the next century, the Wars of the Roses and the gradual eviction of the English, under Henry VI, from France. But it was also a time of growing wealth and learning and, as the General Prologue to the *Canterbury Tales* shows, of a diversification of the English class system almost to its modern complication. Chaucer who, among his other gifts, was a great comic poet did not miss the opportunity to use the pride and satisfaction of all Englishmen with their own class as a source of comedy, in which he has had many followers.

II Moral Gower

Let us turn to a slightly older contemporary of Chaucer, the author of the English *Confessio Amantis*, but also of the French *Mirour de L'Omme* and the Latin *Vox Clamantis* – John Gower. *Vox Clamantis* is a long, and very sincere poem in its moral and religious didactic appeal to sinners to ask Mary to intercede for them with Christ. (Both a devotion to Our Lady, as marked by the cult of Our Lady of Walsingham, and an instinctive preference for the theology of grace, the Augustinian tradition, to the theology of works or merits as the necessary fruits of grace, seem rather unexpectedly recurrent in medieval England. The opposing doctrine of Pelagianism, denying original sin and salvation through grace, had surprisingly little sway in England.)

Vox Clamantis was inspired by the Peasant's Revolt of 1381 in which the young Richard II played a brave part, dispersing the rebels by promising that their grievances would be seen to. When they returned to Kent, Gower's own county, several were put to death for their pains. The poem, mainly an account of the rebellion, is in Latin elegiac couplets, five thousand of them. It is no worse than other medieval attempts to revive classical metres, but its interest is mainly historical.

By the time he wrote in 1390 *Confessio Amantis* – in 1963 the poet Terence Tiller brought out a good modernisation for Penguin Classics – Gower had decided that English was a respectable enough language in which to write, and also that one can be 'moral' without moralising all the time. The poem is a collection of a hundred love stories from various sources, never of course concise or very dramatic but in a quiet way readable and interesting.

One of the great technical interests of *Confessio Amantis* is that both Gower here and Chaucer in *The Boke of the Duchesse* translate or paraphrase the same story, that of Ceyx and Halcyone from Ovid's *Metamorphoses*. The high poetic point of this story of Ovid's is generally admitted to be the description of the Cave of Sleep and to set a few lines of Gower's before a few lines of Chaucer's is to have a living demonstration of the difference between decent talent and rare genius in poetry. It should be remembered, also, that Chaucer is writing as a beginner in poetry, Gower as a man in late middle age. Experience cannot quite make up for freshness. Here is Gower:

> Ther stant no gret tree nyh about
> Where on ther myhte crow or pie
> Alihte, for to clepe or crie:
> There is no cok to crowe day,
> Ne beste non which noise may;
> The hell bot al aboute round   *hill*
> There is growende upon the ground
> Popi, which berth the sed of slep,
> With other herbes suche an hep.
> A stille water for the nones
> Rennende upon the smale stones,
> Which hihte of Lethes the rivere,   *is called*
> Under that hell in such manere
> There is, which gifth gret appetit
> To slepe. And thus full of delit
> Slep hath his hous . . .

Here is the young Chaucer:

> Til he cam to the derke valeye
> That stant bitwixe rokkes twaye,
> Ther nevere yit grew corn ne gras,
> Ne tree, ne nought that on live was –
> Beest ne man ne nothing elles–
> Save that ther were a fewe welles
> ·Come renning fro the clives adown,
> That made a deedly sleeping soun,
> And ronnen down right by a cave
> That was under a rok ygrave,
> Amid the valeye, wonder deepe,
> Ther thise goddes lay and sleepe . . .

Chaucer's lines should of course be compared with the lush landscape of his actual dream in *The Boke of the Duchesse*: the contrast of the total setting accentuates their grim bleakness. Clearly, also, he is condensing or summarising where Gower is giving either a straight translation or a slightly expansive paraphrase. Still, compare the sinister magic of

> Save that ther were a fewe welles
> Come renning fro the clives adown,
> That made a deadly sleeping soun,

with the modest competence, no more, of

> A stille water for the nones
> Rennende upon the smale stones.

Gower, however, is worth attention because he and his friend the 'philosophical Strode' – whose philosophical poems, alas, have vanished – clearly constituted for Chaucer part of what every poet needs: the small group of poet friends who may not be successes themselves but know the toil of it all: 'the lyf so short, the craft so long to lerne'.

III Chaucer's Three Phases

Because Chaucer was what we would now call an administrative civil servant, we know a great deal about his public duties but comparatively little about his private life. His self-portraits in his earliest original work, *The Boke of the Duchesse*, and in *The Canterbury Tales* is of a good-natured, slightly inept little man, of the sort of whom people like to make kindly fun. We have no autograph manuscripts, and modern scholars agree that the surviving text of Guillaume de Lorris's and Jean de Maun's *Roman de la Rose*, a much abridged version, is not the version, perhaps fuller, which the young Chaucer made; it may have Chaucerian contributions. His earliest period, which includes his own translation and his contributions to the surviving translation of the *Roman de la Rose* and has its climax in the poem on the death of John of Gaunt's first wife Blanche, *The Boke of the Duchesse* – 1369 – has been called his French period. He uses current French conventions of dream, allegory, and vision and the favourite French rhyme form of the octosyllabic couplet. In his diplomatic journeys he could have met Boccaccio and Petrarch (Dante had been dead for fifty years) and would have become aware at least that Italy was producing a less conventional and more psychologically penetrating literature than France. Since the Knight's tale in *The Canterbury Tales* is adapted from Boccaccio's *Il Teseide* and probably precedes the *The Canterbury Tales* (where the Prologue and the characters are used partly to provide a framework for some stories, some at least of which may have been previously written) and *Troilus and Criseide* is much expanded – with a subtlety of character portraiture and a humour that are all Chaucer's own – from Boccaccio's *Il Filostrato*, the second period, beginning about 1332 but reaching full maturity between 1380 and 1385, can be called the Italian period. Chaucer here on the whole prefers a five-stress line (mostly of ten, sometimes of nine, and if one pronounces a final extra-metrical-e, sometimes of eleven syllables) to the octosyllable and is very fond of the seven-line stanza rhyming ababbcc in which *Troilus and Criseide* is written. (This form of stanza was later called 'rhyme royal' because used for his long Petrarchan love poem *The Kingis Quhair* by James I of Scotland.)

The period of *The Canterbury Tales*, from 1386 till near his death in 1400 may be called Chaucer's English period. He allows his humour and his powers of sharp but tolerant social observation full play. Like many poets of social observation (Pope or Crabbe, say) he now finds the couplet, on the whole, a handier instrument than the stanza; a stanza has, in the poet's head, to be at least roughly planned before he writes a first draft of it. A succession of couplets allows more scope for the suddenly occurring thought or the newly observed detail. But Chaucer uses rhyme royal when he wants a pathetic or lofty effect, as in the Clerk's tale of patient Grisilde, or as in the Prioress's tale of the little boy murdered by the Jews. Matthew Arnold – who was worried by Chaucer, as by Burns (can great poetry deal with common or homely things?) – clung to one line of this as an example of Chaucer's capacity, at least, for 'high serious-ness' and the grand style:

> O martyr souded to virginitee . . .   *soldered to*

The homely metaphor of 'soldered to' for 'enlisted in the service of' might have disconcerted Arnold had he under-stood it.

For a modern reader, whose demands of poetry are less narrow and exclusive than Arnold's, Chaucer's homeliness, like his broad, sometimes coarse humour, is a mark of his greatness. Chaucer in the retraction of his poems, and of anything in them tending to sin, with which he takes his leave of *The Canterbury Tales*, is more severe on himself than Arnold, but writes from the point of view of an elderly man shortly to face his Maker and give an account of all his works. He revokes of his poems 'thilke that sounen (*sound, tend*) unto sinne' and also – they have not survived – many a song and many a lecherous lay. A great modern poet, Ezra Pound, has been enchanted by the musicality of a poem like *Merciless Beauty*,

> Your yen two wol slee me sodeinly:
> I may the beautee of hem nat sustene,

but on the whole critics have been too much occupied with the narrative poems to equal Pound in his freshness of response here.

The purpose of a primer of English poetry like this is to give readers the flavour, the first impact of poets, such as one felt oneself on one's first reading of them, not to provide a catalogue of dates and titles. It is enough, I think, if I illustrate Chaucer's development by extracts and comments from his earliest and his two greatest later original works, *The Boke of the Duchesse, Troilus and Criseide*, and *The Canterbury Tales*. Though he served John of Gaunt's brother Lionel as a boy, and later became nominally *valet de chambre* to Edward III, it is not known whether Chaucer was in the service ever, directly, of John of Gaunt: we know that his sister-in-law, Katherine Swynford, governess to John of Gaunt's children, became, first John of Gaunt's mistress and then his wife, her children the founders of the Beaufort family. We know, also, that the date of the vision poem about the dead lady called White must be 1369, not long after the death of Blanche, the beautiful young Duchess of Lancaster, and not too near Gaunt's next dynastic marriage. Henry IV's doubling of Chaucer's pension and confirming of his yearly grant of a butt of wine, like the legacies from John to Chaucer and his wife Philippa, suggest that the great magnate, in any case known as a patron of poets and the arts, had a kindness for Chaucer.

In *The Boke of the Duchesse* Chaucer is faced with a problem of social tact. He must show appreciation of the depth of Gaunt's grief and of the virtues and graces of the dead young duchess without presuming to offer direct consolation as a social equal. He solves this tricky problem by writing a vision poem in which the meaning of the vision is clear to the reader (and to John of Gaunt) but not to the obtuse narrator himself. The danger of this technique of the 'fictional narrative' is obvious. Professor E. T. Donaldson remarked in his excellent Chaucer anthology for the modern reader, in 1958:

> He seems at times almost too stupid to be true: though he has initially overheard the Knight lament his lady's death, he keeps pestering the mourner to reveal the cause of his grief . . . Nevertheless, this stupid character accomplishes his mission of consolation and that is what he is intended to do. His very density forces the Knight to sing the praises of his lady ever louder and louder, and his literalism makes the Knight eventually bow to the fact of her death.

Here is the Knight, after a long and lovely description of

the lady's beauty of manner and figure and heart, suddenly
revealing, so that the obtuse narrator can at last understand
it, that this paragon is dead:

> 'Sire,' quod I, 'wher is she now?'
> 'Now?' quoth he, and stinte anoon.
> Therewith he weex as deed as stoon,
> And saide, 'Allas that I was bore,
> That was the loss that herbifore   *heretofore*
> I tolde thee that I hadde lorn.   *lost*
> Bithenke how I saide herbiforn,   *Bethink*
> 'Thou woost ful litel what thou menest;   *knowest*
> I have lost more than thou weenest.'   *supposest*
> God wot, allas, right that was she.'
> 'Allas, sire, how? What may that be?'
> 'She is deed.' 'Nay!' 'Yes, by my trouthe.'   *troth*
> 'Is that your los? By God, it is routhe.'   *ruth, pity*

Chaucer or the narrator's 'By God, it is routhe' is in fact in
its gruff abruptness more moving than a flood of words
would be. And, of course, the narrator's very thickness has
already released from the lips of the Knight pages of healing
praise of the dead lady:

> But swich a fairnesse of a nekke
> Hadde that sweete, that boon nor brekke   *bone, flaw*
> Had ther noon seene that missat: *sat clumsily*
> It was smoothe, straight, and pure flat   *entirely*
> Withouten hole – or canel-boon: *collar-bone*
> As by seeming, she hadde noon.
> Hir throte, as I have now memoire,
> Seemed a round towr of ivoire
> Of good greetnesse, and nought too greet.
> And goode, faire Whit she heet.   *White (Blanche)*
>   *was called*

The odd unemphatic 'as I have now memoire' adds to the
beauty of the description the sudden sense, and pathos, of
John of Gaunt's momentary remembering, there and then.

Troilus and Criseide is, of course, a much richer and more
mature poem, though certain gifts of Chaucer's – vividness,
pathos, the power of evoking pity – are there from the
beginning in *The Boke of the Duchesse* and could reach no

greater intensity. What did mature were Chaucer's power of telling a story, of presenting a character, with all its oddities and contradictions, in the round, the range and exuberance of his humour, his pitying acceptance of the world's sadness and disappointments, and a kind of Christian piety that comes with that acceptance. The three almost unbearably beautiful and intense stanzas from towards the end of the last book, given below, illustrate the qualities that I have mentioned (notice that Chaucer, at his greatest, is free from the fault which for a modern reader makes longer medieval poems difficult to read through to the end: prolixity). Troilus, deserted by Criseide, fiercely slays many Greeks, though he never tracks down his betrayer Diomede, but is in the end himself slain by the 'fierse Achille'. He faces the judgment of eternity: his great love, and his great betrayal, far less important. And Chaucer gently tells young people like Troilus that, in setting their hearts on anything but salvation, they set them on nothing. In this life, Fortune's wheel will carry them up and carry them down again, but what does earthly Fortune matter?

Swich fin hath, lo, this Troilus for love;   *end*
Swich fin hath all his grete worthinesse;
Swich fin hath his estaat real above,
Swich fin his lust, swich fin hath his noblesse;
Swich fin hath false worldes brotelnesse:
And thus began his loving of Criseide,
As I have told, and in this wise he deide.

O yonge fresshe folkes, he or she,
In which that love up groweth with your age,
Repaireth hoom from worldly vanitee,   *Repair*
And of your herte up casteth the visage
To thilke God that after his image
You made; and thinketh al nis but a faire,
This world that passeth soone as flowres faire;   *faire flowers*

And loveth him, the which that right for love
Upon a crois, oure soules for to beye,   *cross, buy*
First starf, and roos, and sit in hevene above;   *died, arose*
For he nil falsen no wight, dar I saye,
That wol his herte all hoolly on him laye:
And sin he best to love is and most meeke,
What needeth feined loves for to seeke?

But Chaucer, of course, knew that the love of the shy, brave Troilus for Criseide, her more calculating, more hesitant, more self-deceiving but genuine, if transient and shallow, love for him, her uncle Pandar's vicarious love for the love of the 'yonge fresshe folke', his genuine, mischievous but sexless love for each individually, were not 'feined loves': he enters with full sympathy into all his characters and this is why *Troilus and Criseide*, though in verse, has sometimes been called the 'first English novel'. It certainly allows more room for the deep exploration of character than *The Canterbury Tales*, and though one cannot rob the latter, with its magnificent pageant of English life in Chaucer's time, and its magnificent variety of verse tales from the broadly comic to the nobly romantic, of the title of Chaucer's masterpiece, the grand climax of his life's work, I am not alone in finding more personal enjoyment, and more depth if less breadth of perception, in *Troilus and Criseide*.

Chaucer had no doubt been on the pilgrimage to Canterbury, to the shrine of St Thomas à Becket, and his house at Greenwich also lay on the pilgrims' way. It was chiefly on these pilgrimages that, in a rapidly changing but still very hierarchical society, men of every class would meet each other and treat each other with a kind of equality in the face of God and his saints and martyrs who transcended all earthly hierarchies. But the nicities and courtesies of degree were, among the pilgrims, still closely observed among the lower ranks, towards each other even if not towards the well-born and the rich, like the Franklin:

> It snewed in his hous of mete and drink.

who represents (like Chaucer, in his own very different way) a new rising class, below the aristocratic Knight and Squire, but somehow a little above the still prosperous guildsmen in the uniforms of their guilds. The Wife of Bath, apparently as prosperous as the Franklin, does not make the kind of claims to be a lady that he makes to be a gentleman. Her prologue and her tale, with their emphasis on the ideas of 'maistrye' – the woman's desire to dominate the man – contrast strangely with the Knight's tale of Palamon and Arcite, the two close friends divided by their humble love for Emelye.

As in the Knight's tale and the Wife of Bath's tale, the stories sometimes seem to suit their tellers or to enlarge our idea of them. The Prioress, for instance, is presented with kindly satire as a pleasant and gentlewomanly person, but aiming at a little more refinement and delicacy than naturally belong to her: her tale of the little boy murdered by the Jews shows that, under her affections, her piety is simple and deep (it is better, when reading this moving story, to ignore the nasty legend about the Jews and their custom of sacrificing Christian children: Chaucer's Jews, and later Shakespeare's and Marlowe's, were creatures of the imagination, the Jewish community having been expelled as a body from England and permitted to return only by Oliver Cromwell). Noting signs of historical change, we can see that, though Chaucer reverses the secular priest, the 'poor parson', he thinks the monk a hypocrite, and the summoner and the pardoner positively evil and corrupt. He notes the financial ambition and sometimes dishonesty of the rising middle classes, the merchant, the reeve, the manciple, the sergeant of law: he paints a society, in fact, full of worldly ambition in which the unworldliness of the learned 'clerk of Oxenford' astonishes the host and where Chaucer's own apparent unworldliness earns him good-natured mockery:

> Till that our Hoste japen he bigan.
> And thanne at erst he looked upon me,
> And saide thus, 'What man artou?' quod he.
> 'Thou lookest as thou woldest finde an hare,
> For ever upon the ground I see thee stare.
>
> 'Approche neer and looke up merrily.
> Now ware you, sires, and lat this man have place:
> He in the wast is shape as wel as I –
> This were a popet in an arm t'enbrace,   *doll*
> For any womman, smal and fair of face:
> He seemeth elvvish by his countenaunce,
> For unto no wight dooth he daliaunce.

Chaucer, as we have seen in studying *The Boke of the Duchesse*, seems to delight in self-mockery. He carries it on by giving himself deliberately the most tedious of all the tales, *Sir Thopas*, a parody of the see-saw metre, the improbable incidents, and the insufferably redundant verbosity of the old verse romances that were beginning to go out of fashion: it comes to no point nor shows any signs of coming to one. No wonder the explosive Host interrupts:

'Namore of this, for Goddes dignitee!'

On the whole, then, *The Canterbury Tales* is rightly Chaucer's most famous work, exhibiting the variety of his gifts including a gift, anticipating Pope, for the satirical sketch of character, with much richness and variety. But of its very nature it cannot have the organic unity of *Troilus and Criseide*, and though the General Prologue is rightly famed as a panorama of English society in Chaucer's time its characters, with a very few exceptions like the Prioress, the Wife of Bath, and possibly the Knight, are types done in the flat rather than rounded individuals (one would make an exception, also, of the Host at the *Tabard*). The General Prologue offers us a kind of Dramatis Personae, of a play, but the interaction both there, and very largely thereafter, between the various characters is minor. In a sense the device of the pilgrimage, and the various social classes and moral characters of the pilgrims, is a hollow structure to contain a succession of stories, some related by dealing with chivalry, marriage, or the humours of low life, but on the whole not very closely tied to each other. *The Canterbury Tales* remains, if not an organic work, a very rich work. No other English poet of Chaucer's date is at once so intelligently observant and such a master of the craft and art of verse, from vivid presentation, with much humour, of character and speech to plain narrative and occasional passages, when they are needed, of eloquence and pathos. Perhaps no other English poet at all gives Chaucer's unique effect that, whatever he does, he is doing it never with slackness but always with ease of control: never straining himself. The personality that comes shyly or slyly through the poems is a modest, gay, affectionate and endearing one. Finally, we do not need to make special historical allowances, as we have with some other poets we have dealt with, for his time: he is just as sophisticated and civilised as any poet who has succeeded him. The society sketched out in vivid and brightly coloured outline in the General Prologue is not a society cruder, less sensitive, or less intelligent than our own. One might even say that in the uncomfortable preoccupation of its less sympathetic characters with degree, power, money, and the prospect of putting one over on people and rising in the world, it is very much our modern world in embryo. We lack, of course, the religion that unified it and the codes of common courtesy that tended to make encounters on the road agreeable.

4

The High Middle Ages: II

I William Langland

William Langland, of whom very little is known apart from
some autobiographical touches in his poem, had a biographical note scribbled at the back of the manuscript of his
poem now in Dublin: 'Memorandum quod Stacy de Rokayle
pater willielmi de Langlond qui stacius fuit generosus &
morabatur in Schiptoun vnder whicwode tenens domini le
Spenser in comitatu Oxoniensi qui predictus willielmus fecit
librum qui vocatur Perys ploughman.' In modern English:
'Note – Stacy de Rokayle was the father of William Langland who lived at Shipton-under-Wychwood with the status
of a gentleman as a tenant of Lord Despenser in Oxfordshire, which aforesaid William made the book called Piers
Ploughman.' He was born sometime early in the 1330s, most
probably Rokayle's illegitimate son (or he would have
inherited some land, some money, and probably, though the
handing on of surnames was not universal, the name de
Rokayle). He was most likely educated at Great Malvern
monastery but could afford only to take minor orders. He
travelled about the country and in London lived with his
wife Kit and his daughter Colette near Cornhill. Without
any parsonage or even curateship, he earned a meagre living
by singing the Office of the Dead. Those in minor orders
were in a sense the proletariat of the Church, enjoying
unusual freedom, more or less their own masters, but with
no hope of advancement. Where Chaucer was all his life at
the comfortable centre of things, Langland was at the harsh
outer edges.

Apart from earning enough bread for his family and keeping a roof over his head, Langland devoted his whole life to the steady extension of his single work. The A text was composed about 1370, the B text between 1377 and 1379, the final C text when Langland was an elderly man and part at least of the C text had been written by 1388. The three versions do not aim at greater perfection of form but at packing in more matter, matter which switches bewilderingly from religious and even mystical vision to straight moral exhortation, such as Langland might have used in his sermons, and to sharp and often very amusing political and social satire. Langland was undoubtedly a great poet but he differs from most great poets in that one approaches him more through, and for, the matter than through, and for, the form, and that, though he is always readable, the loose alliterative line he used told against any passages of striking poetic concentration; the use of the form for him was its flexibility, what Elizabeth Salter in *Piers Plowman, an Introduction* (Blackwell, 1963) calls 'rapid contraction and expansion of reference'.

The poem begins with a vision of a plain set between the Tower of Truth (which in the Middle Ages meant Troth, Loyalty, Trustworthiness, the word for our main sense of truth being Sooth) and Falsehood. On the plain full of folk, Langland spies all sorts of dishonesties and a reckless king, a cat whom the mice dare not bell. The Lady Holy Church exhorts him to save his soul by pursuing Truth and Love, which are one. He is also warned against the Lady Meed (broadly Bribery), the daughter of Falsehood. Meed is arrested, is to be pardoned if Conscience will marry her, but Conscience refuses. On Conscience's appeal, the king calls Reason to court, who denounces Meed's protection of Crime. The dreamer then awakes, only to sleep and have another vision of the Seven Deadly Sins, all of whom are absolved after confession. Piers the Ploughman (who is an allegorical figure of Christ, but who also represents the need for honest labour in the world) offers to take charge of pilgrims and lead them in the right path if they help him to clear his small half acre of land first. (Since the Black Death, labour had been dear and scarce.) The pilgrims are unwilling but are driven to work by hunger. The Truth then sends for Piers a pardon for all who have worked honestly with him.

The vision of Piers Ploughman, proper, ends here and William sets out on his more solitary quest for the vision of Do-Well, Do-Better, and Do-Best. He is first led astray by two Friars who assure him of the inevitability of sin but, falling asleep, has a vision of Thought, a questing spirit, very like himself. Thought has the theory of Do-Well but not any practical advice. They go in search of Intelligence who speaks mainly about Good Sense governing the Flesh. He is sent by Intelligence in search of Learning, but Learning himself attacks the learned, and William says Learning cannot help men predestined to damnation or salvation.

This rejection of study and learning has very startling results. The dreamer falls asleep again and follows Fortune for forty-five years, till in his old age she deserts him. He is seized with a sudden fear of damnation which is eased a little by Scripture and by the thought of the good pagan Emperor, Trajan, who was set free from Hell. But he goes on arguing even with Nature and Reason till he awakes, and finds himself under the guidance of Imagination. He falls asleep again and is invited to dine, but at a humble side table, accompanied by Patience, at a dinner given by Conscience, Scripture, and Learning and a non-allegorical figure, a great churchman, whose greediness drives him into a rage. Conscience accompanies William, moved by the words of Patience, on a pilgrimage, where they meet Haukyn, the active as against the contemplative man, rich, successful, but his garments, signifying Baptism, soiled by all the Seven Deadly Sins. Haukyn is told to save his soul by embracing poverty, to which he is at last persuaded. Langland has now discovered Do-Well and is assisted on his quest for Do-Better, or Charity, by the mysterious figure of Anima, who tells him that Piers is Christ (and denounces Christ's corrupt priests). Anima advises him to seek a precious tree on which the fruits of charity grow, but the Devil snatches the fruits away from Piers who pursues him. William has a vision of the life of Christ till his victory over the Devil on the Cross. William awakes again and meets Abraham, who explains Faith and the mystery of the Trinity to him. He falls asleep again, witnesses the Passion, and flees in horror from it to the borders of Hell where he sees Christ harrowing Hell. The poet is awakened by the bells of Easter morning and calls his family to come to Mass. At Mass, however, he falls asleep again and witnesses Christ bestowing on Piers – who is now no longer Christ but his representative, St Peter – the power to plough the field of the world. But even when Christ offers them the Eucharist, some Christians are unwilling to make reparation of the wrongs they have done to others to make themselves fit to receive it. The last book is grim. Antichrist has come and Conscience is left with few followers to defend the castle of Unity, though age, death, and the plague attack Christ's enemies; but old age attacks all men and Will who is perhaps Langland himself, stricken with age, seeks refuge in the Castle of Unity. All is not well: a Friar, who has been let into the Castle of Unity, makes penance too easy and the people again relapse into spiritual sloth. Conscience is not strong enough, nor is the Castle of Unity impregnable enough, to be a sufficient defence against Antichrist. Conscience and the Dreamer take to the roads again, to find Piers, their only champion. And Langland awakes for the last time.

I emphasised, in the last chapter, the modernity of Chaucer. Langland is not modern in that sense. He is not, however, merely medieval; like Bunyan in *The Pilgrim's Progress* he presents to us a world in which the things of the spirit are as real and homely as the things of the body, in which abstract ideas – Meed, Conscience, Reason, Learning – become real people, like Bunyan's Greatheart or his Pliable or his Mr Worldly Wiseman, and in which, on the other hand, 'real' people, ignorant or corrupt or greedy clergymen, become personifications of abstract ideas. We are on the borders of heaven and hell, but we are also in Cornhill or the Malvern Hills. The poet himself is not a mere passive recipient of wisdom but often argumentative and wrong-headed. There is human interest all through.

But what of Langland as a poet? Elizabeth Salter and Derek Pearsall in their very useful selection for sixth-formers and undergraduates (*Piers Plowman*, York Medieval Texts, Edward Arnold, London, 1967) point out that in his direct conversational speech,

'What manere mynstralcie, my dear friend,' quath Conscience,
'Hast thou used other haunted all thy life-time?'

Langland is in a sense easier to read, more like our current speech today (and more like 'modern accentual verse', by which I take it they mean the stress verse, as distinct from foot verse, used in Auden's *The Age of Anxiety* and parts of Eliot's *Ash Wednesday*) than Chaucer. Yet, they also point out, he is not a naif poet, he can in his revisions polish for special effects: as in the C version of Christ's words to Lucifer,

> 'May no pyement ne pomade, ne presiouse drynkes,
> Moiste me to the fulle, ne my furste slakke . . .'

compared to the simpler version of B,

> 'May no drynke me moiste, ne my thruste slake . . .'

Literally the meaning of the C version is: 'May no spiced drink or apple-juice or any precious drinks moisten me to the full nor slake my thirst'; the meaning of the B version: 'May no drink moisten me, nor slake my thirst . . .'. I feel myself that the directness of the B version is preferable, the C version an elaboration without improvement, and indeed a rather thoughtless elaboration: spiced drinks increase one's thirst rather than slaking it. It is best, I think, to praise Langland more for the ease, naturalness, and flexibility of his verse (though unlike rhymed stress-syllable verse it has to proceed at an even jogtrot throughout, cannot make its rhythms suddenly rapid or make them pause in grave solemnity) than for its beauty: and depth and detail and homely humanity touching even the deepest things of the spirit are again what please us in the poem as a whole, not a structural mastery or beauty of design but spontaneous naturalness of development. In a work which lasted him for a lifetime Langland was seeking, and perpetually renewing his seeking, for truth rather than, like Milton in *Paradise Lost*, designing a masterpiece. It is difficult in fact to make a final assessment of *Piers Plowman*: it perhaps expresses the affection and respect which its lovers feel for it to say that, like *The Pilgrim's Progress* with which I have compared it, it is one of the most purely English of those works of our people that last.

II The *Gawain–Pearl* poet

There are four late fourteenth-century poems in one manuscript, none of them with a title, but all in a North-Western dialect. It is possible that a poet like Chaucer, with a gift for languages, might have understood them, just as it is possible that a modern English reader might understand Burns, even when his Scots is richest: it is equally possible in both cases that the reader accustomed to standard East Midlands might catch a general drift but be bewildered by details. The East Midlands dialect developed into our modern English and the North-Western dialect of the poet we are considering had no important literary progeny. Yet printing slightly misleads us since we do not know how the poem originally sounded in the poet's own voice. The Elizabethan poet, Sir Walter Raleigh, is reputed to have spoken in broad Devonshire, the Victorian poet, Tennyson, with a Lincolnshire burr.

In the Middle Ages, if one avoided pilgrimages and crusades and had no political business that drew one to London, it was possible to be perfectly confident and assured spending most of one's life in what we would now call a provincial culture. This seems to be true of the great author of the four untitled poems, with crude but moving illustrations, that we call *Purity* (or *Cleanness*), *Patience*, *The Pearl*, and *Sir Gawain and the Green Knight*. Linguistic scholars guess that he flourished in south rather than north Lancashire (he never uses the north Lancashire term *beck*, used by Wordsworth and Hopkins, for a stream) and on the borders rather than deep into Cheshire (since he never uses the similar Cheshire word *bach*: yet he loves writing about running water). In *Sir Gawain* the hero rides north from a Camelot which seems to be Caerleon on Usk rather than the Cornish Camelford, skirting Anglesey on his left, yet arriving at a place called Holyhead (it might be Saint Winifred's well, where a virgin saint was decapitated in resisting rape). The castle at which he finally arrives in thick woodland country, strong but ornate, has been thought to resemble the castle of Caernarvon, well to the south of him. The heavily wooded, tacky, watery landscape in which the poet, both in *The Pearl* and *Sir Gawain* delights, reflects features of the Pennine chain. He evokes natural landscape with a beauty which neither Chaucer nor Langland in this field aim at: the vision of the Paradise from which the lost Pearl, now a Queen in Heaven, speaks to him across a river, containing some features of the natural landscape (though it is also a dream landscape) in which he has been wandering. The three hunts in *Sir Gawain* conform to all the medieval rules of manuals of hunting – the three preys are the deer, the wild boar, the fox – but have a fierce, primitive force. The elaborate courtesies of the scenes in the castle, the feastings and the three temptations of Sir Gawain by the lady, are at once the stuff of romance and yet seem to reflect a contemporary, surviving way of life. A colleague and friend of mine, Professor Jack Simmons, tells me that when he crosses the Scottish border he goes back fifty years in time; perhaps in north-west England one went back two or three hundred years in time.

The primitive force is reflected in the metre of these poems, basically the old English stress metre, but in *The Pearl* worked up into stanzas linked to each other by a key word and in *Sir Gawain* winding up long passages of long alliterative lines with a single iambic foot followed by a quatrain in iambic trimetres:

> so gode.
> 'Inogh,' quoth Sir Gawayn,
> 'I thonk yow, by the Rode,'
> And how the fox was slayn
> He tolde hym as thay stode.

Such a quatrain may not seem very brilliant in itself, but it should be taken with what leads up to it, the Green Knight's (though Gawain does not know he is the Green Knight) account, boisterous and vivid, of the profitlessness of the hunting of the fox. There is an agreement that Gawain and the Green Knight should each exchange with the other any prizes they have won during the day, Gawain waiting in the Knight's castle while the Knight hunts. On the morning of the first day of hunting, the Green Knight's wife comes to Gawain's bed, and tempts him. To preserve both courtesy and chastity he kisses her once. On the second day, he is more severely tempted, and kisses her twice. These kisses he loyally gives to his host: on the third day (and as the boar symbolises the fierceness of temptation, the fox symbolises cunning) the lady offers Gawain a girdle which, she says, will protect him in his encounter at the Green Chapel the next day. Largely out of cowardice, he hangs on to this gift and is wearing it when he encounters the Green Knight (utterly transformed in appearance from his host at the castle) in the Green Chapel – a natural cave in the woods – the next day. The Green Knight twice brings the axe down on Gawain's neck without hurting him but the third time very slightly cuts the skin. This is a penalty for Gawain's failure at the third temptation. A year before, the Green Knight had ridden into Camelot and asked King Arthur or his representative (Gawain offers himself) to cut off his head, if he would meet him to face the challenge the next year at the same time, during the Christmas festivities. When we know all this we can appreciate the Knight's tone of disgust with the fox, which is also disgust with Gawain for having failed at the third temptation (and failed not out of desire for the lady, but out of desire for a magical talisman of self-protection):

> 'Mary,' quoth that other man, 'myn is bihynde, *my gift*
> For I haf hunted al this day, and noght haf
> I geten
> Bot this foule fox felle – the Fende haf the *pelt, fiend,*
> godes! *good*
> And that is full pore for to pay for such prys *precious*
> Thinges
> As ye haf thrycht me here thro, suche thre
> cosses *kisses*
>   So gode.'

There is sophisticated irony here; the 'foul fox fell' has, in fact, about the same worth as the three false and lying kisses. And even after forgiveness and reconciliation at the Green Chapel Gawain rides home sadly, in shame not triumph, bearing the ambiguous gift, from the Knight now as well as the Lady, of the protective girdle: but at Camelot the ladies make copies of it and the other Knights of the Round Table wear it in Gawain's honour.

The Three Temptations and the Unbeheadable Knight (who is Nature, and who is still commemorated in pubs called *The Green Man*) are old folk motifs and the descriptions of the three hunts, for all their liveliness, are according to prescription. The deeper seriousness of the poet perhaps is expressed more crudely and directly, though not more effectively, in the earlier, more abstract, less effective poems *Patience* and *Purity*. The three Temptations ostensibly attack Gawain's purity: in the first he slips away easily like a doe, in the second he has to turn at bay like a boar; he is the quarry, and she is the huntress. In the third she insensibly shifts her attack and undermines his patience, his willingness to endure for honour's sake a dreadful death of beheading by a monster. To this third temptation he yields, and for all its atmosphere of gaiety and courtesy, for all the Green Knight's own courtesy and forgiveness, there is the medieval sense that inevitably, by Christian standards, the highest natural virtue will fail. The mood is not tragedy, but neither is it comedy, the prize quite cleanly won, the task accomplished; rather the Knights of the Round Table who share Sir Gawain's fallen nature choose to wear with him the girdle which is a badge of humility rather than triumph.

The Pearl, which probably preceded *Sir Gawain and the Green Knight*, is an extraordinarily beautiful and profound poem without, however, the range and action of *Sir Gawain*. It will always find some readers (I am among them) who because of their attraction to the spirituality of medieval writing, as well as for a certain inwoven intricacy in its art, prefer it. It can very deeply touch the heart. The poet has lost a perfect pearl, a child of two years old, buried, and his heart cannot be consoled for her. He falls asleep beside a mound that is her grave and has a vision of her standing, adult, arrayed as a queen, with a crown and a white robe, all embroidered in pearls, on the other side of a river bank. Her manner to him is a little stern. He wants to cross the river and join her but of course he can only do so after death, and it is presumption to suppose that anyone will cross the river to heaven. He is also, in spite of himself, astonished and a little angry that she should be made a queen on her very first day in heaven, as she was too young when she died to have acquired, other than her baptised innocence, any merit in God's eyes. She explains this by an unusual interpretation of the parable of the vineyard, that the last who come to labour shall be the first to be paid, and that her being a queen in heaven is no reflection on the Virgin as Queen of Heaven since it is the delight and chief pleasure of all the other queens to serve her and Christ, the lamb of God, who is the source of all the light in heaven – of whose jewelled streets the poet is given a vision – and the reward of all the faithful is equal. (The orthodox view of paradise was that the plenitude of bliss, or capacity for receiving bliss, was hierarchical, like medieval society on earth. This is to be found in Dante, for instance, and as late as Dr Johnson, who said in conversation with Boswell that a worthy carter would be as happy in heaven as Sir Isaac Newton, but according to capacity: just as a pint pot of beer can be full, but not, in Johnson's homely illustration, contain as much beer as a full quart pot. The heresy of democracy in heaven or equality of bliss and glory is not, in any case, likely to trouble modern readers.) And the poet is reassured, above all perhaps, by the Pearl's insistence on the safety, after death, of children:

> Jesus thenne hem swetely sayde:
> 'Do way, let chylder vnto me ticht,   *come*
> To suche is hevenryche arayed':   *the kingdom of heaven*
> The innocent is ay saf by rycht.

Having had his bejewelled and glittering glimpse of heaven and been counselled by the heavenly wisdom of his transfigured daughter, the poet is turned from the hopeless grief for the 'pearl withouten spot' of the beginning of the poem:

> Forsothe ther fleten to me fell,   *floated, many* (sad
> To thenke her color so clad in clot.   *clay*   thoughts)
> O moul, thou marres a myry iuele,   *mould, marrest, jewel*
> My privy perle wythouten spotte,

to the calm resignation of the end:

> To pay the Prince other sete sachte   *cause to be a peace*
> Hit is full ethe to the god Krystyn,   *easy, good*
> For I haf founden hym, bothe day and
>   nachte,   *night*
> A God, a Lorde, a frende full fyin,   *excellent (fine)*
> Over this hyiil this lote I lachte   *mound, lot, received*
> For pyty of my perle enclyin,   *lying prostrate*
> And sythen to God I hit bytachte,   *since, committed*
> In Krystez dere blessyng and myn,
> That in the forme of bred and wyn   *That Christ's blessing*
> The preste vus schewez vch a day.   *everyday*
> He gef vus to be his homly hyne   *hinds, labourers*
> Ande precious perles unto his pay.

>   Amen.   Amen.

In outlining the argument of these poems, I have failed to illustrate the passages of sheer glittering and ornate beauty. Here is part of the description of the Pearl in her queenly adornments:

A pyght coroune yet we that gyrle	*adorned*
Of mariorys and non other ston,	*pearls*
Highe pynakled of cler quyt perle.	*white*
Wyth flurted flowrez perfet vpon.	*figured, perfectly worked*
To hed hade ho no other werle;	*she, circlet*
Her here leke, all hyr umbegon,	*enclosed, lying around*
Her semblaunt sade for doc other erle	*grave enough for, duke*
Her ble more blacht then whallez bon	*complexion, white*
As schorne golde schyr her fax thenne schon,	*hair*
On schylderez that leghe unlapped lyghte.	*shoulders, unbound*
Her depe color yet wonted non	*deep white of her com-*
Of precios perle in porfyl pyghte.	*embroidery, set* [*plexion*

Whistler might have called this a 'symphony in white'.

John Speirs has called attention, similarly, in reference to *Sir Gawain*, to the first description of the Green Knight's castle (or rather the castle of the Green Knight in human disguise) whose delicacy of outline (by the fourteenth century castles had become works of art and places of revelry, not merely defensive keeps) becomes even more magical because of the suggestion that it might have been cut out of white paper:

And innermore he behelde that hall full hyghe,	
Towers telded betwene, trochet full thik,	*set up, pinnacle*
Fayre fylyolez that fyyed, and ferlyly long,	*pinnacles, fitted*
With coruon coprounes craftyly cleghe,	*carved tops, made*
Chalk-whyte chimnées there ches he innoghe	
Upon bastel rovez, that blenked full whyte:	*roof towers;*
So many pynakle payntet was poudred aywhere,	*everywhere*
Among the castel carnelez clambred so thick	*embrasures*

That pared out of papure purely hit   *Cut out of (like*
  seemed.   *paring an apple)*

What sort of castle had the poet in mind? One, perhaps, rather like Carnaervon in design or the unfinished castle at Beaumaris in Anglesey, with elaborate battlements, pinnacles, pepper-pot towers, built for defence, but also to make a fine show? And because built of some rather dull stone, or even brick, showily whitewashed all over? That last line, 'that pared out of paper purely it seemed', is genius. There never was such a castle except in the world of the imagination: it is the poet who has pared out of paper, purely.

III Barbour's *The Bruce*

Scottish poetry might not seem to have a place in these pages, and indeed Scottish poetry in Gaelic like Irish poetry in Irish Gaelic or Welsh poetry in Welsh is, both from my ignorance of the Celtic languages and the lack of direct contact and influence between Celtic and English literature (there are a few late exceptions, like the poetry of Hopkins, or, in the later eighteenth-century, the influence of Mac-Pherson's half-fraudulent but only half-fraudulent – he was making a showy literary use of genuine oral traditions – *Ossian*) outside my brief. Matthew Arnold, to be sure, thought that the English got their touch of poetic magic, so different from Germanic lumpishness, from the Celtic blood in their veins. And it seems fairly obvious that some of the earliest Germanic invaders of Britain must have come over in all male groups and taken their women from the Cymric peoples they drove to the West. I know that I myself have Highland Scottish, Welsh, Northern English, and so far as I know no Lowland Scottish blood. Yet I was brought up largely in Aberdeen, the capital of the north-east thrust of the Lowlands. In the town hall there, there is still the armour of the short bandy-legged Provost of Aberdeen who took part in the battle of the Red Harlaw, which prevented MacDonald, the Lord of the Isles, from making Scotland a mixture of Norsemen and Gaels. Edinburgh, Edwin's burough, is the capital of those Lowland Scots whom a Highlander would call Sassenachs: remote England might hardly come into his mind. The medieval poetic language of Lowland Scots was in fact a north-eastern vernacular of English, as the language of the *Gawain–Pearl* poet was northish-western, and that of Chaucer east-midland. All in verse were 'poetic' dialects – never exactly the language of everyday speech – and poets from different regions would borrow phrases from each other. The use of a local vernacular had nothing to do with what we call today literary nationalism; the greatest Scottish poet of the fifteenth century, Dunbar, wrote a poem in praise of London and addressed comic verse to the English laureate, Skelton; Robert Henryson's greatest poem *The Testament of Cresseid*, though very different in tone, was a kind of complimentary sequel to Chaucer's *Troilus and Criseide*. Modern historians of Scottish literature dislike the phrase 'the Scottish Chaucerians', but certainly the late medieval (or early Renaissance, as one likes to think of it) Scottish poets were great admirers of Chaucer. In spite of the differences in vernacular usage, it might be said that the literature of this island was more closely linked in the late Middle Ages than it is today. Does the name of Ian Crichton-Smith mean much to many readers out of Scotland, the name John Montague to many out of Ireland, the name Anthony Conran to many out of North Wales, or the name H. J. Prynne to many, even in England, out of Cambridge? Common assumptions about what poetry was and did, and difference of accidence and syntax not serious enough to act as barriers to understanding, made the non-Celtic poetry of our island into a kind of unity. Today, apart from experiments in Lowland Scots, there is a single standard literary English: but there are no common assumptions about what poetry is and does.

Scotland was a poorer country than England and also a very much more divided one. An alliance of the Norsemen who held the Orkneys and much of the Western islands and the North-Eastern plain of Scotland (the surnames and place-names of Caithness are Norse; the country of Sutherland is well to the north of Scotland but well to the south of Norway) and the Gaelic-speaking Scots, originally from Ireland, was a perpetual threat to the Sassenach, or Saxon, kingdom of the Lowlands. The feudal system had never caught on: in the Highlands, the clan or tribal system, torn by internecine feuds, prevailed. In the Lowlands, unless circumstances demanded a strong King like Robert the Bruce or unexpectedly brought one, like James I, who spent his youth as a royal hostage in England, learning something both of the art of politics and the art of verse, the great magnates, Douglases, Kennedys, Hamiltons, Gordons, Forbeses, Ruthvens, Beatons, at feud with each other as well as disloyal to their kings, held sway. When James I was assassinated for trying to bring some order into this turmoil, there was a general sense of shock when his English queen rounded up the high-born assassins and had them slowly tortured to death. There was a feeling that the lady was not playing according to the traditional rules of the game.

One feeling, and one alone, could unit the turbulent and divided Scottish people, a fear and hatred of their powerful English neighbours to the South. About fifty-two years after the battle of Bannockburn, in which Robert Bruce in 1314 drove Edward II and the English invaders from Scotland, John Barbour (c.1320–95) published his great *chanson de geste, The Bruce*. It was a rough, powerful poem, a stripped, bare language with nothing ornate about it, with no element of courtly romance or picturesque description. Its subject was war, the character of a leader, and the passion for freedom which made a people so divided among themselves follow that leader loyally. One great passage has echoed down the ages:

A! fredome is a noble thing!	
Fredome mays man to haiff liking;	*makes*
Fredome all solace to man giffis:	
He levys at es that frely levys.	*lives*
A noble hart may haiff nane es,	*ease*
Na ellys nocht that may him ples,	*please*
Gyff fredome failyhe: for fre liking	*fail*
Is yharnyt our all othir thing,	*yearned for over*
Na he that ay hass levit fre,	
May nocht knaw weill the propyrte,	
The angyr, na the wretchyt dome,	*doom*
That is couplyt to foule thyrldome.	*thraldom*
Bot gyff he had assayit it,	
Than all perquer he suld it wyt;	*by heart, know*
And suld think fredome mar to prys,	*prize*
Than all the gold in warld that is.	
Thus contrar thingis evir-mar,	
Discoveryngis of the tothir ar.	

Strong and fine as this is, heroic in its simplicity, it seems to belong (and indeed does belong) to a time two or three hundred years earlier than that of Chaucer: to the last of the heroic age, rather than to the flowering of the age of allegory, romance, and verse comedy. Barbour's tradition did not die. A hundred years after his time, Henry the Minstral or 'Blind Harry', who flourished around 1470, produced a similar but not so powerful heroic lay, *The Wallace*. But his very name suggests that in the century of elaborate and courtly Scottish poetry, he appealed to simple folk and cottagers, not, like Henryson and Dunbar, to a courtly and highly literate audience.

IV Lyric and Drama

I have decided, very reluctantly, to leave verse drama out of this survey. Shakespeare, our greatest poet, happens also to be our greatest dramatist; but he uses great verse in his plays when he needs it, and not at other times. The second scene of *Macbeth*, for instance, that of the 'bloody sergeant', is a first rate piece of stagecraft but the language is, deliberately, inflated rhetoric rather than anything that could be called poetry. High poetry was at Shakespeare's call when he needed it, which was not always. The various medieval cycles of miracle plays, traditionally associated with towns such as York, Wakefield and Towneley, covering the whole story of Creation, the Fall, the Redemption, and the Last Judgment are moving either to watch (as in an excellent BBC production of one of the cycles in 1975) or to read, noting both the simple and unquestioning faith and the broad, earthy humour which seems to make the sacred story repeat itself eternally on the homely streets of English towns. It is easier, perhaps, to get the everyday flavour of prosperous, likely *bourgeois* life in late medieval England from the miracle plays than anywhere else. Their successors, the morality plays, *Everyman*, *The Castle of Perseverance*, which continued as a fairly popular mode into late Tudor times (and influenced Elizabethan drama itself, so that Falstaff has been seen as the Vice of the Moralities and the easiest way to understand that unsatisfactory play *Measure for Measure* is to think of it as a belated morality in which Shakespeare spoiled the pattern by turning his allegorical types into real people) are edifying but obvious in their development and lacking in poetic excitement . . . In contradiction to this policy, I shall deal at some length with later poems like Shelley's *Prometheus Unbound*, which could not hold the attention of any audience in a theatre, but as long, well modulated, lyrically meditative poems have great purely poetic importance.

My decision to leave out verse drama is not based on any theory of what poetry is, or is not, but on convenience. If there were, for instance, as many long poems of the merit of *Paradise Lost*, *The Prelude*, *Don Juan* as there are important English prose novels, I would clearly leave the long poem out and call this book *A Short History of Shorter English Poems*. Fortunately, if one includes *Beowulf*, there are not more than six or seven really important long poems in the English language and even of these six or seven a number are either not wholly successful in achieving their aims or are successful in a way which verges on the trivial. Tennyson's *The Princess* is quite successful in its way, but verges on the trivial: Browning's *The Ring and the Book* and Pound's *Cantos*, on the other hand, are nobly ambitious in their aims but seem in the end not successful. There are few enough of such poems, in any case, to include in a primer like this: but, if one considers not only Shakespeare but his contemporaries, and also all that one demands of a good play *apart* from mastery of language and sincerity of feeling, verse drama must clearly be left out. Shakespeare's sonnets – if not, with the same certainty, his narrative poems – give him, in any case, a place in the first rank of English poets.

English lyric poetry in the fourteenth century remained on the whole a popular form, as, in our second chapter, we have seen it was in the two centuries after the Conquest. Chaucer introduced two highly 'literary' forms, the ballade and the rondel, both depending a great deal on the refrain (in the rondel a pair of refrains) and the ballade sometimes making a rich use of the poetic associations of proper names:

Hid, Absalon, thy gilte tresses clere;	*gilt, golden*
Ester, lay thou thy mekeness al adown;	*Esther*
Hid, Jonathas, all thy freendly manere;	*Jonathan*
Penolopee, and Marcia Catoun,	*Cato's wife*
Make of your wifhood no comparisoun;	*womanliness*

Hid ye youre beautees, Isoude and Elaine: *take the shine out of* Alceste is here that al that may distaine.

Chaucer's acquaintance with Italian did not lead him, however, to introduce the sonnet, and such poems of courtly flattery lack the fusion of bitterness and adoration, the sense of love as a deadly but desirable sickness, which is at the heart of the *dolce stil nuovo* ('sweet new, or novel, style') tradition of which Petrarch, and Petrarchanism, is the culmination. Looking for something really English, original, and magic the casual reader is much more likely to turn to the mysterious:

> Maiden in the mor lay,   *moor*
> In the mor lay;
> Sevenight fulle,
> Sevenight fulle,
> Maiden in the mor lay;
> In the mor lay,
> Sevennightes fulle and a day . . .

Throughout English poetry – it is to be noted even and especially in the rhythms – there is this clash between rooted nature and polished convention. I prefer, myself, the maiden in the moor to Absalom's 'gilte tresses clere'.

5

The Fifteenth Century

I Linguistic Changes in England, Linguistic Stability in Scotland

It is generally agreed that the fifteenth and early sixteenth centuries are the greatest period of Scottish poetry in English, or 'Inglis', as the Scots poets in what we now call Lowland Scots called their language, to contrast it with the 'Irisch' of the Gaelic Scots. It is equally generally agreed that English poetry of the fifteenth century is, with the exception of the very outstanding and personal work of John Skelton (his date of birth is uncertain but he was writing between 1489 and 1529, the year in which he died) is, if not wholly dull, at least quite remarkably lacking in poets of interesting temperament and original talent. The most original were King James I of Scotland whose *The Kingis Quhair* is a long courtly love poem arising from a glimpse from his window of the Lady Joan Beaufort whom he ultimately married (and who was beautiful, passionately loyal, and had James's assassins put to death, as we have seen, with a prolonged cruelty that shocked even the rough and murderous nobility of Scotland). The other was the French prince, Charles d'Orleans, who is also a minor classic in his own language. He succeeded Chaucer in naturalising forms like the rondel and this example has delightful humour and charm:

> My gostly fadir, Y me confess,   *spiritual father*
> First to God and then to yow,
> That at a wyndow, wot ye how,   *you know how*

I stale a cosse of gret swetnes,   *stole a kiss*
Which don was out avisyess (–)   *deliberately*
But hit is doon not undoon now.
    My gostly fadir, Y me confess,
    First to God and then to yow.
But I restore it shalle, dowtles,
Ageyn, if so be that I mow;   *may*
And that to God Y make a vow
And ellis I axe foryefnes.   *forgiveness*
    My gostly fadir, Y me confesse,
    First to God and then to yow.

The humour is delicate. It is from her ghostly father, her confessor, that she has stolen a kiss and she begs God's forgiveness unless she makes reparation by restoring it to him; the combination of demureness and naughtiness is delightful but one wonders if Charles, a prisoner of war or hostage in England (1394–1465), is typically English at all or is bringing into our language a sly and graceful French mischievousness.

Some critics have doubted James I's authorship of *The Kingis Quhair*, perhaps contrasting the romantic tenderness of the poem with the sternness with which James, restored to his Kingdom, attempted to bring law and order into Scotland. But the knightly character, of which this first and greatest of the Jameses ('They were all called James', said Lord Melbourne slightly inaccurately to Queen Victoria, 'and they were all murdered!') was a high exemplar, combined courageousness and sternness to enemies with submissive grace to ladies. The style of *amour courtois* James had certainly not acquired during his early days in England: yet the poem by this man who attempted to unify a broken kingdom – his dates are 1394 to 1437 – shows the same determination and order as his efforts in kingship. Written by a long exiled Scotsman in England, and also the personal love poem of a royal person, *The Kingis Quhair* has, in period, a unique flavour of its own. (*Quair* or *Quhair* is, of course, the equivalent of the French *cahier*, today a schoolboy's exercise book, formerly any book to write in, or written in.) An example of James at his best is near the beginning of the poem, the song of the nightingales in praise of love:

And on the smallé grene twistis sat   *twigs*
   The litill sweté nightingale, and song
So loud and clere the ymphis consecrat   *hymns*
    Off lufis use, now soft, now loud, among   *in turn*
    That all the gardyng and the wallis rong
Ryght of their song, and on the copill next   *couplet*
Off thaire swete armony, and lo the text:

'Worschippe, ye that loveris bene, this May,
   For of your blisse the calendis are begonne,
And sing with us, away, winter away!
    Cum, sumer, cum, the swete sesoun and sonne!
    Awake for schame! that have your hevynnis wonne,
And amourously lift up your hedis all,
Thank lufe that list you to his merci call.'

I have marked, in the first two lines, the only mute -e's that have to be pronounced for scansion. The Scottish '-is' plural (equivalent of the English '-s' or '-es') as in 'loveris' is always pronounced. The metrical movement in fact (and James's early years in Scotland may have something to do with this) is, like that of Charles d'Orleans, perfectly regular to a modern ear (notice that 'sesoun' is stressed on the second syllable, 'sesoun').

What is interesting is that, where the versification of Charles d'Orleans and James I is perfectly regular to our ears, the versification of poets born and brought up in England seems to limp, as if the poet were counting his syllables carefully but had no clear idea of where to put his stresses. We should get this problem clear in our heads. Medieval poets had no theory of metrics, beyond counting syllables (and even Chaucer has many nine-syllable lines and a number of lines which seem to invite stressing, in the manner of Langland, rather than division into stress-syllable feet). The existence of the iambic foot (as a stress-syllable foot, not a classical quantitative foot) was discovered by the early Elizabethan poet, George Gascoigne, in the first English treatise on prosody, *Certain Notes on Instruction*, published with Gascoigne's *Posies* in 1573. If Scottish poetry of the fifteenth century moves with a marvellous vigour, the basic reason must be that some changes were taking place in the English language but not the Scottish. (I take it that the foreigners in England, James I and Charles d'Orleans, write correct verse partly because their spoken English was slightly old-fashioned: an intelligent foreigner sticks to the language he has learned and does not attempt to keep up with changes in pronunciation and intonation.)

It may make my point here clearly if I take two short stanzas from the greatest technician among Scottish poets of the fifteenth century, William Dunbar (c. 1460–c. 1513) and one longer stanza from an English poet of some reputation in his time, Stephen Hawes (c. 1475–?1523). They are roughly contemporary, their working lives overlap, so the comparison is a fair one. I shall divide the quotations into two syllable units but not mark the stresses. Dunbar is speaking of his fear of death which oppresses him particularly in the long wet dark Scottish winters:

For feir/ of this/ all day/ I drowp;
Nor gold/in kist,/nor wine/ in cowp.   *chest, cup*
   No lad/ eis bew/ tie nor/ luiffis blys,
   May lat/ me to/ rememb/er this   *prevent me from*
How glad/ that ever/I dyne/ or sowp.

Yit quhone/ the nycht/ begynnis/ to schort   *when*
It dois/ my spreit/ some pairt/ confort,
   Off thocht/ oppress/it with/ the schowris: *Often*
   Cum, lust/ie sym/mer, with/thi flowris,
That I/may leif/ in sum/ disport.   *live*

It will be noticed that, unlike James I, born about a century earlier, Dunbar does not pronounce the plural or genitive '-is': if he does at the end of a line, as in 'schowris' and 'flowris', the '-is' is extra-metrical. 'Ever' is metrically a monosyllable (as 'heav'n' often is) and the stress comes, in the French fashion, on the second syllable of 'con*fort*'. Making these allowances, we get what a modern reader would recognise as vigorous and correct iambic tetrameters (four-feet line in a rising rhythm, that is with the second syllable of the two-syllable foot stressed more than the first). The regular dancing beat of fifteenth-century Scottish poetry makes it easier to get in touch with, even for the English-born student, than English poetry in the East Midland dialect.

Here is a stanza from Stephen Hawes's *The Pastime of Pleasure* divided into two-syllable feet in the same manner, but again with the stresses not marked:

And yet/ also/the per/fite/ physike,
Which ap/pertain/ eth well/ to the/ body,
Doth well/ resem/ble un/ to the/musike;
Whan the in/warde in/ trailes tourn/eth con/trary,
That nat/ure can/ not werk/ e dir/ ectly.
Than doth/ phesike/ the part/ es int/ eriall
In ord/re set/ to their/ orig/ in all.

The meaning is that medicine for the body resembles music for the soul. When we are upset inwardly so that our natural forces cannot work in their ordinary straightforward way, then medicine restores our inward parts to their original orderly working. The comparison of the soothing effect of music on the soul to the corrective effect of medicines for constipation may strike us as unpoetical (the lofty is compared with the base, but Hawes might say that an excessively abstract idea is given a homely and familiar illustration). What is odd and wearisome is the scansion, with its weak end-rhymes and its limping feet which sometimes seem iambic only by a distortion of pronunciation ('body', 'contrary') and sometimes pyrrhic (two light syllables) or trochaic (a heavier followed by a lighter syllable) where they should be iambic. The sounded mute e's are clearly put in merely to fill out the ten syllables and the genuinely iambic feet are themselves weak ('And yet/also . . .'). There is none of the dancing quality of Dunbar. I would say that Hawes and other English fifteenth-century poets, like the more famous Lydgate, were neither unconsciously writing foot-verse, stress-syllable verse, like Chaucer, nor consciously writing stress-verse, like Langland and in his different way the *Pearl-Gawain* poet. They were counting the number of syllables in a line.

They were doing so, I think, because of changes (which are the most difficult kind of changes to trace by written documents) in the stress pattern of spoken English. Since the spelling of the word has not changed and it is rarely if ever used as a rhyme ending, it might well remain unrecorded that in my own lifetime of sixty years the French word 'garage', as it was at first pronounced, has moved from 'garage' to something like 'garij'. We have seen already that between James I and Dunbar the Scottish plural and genitive '-is' had become silent even in verse, but we can imagine a period when it was still used in verse but not in ordinary speech (this happens also in prose: Henry Fielding nearly always wrote 'hath' but probably nearly always said 'has'.) There has been from very early on a tendency for the stressed syllable in borrowed French words to move back: we can imagine that Chaucer said 'se*soun*' or 'con*fort*', that these remained accepted poetic pronunciations, but that the spoken words were becoming more like our own 'season' or 'comfort'. Clearly the mute '-e' is used twice in Hawes as a pronounced syllable ('Werke', 'partes') not because that is what he would have said, but to get the right syllable count in his line.

It seems to me that if we bear this idea of poets writing a basically syllabic verse in mind – like Marianne Moore, like the later Auden often, like Thom Gunn in some of his poems, like the late B. S. Johnson, or like Robert Bridges's daughter, Mrs Elizabeth Daryush – we might read much more English fifteenth-century poetry with interest and sympathy, and not see it as so utterly overshadowed by my own countrymen, the Scots. John Lydgate (1370–1450) is often considered as the most distinguished, as he was certainly one of the loyalest, disciples of Chaucer. His total extant works extend to 140,000 lines and, as this suggests, he had the typical medieval vice of prolixity in excess. His longest works are *The Troy Book, The Siege of Thebes,* and *The Fall of Princes* (36,365 lines). But he could write shorter, humorous and satirical poems too. Since he was nearer to Chaucer's time and spoken language than Hawes, his verse is richer and smoother. From *The Life of Our Lady* I have found one stanza which strikes me as exceedingly beautiful, and other desperate dippers might have similar luck: it is the second of these two, the first being necessary to explain its sense, and not a bad stanza in itself either:

And to oppresse the derkenesse and the doole
Of hevy hertes that soroen and syghen ofte –
I mene the sterre of the bright poole   *Spica*
That with her bemys when she is alofte
May all the trowble aswagen and asofte
Of worldly wawes, which in this mortal see   *waves, sea*
Have us byset, with grete adversitee,
The rage of whiche is so tempestyuous
That whan the calme is moste blandyshing,

Then is the streme of dethe most perylous,
If that we want the light of hir shyning
And but the syght, allas, of her lokying;
From dethes brinke make us to escape,
The haven of lif of us may not be take.

I find the deliberately weak rhymes of 'tempestyuous', 'perylous', 'blandyshing', 'shynyng', 'lokying', moving, somehow expressive of the speaker's dependence on the Virgin Mary, represented by the star Spica. And the one strong and bad rhyme 'escape', 'take', somehow seems to express a desperation that, on the verge of drowning in damnation, cannot spare time to find the proper word.

Thomas Hoccleve (c. 1368–c. 1450), Lydgate's almost exact contemporary, was trained to be a priest but became, like Chaucer, a civil servant. He is a much less prolix and more amusing poet than Lydgate, and what we know of his life is touching and interesting. As a young man, he lived or wanted to live a wild, Villonesque life, and his *La Male Regle* is a funny but often moving mockery of this ambition. In 1410, he married and in 1412 wrote a didactic poem, addressed to the Prince of Wales, afterwards Henry V, called *The Regement of Princes*: a mere 2000 words long (think of Lydgate!) it is more cheerful and entertaining than most medieval didactic poems. In 1412, he also had a nervous breakdown from which he recovered and which he made the subject of his most psychologically interesting poem, *The Complaint*, written around 1420. In 1424, he retired from the Civil Service and spent the rest of his life, well provided for, at the Priory of Southwick in Hampshire, where he died some time before 1450. In his ability to display his own character humorously in verse, he is much more like Chaucer than Lydgate. William Tydeman, whose scholarly anthology *English Poetry, 1400–1570* (Heinemann, 1970), I am largely relying on here, describes him as 'possibly the most seriously underrated poet in this book'.

Here, from *The Regement of Princes*, the prologue, an account of troubled sleeplessness, is an example of the dramatic power that was at Hoccleve's command:

Musing upon the restles bisinesse
Which that this troubly world hath ay on
honde,

That other thing than fruit of bittirnesse
   Ne yeldeth nought, as I can undirstonde,
     At Chestre inne, right fast be the stronde   *close*
      As I lay in my bed upon a night,
       Thought me bereft of sleep with force
        and might.   *grief*

And many a day and night that wicked hine   *thrall*
   Hadde biforn vexid my poore goost   *spirit*
So grevously, that of anguish and pine
     No richere man was nougher in no coost: *nowhere, coast*
     This dar I seyn, may no wight make his
      boost
     That he with Thought was bettir than I
      aqueinted,
     For to the deth it well nigh hath me
      feinted.   *weakened*

There is a kind of direct self-examination there that we are
not used to in medieval poetry, a piercing, unornate intro-
spection. We can contrast Hoccleve in a humorous vein:
from the early *La Male Regle de T. Hoccleve* (not so easy to
translate as it looks: ill discipline, bad example, wrong rule):
Hoccleve describes how he frequented taverns, stood the
girls free drinks, but was too shy to go farther than a kiss: he
was uneasily aware that he was sexually impotent or a
fumbler. He married later, and no doubt he is speaking of
his late youth. The company of pretty women was a satisfaction enough in itself, but he got angry when other people
boasted of their sexual exploits.

    Again, as in the previous passage, there is a clear intro-
spective self-knowledge unusual in medieval poetry:

Of loves aart yit touchid I no deel –
I cowde nat and eek it was no neede:
Had I a kus, I was content full weel,   *kiss*
Better than I wolde han be with the deede.
Thereon can I but smal, it is no dreede: *I am no adept, no*
Whan that men speak of it in my presence,   *doubt of that*
For shame I wexe as reed as is the gleede . . . *red, coal*

The *persona* in *La Male Regle* is not, of course, necessarily
Hoccleve himself but a young man who wastes time and

money on pleasures he is either unfit to enjoy or knows to
be not worth the money. He is like a painfully shy man
today who frequents pubs in the hope of getting into a gay
and rowdy set, and becoming one of them, but is accepted
only because he stands free drinks. He is behaving like a
fool, and is intelligent enough to know it. He would like to
be wild, if not wicked, but is essentially innocent: what he
really likes, the good looks of girls, their easy conversation,
a friendly kiss, is innocent. Lecherous talk makes him blush
not only with shame (he knows he is not gifted that way)
but with a kind of indignation. Hoccleve may not be a great
poet, but he is a very interesting person.

John Skelton, who was probably born in the 1460s and
died in 1529 is too important a writer to be added to our
list here and will later have a section to himself. Alexander
Barclay (1472–1552) has both been described by one notable scholar as exemplifying the poetry of his time at its
worst and praised by another for his tough, realistic language. Like almost all the poets of this period, he raises
problems of scansion. He introduced the Eclogue or Pastoral Dialogue (he spelt it *Egloge*) into English, adapting
his work from two writers in Renaissance Latin, Aeneas
Sylvius Piccolomini, a devotee of humane rather than divine letters who became Pope Pius II, and Mantuan, whose
imitations of classical Latin verse were so good that he was
taught alongside Virgil in the grammar schools. Tydeman
notes that he turned the Italian landscape of his originals to
a rough northern one. Here are a few lines: though they
rhyme, it seems to me that they are basically in stress
verse, and I have marked the two stresses on each side, and
the central break:

> The wińter snówes,/ all covéred is the groúnde,
> The nóřth wind blówes/ sharp and with ferefull sound.
> The lońg isésicles/ at the ewes hang,
> The streame is frośen,/ the night is cold and lóng;
> Where bótes rówed,/ now cartes have passage,
> From yóke the oxen/ be loséd and bondage . . .

There is a certain vigour here, but it we compare it with, for
instance, the rhymed stress-verse of *Pearl* it lacks grace and
beauty and threatens monotony. Barclay, however, com-

pared to the feeble Hawes, has muscle, and should be praised for that.

The lyric carried on through the fifteenth, as through the previous three centuries, apparently at its best natural, anonymous, and totally unaffected by fashions in feeling like Petrarchanism and fashions in form like the rondel and the ballad. This very famous quatrain, for instance, has the air of having strayed into an early Tudor court song-book by accident:

> Westron wynd, when wyll thou blow,
> The small rayne down can rayne?
> Cryst, yf my love were in my armys,
> And I in my bed agayne!

The court poems properly belong to our next chapter on the Renaissance. The anonymous poems should not be thought of as artless, in spite of their astonishing glowing innocence. I know no more beautifully shaped poem, of its length, in the English language than this, and I am not, I think, allowing the subject to affect my judgment:

> I syng of a mayden/that is makeles,
> Kyng of alle kynges/to her sone she ches.
>
> He cam also stylle/ther his moder was,
> As dew in Aprylle,/that fallyt on the gras.
>
> He cam also stylle/to his moderes bower,
> As dew in Aprylle,/that fallyt on the flour.
>
> He cam also stylle/ther his moder lay,
> As dew in Aprylle,/that fallyt on the spray.
>
> Moder and mayden/was never non but she –
> Well may swych a lady/Godes moder be.

The skill of repetition and variation there is matchless, and quite unmatched in the consciously artful court lyrics. There is a stronger case for the purely English (leaving the Scots out) poetic achievement of the fifteenth century than has yet been made out. Fifteenth-century English poets have suffered from coming between the age of Chaucer and the age that was to be crowned by Shakespeare, just as the English poets of the Victorian age have suffered until recently by coming between the age of Wordsworth and Keats and the age of Yeats and Eliot. Poets today in their fifties, like Philip Larkin, suffer from having behind them not only the great poets of the modern period, like Yeats, Eliot, Lawrence, and (as we are now recognising) Hardy, but the major talents of the 1930s, Auden, MacNeice, Empson. To come between two great ages is perhaps the worst fate that can befall a poet of talent. Not that, of course, in our growingly less literate world, we have any guarantee that a great age will succeed the age of Philip Larkin, Donald Davie, Thom Gunn, and Ted Hughes, or that people will go on reading or writing poetry at all.

II The Great Age of Scottish Poetry

In the fifteenth and early sixteenth century, Scotland produced three great poets, Robert Henryson (c.1425–c.1506), William Dunbar (c.1460–c.1515), and Gavin Douglas, Bishop of Dunkeld (c.1474–1522). On the evidence of Dunbar's great poem, *The Lament for the Makaris*, they were three of many, and, poetically and culturally, he considered England and Scotland 'this countrie': he begins his lament, in fact, thus:

> He hes done petuously devour
> The noble Chaucer, of makaris flour,
> The Monk of Bery, and Gower, all thre;
> *Timor mortis conturbat me.*

'Bery' is Bury St Edmunds in whose priory Lydgate died after retiring from the Civil Service. The fact that Dunbar begins his great lament by naming Chaucer and Chaucer's most distinguished disciple suggests that the phrase 'the Scottish Chaucerians' is not so inept as modern Scottish critics, inspired by nationalistic feelings, sometimes suggest. It is true that the latest of these poets, Gavin Douglas, in his version of the *Aeneid*, seems deliberately to write a rougher and thicker Scots than Henryson or Dunbar. The battle of Flodden, like the battle of Pinkie Heugh after Douglas's death, may have created a conscious anti-English feeling, extending to culture. Scotsmen attached to the Roman communion attacked the Reformers for writing in standard English, rather than in standard Scots: 'I knap not your suddroun' wrote one Roman Catholic polemicist ('I do not understand your southern dialect'). Till the end of the century, good poems were written in Lowland Scots, which was the language of Edinburgh, the court, the law, and the professions. James VI of Scotland even wrote a treatise on the art of verse in Scots, and some Scots poems. But when he became James I of England and his greatest courtiers followed him to London, he picked up standard East-Midlands readily enough, and so far as Scots remained alive as a literary language, it was as a vernacular for comic pastoral. That was what T. S. Eliot, a critic of piercing historical insight, meant when he called Robert Burns a great poet in a decadent tradition. Burns could write great poems in Scots because he was a peasant: literary Scottish gentlemen of his time (and even Burns himself, in his letters) wrote and spoke in a slightly stilted, rather too consciously correct standard English. (Boswell shuddered at Scotticisms like 'jeelly' for 'jelly'.)

Let us consider, however, the short great age of Scottish poetry, of which Henryson is the senior representative. Most (according to a leading expert on him, Professor John MacQueen) of his life belonged to the fifteenth century, the last three-quarters of it. We think of this as a very violent time in both England and Scotland though it is a general belief of historians now that the Wars of the Roses, essentially a set of squabbles between magnates for political power, did not much interest the common people or interfere with the growth of a *bourgeois* class or the growing prosperity of the realm. (The twenty years reign of Edward IV, drastically foreshortened by Shakespeare because it was successful and undramatic, relied for its success on the King's practical interest in trade and finance and his ability to get on with the new merchant class.) Nonetheless, it was violent. In Scotland James I was murdered, James II blown up by a cannon, James III stabbed on the battlefield, James IV unnecessarily killed (though after the turn of the century) by moving with absurd chivalry from an advantageous hill top position at Flodden. But no more than in England did this violence, in which they took no active part, interfere with the growing prosperity of the merchants. Apart from a more luxurious way of living, the century was marked by the founding of universities (in order, St Andrews, Glasgow, and Aberdeen) and a growing interest in education (Henryson is believed to have been a schoolmaster at Dunfermline: and his poems show a thorough knowledge of a number of Latin texts, of Greek myths through Latin sources – his first poem was on Orpheus and Eurydice – and of both English and Scottish vernacular poetry). His tragic *The Testament of Cresseid* is a sequel to Chaucer's *Troilus and Criseyde*, without Chaucer's psychological depth and ranging humour, but with a tragic Dantesque concision that lay outside Chaucer's range. His fables have a humour all their own and a special affectionate feeling for animals that is characteristically Scottish (think of Burns's dialogue between the rich man's dog and the poor man's dog or his *To a Mousie*).

The first stanza of *The Testament of Cresseid* perhaps shows the good schoolmaster in Henryson, the gift to put things plainly, and yet the liking for a long latinate word (one such word, to make it easier for the boys, used to explain another) and for the astrological allusion, easier to grasp then than now, but also the proper setting of an atmosphere for a sad story:

Ane doolie sessoun to ane cairfull dyte	*gloomy, sad, tale*
Suld correspond and be equivalent:	
Richt sa it wes quhen I began to wryte	
This tragedie – the wedder richt fervent,	*severe*
Quhen Aries, in middis of the Lent,	
Schouris of haill can fra the north discend	*can=made*
That scantlie fra the cauld I micht defend.	

This, unlike English poetry of the same period scans perfectly to the modern ear, but notice that Henryson, an older man, unlike Dunbar sounds the '-is' of 'middis' and 'schouris'. 'Tragedie' is any tale that ends sadly, just as 'comedie' is any that ends happily. 'Dyte' for a tale (here in verse) recalls the German word for an imaginative writer, *dichter*.

This tragic story, Henryson's greatest work, has a simple plot. Cresseid, having betrayed Troilus, is deserted by Diomeid:

> Quhen Diomeid had all his appetyte,
> *And mair*, fulfillit of this fair ladie,
> Upon ane-uther he set his haill delyte . . .

The 'And mair', which I have italicised here, has a special Scottish grimness of understatement that lies on the whole outside the English range; and the compassion of the next stanza is mingled with a sort of brutal realism that is un-English too. Cresseid becomes a professional whore:

> O fair Cresseid, the flour and *A per se*
> Of Troy and Grece, how was thow fortunait!
> To change in filth all thy feminitie,
> And be with fleschelie lust sa maculait,   *stained, soiled*
> And go amang the Greekis air and lait   *early and late*
> Sa giglotlike, takand thy foull plesance!   *whorishly*
> I have pietie thow suld fall sic mischance!   *pity*

The gods, particularly Venus, Cupid, and Mars (the gods of love and chivalry), determine to punish the disloyal and frivolous Cresseid and she is stricken with incurable leprosy, and has to earn her living as a beggar. Troilus, riding round the Trojan walls, sees this leper and flings her his purse, not because he recognises her, but because he is generous, and because an image of the lovely lady who has betrayed him comes inexplicably into his mind:

> For knichtlie pietie and memoriall
> Of fair Cresseid, ane gyrdill can he tak
> (Ane purse of gold, and mony gay jowall),   *jewel*
> And in the skirt of Cresseid doun can swak;   *throw*
> Than raid away and not ane word [he] spak,
> Pensive in hart, quhill he come to the toun,
> And for greit cair oftsyis almaist fell doun.

Cresseid, as a leper, is too blind to recognise him, but when she is told that her benefactor is Troilus her heart breaks. She makes a long lament, dies, and 'sum said' that when Troilus heard her whole story he 'maid ane tomb of merbell gray', with this inscription on it:

> Lo, fair ladyis! Cresseid of Troyis toun,
> Sumtyme countit the flour of womanheid,
> Under this stane, lait lipper, lyis deid.'

A. C. Spearing in his very illuminating *Criticism and Medieval Poetry* (Edward Arnold, second edition, 1972) remarks on the unmedieval conciseness of this (Dante, one might say, is as concise, but no other medieval poet, English, French, or Italian is): 'Henryson's conciseness depends upon precision and completeness; it compresses much explicit meaning into as few words as possible.'

Henryson's fables are, of course, comic-satirical and not tragic, and humour, which often depends on the apparently irrelevant detail, does not lend itself to this sort of conciseness: in *The Taill of the Uponlandis Mous and the Burges Mous* (the old fable of the Country Mouse, living frugally and peacefully, and the Town Mouse, living richly and in danger), it is the comfortable detail that makes the stanza so pleasing when the Uponlandis Mous has, at last, left the town and got safely home:

Bot I hard say scho passit to hir den,	*heard*
Als warme as woll, suppose it wes not greit,	*allowing that*
Fully beinly stuffit, baith but and ben	*furnished, without, within*
Off beinis, and nuttis, peis, ry, and quheit:	*beans, wheat*
Quhenever scho list, scho had aneuch to eit,	
In quyet and eis, withoutin ony dreid;	
Bot to her sisteris feist na mair scho yeid.	*went*

William Dunbar was a greater technician than Henryson. Professor James Kinsley, the editor of an excellent selection of his poems (*William Dunbar, Poems*, Clarendon Press, Oxford, 1958) remarks: 'In craftsmanship Dunbar surpasses most medieval poets and all other Scots poets – a passion for form and finish is not conspicuous in Scottish literature'. (What other very great novelist, for instance, writes in such rambling and digressive prose, and brings his novels to such a rapidly huddled conclusion, as Sir Walter Scott?) Kinsley goes on to point out that Dunbar pays for his technical polish with a lack of human and intellectual interest: 'He expresses the melancholy temper of his age with fine simplicity, but there is no provocative questioning, no restless seeking "after the whyes"'. Kinsley adds that Dunbar lacks the compassion of Chaucer and Burns (he might have added, of Henryson) but is not like Dryden a mere first-rate craftsman: 'Dunbar's energy is not only, like Dryden's, an energy of utterance: it is also an energy of imagination'. 'The people of Scotland', Kinsley agrees with Sir Herbert Grierson, '"have never taken Dunbar to their hearts: he wants the natural touch." But he is their finest artist, if not their greatest poet.'

It is best, therefore, to illustrate Dunbar's qualities with a number of isolated quotations, exemplifying the fine art that makes up for the natural touch, or for the lack of it. Here, from *The Golden Targe* is an example of the 'aureate style' (it has something in common with the flamboyant style in Church architecture that was becoming popular in the later Middle Ages). The poet makes no attempt to express either sincerity of feeling or complexity of thought. By the use of particularly latinate words and such devices as alliteration he makes the stanza, quite apart from its meaning, a shining and ornate object in itself:

Ryght as the stern of day begouth to schyne,
Quhen gone to bed war Vesper and Lucyne, *evening star, moon*
   I raise, and by a rosere did me rest; *rose tree*
Up sprang the goldyn candill matutyne *of morning*
With clere depurit bemes cristallyne *purified*
   Glading the mery foulis in thair nest; *fowls (wild birds)*
   Or Phebus was in purpur cape revest *purple, clothed*
Up raise the lark, the hevyns menstrale fyne, *minstrel*
   In May, in till a morrow myrthfullest.

Let the reader who feels this is merely richly vapid, attempt an equivalent himself. But compare that artificiality with the evocation of natural beauty at the beginning of *The Tretis of the tua Marrit Wemen and the Wedo*. In this poem, against a lovely and vivid background, the three ladies tell stories that would make the Wife of Bath blush. Dunbar here uses old English stress metre with beautiful skill:

Ápon the Midsummer évin,/mirriést of nichtis
I múvit furth alláne/neir as midnicht wes pást,
Besyd ane gúdlie grein gárth,/ full of ǵay flóuris,
Hégeit of ane húge hicht/ with háwthorne tréis,
Quhairon ane bird on ane bransche/ so birst out her notis
That never ane blythfullar bird/ was on the beuche hárde . . .

The metre was almost dead by Dunbar's time: notice that he never makes the common medieval mistake (even Langland is sometimes guilty of it) of having two alliterating stresses in the second half-line.

I have already, in the first section of this chapter, given an example of Dunbar's skill in expressing the melancholy mood brought on by Scottish winter weather, and it is time to move on to Gavin Douglas, the most difficult for an English reader of all these three poets, and one who is perhaps deliberately turning away, out of the bitterness that followed Flodden, from the English tradition. Scotland and England had been at peace since the Battle of Bannockburn in 1314; apart from border cattle rustling, a fault of which both sides were guilty, there was no particular danger to England from her poor northern neighbour and more glory to be won from the long war in France than from any attempt to conquer Scotland. The two battles of Flodden and Pinkie Heugh were, as much as anything else, to put the Scots in their place, and to let them know which was the more powerful nation: but they interrupted what could have been a period of fruitful cultural collaboration. It is significant that where a younger man, Sir David Lindsay, the author of the *Satire of the Three Estaitis* still calls the language of his poetry 'Inglis', Gavin Douglas, in the prologue to his first book of the *Eneados* (his version of Virgil's *Aeneid*), announces a deliberate Scotticising policy, like that, early in this century, of 'Hugh MacDiarmid' (Christopher Grieve). He wants in his diction

> to mak it braid and plane,
> Kepand na sudroun, bot out awin langage,
> And speikis as I lerit quhen I wes page.

But even today broad Lowland Scots and, say, Cockney English are local dialects of one language, not separate languages: the test is that speakers of both can understand each other without much difficulty. The syntax and the bulk of the vocabulary are the same: the ear can quite rapidly pick up the phonetic differences and the few characteristic and specific differences of vocabulary. That what you as an Englishman call a meat dish, I as a Scotsman call an ashet, does not make us incomprehensible to each other. And the

Scottish burn is no more different from the English stream
than the northern English beck.

Even Gavin Douglas in a sense realised that he was
undertaking an impossible task:

Nor yit sa clene all sudroun I refuse,
Bot sum word I pronunce as my nychtbour doise.
Like as in Latyne bene Grew termes sum,   *Greek*
So me behuvit quhilum, or than be dum,
Sum bastard Latyne, Frensch, or Inglis oiss: *use*
Quhar scant war Scottis, I had nane wther choiss.
Nocht for our toung is in the selfin scant,   *poor in itself*
But for that I the foutht of langage want;   *abundance*
Quhar as the colour, of his propirte
To keip the sentence, thairto constrenit me,   *meaning*
Or than to mak my sang schort sum tyme,
Mair compendious, or to liklie my ryme.   *go with (likely)*

Douglas, of course, was completely mistaken in supposing
that Scots or any language in the world exists in a pure state,
without bastard terms. But there *is* a Scottishness in Scots, a
tendency towards the expressively harsh, just as there is an
Englishness in English, in prose a tendency towards elegance, in verse towards richness rather than roughness of
sound: even the forcible, as in Milton or Donne, must have
its own music. It is not exactly music that we hear in Gavin
Douglas's description of winter (the prologue to Book VII
of the *Eneados*):

The dowie dichis war all donk and wait,   *dreary, dank, wet*
The law vaille flodderit all with spait,   *low, flooded*
The plane stretis and every hie way
Full of fluschis, doubbis, myre and clay.   *pools, puddles*
Laggerit leys wallowit fernis shew,   *muddy, withered*
Broune muris kithit their wisnit mossy hue,   *showed, withered*
Bank, bra and boddum blanchit wolx and bare:*bottom*
For gurll weather growit beastis haire . . .   *rough*

Nothing could be more vivid (almost too insistently so) but
after a few pages little could be more grating on the ear:
notice that Douglas's habit of heavy alliteration is purely for
emphasis (for rather undiscriminating emphasis) and if
anything adds to the unmusical effect. Of these three poets,
Henryson's spirit appeals to me most: I admire Dunbar's

extraordinary skill while feeling no personal attraction to him: Douglas arouses my admiration, and even a kind of liking, by his dogged determination – and in the prologues he shows that he has a most intimate feeling for Scottish weather – but I always find reading him a duty rather than a pleasure. (This is also true of very much, at least, of the over-voluminous and over-emphatic writing of our most distinguished living Scottish poet, Hugh MacDiarmid: he must almost equal Lydgate's 140 000 lines in his total verse production.)

This chapter is already a little over long. But John Skelton the most original English poet of the late fifteenth and early sixteenth century (he does not resemble anybody who came before him nor, till he had some influence on Graves and Auden in our own time, anyone who came after him) deserves a short section to himself.

III The Vicar of Hell

John Skelton, till our own time, has had a bad press with subsequent poets. Because Skelton held the Rectorship of Diss, in Norfolk, Henry VIII jocularly described him as his 'Vicar of Hell': Milton took this classical pleasantry as a serious reflection on Skelton's character. Pope, wishing to suggest that a prurient antiquarianism was destroying taste in Oxford and Cambridge wrote:

> And beastly Skelton Heads of Houses quote.

(Heads of Houses are what we would more commonly call Principals of Colleges.) But, though Skelton's humour is often free-spoken, it would be possible to find much more real nastiness in Pope and his friend Swift themselves. What are the real reasons for this genuine dislike he has aroused (in for instance, a fine scholar – if not always a very discriminating critic – C. S. Lewis, in *English Literature in the Sixteenth Century*, Oxford University Press, 1954)?

Perhaps it is the lack of something. During his period as a Rector of Diss (1502–12), he appears to have been a most conscientious clergyman – involved, for instance, in an inquiry into the 'health of the soul' of a parishioner, just as much later he was in 1527 to be a witness against a

Colchester heretic – but though he was undoubtedly a soundly conservative churchman, there is no sign in his poetry of personal religious feeling. He had a feeling for gallant naughtiness and, in later life, for the sheer prettiness of young girls, but even his most graceful lyrical poems are without passion. The fact that he had been Henry VIII's tutor probably made him bolder in his satires on Wolsey, though he is once recorded as living in sanctuary in Westminster. But we wonder whether it was Wolsey's low birth and coarse ostentation that annoyed him even more than the Cardinal's policy. His hostile poems are more like what the Scotch call 'flyting', directed against a person, rather than like satire proper, directed not against the man but the vice. Because of the personal nature of the attack many of his poems, like *Speke, Parot* are exceedingly obscure. The metre which he invented, Skeltonics, has been considered an uncouth sort of doggerel: made up of successions of short lines, rather like the half-line of Anglo-Saxon verse, but linked by rhymes carried on as long as possible rather than by alliteration. The Skeltonic in fact restored to the English language the sense of the vigour and bounce of the stress in verse which it had been losing during the last century. A poem like *The Tunning of Eleanor Rumming*, a description of the goings on in a low ale house, has been reproached for lacking a moral: grotesque and richly farcical in detail, it has as broad and obvious a moral, and as little artistic need of one, as a drawing by Rowlandson. Again critics have wondered whether Skelton (praised by Erasmus) is our first Renaissance or our last Medieval poet. Essentially conservative, he is treated as the latter here. He was given at Oxford for his post-bachelor degree the degree of laureate (for his excellence in rhetoric), and Cambridge later gave him the same honorary degree. He was allowed, in 1512, to use the title Orator Regius. So, if not exactly our first Poet Laureate, he is on the verge of being so.

It is difficult to illustrate Skelton's qualities briefly, but this stanza from a naughty early poem (based on the traditional Christian lullaby, about Mary and her Child, but here about a woman who leaves her drunken snoring husband to pick up a lover) shows how he could combine a haunting lyricism with broad sexual humour:

The river routh, the waters wan;   *rough, dark-coloured*
She sparyd not to wete her fete.
She wadyd over, she found a man
That halsyd her hartely and kyst her
   swete;
Thus after her cold she cought a hete.   *was 'on heat'*
'My lefe,' she sayd, 'rowtyth in hys bed;   *sweetheart, snores*
Iwys he hath an hevy hed,'
     With hey, 'Lullay, lullay,' lyke a
       chylde,
      Thou slepest to long, thou art begylde!

Contrast the graceful innocence of this late poem: to
'Mastres Margaret Hussey':

      Mirry Margaret,
    As mydsomer flowre,
    Jentill as faucoun
    Or hawke of the towre:
      With solace and gladnes,
    Much mirth and no madnes,
    All good and no badnes;
    So joyously,
    So maydenly,
    So womanly
    Her demenying:
    In every thinge
    Far, far passynge
    That I can endyght
    Or suffice to wryght
    Of mirry Margarete,
    As midsomer flowre,
    Jentill as faucoun
    Or hawk of the towre.

And here finally is the Rowlandsonian touch (and incidentally a good example of Skeltonics) in the grotesque picture
of Elynour Runmying:

    Her lothely lere   *face, complexion*
    Is nothynge clere,
    But ugly of chere,   *face (as good cheer)*
    Droupy and drowsy,
    Scurvy and lowsy;
    Her face all bowsy,   *boozy*

Comely crynklyd,
Woundersly wrynklyd,   *wondrously*
Like a rost pygges eare
Brystled with here.   *hair*
Her lewde lyppes twayne,
They slaver, men sayne,
Like a ropy rayne,
A gummy glayre,   *beaten egg whites*
She is ugly fayre: *(used as cosmetic)*
Her nose somdele hoked
And camously crooked,   *concavely*
Never stoppynge,
But ever droppynge;
Her skynne lose and slacke,   *loose*
Greuyned like a sacke;
With a croked backe.

This (and it goes on for another two pages) could be cruel; reading, we do not feel it so, any more than gargoyles in medieval cathedrals. And in Skelton, an age strangely foreign to us (more foreign than ancient Greece or Rome) looks at us with a wanton's face, a lovely child's age, a face that seems to rejoice in its own exaggerated hideousness: and is gone. From now on, we are on growingly solid and familiar ground.

6

The English Renaissance

The English Renaissance is generally thought of as beginning with two short-lived courtly poets, Sir Thomas Wyatt (1503–42) and Henry Howard, Earl of Surrey (1517–47). Wyatt had been imprisoned in 1536 because of a quarrel with the Duke of Suffolk at the time of Anne Boleyn's downfall. He may have been one of Anne's lovers (there is a sonnet, adapted from Petrarch, that suggests that he at least loved her, and there is a passage about Cato and Caesar in one of his satires that seems directly aimed at the King) but he had talents which the King could make use of. He was ambassador in Spain for three years and though he was imprisoned in 1541 charged with treason during this mission, he was cleared and pardoned. In the last year of his life he was a member of Parliament and was about to be promoted to a Commandership of the Fleet, the new English navy that had been created by Henry VII. He died suddenly of a fever caught on a journey to Falmouth to greet the Spanish Ambassador. His friend lamented him nobly.

The Earl of Surrey was of grander stock and his Plantagenet blood made him an object of suspicion to Henry VIII. The Tudors had very little of the old royal blood, and a steady weeding out of magnates with more of the Plantagenet seed than himself was one of the policies of Henry's reign. His obsession to have a male heir, which was at least one of the motives behind the execution of Anne Boleyn and Katherine Howard as it was behind the 'great matter' of the divorce from Katherine of Aragon, which led to the break with the Pope, sprang from the same wish to establish a new line. He may have been sexually demanding but he must have been singularly sexually unattractive for two of his wives to risk their necks by a series of almost flaunted adulteries. On the other hand, Henry VIII, himself a poet and musician, unlike his much more capable but quite philistine father, encouraged courtly love poetry in the Italian tradition, which was at last reaching England. H. A. Mason, among others, has pointed out that it is very hard to distinguish between purely conventional poems by Wyatt and Surrey (the equivalent of smoothly turned modern jazz lyrics, such as 'Smoke gets in your eyes' or 'I hates to see that evening sun go down') and the expressions by these poets and their minor contemporaries of personal passion. With both Wyatt and Surrey, we must judge by tone.

From his father's and mother's side, the young Earl of Surrey could boast descent from Edward the Confessor and from Edward III. He had an excellent education and was brought up as companion of Henry VIII's illegitimate son, Henry Fitzroy, Duke of Richmond. Unlike Wyatt's, Surrey's gifts were for war rather than diplomacy and he took part in campaigns against Scotland and France, in one of which, as he records in his poetry, he received the surrender of Boulogne. Though it does not show at all in his poetry, he was famous for pride and quarrelsomeness, and imprisoned twice for rows with fellow courtiers and once for street riots and eating meat in Lent (H. A. Mason thinks he may have had Protestant sympathies). His execution, a week before the King's own death, was the result of his quartering the arms of Edward the Confessor on his crest, which the sick and dying Henry took as implying a treasonable claim to the crown. These biographical details are not irrelevant to the atmosphere of the English Renaissance, or the Renaissance elsewhere. Where the atmosphere of the Middle Ages, as typified either by Chaucer or Langland, is one of very wide social sympathy, the atmosphere of the Renaissance is aristocratic: its poets write, like Castiglione's *cortegiano*, or ideal courtier, with a certain *sprezzatura* or noble scorn for mere professionalism. For both Wyatt and Surrey poetry must have been one aspect only of a noble and active life, in which the risks of execution or imprisonment were to be regarded with *sprezzatura* too. This basically aristocratic attitude lasts right through the century, even in poets of humble birth or circumstances like Marlowe, Ben Jonson, Spenser, and the 'university wits' who were our earliest dramatists. It could involve not only *sprezzatura* but, as in the 'golden' period of Elizabethan poetry, the deliberate creation of an unreal and romanticised ideal pastoral world. There is, in fact, more pain and psychological realism in Wyatt, and even sometimes in Surrey, than in many of the more famous poets of the end of the century. A penetrating bitterness like Wyatt's is combined strangely in the poems of one of the last really great courtier poets of the end of the sixteenth century and the beginning of the next, Sir Walter Raleigh. Donne's fame rests partly on turning against the courtly tradition to one of harsh 'moral realism', but in the best of the earlier Tudor poets, even in the great technical inventor, Sidney, with whom Donne is so often contrasted, there is much more moral realism, much more bitterness of penetration and painful self-knowledge, than traditional opinion allows. Because Sidney's lines move with a mellifluous sweetness, new in English poetry, it does not follow that he has not looked searchingly into his heart. And it was a better heart than Donne's, who, in his own self-dramatising way, is perhaps the more 'rhetorical' of the two poets. Donne always gets his feelings across with tremendous punch: but *are* they his feelings?

I Wyatt and Surrey: the Innovators

Wyatt and Surrey have equal credit for introducing the sonnet into English. Surrey, in his translation of Books II and IV of Virgil's *Aeneid*, may be said to have 'invented' English blank verse. In his satires, partly adapted from Italian originals, Wyatt introduces Dante's difficult rhyme-scheme of *terza rima*: aba bcb cdc ded, and so on indefinitely; it was not to be used successfully again till Shelley's last great unfinished poem, *The Triumph of Life*. The metre is difficult in English simply because of the comparative paucity of satisfying full rhymes in English (the important word 'love', for instance, has only 'dove' and 'glove' though 'move', 'prove' and recently 'of' are accepted as courtesy rhymes), easy in Italian because of the abundance of rhymes through the existence of so many words with echoing vocalic endings. What is difficult in Italian is to write blank or free verse that avoids rhyme. Surrey was the more admired in the later sixteenth century, and throughout the Victorian age, because of the greater regularity of his metres, but it should be noted that his iambics often move with too mechanical a regularity, though Richard Tottel, in *Songs and Sonnets*, 1557, may have attempted to smooth Surrey out as he certainly did Wyatt. Here are the opening lines of *Description of spring, wherein each thing renews save only the lover*. It is adapted from Petrarch's *Sonetto in morte di Madonna Laura* (cccx), but substituting freshly an English for an Italian spring:

> The soote/ seasón/ that búd/ and bloom/ forth brings
> With greén/ hath clád/ the hill/ and eké/ the vále,
> The night/ ingalé/ with feath/ ers new/ she sings,
> The túrt/ le tó/ her maké/ hath tóld/ her tale. . . .

The effect of monotony comes from the over-abundance of monosyllabic words which give the effect of the poet counting the feet of the line on his fingers. 'Soote' was archaic but preserved in poetry because of Chaucer's use of it in the first line of the General Prologue to *The Canterbury Tales*:

> Whán/ that Áp/ ril with/ his shówr/ es sóot(e),

though the final *e* is not pronounced, as it probably is in Chaucer, though extra-metrically. The stress on the second syllable of 'season' probably again represents poetic tradition rather than the current pronunciation of the word in ordinary speech in Henry VIII's time. Contrast, on the other hand, Sir Thomas Wyatt's version of the first four lines of Petrarch's *Sonetto in vita di Madonna Laura* (clvi): Wyatt is trusting his ear, which is a perfect one, rather than chopping his lines mechanically into feet. It is impossible not to feel that his lines are more forceful and moving than Surrey's (and, indeed, our Italian Professor at Leicester, Dr McWilliams, has admitted to me in this case more so than Petrarch's original). The images of the galley, the sharp seas, the winter nights, the rock, love as the master of the galley slaves who pull the oars, all conventional to Petrarch, are concrete and real to Wyatt: he gives us not merely an allegory but a dangerous seascape:

My galley chargëd with forgetfulness
Thorrough sharp seas, in winter nights, doth pass
'Tween rock and rock; and eke mine enemy, alas,
That is my lord, steereth with cruelness . . .

If one did attempt to scan this as iambics one would get an extraordinary freedom of handling these, rather like the 'common rhythm counterpointed' of an early modern innovating poet, Gerard Manley Hopkins:

My gál/ ley chárg/ ëd wíth/ forgét/ fulnéss
Thórroủgh/ shárp seás/ in wínt/ er níghts/ doth paśs
'Twéen ròck/ and róck/ and ęke/ mine eń/ emỷ alás
Thát ìs/ mỷ lórd/ stéereth/ with cŕu/ elnèss . . .

The second line begins with a trochee (stress, unstress, marked `'°`) and a spondee (double stress, `''`). The last foot of the third line has two or possibly three unstressed syllables (or, if one prefers to put it that way, syllables of minimal stress). The first foot of the last line is interestingly ambiguous ('*That* is, my lord . . .' or 'That *is* my lord' or some fusion of these). The trochee 'steereth' is in a most unusual place. Ignoring rules, Wyatt is in fact discovering freedoms of metrical fingering which we associate with metrical experimenters of our own time, such as the young T. S. Eliot or the young Ezra Pound in their syncopations of the iambic line in *Prufrock* or *Hugh Selwyn Mauberley*. Sensitive readers have also today felt a 'modernity' of feeling as well as handling in Wyatt. Surrey may have excelled him in smoothness but Wyatt is much the more interesting personality.

Not that Surrey lacks his own interest. This epitaph on Thomas Clere, his faithful friend and follower, shows, as Robert Graves has remarked, the aristocratic virtues and vices with absolute honesty. There is the pride of ancestry and of martial achievement combined with the chivalry, the gratitude to a brave follower who had saved Surrey's life. The aristocrat's sympathies are, as it were, narrow or circumscribed but also true and intense. And the names of great families or of great cities sacrificed in war make a clangour in our ears as they did in Surrey's:

Norfolk sprung thee, Lambeth holds thee dead;
Clere, of the County of Cleremont, thou hight;

Within the womb of Ormond's race thou bred,
And saw thy cousin crowned in thy sight.
Shelton for love, Surrey for lord thou chase,   *chosest*
(Aye me! while life did last, that league was tender)
Tracing whose steps thou sawest Kelsel blaze,
Landrecy burnt, and battered Boulogne render.
At Montreuil gates, hopeless of all recure,
Thine Earl, half dead, gave in thy hand his will;
Which cause did thee this pining death procure,
Ere summers four times seven thou couldst fulfill.
   Ah! Clere! if love had booted, care, or cost,
   Heaven had not won, nor earth so timely lost.

It mattered where one was born, where one was buried, who
were one's mother's family as well as one's father's, whom
one married, what great magnate one attached one's fortunes to: otherwise one was nobody. (Clere's cousin was
unlucky Anne Boleyn whom Surrey's friend Wyatt, perhaps
not vainly, loved.) The burning and battering of towns was
glory not brutality. At the same time, it is a wicked world,
and God takes the good young. And Surrey loved this loyal
young man, who had attended him when he thought he was
dying and died perhaps from the lingering effects of wound
or fever suffered in Surrey's service. If we can transfer our
imaginations to a quite other world than ours we shall be
profoundly moved: moved also when Surrey is imprisoned
in Windsor and remembers he was brought up there, in
splendour, chief companion to a king's bastard son; memories of royal tennis:

   The stately seats, the ladies bright of hue,
   The dances short, long tales of great delight;
   With words and looks that tigers could but rue,
   Where each of us did plead the other's right;
   The palm play where, despoilëd for the game,
   With dazëd eyes oft we by gleams of love
   Have missed the ball and got sight of our dame,
   To bait her eyes, which kept the leads above. . . .

   Wherewith, alas, reviveth in my breast
   The sweet accord; such sleeps as yet delight,
   The pleasant dreams, the quiet bed of rest;
   The secret thoughts imparted with such trust,
   The wanton talk, the divers change of play,

The friendship sworn, each promise kept so just,
Wherewith we passed the winter night away.
And with this thought the blood forsakes the face,
The tears berain my cheeks of deadly hue . . .

It was a man still a boy at heart, with all a boy's recklessness, generosity, capacity for delight, who had his head cut off a week before the wicked old king's death. It is ironic that the son for whom Henry VIII sacrificed so much, and so many, died young without children, Mary Tudor married but barren, and Elizabeth, the last of that line of capable Welsh usurpers, a great and brave woman but a 'barren stock'.

The pleasure that Wyatt offers us is a different one, that, though he was not yet forty when he died, of intense but considered and mature emotion. It was perhaps sheer luck that he did not die like so many other admirers of Anne Boleyn; or it may have been caution, as this sestet of a sonnet, *Whose list to hunt*, suggests (even though the sonnet as a whole is adapted from Petrarch):

Who list her hunt, I put him out of doubt   *wishes to hunt*
  As well as I, may spend his time in vain.
  And graven with diamonds in letters plain
There is written her fair neck round about:
  '*Noli me tangere*, for Caesar's I am,   *Fear to touch me*
  And wild for to hold, though I seem tame'.

Yet what he thought of 'Caesar' comes over clearly enough in the satire *Of the Courtier's Life*, adapted from Alamanni and addressed to his friend John Poins:

> I am not he that can allow the state
> Of high Caesar, and damn Cato to die;
> That with his death did scape out of the gate
> From Caesar's hands, if Livy doth not lie,
> And would not live where liberty was lost,
> So did his heart the commonwealth apply.
> I am not he, such eloquence to boast,
> To make the crow in singing as the swan,
> Nor call the lion of coward beasts the most,
> That cannot take a mouse as the cat can;
> And he that dieth for hunger of the gold,
> Call him Alexander, and say that Pan
> Passeth Apollo in music manifold . . .

The satire is general, but in regard to Henry's fierce despotism, his eloquence (the long anti-Lutheran pamphlet which earned him from the Papacy with which he was so soon to quarrel, the title of *Defensor Fidei*, Defender of the Faith), his attempts at music and poetry, which are respectable for a king but do not put him in Wyatt's or Surrey's class, his successful wars against the French, his love of chivalric show (the Field of the Cloth of Gold) and his failure to take any active part in war, the lines would have stung; if Wyatt has primarily Henry in mind the only wrong hit is 'hunger for the gold'. Henry could be predatory enough but his foible was lavishness not, like his father's (for the money is the kingdom's and a main source of the king's strength) the more excusable royal vice of avarice.

What has given Wyatt his most lasting admiration is, however, his treatment, tender or bitter, but always true to his heart, of the passion of love. Here is the tenderness and the sadness of being forsaken:

> They flee from me, that sometime did me seek,
> With naked foot stalking in my chamber.
> I have seen them gentle, tame, and meek
> That now are wild and do not remember
> That sometime they have put themselves in danger
> To take bread at my hand; and now they range,
> Busily seeking with a continual change . . .

One remembers the use of the adjectives 'wild' and 'tame' in the sonnet on Anne Boleyn and wonders if this might refer to an earlier time before she had *Noli me tangere* round her neck. He is talking of course about one woman. He says 'they' as we sometimes today say: 'Some people . . .' In the Anne Boleyn poem the beloved one is compared to a hunted hart; here one thinks more of a timid fawn straying into an open chamber looking on a great royal park, to be fed on bread. But Anne, if it is she, found herself after her marriage, not in fear of her husband but in weariness and disgust of him, behaving promiscuously, 'busily seeking with a continual change . . .'

If for sad tenderness that poem, which develops into greater complexity a dialogue between love and resentment, is hardly to be excelled in English, for concentrated bitterness (yet bitterness to the lute, beautifully musical), this next one is unique (many qualities that readers admire in Donne they might find – the strength without the contortion, the energy without the posture – in a more distilled form in Wyatt). I quote the final stanzas of *The lover complaineth the unkindness of his love*:

> Proud of the spoil that thou hast got
> Of simple hearts, thorough love's shot;
> By whom, unkind, thou hast them won,
> Think not he hath his bow forgot,
> Although my lute and I have done.
>
> Vengeance shall fall on thy disdain
> That makest but game on earnest pain;
> Think not alone under the sun
> Unquit to cause thy lovers plain,
> Although my lute and I have done.
>
> Perchance thee lie withered and old,
> The winter nights that are so cold,
> Plaining in vain unto the moon;
> Thy wishes then dare not be told.
> Care then who list, for I have done.
>
> And then may chance thee to repent
> The time that thou hast lost and spent
> To cause thy lovers sigh and swoon;
> Then thou shalt know beauty but lent,
> And wish and want as I have done.
>
> Now cease my lute, this is the last
> Labour that thou and I shall waste,
> And ended is that we begun.
> Now is this song both sung and past,
> My lute, be still, for I have done.

There were other, but rather minor, courtly makers in the first half of the century, like Thomas, Lord Vaux. But Wyatt and Surrey stand out as the first properly Renaissance English poets, not merely because of the new forms and formal attitudes they introduced, but because of their spirit.

II Plain Style, or Drab Style?

Tudor poetry between Wyatt and Surrey and Sidney and Spenser has been described rather deprecatingly by C. S. Lewis as poetry in the drab style, and by a fine American critic and poet as poetry in the plain style, the only style which this critic, Yvor Winters, admires. The old rhetoricians made a distinction between the high style, suitable, say, for choruses in tragedy or formal panegyric; the middle style, more familiar and easy but aiming also at a certain grace and ornament; and the low style, suitable for a naturalistic kind of pastoral verse, and imitating the simple speech and sometimes the uncouth dialect of shepherds, farmers, or fishermen. In English, for instance, much of Milton's *Paradise Lost* is in the high style, Shakespeare's sonnets are the perfection of the middle style (as, in a quite different way, are Pope's imitations of Horace), and Wordsworth in the *Lyrical Ballads*, or those of them that carry out his theory, is aiming at a rustic naturalness of speech, as free from poetic ornament as possible, the low style, but used for high purposes.

Winters uses 'the plain style', however, as a term not merely of description but of praise as we speak of a plain honest man. C. S. Lewis similarly uses 'drab' (as for Elizabethan poetry from Sidney and Spenser on he similarly uses 'golden') evaluatively rather than descriptively. Winters and Lewis recognise the same phenomena. They admire (and ultimately there is no arguing about taste) opposite kinds of things. Lewis admires what one can call the magic or the transformatory power of poetry; Winters admires poems that make a concise and exact moral judgment on common experience (and a judgment with which he can rationally concur). In dealing with the drab or the plain period, since his admiration for the tradition of the plain style is genuine, Winters is a better guide than Lewis, who is bored and anxious to get on to what he really likes. But one should add that Winters, since it characterises his own verses, was probably quite unaware of or positively responsive to a feature that puts many readers off mid-Tudor poetry: a thumping monotony of rhythm.

Barnabe Googe (1540–94), Thomas Churchyard (1520–1604), Thomas Howell (1568 fl.), George Turberville

(1540–95) and, the most individual of all these in voice, George Gascoigne (1542–77) (a professional soldier and almost a professional man of letters, and in his *Certain Notes of Instruction* the first English theorist of prosody and definer of the English stress-syllable iambic foot) are all typical of this drab or plain period. Googe, who was especially interested in translation, like the fourteener and the alternation of fourteener and alexandrines that was called 'poulter's measure' (because poulterers, if one bought several dozen eggs, would give thirteen for the dozen, but do this by alternating twelve eggs with fourteen). The measure is a very monotonous one, which Googe cannot help much by breaking it always at the caesura (line break) into two lines: here is an example of these broken lines, alexandine regularly followed by fourteener:

Once musing as I sat.	6 syllables
and candle burning by,	6
When all were hushed, I might discern	8
a simple, silly fly,	6
That flew before mine eyes	6
with free rejoicing heart,	6
And here and there with wings did play	8
as void of pain and smart.	6
Sometime by me she sat,	6
when she had played her fill	6
And ever when she rested had	8
about she flittered still . . .	6

The poet goes on to draw the moral that the thoughtless fly has a happier life than its reasonable observer. If God were to enable Googe to change places with the fly,

Then I should joy, as thou dost now	8
and thou shouldst wail thy case.	6

The language is clear and pure, the example vividly presented, and the moral clearly drawn from it. The complete lack of poetic ornament may convince us of the poet's plain honesty. Yet few would guess from Googe's work, and that of most of his contemporaries, that England was on the verge of one of her grand periods. One does not despise such a poem, but it is good journeyman's work: 'honest yeas and russet kersey noes'.

From the *First Part of Churchyard's Chips*, 1575, we can demonstrate that even the staple line of subsequent English poetry, the iambic pentameter, or five foot stress-syllable line in rising rhythm, the most flexible of all English lines, had in the early Elizabethan age a wooden stiffness: Thomas Churchyard writes in praise of soldiers thus in his poem, *The Siege of Edinburgh Castle*:

> Yŏu wárd/ thĕ dáy/ aňd wátch/ thĕ wín/ tĕr's níght,
> Iň fróst,/ iň cóld,/ iň sún/ aňd héat/ ǻlsó;
> Yŏu aře/ sŏ bént/ thǎt láb/ oŭr seém/ ĕth líght
> Aňd iň/ thĕ stéad/ ŏf jóy/ yŏu wél/ coňe wóe . . .

What makes this dreary to read is the predominance of monosyllables. Churchyard knows what an iambic foot is but mistakenly thinks that its main stress must fall on a word or root of main sense-stress whereas in fact it need only fall on a syllable slightly stronger than that which precedes it, as in Sidney's

> Sure, if that long-with-love-acquainted eyes.

And even a monosyllabic line can become melodious when, as in the same sonnet, Sidney allows the first syllable of a foot to be almost as strong as the second: I shall exaggerate this by marking it as *just* as strong:

> Wíth hoẃ/ sád stéps/ Ó moón/ thóu clímb'st/ thĕ skíes . . .

The most one can say, it seems to me, for a poet like Churchyard is that on his rough foundations Spenser and Sidney learned how to build, but after Wyatt and Surrey the mid-Tudor period, till we reach Sidney and Spenser, seems a period of trite thoughts, mechanical metres, and a desperate lack of assurance and style.

Howell is more attractive than those others I have named because sometimes he goes back to the mood of Wyatt and a repeated rhyming on weak syllables that recalls Skelton in his more tender moods:

To his lady, of her doubtful answer

'Twixt death and doubtfulness,
'Twixt pain and pensiveness,
'Twixt hell and heaviness,
Rests all my carefulness.

Oh, vain security,
That will not liberty,
Fie on that fantasy
That brings captivity!

My life is loathesomeness,
My pleasure pastimeless,
My end your doubtfulness,
If you be merciless.

In doubt is jealousy,
Hope helpeth misery;
Most women commonly
Have answers readily.

Howell, as his name suggests, was of Welsh ancestry – he was a member of the household of the Earl of Shrewsbury, who takes his title from a town on the English marches of Wales – and, as examples in our own time show, a Welsh poet may be at a loss for matter, but is never at a loss for music.

The most important poet of this period, however (and for a short time his translations of plays, his satire in blank verse (*The Steel Glass*), and his long narrative poem, harshly realistic, about his experiences as a soldier in the Dutch wars (*Dulce Bellum Inexpertis*), made him the most variously gifted poet in England) was George Gascoigne. He is a difficult poet, however, to represent adequately in quotation: his effect is cumulative, the effect of honest steady effort, rather than one that expresses itself in the individual line. The last stanza, for instance, of *Gascoigne's lullaby* (the reader has already seen Skelton's use of this popular traditional form) is very moving if one has read the rest of the poem. Gascoigne is lulling to sleep, not any baby, but the will to live: he writes as a man prematurely old, disappointed in everything:

Thus lullaby, my youth, mine eyes,
My will, my ware, and all that was,

I can no mo delays devise,
But welcome pain, let pleasure pass;
With lullaby, now take your leave,
With lullaby, your dreams deceive,
And when you rise with wak ng eye,
Remember Gascoigne's lullaby.

Rather similarly, the following passage from *The Steel Glass* makes its effect not by the strikingness of any individual line but by the pounding repetition of the line pattern and the steady, unvaried mood of denunciation. The strength comes from a relentless monotony:

This is the cause (believe me now, my lord)
That realms do rue from high prosperity,
That kings decline from princely government,
That lords do lack their ancestors' good will,
That knights consume their patrimony still,
That gentlemen do make the merchant rise,
That plowmen beg, and craftsmen cannot thrive,
That clergy quails and hath small reverence,
That laymen live by moving mischief still,
That courtiers thrive at latter Lammas Day,
That officers can scarce enrich their heirs,
That soldiers starve, or preach at Tyburn cross,
That lawyers buy, and purchase deadly hate,
That merchants climb, and fall again as fast,
That roisters brag above their betters' room,
That sycophants are counted jolly guests,
That Lais leads a lady's life aloft,
And Lucrece lurks with sober bashful grace.

Gascoigne's poems are those of a disappointed man and a discontented man, who, however, has a soldierly reticence in expressing his deepest feelings, except in an oblique, formal, and indirect way. While many late Elizabethan poems strike one as poems of delightful artifice pretending, but not very hard, to be personal feeling, Gascoigne's best work is in poems of often sour personal feeling pretending to be artifice. The artifice, of course, is of a much plainer sort than we associate with later Elizabethan poetry. Gascoigne never delights or enchants us. He never felt, or cannot express, joy. His verse never catches fire. But in his dogged, bitter, and restrained way he is the one poet of this mid-Tudor period who remains alive in his poetry as an enigmatic and rather formidable personality.

Two other poets of this period, who do not quite fit into the drab or plain pattern, should be mentioned. Arthur Golding (1536–1606) published in 1565 the first four books and in 1567 the whole fifteen books of Ovid's *Metamorphoses*. In spite of the jog-trot effect of the fourteener in which he wrote, Golding had a sense of the vividness and surprisingness of Ovid's imagery; he was good enough for Shakespeare to steal from, in *The Tempest*, and for Ezra Pound to praise. Thomas Sackville (1536–1608), first Earl of Dorset and Baron Buckhurst, was co-author with Thomas Norton of the first English tragedy in blank verse, *Gorboduc*, which was performed before Queen Elizabeth at Whitehall in 1561 and in 1563 he contributed the dignified 'Induction' and the life of Henry Duke of Buckingham (Shakespeare's 'deep-revolving, witty Buckingham', the assistant and then the enemy of Richard III) to the *Mirror for Magistrates* (magistrates meaning magnates or rulers, not petty justices, as today). The work was planned as a continuation of Lydgate's *Falls of Princes* and the various narratives were spoken by the hosts of these great men who had fallen, by the turns of fortune's wheel, from great estate. Something grander than the plain style was obviously required and in the 'Induction' particularly Sackville did his best to supply this. I quote one stanza, almost at random:

> And first, within the porch and jaws of hell,
> Sat deep Remorse of Conscience, all besprent
> With tears, and to herself oft would she tell
> Her wretchedness, and cursing never stent   *stinted*
>   With thoughtful care as she that, all in vain,
>   Would wear and waste continually in pain.

Sackville was too busy as a politician, after the early 1560s, to find time for verse, but he deserves credit for introducing in the 'Induction' a new quality into Elizabethan poetry, a plangent and public eloquence.

III The Late Elizabethan Period: Lyrical Poems

The comparative drabness or the lack of spring of the earlier

Elizabethan poetry we have just been considering may reflect the uncertainty of the queen's subjects about being ruled by a woman, the turning back from the Papacy after the return to it under Queen Mary, the comparative traditionalism and compromise of the new Anglican settlement as compared with European Calvinism and Lutheranism, the tepidity and moderation, to say the least, of the queen's interventions in the Low Countries on behalf of the Dutch Protestants, the drawbacks of her marriage either to a French Catholic like the Valois Duke of Anjou, or the equal danger of her marriage to a noble over-powerful English subject like Robert, Earl of Leicester. The rather ugly and mysterious circumstances of the death at Kenilworth of Leicester's wife were also dangerous to the queen's popularity though, in the end, they made any marriage with Leicester impossible. Though the queen had a succession of favourites from Raleigh to Essex and enjoyed the formal and extravagant homage paid by young courtiers and by poets to her ageing beauty, to the image of herself as the Virgin Queen, Diana, Cynthia, she enjoyed power even more: the Virgin Queen may have been irked by her virginity, and by the problem of an heir after her death, but the death of Mary Queen of Scots at Fotheringay and the defeat of the Spanish Armada in 1588 increased her security and popularity in her later years. That popularity did not quite last to her death, as Essex's rebellion, though it was easily quelled, showed. It was becoming more difficult to treat a painted old woman as an eternally beautiful goddess, the problem of an heir was really worrying, and the ignoble James VI was welcomed from Scotland by many subjects of Elizabeth who had no illusions about James's character: at least he secured a succession. Spain was still a very formidable power and the loss of the Netherlands and the defeat of the Armada had mattered less to Philip II than Englishmen supposed. But there was a period of triumph and new wealth from the new English plantations in North America, from trade with the Indies, and from the raids on Spanish treasure ships by British privateers. The early part of Elizabeth's reign had been, like its poetry, a grey period. The atmosphere changed from the 1580s onwards, a change reflected not only in the more ornate language of poetry from about 1580 onwards but in the showy dress of courtiers, the building of great houses, the giving of splendid entertainments, a general fondness for show and pageantry and, above all, perhaps, the new professionalism of the theatre, in its acting, its presentation, and the quality of its plays. Life was largely a disguise. A new merchant class was rising to wealth but not thrusting itself too ostentatiously forward; the gallantries and revelries of the court were partly competitions by ambitious young men for place and favour. The greatest long poem of the age, Spenser's *The Faerie Queene* was partly a glorification of Elizabeth but even more a fierce defence of extreme Protestantism and an attack on Roman Catholicism, figured by the fair but false Duessa, who is at once the Church of Rome (the whore of Babylon) and Mary Queen of Scots. Yet the colouring of the poem is wholly medieval, its language is often mock-medieval, and it is in fact a longer, more elaborate, and grander verse allegory than the English Middle Ages have left us. A time of radical change, in England, is often marked by an attachment of a romantic but unreal sort to picturesque and out-moded forms.

The great achievement of the Elizabethan and the earlier Jacobean period was in drama, but for reasons that have been explained, drama does not come under our purview in this survey. William Shakespeare (1564–1616) was our greatest dramatist and he happened also to be our greatest poet, but he uses his poetic gift at full pressure in his plays only when dramatically he needs to. The second scene of *Macbeth*, for instance, the 'bloody sergeant' episode, is very effective theatrically, but considered in cold blood the language is pure rant. The only one of Shakespeare's tragedies in which the language has the quality of pure poetry all through, *Anthony and Cleopatra*, is strangely enough *also* that in which the language throughout has the quality of easy, natural, and highly individualised speech. His last play, *The Tempest*, though the most poetical of his comedies, is that in which the characters and the episodes are at the farthest remove from real life and two of the most eloquent characters, Ariel and Caliban, are not human beings but a spirit and the monstrous offspring of a witch. T. S. Eliot might have counted Thomas Middleton (1580–1627) as one of the very greatest dramatists of Shakespeare's time outside Shakespeare for his psychological realism; but except in a few passages of climax, which have a quality of freezing horror, Middleton's language, though perfectly transparent and fully adequate to its dramatic purposes, lacks the memorableness of poetry. And Beaumont and Fletcher, full of pretty and very poetical flowers of language (like cut flowers stuck in a vase, Eliot thought) are completely intent in their plotting and characterisation not, like Middleton, on reality but on effective theatrical artifice. For these reasons, in dealing with the Elizabethan period at its heyday, we leave drama out. This leaves us with three kinds of poem to consider: the usually, but not always, short poem of the type we call lyrical or meditative; the short romantic narrative poem (like Shakespeare's *Venus and Adonis*, Marlowe's two sestiads of Marlowe's and Chapman's *Hero and Leander*, or Lodge's *Scylla's Metamorphosis*) which is called the epyllion; and one very long poem, Spenser's *The Faerie Queene*, which can be considered as perhaps the master poem of its age. Along with the last kind, historical narrative poems like Drayton's *The Barons' Wars* and Daniel's *Civil Wars*, rhymed chronicles of medieval history, will deserve mention but it must be admitted that, outside drama, the longer an Elizabethan poem is the less likely it is to have been generally read, and that the kind of Elizabethan poem which has kept, as frequent anthologies show, a general popularity is the short lyric (in which the sonnet, of course, is included).

Sir Philip Sidney in his short life (1554–86) earned the kind of reputation as a soldier, a courtier, a poet, and a man of virtue, honour, and courtesy which made him the very type of the Renaissance hero. Thus Yeats, in our own century, wishing to praise the dead Robert Gregory could find no grander phrase than 'our Sidney and our perfect man'. Before his heroic death at Zutphen, he had travelled widely in Europe and he introduced into England many European stanza forms, such as the elaborately difficult sestina, which he uses in one famous poem examined by Empson the 'complaints eclogue-wise' of Strephon and Claius from *Seven Types of Ambiguity* in Book 2 of his prose romance *The Countess of Pembroke's Arcadia*, and the trochaic foot, or reversed iambus, which is much more suitable for songs and verse to be set to music than the iambic foot. It was appropriate that he should die at

Zutphen, in the Low Countries, wounded in the Protestant cause, for like his patron, Leicester, he was a much more militant Protestant than the cautious queen. He also experimented, but not very seriously, with attempts at quantitative verse in English. He was the most scholarly and adroit craftsman and inventor in verse yet to appear in sixteenth century England, though he never appears strained or difficult but always easy and natural. His greatest collection of poems, *Astrophel and Stella*, is based on his love for Penelope Devereux, the daughter of the first Earl of Essex (not, of course, Elizabeth's later favourite) who had been married to a man apparently universally disliked and despised, Lord Rich. This series of sonnets, interspersed with short lyrical poems in various stanza forms is, for all its glowing beauty and courtly wit, a painfully honest account of the struggle in both Sidney and Penelope between a passionate love and a sense of honour and conscience which forbade both of them to yield to this love. It tells a much clearer story than Shakespeare's sonnets, whose story, if there is one, still distracts commentators from their poetry, and it is at least as psychologically honest as the love poems of John Donne. Donne is often seen, as by A. Alvarez in *The School of Donne*, as reacting against the Petrarchan artificiality of Sidney and the more courtly late Elizabethan poets generally; but Sidney had truly obeyed his own injunction:

Fool, said my muse to me, look in thy heart and write.

With the English High Renaissance, of which Sidney is so centrally representative, we reach a stage in which the material discussed is more generally accessible and the poets are much less in need of illustration by extensive quotation and glossing. We are dealing, now, with what in a very broad sense can be called 'modern' times: from late Elizabethan times onwards we are aware of the growing centralised power of the nation state, the growth of new methods of technology, the discovery and colonisation of new countries, the polarisation, unknown in the Middle Ages, of 'right' and 'left' (Papist, or Puritan and Anglican, the gentry and the merchants, 'court' and 'country' parties, Tories and Whigs, Conservatives and Liberals, Conservatives and Labour) which continues to our own times. Very roughly, if medieval poetry reflects a deep inner harmony and faith, in which even sad and disastrous events are accepted as part of God's hidden purpose and the divine order of things, from the Elizabethan age onwards what gives both English society and poetry its life is an awareness of tension, of the willed unity of contraries. This unity in tension can be seen in the eleventh song of *Astrophel and Stella*, in which the first two lines of each stanza are imagined as spoken by Stella, the remainder by Astrophel. Stella, gently, is telling Astrophel that absence and other beauties will gradually cure Astrophel of the love for her which in her heart she returns but in honour cannot reward:

> 'What if you new beauties see,
> Will not they stir new affection?'
> 'I will think they pictures be,
> Image-like, of saint's perfection,
> Poorly counterfeiting thee.'

> 'But your reason's purest light
> Bids you leave such minds to nourish.'
> 'Dear, do reason no such spite,
> Never doth thy beauty flourish
> More than in my reason's sight.'

> 'But the wrongs love bears will make
> Love at length leave undertaking.'
> 'No, the more fools it do shake,
> In a ground of so firm making,
> Deeper still they drive the stake.'

Under the polish we can feel the pain: the poem from which these stanzas are taken is, incidentally, an instance of a triumphant use of the trochee, the foot which Sidney introduced into English verse. It is a foot perfectly adapted to the expression of melancholy:

> Ín å/ g.round ôf/ só firm/ mákin̊g,
> Déepe̊r/ still the̊y/ driv́e the̊/ stáke

Sidney wrote two poems in which, for love of heaven, he bids farewell to earthly love. Ironically enough, their dic-

:ion, full of monosyllables and faintly suggesting the drab
style, though the drab style transfigured, implies that they
were written *before Astrophel and Stella*, whose metrical
fingering is much more subtle. Here is the second and more
famous of the two:

> Leave me, O love which reachest but to dust;
> And thou, my mind, aspire to higher things;
> Grow rich in that which never taketh rust,
> Whatever fades but fading pleasure brings.
> Draw in thy beams, and humble all thy might
> To that sweet yoke where lasting freedoms be:
> Which breaks the clouds and open forth the light,
> That doth both shine and give us sight to see.
> O take fast hold; let that light by thy guide
> In this small course which birth draws out to death,
> And think how evil becometh him to slide,
> Who seeketh heav'n, and comes of heav'nly breath.
>> Then farewell, world; thy uttermost I see;
>> Eternal Love, maintain thy life in me.

Splendidis longum valedico nugis

The Latin means, 'I bid a long farewell to shining trifles',
and the renunciation of earthly for heavenly love is part of
the Petrarchan tradition. Nevertheless the style of the poem
does suggest that it is early in Sidney's development, and it
would be typical of the irony which seems to attend the
emotional development of poets if the young Sidney should
have bidden farewell to love poetry before he seriously fell
in love.

A number of very interesting poems adorn his prose
romance, *The Countess of Pembroke's Arcadia*: the following lines, for instance, are a very gallant attempt at classical
quantitative verse in English. (The metre is called the
shorter asclepiad.) When the reader has seen what Sidney is
attempting to do he will find in the slow, dragging
movement of the line a peculiarly haunting quality which
perhaps neither stress-syllable verse nor pure stress alliterative lines can attain. At the same time, there is a sense of
artifice and of difficulty just conquered:

> Ō sweēt/ woͦods thĕ dĕlighͫt/ of sŏlĭtar/ iñess!
> Ōh, hoͦw/ muͦch Ĭ dŏ liͤke/ your sŏlĭtar/ iñess!

Whēre mān's/ mīnd hăth ă freēd/ cōnsĭdĕrăt̄/ioň,
Ōf goōd/nēss tŏ rĕceive/ lovelў dĭřect/ĭon.

Notice that the long syllable in this method of scansion does
not always (more often than not, does not) coincide with the
syllable of first or secondary stress in ordinary pronunciation. The scansion also depends on the pronunciation (common in verse, though probably not in ordinary speech) of
the 'ion' at the end of words like 'consideration' and
'direction' as two syllables. The classical scansion also
involves slightly unnatural prolongation of what in speech
are insignificant words, like the 'of' at the beginning of the
last line, and while we can accept Sidney's quantitative
scansion of 'cōnsĭdĕrăt-' that of 'sŏlĭtar-' strikes us as dis-
tinctly odd. Sidney's long syllable is one we might slur in
ordinary speech: 'solit'riness'. Nevertheless, these experiments in quantitative verse are part of Sidney's fine bold-
ness. When this young man died at thirty-two, refusing a cup
of water and offering it to a dying soldier with the words,
'His need is greater than mine', he was not only the
Protestant paragon; he had opened out the possibilities of
English verse in a dozen new directions. His *Defence of
Poesy* also answered the attacks of Puritans who claimed
that poetry told lies and was a trifling and useless pursuit by
saying that, in the fallen state of man, poetry alone delivers
us a golden world. And by describing how the old ballad of
the Percy and the Douglas (he probably meant the English
version, *The Perse owte of Northumberland* rather than the
Scotch) roused his heart like a trumpet, he was recalling
attention, in an age whose poetic danger was a suave
unreality, to the roots of poetry (Prospero's 'rough magic')
in the folk.

Sidney's friends among the courtly makers of Elizabeth's
time mourned his death. One was Fulke Greville, Lord
Brooke, whose quatrains have a passionate plangency:

> Silence augmenteth grief, writing increaseth rage,
> Staled are my thoughts, which loved and lost the wonder
> of our age;
> Yet quickened now with fire, though dead with frost ere now,
> Enraged I write I know not what; dead, quick, I know
> not how.

Hard-hearted minds relent and rigour's tears abound,
And envy strangely rues his end, in whom no fault was found.
Knowledge her light hath lost, valour hath slain her knight,
Sidney is dead, dead is my friend, dead is the world's delight.

The savage, monotonous emphasis of this is like a man tearing at his own flesh. Brooke had a powerful but self-tormenting mind, as is shown in his most famous lines, from a chorus of priests from his tragedy, *Mustapha*, 1609:

Oh, wearisome condition of humanity,
Born under one law, to another bound,
Vainly begot, and yet forbidden vanity,
Created sick, commanded to be sound . . .

Born in 1554, Brooke was murdered in 1628 by a servant, who immediately killed himself. His verses suggest that he was a moody man, of cloudy temper, yet he held many high offices but disdained them in comparison with his friendship with Sidney; he wrote his own epitaph: 'Servant to Queen Elizabeth, councillor to King James, and friend to Sir Sidney.'

Of far grander and more various talent, and at his best a great poet, was Sir Walter Raleigh (1552–1618). This Devonshire gentleman who wrote his poems always, as his surviving manuscripts show, in the broad Western dialect of his native county, was as different from Sidney as could be, a man famous for being 'damnable proud', startlingly in and out of favour both with Queen Elizabeth and King James (he lost the favour of the first by his marriage to Elizabeth Throckmorton in 1592, and was found guilty of treason, on very dubious grounds, against the latter and imprisoned in the Tower for thirteen years, until the king's greed released him to set off on a voyage of exploration to discover El Dorado on the impossible condition that he avoided clashes with the Spaniards). On his return from an exciting but vain voyage, Raleigh was again imprisoned, brought to trial, and executed. During his earlier and longer imprisonment in the Tower, he had written in prose the first English universal history. 'Only my father,' said Henry, the Prince of Wales, who visited Raleigh often and died tragically young, 'would keep such a bird in a cage.'

Raleigh was a poet who could master quite various styles. C. S. Lewis thought him an overrated writer, without a real style or personality of his own, starting as a drab poet, and never quite mastering the golden manner. One can only briefly quote from very various kinds of poem to demonstrate the assurance (it went with being 'damnable proud') that unifies his work in various kinds. First, here is the last stanza of an adapted ballad, *As you came from the holy land*:

> But Loue is a durable fyre
>   In the mynde ever burnynge:
> Never sycke, never ould, never dead,
>   From itt selfe never turnynge:

And here his answer to Marlowe's famous pastoral, *The Nymph's reply to the Shepheard*:

> If all the world and love were young,
> And truth in every shepheard's tongue,
> These pretty pleasures might me move,
> To live with thee and be thy love.
>
> Time drives the flocks from field to fold,
> When rivers rage, and Rocks grow cold,
> And Philomell becommeth dombe,
> The rest complains of cares to come . . .

Marlowe, it will be remembered, had written:

> Come live with mee, and be my love,
> And we will all the pleasures prove,
> That hills and valleys, dales and fields,
> Woods, or steepie mountaine yeeldes.
>
> And wee will sit upon the Rocks,
> Seeing the shepheards feede theyre flocks,
> By shallow rivers, to whose falls,
> Melodious byrds sing Madrigalls.

Here is the 'damnable pride', perhaps, from a poem that provoked many answers, *The Lie*:

Say to the court, it glowes
    and shines like rotten wood;
Say to the church, it showes
    whats good, and doth no good:
If church and court reply,
    then give them both the lie . . .

Tell men of high condition,
    that mannage the estate,
Their purpose is ambition,
    their practice only hate:
And if they once reply,
    then give them all the lie.

Of the many answers to *The Lie* the most logical is that from
MS. Chetham 8012, p. 107, of which these are two stanzas:

admitte some man of state
do pitche his thoughts to hie;
is that a rule for all the rest,
their loyall hearts to trie?

your wittes are in the waine;
your autumne in the bud;
you argue from particulars;
your reason is not good.

But Raleigh, no doubt, knew perfectly well that he was
being sophistical and knew that the gay and insolent assurance of his rhetoric made mere logical quibbling (making
universal inductions from a few scattered instances) a par-
donable fault. He was, one presumes, out of favour for the
time being, and the Court was going to feel it. But the poem
is more than a mere insolent joke: the refrain rings like a
hammer on iron. Raleigh had known, too well, the hollow-
ness and pretence of friendship in high places.

Raleigh's most important, beautiful, and mysterious
poem is, however, *The 11th: and last book of the Ocean to
Scinthia* (meaning Cynthia) which was clearly written to
Queen Elizabeth at some time when he was out of favour
with her. Everything about the poem is mysterious. It has,
to quote Raleigh's editor, Miss Agnes Latham, an 'urgency
and desperation' about it which makes it unlikely that it is
the same poem to Cynthia which Spenser describes Raleigh

as reading to him during their Irish service. Can there have been an earlier ten books (the book that we possess has no narrative content), and could ten earlier books of the same length have been made out of mere praise of Elizabeth? The poem again reads like a desperate and real love poem, but can the young Raleigh, however besotted with the glamour with which she surrounded herself, really have been in love with a withered, painted, masculinely dominating *demi-vierge*, middle-aged with dyed hair? He is in love, Donald Davie has suggested, with courtly favour and all the power and glory it can bring to him, and poetically transforms this vain but passionate desire into the image of the eternally youthful, eternally beautiful Elizabeth. There are other problems. Miss Latham thinks the manuscript that we have in Raleigh's hand, with his phonetic broad Devonshire spellings, is a fair copy of a rough draft. Why then are there syntactical tangles and gaps, a feeling of inspired groping? Miss Latham, wisely leaves the final interpretation of this strange poem, the most beautiful long poem of its age, I think (522 lines, longer than *The Waste Land* or Valéry's *La Jeune Parque*), to the reader. It is the only long poem of its age which has a sense of a profound and difficult meaning eluding and yet attracting the reader, as *The Waste Land* and *La Jeune Parque* do.

Here are some brief examples of the beautiful images and perhaps deliberately confusing syntax that so fascinate me. The reader must make up his own mind whether I am over-fascinated:

My love was falce, my labors weare desayte

Not less than such they are esteemde to bee,
A fraude bought att the prize of many woes,
A guile, whereof the profitts vnto mee –
Coulde it be thought premeditate for thos? . . .

To seeke for moisture in th'Arabien sande
Is butt a losse of labor, and of rest
The lincks which time did break of harty bands

Words cannot knytt, or waylings make anew.
Seeke not the soonn in clovdes when it is sett . . .
On highest mountaynes where those Sedars grew,
Agaynst whose bancks, the troblcd ocean bett,   *beat*

And weare the markes to finde thy hoped port,
Into a soyle far off themsealves remove,
On Sestus' shore, Leanders late resorte,
Hero hath left no lampe to Guyde her love . . .

Shee is gone, Shee is lost! Shee is fovnd, she is
    ever faire!
Sorrow drawes weakly, wher love draws not too.
Woe's cries, sound nothinge, butt only in loves eare.
Do then by Diinge, what life cannot doo . . .   *dying*

There is a strange haunting music, which comes, for instance, in two earlier lines: the end of a stanza and the beginning:

      Like to a fallinge streame which passing sloe
      Is wovnt to nurrishe sleap, and quietness . . .

Such quotations should tell the reader whether the poem will haunt him, too.

7

The Seventeenth Century

I. The Adventurous History

The seventeenth century is the most interesting and surprising of all the centuries of European history, including our own. It laid the foundations, through Galileo, Pascal, and Newton for that orderly and mathematical concept of the physical universe which is still our concept today. It led, through men's weariness of the Thirty Years' War, to the reluctant acceptance of a kind of tolerance (a man's religion should be that of his ruler) and in many minds of a kind of scepticism about religion in general, called in England free-thinking and in France libertinism. In North America, Canada, and the Dutch East Indies it saw the beginnings of colonialism. In Europe, the stronger nation states tended to become more centralised and more concerned with their own power: in England, as a result of the Civil Wars, the philosopher Thomas Hobbes preached in *Leviathan* that any strong ruler, be he Cromwell or a Stuart King, was better than anarchic disorder.

Because of its Civil Wars and religious disagreements which partly led to these and ultimately to the flight and dethronement of James II, a staunch Roman Catholic, in 1688 England played a minor part in European politics. She did poorly in her naval battles with the Dutch. The foundation of the Royal Society after the Restoration gave her a lead in science. But Charles II took bribes from Louis XIV, in architecture and the visual arts England was backward, and to French visitors the English seemed rustic. It was not until the reign of William of Orange and Mary, the daughter of the deposed James II, that William, a soldier by nature and a bitter enemy of Louis, was able (partly through the foundation of the Bank of England and the institution of the National Debt) to fight Louis with a doggedness that led to the Peace of Ryswick and in the next century was to lead to Marlborough's great victories. Hobbes, as a fashionable political philosopher, was replaced at the same time by the duller but more sensible Locke.

Locke justified a mixed rule of king and parliament aiming above all at the protection of property. In philosophy proper, he was the founder of that British empirical tradition which, basing knowledge on sensory experience rather than innate ideas, fostered the growth of British science. Religious dissensions, which had been very fierce throughout the seventeenth century, were tending by 1700 to blur into a general reverence for a benevolent God who had created an orderly universe, and politics, too, lost its fanaticism. Yet the fierce passions of religion and politics had lain behind much of the greatness of English seventeenth-century poetry. The reign of Reason was to prove in some senses the death of Imagination.

Dryden spoke of the earlier seventeenth century as 'the giant age before the flood'. Yet, though looking back particularly in his religious poems like *Religio Laici* and *The Hind and the Panther,* to the complicated argumentation of the metaphysical mode, Dryden is rightly thought of (with two minor figures, Denham and Waller) as the founder of the Augustan mode which was to dominate at least the first half of the next century, the age of Pope, of the Gray of the *Elegy*, of Goldsmith, of Johnson, and belatedly of Crabbe. Though Dryden had a natural taste for the wild and extravagant, a hearty raciness, which looks backwards to the beginning of his century, he had also a logical and what he himself would have called a 'sequacious' mind.

One critic has called Dryden the 'last English poet with a sense of history', having in mind, I think his Jacobitism as well as his ability to appreciate Chaucer and in *Fables* to invent a modern version of the medieval mode. In spite of his youthful parodies and his 'versifications' of Dr Donne's satires, Pope lacked Dryden's sense of the past just as he lacked what Gerard Manley Hopkin's called Dryden's feeling for the 'naked thew and sinew of the language'. More delicate and more observant (Wordsworth observed of Dryden that no other major English poet has had his eye less on the object) than Dryden, Pope lacks his strong continuity of thought and his careless, felicitous energy. Donne, at the beginning of the century has the same energy, sometimes harsh and rough: for the critic of poetry, the English seventeenth century is certainly 'the century of genius' (though not the only such age in our poetic history) but even more strikingly it is the age of strength.

II The School of Donne

In the three and a half centuries since his death, Donne has never been exactly ignored. His difficulty, the oddity of some of his ideas, and the harsh counter-pointing of speech stress and metrical stress in some of his lines, were all noted in his own lifetime. One of the few witty remarks attributed to King James I of England and VI of Scotland is, 'Dr Donne's poetry is like the peace of God; for it passeth all understanding'. Ben Jonson is reported by Drummond of Hawthornden, a Scottish gentleman who wrote melodious English verse in an old-fashioned late Elizabethan mode, as saying that 'Donne's *Anniversary* was profane and full of blasphemies: that he told Mr Donne, if it had been written of the Virgin Mary it had been something; to which he had answered, that he described the idea of a woman, and not as she was', that 'Donne for not keeping of accent, deserved hanging', and yet that 'he esteemeth Donne the first poet in the world, in some things; his verses of the lost chain he hath by heart; and that passage of *The Calm*, that dust and feathers do not stir, it was all so quiet. Affirmeth Donne to have written all his best peices ere he was twenty-five years old.' The date was 1619, so it is likely that Jonson had seen some of Donne's later religious poems, though this depends upon what degree of intimacy still subsisted between the two men: Donne born in 1571 had taken orders, became Dean of St Paul's in 1621, died in London in 1631, and his poems were not published till 1633. What Jonson will have seen of the poems he judges would be manuscript copies, made by or for Donne's friends.

Jonson was far and away the best critical mind among the poets of his time. He was also Donne's contemporary and friendly acquaintance and could connect the man with the poet in a way we cannot. It is impossible, for instance, to be certain which of Donne's love poems are addressed to real women and which represent the play of wit or fancy on imaginary situations; similarly in his religious poems it is often hard to know how deeply he has the fear of God in his heart and how much he is carried away by his own wit and eloquence. A delight in his own rhetoric of surprise is, perhaps, the only emotion in Donne we can always be quite sure of. We may feel also that, even where his wife or a real mistress, or where a real devotion to God, are genuinely involved, Donne, unlike George Herbert, can never escape from a preoccupation with the paradoxes of his own personality. It is not a question of insincerity. Donne is first and foremost a poetical performer and his poems, though we hear only his side of the conversation, have often the abruptness and violence of dialogue in Jacobean drama. In a famous poem, T. S. Eliot classed him with Webster, seeing them both obsessed with death, and certainly there is a family resemblance between Donne's

> A bracelet of bright hair about the bone,

and Webster's:

> Cover her face; mine eyes dazzle; she died young.

What we find in the poems in fact is not Donne's profoundest and most secret self – God alone, literally, knows what that was – but those aspects of Donne's personality that lent themselves to witty dramatisation. Who knows the soul of a great actor? Not the actor himself probably.

Following Jonson, let us look first at the extravagance of the two '*Anniversaries*': '*An Anatomie of the World*' and '*The Progress of the Soul*', which commemorate a girl of fifteen, Elizabeth Drury, whose father Sir Robert Drury was thought to have been Donne's generous patron. John Hayward, whose Nonesuch edition is the best modern collection of Donne's poems and selection of his prose, agrees with Jonson in describing the poems as 'preposterous' but adds that they mark an important stage in Donne's progress 'from poet to divine'. A later critic, Dr Johnson, who gave Donne and his fellow-poets the label 'metaphysical' analysed their method in the conceit as 'the violent yoking together of heterogeneous ideas.' The conceit at the centre of the poem is that of Elizabeth Drury as the pure soul of the world in whose absence nothing awaits the world but decay. Here are the most famous lines in which the death of Elizabeth Drury, the symbol of primordial purity unblasted by original sin, is somehow the cause of the complete reversal of the medieval world picture:

> *Science*
> And new Philosophy calls all in doubt,
> The Element of fire is quite put out;
> The Sun is lost, and th'earth, and no mans wit
> Can well direct him where to looke for it.
> And freely men confesse that this worlde's spent,
> When in the Planets, and the Firmament,
> They seeke so many new; then see that this
> Is crumbled out againe to his Atomies.
> 'Tis all in peeces, all cohaerence gone;
> All just supply, and all Relation:
> Prince, Subject, Father, Sonne, are things forgot,
> For every man alone thinks he hath got
> To be a Phoenix, and that then can bee
> None of that kinde, of which he is, but hee.

The earlier lines describe the effect of the Copernican philosophy (which makes the earth no longer the centre of the created universe but one of many planets moving round the sun) on the medieval Ptolemaic view that all the spheres revolve round our planet, which is fallen but nonetheless the centre of God's attention. The passage beginning

> All just supply, and all Relation . . .

describes the new and ruthless kind of individualism of a character like Edmund in Shakespeare's *King Lear*: Machiavelli had made the old hierarchies of society and family seem mere conventions for the ambitious man and Montaigne (interested in his thoughts because they were his own thoughts, not anybody else's) had encouraged that introspective self-absorption that made every man his own phoenix. Denouncing as destructive all these modern heresies, Donne, in his intimate fascination with them, seems nevertheless very modern himself.

One can see that Jonson with his strong and solid but inelastic mind would shy away from Donne's agility in paradox; from the sense that what Donne denounces here he also, with another part of him, admires. What did Jonson, whose own verse often moves with a burly stiffness, mean by 'not keeping of accent'? Part of the answer is that Donne, especially in his satires, often does this deliberately, playing the formal correctness of accent against the scorn of the sense stress: here are two lines from a satire on a vapid babbling traveller where I have marked the feet conventionally but underlined words where sense plays against metrical stress:

Yŏur eáres/ shăll héare/ no̱u̱g̱ẖṯ, bút/ Ḵi̱ṉg̱s̱; yoúr/ e̱y̱e̱s̱ méet
Ḵi̱ṉg̱s̱/ oń/ lў; Thĕ wáy/ tŏ ĭt iś/ Ḵi̱ṉg̱stréet.

The effect of the wrenching of rhetorical stress against metrical stress five times in one couplet is of a barely controlled scorn (the rhetorical stress) fighting against a conventional politeness due even to fools (the metrical stress). Donne knew what he was doing in such lines, if few of his commentators to this day have attained that knowledge. He does 'keep accent' in his lyrical poems and to think that he does not is a mistake in scansion. I have heard such a fine poet as William Empson maintain that the third of these lines from *A Valediction: Of Weeping*, should be scanned as anapaests (two short syllables followed by a long one) – the first having the two opening light stresses left out:

Ŏ móre/ thăn Moóne,
Drăw ńot/ ŭp seás/ tŏ drówne/ mé iň/ thў sphéare,
Weépe/ mĕ nŏt deád,/ iň thĭine arḿes,/ bŭt fŏrbeáre
Tŏ teách/ thĕ séa,/ whăt iť/ máy doé/ tóo soóne . . .

But Donne, as I. A. Richards has said, is the 'slowest mover' in all English verse and this anapaestic gallop is quite unlike him, jarring terribly against the double spondaic ending of the next line. If one remembers that 'me' and 'thine' express the key concepts of the poem, the obvious scanning is clearly also the correct one:

Weêpe m̲e̲/ nôt deád,/ iñ t̲h̲i̲n̲e̲/ armes, bût/ fórbeare. . . .

As for 'armes, but' remember that the two-syllable foot may be freely reversed in any place but the second and fifth. Donne perhaps made a freer use of this liberty than most of his contemporaries outside dramatic blank verse. Nevertheless he seems to me in his own unique way a musical poet; a way that was unforgettably expressed by George Saintsbury when he spoke of Donne's 'sad clangour'. If I am not impressed by Jonson's metrical criticisms, I am not very much impressed either by what he singles out for admiration, which are examples not of Donne at his most moving but at his cleverest. The couplet he admires from *The Calme*:

> No use of lanthornes; and in one place lay
> Feathers and dust, today and yesterday,

certainly remains in one's head for ever when one has read it once but, lodged there, it does not seem to do much to one. Beneath the vividness and verbal ingenuity, the idea of life as transitory is a trite one. As for *The Bracelet: Upon the Losse of his Mistresses Chaine, for which he made Satisfaction,* I am surprised that Jonson should have it by heart. Ingenious, it nevertheless seems to me the least sensual and passionate of the *Elegies*:

> Not that in colour it was like thy haire,
> For Armelets of that thou maist let me weare:
> Nor that thy hand it oft embrac'd and kist,
> For so it had that good, which oft I mist:
> Nor for that silly old moralitie,
> That as these linkes were knit, our love should bee:
> Mourne I that thy seavenfold chaine have lost;
> Nor for the luck sake; but the bitter cost.

Though he was an acute critic and in his own right a poet as much admired and imitated as Donne (and a poet whom some fine modern American critics and poets, Yvor Winters and J. V. Cunningham and their followers, admirers of the 'plain style', have preferred to Donne), Jonson was perhaps too temperamentally different to see what Donne was after. Jonson is at his best in either a lyrical or discursive vein, when he is straightforward; he is a poet with a great deal of self-control and cool good sense, whose feelings and ideas are never likely to run away with him. Donne is a poet of passionate feelings and extravagant ideas, as in the first stanza of *A Feaver*:

> Oh doe not die, for I shall hate
>   All women so, when thou art gone,
> That thee I shall not celebrate,
>   When I remember, thou wast one . . .

or as in *Twicknam Garden*

> Hither with christall vyals, lovers come,
>   And take my teares, which are loves Wine,
> And try your mistresse Teares at home
> For all are false, that tast not just like mine;
>   Alas, hearts do not in eyes shine,
> Nor can you more judge womans thoughts by teares,
>   Than by her shadow, what she weares.
> O perverse sexe, where none is true but shee,
>   Who's therefore true, because her truth kills mee . .

or from *Love's Deitie*

> I long to talke with some old lovers ghost,
>   Who dyed before the god of Love was borne:
> I cannot thinke that hee, who then lov'd most,
>   Sunke so low, as to love one which did scorne.
> But since this god produc'd a destinie,
> And that vice-nature, custome, lets it be;
>   I must love her, that loves not mee.

Donne's love convinces us most when it is most fused, as in these passages, with grief and resentment. A thought almost too painful to express, as in the first quatrain – if the woman he loves dies of her fever, he will hate all women – is logically extended to a bitter witticism: so when she is dead he will hate her too (and, by hating all including the dead love, lose his logical reason for hating any). He writes, on religion as well as love, a poetry of shock-tactics: as in his love poems he seems, in Dryden's phrase, 'to affect the metaphysics' (not suitable, Dryden thinks, to allure the soft sex) in his religious poems he is drawn to amorous conceits. Addressing God he writes:

Yet dearely' I love you, 'and would be loved faine,
But am betroth'd unto your enemie:
Divorce mee, 'untie, or breake that knot againe,
Take mee to you, imprison mee, for I
Except you'enthrall mee, never shall be free,
Nor ever chast, except you ravish me.

(The apostrophes there are not quotation marks but the Jacobean printers' convention for the metrical elision of two adjacent short vowels.) He asks himself (he had been born and bred a Roman Catholic and it was after long hesitation that he became ordained in the Church of England and ended what had been a life of adventurous and uneven fortunes illustriously as Dean of St Paul's) which is the true Church. His answer seems here still, quite late in his career, to incline towards the Church of Rome:

Doth she, and did she, and shall she evermore
On one, on seaven, or on no hill appeare?
Dwells she with us, or like adventuring knights
First travaile we to seeke and then make Love?
Betray kind husband thy spouse to our sights,
And let myne amorous soule court thy mild Dove,
Who is most trew, and pleasing to thee, then
When she'is embrac'd and open to most men.

The true Church is traditionally the Spouse of Christ, but can also be thought of as the Lady sought by a wandering knight; she is most true to Christ when she is most welcoming, like a harlot, to new lovers. It is not surprising that Donne, quite apart from the sexual frankness particularly of his *Elegies*, has never been a poet with whom orthodox Anglicans have been quite at ease. Their hero has been his contemporary George Herbert, a genuine saint, whose gentle and humble spirit communicates itself even to agnostic lovers of poetry: who are likely to admire Donne's passionate energy of rhetoric, but to feel also that, in love and religion, he is too often seeking to batter down his own doubts.

George Herbert came of a great family (his brother, Lord Herbert of Cherbury, the first English deist, was a very distinguished disciple of Donne's in his own manner) but was content to live a useful and humble life as a country parson, ending up as rector of Bemerton near Salisbury. Promotion in the church could easily have come his way, but he avoided it, and left the decision about publishing his poems *The Temple* and its prose companion, *A Priest to the Temple*, after his death to his friend the saintly Nicholas Ferrars. As Donne is always in the foreground of his poems, and always ready to display himself as an extraordinary man, Herbert seeks to make us aware of his devotion and God, its object, but not of himself except as an ordinary Christian striving to do his duty. Yet he was enough affected by the metaphysical mode to make some use of the riddle and conceit. It is doubtful, for instance, whether his parishioners would have made very much of this short poem:

Hope

I gave to Hope a watch of mine, but he
    An anchor gave to me.
Then an old prayer-book I did present,
    And he an optic sent.
With that I gave a phial full of tears,
    But he a few green ears.
Ah, loiterer! I'll no more, no more I'll bring,
    I did expect a ring.

Many readers will find this little poem more difficult than Donne. Faith, Hope, and Charity are the three cardinal Christian virtues and the poet is giving his time, symbolised by the watch, to Hope. Hope gives him in return an anchor, by which he can fasten himself securely to Hope. He gives Hope a prayer-book, a symbol of the life of Christian prayer, and hope gives him a telescope by which he can have a clearer and longer prospect than most men of what lies before him. He offers Hope a glass full of penitential tears and hope gives him in return a few green ears of corn which will ripen into the divine harvest of repentance. The poet is petulant to Hope because he is waiting for the gift of a ring, a symbol of complete bliss. But if we were given complete bliss on earth the divine virtue of Hope would be unnecessary. Here, as elsewhere, Herbert very gently mocks himself for demanding from God too much, too quickly. A finer spirit, George Herbert has never had the fame of Donne but from readers who can respond to his humble purity of soul he has had more love.

The metaphysical mode, the cult of the conceit instead of the image, of the logical paradox, lent itself in some ways more to religious poetry than to profane love poetry. One thing that is new in the poetry of that mode, found most memorably perhaps in the poems of Henry Vaughan (1621–95), is the sense expressed much later most memorably by Wordsworth, of childhood as a period when man still lives in a state of unfallen innocence:

> Happy those early dayes! when I
> Shin'd in my Angel-infancy.
> Before I understood this place
> Appointed for my second race,
> Or taught my soul to fancy ought
> But a white, Celestiall thought . . .

Thomas Traherne (1637–74) published nothing of interest in his lifetime but became famous in the 1890s with the publication of his religious poems and even more splendid visionary prose meditations. Perhaps because he never seems to have had publication in mind his thoughts (like Vaughan he is much preoccupied with childhood) have an individual strangeness. As a child, looking at reflections in a pool, he thought of the images as a mysterious other world; grown up he sees a reflection of heaven and the thin film of reflecting water as a 'thin Skin' through which by and by he will break into a divine world:

> Look how far off those lower Skies
> Extend themselves! scarce with mine Eyes
> I can them reach. O ye my Friends,
> What *Secret* borders on these Ends?
> > Are lofty Heavens hurl'd
> > 'Bout your inferior World?
> Are ye the Representatives
> Of other People's distant Lives?
>
> Of all the Play-mates which I knew
> That here I do the Image view
> In other Selves; what can it mean?
> But that below the purling Stream
> > Some unknown Joys there be
> > Laid up in store for me;

> To which I shall, when that thin Skin
> Is broken, be admitted in.

The 'thin Skin' is that between earth and heaven, between mortal life and immortal life, teasingly reflected in calm water: what we take for reflection is reality, very near, but not tangible till God breaks the thin skin for us. It is the earth on which we walk as mortal bodies that has the unreality of a reflection in a watery mirror.

Sober piety typifies the English religious temperament. Richard Crashaw (1612–49) was a Roman Catholic convert and the one English poet in what used to be called the Jesuit style. His hymn to Saint Theresa is, in its way a great poem, to many English readers, like the swirling draperies of Bernini's sculpture of her in the Vatican, almost embarrassing in its confusion of the sexual and the religious. Yet its eloquence is unarguable:

> O how oft shalt thou complaine
> Of a sweet and subtile paine!
> Of intollerable *joyes*!
> Of a *death*, in which who *dyes*
> Loves his death, and dyes againe,
> And would for ever so be slaine!
> And lives, and dyes; and knowes not why
> To live; But that he thus may never leave to *dy*.

Bishop Henry King (1592–1669), who lived such a long life in such a troubled age, wrote no poems at all resembling Crashaw's ecstatic self-identification with the agonies of St Theresa. King was passionately loved by his first wife, Anne Berkeley, and is best remembered by his *Exequy* expressing a longing to be reunited with the young woman in death (they were married in 1617, she died in 1624). There is something almost morbid in this desire reaching beyond the grave (for we are told that there is no marrying, or giving in marriage, in heaven, and all the vows of the marriage service are to bind us only 'till death us do part'), which appealed to the sick imagination of Poe:

> 'Tis true, with shame and grief I yield,
> Thou like the *Vann* first took'st the field   *vanguard*
> And gotten hast the victory

In thus adventuring to dy
Before me, whose more years might crave
A just precedence in the grave,
But heark! My pulse like a soft Drum
Beats my approch, tells *Thee* I come;
And slow howere my marches be
I shall at last sit down by *Thee*.

The dead march of the lines is memorable and none would grudge the young woman (who in her seven years of marriage had six children, of whom only two survived) this tribute of grief. Such feelings can be given shape in words but cannot survive for ever in the heart with their first vividness. In 1630, King married for a second time.

Even better evidence than in such quotations as these of how religion dominated the deeper feelings of the age can be found in verses by men whose lives, in general, were worldly or libertine. John Wilmot, second Earl of Rochester, well before his conversion by Bishop Burnet on his final sick bed, wrote, in a lovely poem *Absent from Thee I languish Still*, these moving final stanzas to the wife whom he so perpetually betrayed:

When wearied with a world of Woe,
    To thy safe Bosom I retire,
Where Love and Peace and Truth does flow,
    May I contented there expire,

Lest, once more wandering from that Heav'n
    I fall on some base heart unblest;
Faithless to thee, False, unforgiven,
    And lose my Everlasting rest.

Rochester (1647–80) in the quality of his mind, both in such a lyric as this and in the long pessimistic poem which has at least passages of unsurpassable greatness, *A Satyr Against Mankind*, looks back more to the paradox of the metaphysical mode than forward to the smoothness of the Augustans. His very subject, love, dealt with most delicately in a poem in which he assumes extraordinarily convincingly the role of a sad fastidious woman, *Artemisia in the Town to Chloe in the Country*, is one of the central subjects of the Metaphysicals. The Augustans preferred reason to passion and friendship to love; and even Dryden, who is sometimes still thought of as the first great Augustan poet, has more than a touch of the Metaphysicals in his extravagant conceits, especially in his rhyming plays, and in the abstract vigour of thought of *Religio Laici* and *The Hind and the Panther*. Indeed, Dryden might be defended against Wordsworth's accusation that, of all our poets of note, he has least his eye on the object, by saying that the 'object' in Wordsworth's sense did not interest him: like Donne, though he is consciously reacting against Donne, he is a poet of the concept rather than the image.

Edmund Waller (1606–87) was a man of pleasant manners and a self-centred nature. He wrote a panygyric upon Cromwell after plotting against him and finally receiving a pardon from him. He later became a favourite at Charles II's court. 'Sir', he said excusing his flattery of the Lord Protector. 'We poets never succeed so well in writing truth as in fiction.' Though a master of song – of the sort that seems to hark back to Campion, he is more remembered, along with Sir John Denham for his poems in balanced couplets, smooth but empty, which mark the beginnings of the Augustan style. Compare these lines from *At Penshurst* with Jonson's packed *To Penshurst*:

> Had Dorothea liv'd when mortals made
> Choice of their deities, this sacred shade
> Had held an altar to her power, that gave
> The peace and glory which these alleys have;
> Embroider'd so with flowers where she stood,
> That it became a garden of a wood.

He is best remembered for his graceful *Go, Lovely rose* and for the fine last poem in his volume of 1686 written when death was approaching:

> When we for Age could neither read nor write,
> The Subject made us able to indite.
> The Soul with Nobler Resolutions deckt,
> The Body stooping, does Herself erect:
> No Mortal Parts are requisite to raise
> Her, that Unbody'd can her Maker praise.
>
> The Seas are quiet, when the Winds give o're;
> So calm are we, when Passions are no more:
> For then we know how vain it was to boast

Of fleeting Things, so certain to be lost.
Clouds of Affection from our younger Eyes
Conceal that Emptiness, which Age descries.

The Soul's dark Cottage, batter'd and decay'd,
Lets in new Light thro chinks that time has made.
Stronger by weakness, wiser Men become
As they draw near to their Eternal home;
Leaving the Old, both Worlds at once they view,
That stand upon the Threshold of the New.

We should turn now to the love poems of the Metaphysicals. T. S. Eliot particularly admired a poem by George Herbert's eldest brother, Edward, Lord Herbert of Cherbury, *An Ode upon a Question moved, Whether Love should continue for ever?*' The tone and the subject, the strange union of physical and spiritual love, are very like that of Donne's *The Extasie*, but I am not sure that I do not prefer Lord Herbert's less famous poem. I quote two or three stanzas, which, incidentally, anticipate the rhyme-scheme of Tennyson's *In Memoriam*:

Long their fixt eyes to Heaven bent,
    Unchanged, they did never move,
    As if so great and pure a love
No Glass but it could represent.

When with a sweet, though troubled look,
    She first brake silence, saying, Dear friend.
    O that our love might take no end,
Or never had beginning took!

I speak not this with a false heart,
    (Wherewith his hand she gently strain'd)
    Or that would change a love maintain'd
With so much faith on either part . . .

This is Edward Herbert's longest and greatest poem, but he writes always with an individual and distinguished voice. Born in 1583, dying in 1648, he was only eleven years younger than Donne, whom he knew as he knew Ben Jonson, and sometimes seems nearest to Donne of all his school in the timbre of his voice and the movement of his verse.

Metaphysical love poems are not, however, always or perhaps often as serious as this. Donne's followers sometimes equal him in ingenuity, as Andrew Marvell (1618–78) in *The Definition of Love*:

> My Love is of a birth as rare
> As 'tis for object strange and high:
> It was begotten by despair
> Upon Impossibility.
>
> Magnanimous Despair alone
> Could show me so divine a thing,
> Where feeble Hope could ne'r have flown
> But vainly flapt its Tinsel Wing.
>
> And yet I quickly might arrive
> Where my extended Soul is fixt,
> But Fate does iron wedges drive,
> And alwaies crouds it self betwixt.
>
> For Fate with jealous Eye does see
> Two perfect Loves: nor lets them close:
> Their union would her ruine be,
> And her Tyrannick power depose . . .

And, by the very definition of Fate, to depose her 'Tyrannick power' would be absurd. We do not quite know whether we are reading a love poem or a theorem in mathematics, but Marvell's ingenuity stuns us. Still, for the ordinary reader, *To His Coy Mistress*, with its theme, recurrent in these poets, of the war between love and time, the dangers of delay in fruition, is more immediately moving: the theme moves us and the question, which some critics have thought worth discussing, of whether the coy mistress is a real person or a poetic fiction is a futile one. All reality becomes a poetic fiction when a true poet gets to work on it; and a real problem remains real whether or not the poet has a living example in mind. The patterns of feeling and thought in poetry are more cogent and pungent and concise than the greater but more diffuse richness of life, always straying into irrelevance, ever presents:

> But at my back I alwaies hear
> Times winged Charriot hurrying near:
> And yonder all before us lye
> Desarts of vast Eternity.
> Thy Beauty shall no more be found;
> Nor, in my marble Vault, shall sound

My ecchoing Song: then Worms shall try
That long preserv'd Virginity:
And your quaint Honour turn to dust;
And into ashes all my Lust.
The Grave's a fine and private place,
But none I think do there embrace.

The line there that marks, for me, the Metaphysical mode is 'Desarts of vast Eternity': almost any poet of any other school would have written, 'Vast deserts of Eternity'. What interested Marvell, however, was not the picture of the desert but the thought of eternity. Thomas Hobbes, a philosopher whom Marvell would certainly have disapproved of but as certainly have read, had written in *Leviathan*: 'Eternity is a *nunc-stans*' – a standing Now. From a non-Christian point of view, but one which allows for consciousness after death, we are frozen for ever into the state of awareness in which we die. Eternity is like our physical world if that lacked time and mobility. Marvell had a seriously Christian Protestant temperament, but the Metaphysical poet can play with concepts he does not accept. There are signs that this poem (whose argument, for that matter, is a witty expansion of Catullus's *Vivamus, mea Lesbia, atque amemus*, beautifully rendered by Ben Jonson in *Volpone*) was, though not published before Marvell's death, popular. One of Rochester's best lyrics, *The Mistress*, seems to allude to the couplet about the grave:

You Wiser men, despise me not
  Whose Love-Sick Fancy raves,
On Shades of Souls, and Heav'n knows what:
  Short Ages live in Graves.

I am not, indeed, sure that when one is familiar with Marvell's couplet Rochester's single line is not more concentrated and powerful.

The age of the Metaphysical poem was also an age of political turmoil and intrigue. One is surprised (except for the danger of the time) about how little politics appears in the poems.

There is probably only one great poem, Marvell's *Horation Ode on Cromwell's return from Ireland* which ranks, among English political poems, with Yeats's *Easter, 1916* and with a more flawed poem, which Auden was nevertheless wrong in rejecting, *September 3rd, 1939*. Marvell does full justice to Charles I's dignity and courage on the scaffold and to the 'ancient rights' that Cromwell is destroying: at the same time he sees Cromwell as a preternatural force, a thunderbolt from heaven. No ordinary rules apply to the Lord Protector (or Parliament's chief servant, as he still was). Yet he uses a genuinely Horatian balance rather than Metaphysical paradox to give Cromwell a warning, which the Protector's succession by his weak son, 'Queen Dick', proved all too just. Force must hold what force has gained; and power violently gained is never guiltless and must persist in guilt:

> But thou the Wars and Fortunes Son
> March indefatigably on;
>   And for the last effect
>   Still keep thy Sword erect.
> Besides the force it has to fright
> The Spirits of the shady Night,
>   The same *Arts* that did *gain*
>   A *Pow'r* must it *maintain*.

The cross-hilt of the sword frightened away evil spirits but not all the spirits (for instance, the king's) that haunted Cromwell were evil. 'Arts' was an extremely morally ambiguous word. They had gained Cromwell 'a Pow'r': not Legitimate Authority. One remembers Marvell's remark, as member of Parliament for Hull after the Restoration: 'The cause was too good to have been fought for'. Some accommodation with the king was to the last possible: or patience was.

The short poem I now quote by Sir Henry Wotton was, I would imagine, very cautiously distributed in his lifetime. It is about Robert Carr, Earl of Somerset, who was arrested in 1615 and put on trial in 1616, with his wife Frances Howard, who had been divorced from the Earl of Essex. Carr's friend and adviser Sir Thomas Overbury warned desperately against the marriage (Frances was a wicked woman and in any case Carr had a rival favourite in George Villiers, later Duke of Buckingham). Frances had power enough to have Overbury imprisoned in the Tower, where he was poisoned;

how much did Carr know of his wife's plot, and how far approve? He was arrested in 1615, tried in 1616, and though he was not found guilty nor she, both endured long imprisonment, his favour was over, and so was Frances's pretence of love for him. How sincere is Wotton about Carr's virtue? He certainly seems sincere when he says that 'the Hearts of Kinges are deepe'. He was a man of great experience, who jestingly described an Ambassador as a man sent to lie abroad for the good of his country. He became in later life Provost of Eton, and wrote the first adequate criticism of the young Milton in a prefatory epistle to *Comus*, in 1638: 'Wherein I should much commend the tragical part, if the lyrical did not ravish me with a certain Doric delicacy in your Songs and Odes, whereunto I must plainly confess to you to have seen yet nothing parallel in our language: *Ipsa mollities*. (*Ipsa mollities* means 'sweetness itself' and Doric diction in poetry means a plainly rustic diction but 'Doric delicacy' suggests the subtle art behind Milton's apparent simplicity.)

There is, perhaps, an ironic delicacy, a respect of virtue but an awareness of its ambiguity in Courts in *Upon the Sudden Restraint of the Earle of Somerset, then falling from favour*.

> Dazel'd thus with height of place,
> Whilst our hopes our wits beguile,
> No man markes the narrow space
> 'Twixt a prison, and a smile.
>
> Then, since fortunes favours fade,
> You, that in her armes doe sleep,
> Learne to swim, and not to wade;
> For, the Hearts of Kings are deepe.
>
> But, if Greatness be so blind,
> As to trust in towers of Aire,
> Let it be with Goodness lin'd,
> That at least, the Fall be faire.
>
> Then though darkened, you shall say,
> When Friends faile, and Princes frowne,
> *Vertue* is the roughest way,
> But proves at night a *Bed of Downe*.

One can read this poem three or four times and wonder if

Wotton thought Carr's fall *was* lined with goodness, if 'you that in her armes doe sleep' might be a very oblique allusion to Carr sleeping in the arms of the homosexual King, if the 'towers of Aire' contain an oblique allusion to the Tower of London and just how sinister the reference to James's shifting favours may be:

> No man markes the narrow space
> 'Twixt a prison and a smile.

Wotton was a subtle man and if some accident should have brought the verses to James's hands he might have seen it as a tribute to his Divine Right, to the God-like inscrutable decisions of his Justice, combined with a little harmless moralising about how a fall from favour is made tolerable by the consciousness of virtue. Wotton had not been an ambassador for nothing, and knew that an ambassador's business is not to lie but to set a polite gloss on the most awkward truth.

The other memorable political poem in the Metaphysical vein, *Epitaph on the Earl of Strafford*, who was executed after parliamentary impeachment on 12th May 1641, is attributed very doubtfully to John Cleveland (1613–58), whose verse otherwise is famous, if at all, for its elaborate triviality. Thomas Wentworth, Earl of Stafford, had been the king's deputy in Ireland and was the one strong man in the country willing to champion the king with arms, even Irish arms. His very fierceness and directness might have saved the king but, when Parliament turned against him, he was willing to take all the blame for his plans for defence of the monarchy, to deflect anger from the king. The people loved him because his strong rule seemed to be bringing peace to the Irish, and hated him in case he should be ready to bring Papist Irish troops to England. He is called 'a Papist yet a Calvinist' perhaps because like many Anglicans of his time he thought the government of the Church was one thing and one's private theology another: more likely because he was ready to make military use both of the wild Papist native Irish and the new settlers on the Plantations, largely Presbyterian Calvinist Scots. The timid Charles I dared not save him. Strafford did not wish his blood, like Abel's, to cry from the ground. He made himself an unprotesting martyr to save Charles and the good Royalist, however deeply he felt the rage which this poem expresses, knew that he must not act on it:

Epitaph on the Earl of Strafford

Here lies Wise and Valiant Dust
Huddled up 'twixt Fit and Just:
STRAFFORD, who has hurried hence
'Twixt Treason and Convenience.
He spent his Time here in a Mist;
A *Papist*, yet a *Calvinist*.
His Princes nearest Joy, and Grief.
He had, yet wanted all Releefe.
The Prop and Ruine of the State;
The People's violent Love and Hate:
One in extreames lov'd and abhor'd.
Riddles lie here; or in a word,
Here lies Blood; and let it lie
Speechlesse still, and never crie.

One might call this a special kind of Metaphysical poem, though it is by no means a unique example of the type, in which the difficulty and power come less from the clash of contradictory thoughts than of contradictory feelings.

III The Sons of Ben

Ben Jonson is perhaps the greatest neglected author of short poems of his century; among the young courtiers whom he met when he was collaborating with Inigo Jones (a great man whom, alas, he detested) the burly, frank old man was much more of a friend and favourite than John Donne when he had become Dean of St Paul's. A Devonshire clergyman, Robert Herrick, is his most direct disciple, but court poets like Carew, Suckling, Lovelace and others, though they had learned something from, and admired Donne, also, often called themselves the 'sons of Ben'. They could not be accused (not even a later poet like Marvell, who admired and imitated Donne rather than Jonson) of 'not keeping of accent'. If they have sometimes a conversational bluntness, it is in Jonson's manner rather than Donne's. Oddly enough, Jonson who is almost contemporary with Donne in dates

(1572–1637) differs from Donne in a certain stiffness in versification in his longer poems, though not often in his often very beautiful short lyrics. The same stiffness can be found in his greatest comedy, *Volpone*, if one compares (inappropriately) this classical corrective comedy with the romantic sympathetic comedies of Shakespeare. A great writer may often take great pains; but if he shows it too much he somehow, as Jonson with all the power of his mind and the care of the craftsmanship in his verse does, somehow just misses general fame. Jonson remains, with all the fame of his plays and their occasional very successful revivals, the most unjustly neglected non-dramatic poet of his century.

Socially he was a success, after very inauspicious beginnings. Educated at Westminster School, he acquired enough learning to equip him for Oxford or Cambridge but chose to work at his stepfather's trade of bricklayer and then trailed a pike in Flanders. On return, he became a playwright for Henslowe, killed an actor in a duel in 1598, escaped hanging by pleading benefit of clergy (or adequate literacy which, in those days when it was a very scarce commodity, led automatically to the pardoning of one's first violent crime). His conscience was, however, deeply touched and he became and remained for the next twelve years a devout Roman Catholic. His fame as a playwright led to his being given a title (combined with a pension enlarged later by Charles I) of 'King's Poet' and to his collaborating with Inigo Jones on the new, fashionable royal masques.

The two great men detested each other; for Jones, it was Jonson's business merely to provide words for his costumes and scenery; for Jonson, Jones was merely a stage manager there to carry out his orders. The young courtiers liked the gruff old Ben and their jokes, when he brought out his plays and poems as *Works* in 1616, were good natured:

> Pray tell me, Ben, where doth the mystery lurk,
> What others call a play you call a work.

Jonson's later days were not so happy. The dryness of his comedy became obvious when contrasted with the romantic gaiety (a little anticipating the Restoration) of Beaumont and Fletcher. His self-assertive dogmatism began to pall on a younger generation; he did not manage his money well; and his perpetual heavy drinking told on his health. He died in 1637 neither so popular or so happy as he had been. We hear nothing of his marriage and he could not present love, either romantic or domestic, in his comedies.

Yet the poems, as distinct from the plays, have a warm good-nature and tenderness, as in the touching poem on the death of Salathiel Pavy, one of the boy actors of the time who are raged at in *Hamlet: Epitaph on S.P., a Child of Queen Elizabeth's Chapel.*

> Weep with me all you that read
>   This little story:
> And know, for whom a tear you shed,
>   Death's self is sorry.
> 'Twas a child, that did thrive
>   In grace, and feature
> As Heaven and Nature seemed to strive
>   Which owned the creature.
> Years he numbered scarce thirteen
>   When Fates turned cruel,
> Yet three filled zodiacs had he been
>   The stage's jewel;
> And did act (what now we moan)
>   Old men so duly,
> As, sooth, the Parcae thought him one   *Fates*
>   He played so truly.
> So, by error, to his fate
>   They all consented:
> But viewing him since (alas, too late)
>   They have repented
> And have sought (to give new birth)
>   In baths to steep him;
> But being much too good for earth,
>   Heaven vows to keep him.

The touching, restrained delicacy seems strangely unlike the boastful, burly man. There is a graceful courtesy, also, in Jonson's tribute to the gardens and grand old plain house of Penshurst, where Sir Philip Sidney was born. We get a glimpse also of that plain old English hospitality which, before the tragedy of the Civil Wars, held our country together:

Thou art not, Penshurst, built to envious show,
Of touch or marble: nor can boast a row   *touch: black marble*

Of polished pillars, or a roof of gold:
Thou hast no lanthern, whereof tales are told:
Or stair, or courts; but stand'st an ancient pile,
And these grudged at, art reverenced the while.
Thou joy'st in better marks, of soil, of air,
Of wood, of water: therein thou art fair.
Thou hast thy walks for health, as well as sport:
Thy Mount, to which the dryads do resort,
Where Pan, and Bacchus their high feasts have made,
Beneath the broad beech, and the chestnut shade;
That taller tree, which of a nut was set,
At his great birth, where all the muses met.   *Sidney's*

The compliment to Sidney might seem extravagant but the
insistence that Penshurst, set in good air and soil, is itself a
plain unpretentious house makes the compliment possible.
There is a similar praise of Penshurst's hospitality, decent,
plain, but orderly, and so ready for guests that it is able to
welcome, unexpectedly, King James I:

Whose liberal board doth flow,
With all, that hospitality doth know!
Where comes no guest, but is allowed to eat,
Without his fear, and of the lord's own meat:
Where the same beer, and bread, and self-same wine,
That is his lordship's, shall be also mine.
And am not fain to sit (as some, this day
At great men's tables) and yet dine away.
Here no man tells my cups, nor, standing by,
A waiter, doth my gluttony envy;
But gives me what I call, and lets me eat,
He knows below, he shall find plenty of meat,
Thy tables hoard not up for the next day,
Nor, when I take my lodging, need I pray
For fire, or lights, or livery; all is there;
As if thou, then, wert mine, or I reigned here:
There's nothing I can wish, for which I stay.
That found King James, when hunting late, this way,
With his brave son, the prince, they saw thy fires
Shine bright on every hearth as the desires
Of thy Penates had been set on flame,
To entertain them; or the country came,
With all their zeal, to warm their welcome here.
What (great, I will not say, but) sudden cheer
Didst thou, then, make them! And what praise was heaped

On thy good lady, then! Who, therein, reaped
The just reward of her high huswifery;
To have her linen, plate, and all things nigh,
When she was far: and not a room, but dressed,
As if it had expected such a guest!

'Good old English hospitality' is ready and alert for any unexpected guest from Ben Jonson to the King. Food and service is plain – meat, bread, beer, wine – but generous and abundant with no distinction between the host and his guests. The unexpected guest will find fire and candles and service (perhaps, in Ben Jonson's case, the fetching of another flagon of wine) in his bedroom. When the King arrives unexpectedly after a late hunting session the lady of the house is as ready for him as for anyone, and she is praised not (as Donne might praise a great lady) for her looks and learning but for the most everyday and necessary gifts of someone who runs a great house, those of a good housewife.

T. S. Eliot spoke of a 'certain dissociation of sensibility' that set in towards the middle of the century. Jonson shows us in a great plain poem like this what was really being dissociated: a social bond that held together king, lords, gentry, and those like Jonson with some claim through talent to be treated as gentry, by the sacrament of hospitality. And that reflected itself outwards, for instance, in the willingness and friendliness of a great house's servants. It was a hierarchial society but one linked by generosity and kindness. After the Restoration, something of this lingers, and Rochester mocks it:

The Heir and Hopes of a great Family;
Who with strong beer and beef, the country rules,   *county*
And ever since the Conquest have been Fools.

The sort of family that could produce a Sidney, or any family that had dominated its county since the Conquest, was not foolish. But what Jonson depicts is not a calculated political stratagem but a genuine warmth.

One looks, perhaps, above all in a writer of short poems, for the expression of the passion of love: and we have seen that Jonson with a genius for expressing tenderness, friendship, admiration, and with a quite unusual appreciation as in *To Penshurst* of the social habits and feelings that gave warmth and unity to his age, had not the gift of expressing this passion directly on his own behalf. He could express it, however, in plays: the plangent music of this lyric from *Cynthia's Revels* deserves its fame:

> Slow, slow, fresh fount, keep time with my salt tears:
>   Yet, slower, yet: O faintly, gentle springs:
> List to the heavy part the music bears,
>   Woe weeps out her division, when she sings.
>   Droop herbs, and flowers,
>   Fall grief in showers,
>   Our beauties are not ours:
>   O, I could still,
> Like melting snow upon some craggy hill,
>   Drop, drop, drop, drop,
> Since nature's pride is, now, a withered daffodil.

The short line, 'Our beauties are not ours', for a packed strength that is still musical, for pregnant pathos, is to me unmatchable in Donne. But one fancies that, unlike Donne, Jonson, with his 'mountain belly' and his 'craggy face', though an ideal companion for men in a tavern, can never have appealed much to women. There is a quiet, dry pathos in *Why I Write Not of Love*:

> Some act of Love's bound to rehearse,
> I thought to bind him, in my verse:
> Which when he felt, Away (quoth he)
> Can poets hope to fetter me?
> It is enough, they once did get
> Mars, and my mother, in their net:
> I wear not these my wings in vain.
> With which he fled me: and again
> Into my rhymes could ne'er be got
> By any art. Then wonder not,
> That since, my numbers are so cold,
> When Love is fled, and I grow old.

The loyalest member of the 'tribe of Ben' was probably Robert Herrick (1591–1674), a Devonshire country clergyman, whose wordly poems *Hesperides* and sincere though less effective religious verses, *Noble Numbers* were first published in 1648. Though he lived into his eighties, he published (and perhaps wrote) nothing more. He did not particularly like what he called 'dirty Devonshire' and his epigrams (some of them, like some of Jonson's, rather nasty) show that he personally hated many of his coarse and ignorant parishioners. Yet country festivals pleased him and, like Jonson, he wrote pleasant complimentary verses to his friends. His verse moves with less strength but with less stiffness than Jonson's and, unlike Jonson, he excels as a poet in a light erotic vein. His mistresses are almost certainly all imaginary. Certainly, a rustic parish in Devonshire would not have offered their equivalents nor was he ever involved, as any real pursuit of women would have involved him, in any disciplinary actions of the Anglican Church. He is perhaps a little like an English Horace, treating his remote parsonage as a Sabine farm (where both poets might have preferred to be in London, or Rome) and playing with imaginary flirtations. Real or unreal, his ladies are charming on the page:

To Anthea Lying in Bed

So looks Anthea, when in bed she lyes,
Orecome, or halfe betray'd by Tiffanies:
Like to a Twi-Light, or that simpring Dawn,
That Roses shew, when misted o're with Lawn.
Twilight is yet, till that her Lawnes give way;
Which done, that Dawne, turns then to perfect day.

Tiffany was a kind of thin transparent silk and also a kind of transparent gauze muslin, also called cobweb lawn. It is the precision of such lines, like the sense of the movement of silks in

Upon Julia's Clothes

Whenas in silks my Julia goes,
Then, then (me thinks) now sweetly flowes
The liquefaction of her clothes.

Next, when I cast mine eyes and see
That brave Vibration each way free;
O how that glittering taketh me.

These lines make me wonder, often, how true the accepted

theory of Herrick as an innocent erotic fantasist is. Pure fantasy is never so precise. Some of the ladies, in very polite poems certainly, are named. Around the West country Herrick had many friends and relations on intimately friendly terms; and one does not know what went on in the long dark evenings in these big country houses. To quote a greater poet, Thomas Campion:

> Though love and all his pleasures are but toys
> They shorten tedious nights.

But already, before the end of *Hesperides*, Herrick laments the deaths of his real and fictitious mistresses: and one thinks gloomily of his middle age under the Commonwealth ejected by the Puritans from his Devonshire living and his old age as a forgotten poet under the Restoration.

Apart from Herrick, it is hard to pick out contemporary poets wholly of the 'tribe of Ben'. The best poets of the court of Charles I, Thomas Carew (1595–1639), Sir John Suckling (1609–42), Richard Lovelace (1618–56) owed much also to Donne and a good deal also to the court, which in spite of the example of the king (not quite so certainly of the queen) had, more tactfully and quietly, as libertine an atmosphere as that of Charles II. Two famous poems of Carew's (his name is pronounced Carey), *A Rapture* and *A Second Rapture*, are more vividly and appealingly sensual than anything of Rochester's, for all his greater notoriety, in the next reign: and indeed Carew resembled that poet in concluding a wild life with a repentant death. Suckling and Lovelace are also sometimes very free-spoken poets and have an easy colloquial style, which suggests the conversation of the court rather than any direct literary influence.

Thomas Carew, the richest of these poets, was, according to the letters of Thomas Howell, a member of the 'tribe of Ben' with reservations: 'Ben began to engross all the discourse, to vapour extremely of himself, and, by vilifying others, to magnify his own muse. Tom Carew buzzed me in the ear, that though Ben has barreled up a great deal of knowledge, it seems he had not read the *Ethics* (Aristotle's) which, among other precepts of morality, forbid self-recommendation.' His admiration for Donne, on the other hand, was whole-hearted, as is shown in his *An Elegy Upon the Death of Dr Donne, Dean of St Paul's,* one of the few great pieces of criticism in English verse:

> . . . whatsoever wrong
> By ours was done the Greek or Latin tongue,
> Thou hast redeemed, and opened us a mine
> Of rich and pregnant fancy; drawn a line
> Of masculine expression, which had good
> Old Orpheus seen, or all the ancient brood
> Our superstitious fools admire, and hold
> Their lead more precious than thy burnished gold,
> Thou hadst been their exchequer and no more
> They each in other's dung had searched for ore.
> Thou shalt yield no precedence, but of time
> And the blind fate of language, whose tuned chime
> More charms the outward sense; yet thou may'st claim
> From so great disadvantage greater fame,
> Since to the awe of thy imperious wit
> Our troublesome language bends, made only fit
> With her tough thick-ribbed hoops to gird about
> Thy giant fancy, which had proved too stout
> For their soft, melting phrases . . .

Strangely, Carew is himself a master of the 'soft, melting phrase'. C. S. Lewis has called attention to a lovely poem, *A Song*, in which the English stress-syllable iambics correspond with Latin or Greek short-longs (one should allow for the reversion of the first stress-syllable iambic to a trochee and for the fact that an English stress-syllable trochee may correspond to a Latin quantitative Spondee, a feet of two long syllables). I italicise here the Latin quantities. The English scansion speaks for itself:

> *Ask* me/ *no more*/ where *Jove*/ be*stows*,
> When *June*/ is *past*/ the *fad*/ ing *rose*;
> For in/ your *beau*/ ty's *or*/ ient *deep*
> These *flowers*,/ as in their *caus*/ es *sleep*. . .

Carew, it should be noted, cannot bring off the effect in absolutely every foot: 'in', on the two occasions when it occurs, is a short but stressed syllable.

Carew owed his favour at Court to the Queen, Henrietta Maria. Walking ahead of the king one evening to lead him to her chamber he caught her in a compromising position with Henry St Jermyn and pretending to trip clumsily knocked out the sole candle so that the room was plunged in darkness. From then on, he was a Court favourite. No Court, as such an anecdote suggests, is a place for saints, but Charles I, as is shown by his great collection of pictures, dispersed by Cromwell, was a man of great taste and also of great if slightly cold politeness and the utmost integrity of life. No Court of any English King has equalled his, before or after, in easy refinement of manners. The courtiers rejoiced that England was outside European politics, and the horrors of the Thirty Year War. Carew expresses this happy indifference to European tumult in *In answer to an elegiacal letter, upon the death of the King of Sweden, from Aurelian Townshend, inviting me to write on that subject.* In this he says that Townshend is capable of the heroic vein, but that it does not suit the present happy condition of England:

> Tourneys, masques, theatres, better become
> Our halcyon days. What though the German drum
> Bellow for freedom and revenge, the noise
> Concerns not us nor should divert our joys;
> Nor ought the thunder of their carabins
> Drown the sweet airs of our tun'd violins.
> Believe me, friend, if their prevailing powers
> Gain them a calm security like ours,
> They'll hang their arms upon the olive bough,
> And dance and revel then, as we do now.

It is impossible, when we remember the Civil Wars that were looming ahead, to read these gracefully turned lines, with the picture of a mid-century Arcadia, without a sense of profound pathos. Carew, dying in 1639 (the exact date is a little uncertain), was lucky enough never to feel the bitter irony that time cast back on these buoyant and joyous verses. He remains, both in subtlety of art and power of mind, the most considerable of Charles I's courtly poets.

He was not therefore necessarily the most popular. Perhaps, for his fellows at court, he took too much pains. Suckling says rather coarsely in a squib called *A Sessions of the Poets*:

His muse was hard-bound, and th'issue of's brain
Was never brought forth but with trouble and pain.

Admirers of Congreve will remember that 'natural, easy
Suckling' was Millamant's favourite poet. After a gay youth,
Suckling was involved in a plot to rescue Strafford from the
tower. He fled to France, where he died obscurely, perhaps
killing himself, perhaps murdered by a treacherous servant.
There is no premonition in his poems of this sad ending. No
intellectual, and in his clear, direct way of writing more a
disciple of Jonson than of Donne, but with an ease that
Jonson never attained, he deserved both Millamant's compliment and Dryden's that no poet had in his tone come
nearer 'the conversation of a gentleman'. A brief example of
his light, mocking manner (which yet masks true feeling) is
this little poem:

> Out upon it! I have lov'd
>   Three whole days together;
> And am like to love three more
>   If it prove fair weather.
>
> Time shall moult away his wings,
>   Ere he shall discover
> In the whole wide world again
>   Such a constant lover.
>
> But the spite on't is, no praise
>   Is due at all to me;
> Love with me had made no stays
>   Had it any been but she.
>
> Had it any been but she,
>   And that very face,
> There had been at least ere this
>   A dozen dozen in her place.

Richard Lovelace is the most uneven of all these poets
though a few poems, *To Althea from Prison*, *To Lucasta.
Going to the Wars*, are deservedly famous. He served in the
two Scottish expeditions, in England with the king's armies,
abroad with the French at Dunkirk. He was universally
admired for his courage, fine manners, and good looks
(Aubrey describes him as 'a most beautiful gentleman' and
Wood says he was 'much admired and adored by women').

Chastely gallant as his love poems at their best are, some have a wild libertine spirit. Yet he was lucky to die in 1656 or 1657 for his Sidneyan spirit could not have endured Charles II's witty but gross court. As a staunch royalist he died in hope and was spared the disillusionment of hope fulfilled.

Here are a few lines from one of Lovelace's most charming but lesser known poems, *The Grasshopper*, addressed to his friend (himself an agreeable but unambitious poet) Charles Cotton. He treats his unusual subject with a quaintly delightful minuteness of observation:

> O thou that swing'st upon the waving hair
>   Of some well-filled oaten beard,
> Drunk ev'ry night with a delicious tear
>   Dropp'd thee from heav'n, where now th'art rear'd;
>
> The joys of earth and air are thine entire
>   That with thy feet and wings dost hop and fly;
> And when thy poppy works thou must retire
>   To thy carv'd acorn-bed to lie.
>
> Up with the day, the sun thou welcom'st then,
>   Sport'st in the gilt-plats of his beams,
> And all these merry days mak'st merry, men,
>   Thyself, and melancholy streams. . .

One is reminded of Mercutio on Queen Mab. Lovelace rather rarely writes a poem that is successful all through (he lacked the sense of an ending) but makes up for his unevenness with constant fancy and charm

Sir John Denham (1615–69) in his own famous poem *Cooper's Hill* is by comparison packed with sense and has what the seventeenth century called 'strength' as contrasted with 'smoothness'. The third quality admired by seventeenth century critics, 'sweetness', is hard to define but is to be found, for instance, in my extracts from Marvell and Carew. Denham's strength is best exhibited in some lines concluding a passage on the Thames, lines constantly imitated and parodied. Poets recognised that Denham was pointing the way to something new, a new matching of the balance of sound with that of sense:

> Oh, could I flow like thee, and make thy stream
> My great example, as it is my theme!

Though deep, yet clear; though gentle, yet not dull;
Strong without rage, without o'erflowing full.

Denham, hardly read now, still ranked as a classic
throughout the eighteenth century because it was felt that
without his example neither Dryden nor Pope and his
successors in the couplet could have written exactly as they
did.

III The Restoration: Milton, Dryden, Rochester

John Milton (1608–74) is by general consent the greatest of
all English poets of the seventeenth century, the only one to
be accorded a classic status in the next century (Dryden, by
comparison, seemed, even to Johnson who personally
preferred him to Pope, a writer of great strength who,
because he could always write well and always wrote in haste
for money, rarely wrote at his best).

There are two Milton's the earlier Milton of *Poems 1645*
(actually published in 1646) and the post-Restoration poet
of *Paradise Lost, Samson Agonistes*, and *Paradise Regained*.
Though some of the earlier poems were admired by the
Augustans notably *L'Allegro* and *Il Penseroso*, the Augustan attitude to most of these early works was critical, as
demonstrated by Dr Johnson's very fierce attack on
Lycidas: '. . . the diction is harsh, the rhymes uncertain, and
the numbers unpleasing. What beauty there is we must
therefore seek in the sentiments and images. It is not to be
considered as the effusion of real passion; for passion runs
not after remote allusions and obscure opinions. . . In this
poem there is no nature, for there is nothing new. Its form is
that of a pastoral, easy, vulgar, and therefore disgusting. . .'
(By *disgusting* Johnson means something less strong than
our sense, *unappetising* or *insipid*)'. . . Whatever images
[the pastoral form can supply] are long ago exhausted, and
its inherent improbability always forces dissatisfaction on
the mind.'

To many modern readers, *Lycidas* is the most beautiful
long short poem in the English language. How much real
grief there is for Edward King hardly matters. As in the
Greek pastoral lament for Bion, Edward King as poet is
compared to the dead Orpheus, whose music had creative

power. The death of the fertility god-king or hero in the Greek
myths, such as Orpheus or Adonis makes possible the renewal
of plants and crops in the spring, but not of the dying creator
who makes it possible. Milton interprets the pagan myth in
Christian terms: Lycidas is not dead, but will have everlasting
life in heaven through Christ's redemption of mankind

> So Lycidas sunk low but mounted high,
> Through the dear might of Him that walked the waves:
> Where other groves and other streams along,
> With nectar pure his oozy locks he laves,
> And hears the unexpressive nuptial song. . .

Johnson, according to his own lights, is perfectly coherent in
his judgment. His own only elegy to his humble but worthy
friend, Dr Robert Levitt, *is* a direct expression of grief in a way
that *Lycidas* cannot claim to be. An ear trained to the
'correctness' of Popeian couplets would find a felicitously
invented word like Milton's 'scrannel' harsh in diction, and
one tied all his life to the couplet would find the Italianate
cunning of Milton's verse paragraphs 'unmusical'. The rhymes, of course, *are* deliberately uncertain, and do not appear
in predictable places. What must have troubled Johnson most
deeply, however, was Milton's use of pagan and Christian
images together. There was a long tradition behind this, a
tradition which saw pagan stories of spring deaths as prefigura-
tions of the death and resurrection of Christ. Johnson lived in a
Whiggish, sceptical, at best latitudinarian age in which a
trembling and humble faith like his own could not 'dally with
false surmise'. *Lycidas* is, in fact, the last poem in which Milton
mingles Christian and pagan images in this friendly way. By the
time of *Paradise Lost* the figures of classical mythology are
(with a few exceptions in the similes, like Proserpin and Ceres)
either fallen angels or baseless fables.

Some deep change took place in Milton in middle age. The
young man, though ruining his sight by too much study,
travelled in Italy where he frequented the best company. The
lovely verses of *Arcades* were part of an entertainment
presented to the Dowager Countess of Derby at Harefield,
Comus was presented at Ludlow Castle.

Sir Henry Wotton, whose response to Milton's verses was so
immediate, should, like the noble patrons of *Arcades* and

Comus have gently wooed Milton to the royalist side. *Paradise Lost* is, after all, a poem about the dreadful sin of disobedience and Milton ought to have respected 'the ancient Rights' which Cromwell broke down only by brute force:

> Though Justice against Fate complain,
> And plead the ancient Rights in vain;
> But these do hold or break
> As Men are strong or weak.

Charles I, for that matter, was the most virtuous, and the most gracefully virtuous, of all our kings and Milton's fanatical hatred of him and triumph over his death is hard to understand.

Many reasonable men, like Marvell for instance, were moderate Parliamentarians, but Milton's support for Cromwell was fanatical. It is odd that Milton during the years when he was Cromwell's Latin secretary, and finally blinded himself with official toil and tedious propaganda, should not have noticed a resemblance between the ruthless resource of Cromwell and that of his own already conceived Satan; as in writing *Paradise Lost*, he must have felt in God the Father an uncomfortable resemblance to a Charles I whose actual power equals his claims to legitimate authority.

It is a great poem, but a strange one. Milton was certainly a militant Protestant, and he has sometimes been called a Puritan; but, if we compare *Paradise Lost* with, say, the first part of *The Pilgrim's Progress* or with *Grace Abounding to the Chief of Sinners*, it is the least Puritan work imaginable. The emphasis throughout is on man's free will and on the fact that God, foreseeing the Fall, does not therefore foreordain it. God justifies himself at such length, in fact, that we begin a little to distrust him. Satan is from time to time routinely denounced by Milton, but, except in the second part of the epic, when our sympathies are centred on Adam and Eve and Satan is deliberately diminished in his impact, he retains something impressive about him.

There is his famous speech of admiration, almost of love, on first seeing Adam and Eve:

'League with you I seek,
And mutual amity, so strait, so close,
That I with you must dwell, or you with me,
Henceforth. My dwelling, haply, may not please,
Like this fair Paradise, your sense; yet such
Accept your Maker's work; he gave it me,
Which I as freely give. Hell shall unfold
To entertain you two, her widest gates,
And send forth all her kings; there will be room,
Not like these narrow limits, to receive
Your numerous offspring; if no better place,
Thank him who puts me, loath, to this revenge
On you, who wrong me not, for him who wronged.
And, should I at your harmless innocence
Melt, as I do, yet public reason just,
Honour and Empire with Revenge enlarged
By conquering this new world, compels me now
To do what else, though damned, I should abhor.'

So spake the Fiend, and with necessity,
The tyrant's plea, excused his devilish deeds . . .

Whom is he excusing them to? Angels are incapable of
self-deception (as Satan has shown at the beginning of Book
IV, in his long tragic soliloquy about the hopelessness of his
struggle and the impossibility of a repentance that would leave
him a figure marked by suspicion in heaven, and soon tempted
to the same rebellion again). The idea that civilians must suffer
often in a just war, even one in which they have no direct
concern except as pawns in the game, was current international law – and, if we think of our own bombing of Dresden
in the last World War, still seems current international practice
– and the excuse not only of tyrants but of all rulers and
commanders in the field.

I do not think, and I do not mean, that Milton was Satan's
hero. The Messiah should be that, but Milton does not bring
the Messiah properly to life, perhaps because the Crucifixion
(on which he failed to finish an early poem though that on the
Incarnation, *On the Morning of Christ's Nativity* was a
triumph) was too painful to him. This is still a most distressing
theological puzzle, for while Christ's perfect manhood suffered on the cross, his Godhood, in its nature impassable or
incapable of suffering, could not. Yet He was God in Man not a
dual personality, using his humanity as a mask, God *and* Man.

Perhaps Milton failed with the Messiah because he could not come to terms with these theological puzzles.

Milton had three marriages, of which only the second, soon ended by his wife's death in childbirth, was happy. Where surprisingly he does succeed is in the characters of Adam and Eve. Their innocent splendour in sexual love and their delight in Paradise (which resembles, as Empson remarks, an ideal landscape by Claude or Poussin) are wonderful and are central in the book. Yet one wonders whether Paradise, with the elephant writhing its lithe proboscis to make one sport, would have studied the temperament of Milton himself who wrote, in a prose pamphlet, that the palm is not to be won without dust and heat.

For all the mournful beauty of the lines that commemorate the consummation of the mortal sin,

> Earth trembled from her entrails, as again
> In pangs, and Nature gave a second groan:
> Sky loured, and, muttering thunder, some sad drops
> Wept at completing of the mortal sin
> Original . . .

one feels, perhaps, more of the real Milton in the concluding lines of the epic: in a sense that, after the fall, Adam and Eve, though shattered with grief and shame, are facing and will master with their perhaps disastrous, but certainly sustaining, mutual love a wider and more real world:

> Some natural tears they dropped, but wiped them soon:
> The world was all before them, where to choose
> Their place of rest, and Providence their guide:
> They, hand in hand, with wandering steps and slow,
> Through Eden took their solitary way.

What I am saying, I think, is that Milton was not a diabolist, though he certainly, in the first two books, and in the startlingly honest soliloquy at the beginning of Book IV, gives the devil his due: that his religion (if one compares the tone with that of *On the morning of Christ's Nativity* or even the more ambiguously elaborate *Lycidas*) is real but oddly external: he sets out to justify the ways of God to Man but one agrees with Pope that 'God the Father turns a school divine' and the reader is prone to feel that somebody who justifies himself at such length is suspect: *qui s'excuse, s'accuse*. One might also agree with Bagehot that if we take the story at a merely political level (as the Fall and the war in heaven and God's self-justifications encourage us to) there are in the Messiah's sudden promotion 'symptoms of a job'. What Milton was supremely was a humanist and Adam and Eve and their love for each other (a love which nobody could feel for God as Milton represents him) are the central strengths of the book.

Milton seems to have been so unfortunate in his marriages that the only hint of what love in life meant to him is found in a sonnet commemorating his second, brief, happy marriage, written when blindness was coming upon him:

> Methought I saw my late espoused saint
>   Brought to me like Alcestis from the grave,
> Whom Jove's great son to her glad husband gave
>   Rescued from Death by force, though pale and faint.
> Mine, as whom washed from spot of childbed taint
>   Purification in the Old Law did save,
>   And such as yet once more I trust to have
>   Full sight of her in Heaven without restraint,
> Came vested all in white, pure as her mind.
>   Her face was veiled; yet to my fancied sight
>   Love, sweetness, goodness, in her person shined
> So clear as in no face with more delight.
>   But O! as to embrace me she inclined,
>   I waked, she fled, and day brought back my night.

Alcestis was the wife of King Admetus of Pherae in Thessaly who had acted as a friendly host to Apollo. Apollo warned his friend that he was doomed to die on a certain day unless he could find somebody to take his place. Nobody would consent, not even his aged father and mother, but only Alcestis his young wife. The god Thanatos, or Death, came for her. Then the stricken Admetus had to receive a visit from the roistering Heracles, whom he greeted with courtesy, and explained his robe of mourning vaguely as if worn for some distant relative who had died while visiting him. Puzzled, Heracles enquired farther, and heard from other sources of Alcestis' death. He hurried to her grave at the cross roads at Larissa, wrestled with Thanatos, and in gratitude for hospitality brought Alcestis back to Admetus. Admetus could not at first believe that the veiled woman Heracles brought with him was Alcestis but in her bedchamber she convinced him by unveiling, as Milton's wife, in his dream, has no time to do. The 'Old Law' refers to the elaborate rules in the Pentateuch for purification after childbirth, shortly after which Milton's wife had died. If one knows all this (as a person of moderate education would have, until recently) this seems to me the most personally moving of all Milton's poems.

There has been a tendency, also, to consider Milton, because of the serious, lofty, and utterly dedicated nature of his devotion to poetry and his religious and political loyalties, as an ungenial man. Several little anecdotes contradict this. He 'spoke the letter R very hard, the sure sign of a satirical wit' and there is a rough geniality in his message to Dryden, who wanted to use *Paradise Lost* as the basis for an oratorio, that 'he may tag my verses as he pleases' (tie them up, as with shoe-laces, into rhyme). One of his pleasantest sonnets, *To Mr Lawrence*, has something of the ease (and of the shape, in the unexpected punctuation break in the octave and before the last two lines of the sestet) of an Horatian ode. It gives one the sense of a mild and sober Epicureanism:

> Lawrence, of virtuous father, virtuous son
>   Now that the fields are dank, and ways are mire,
>   Where shall we sometimes meet, and by the fire
>   Help waste a sullen day, what may be won
> From the hard season gaining? Time will run
>   On smoother, till Favonius reinspire
>   The frozen earth, and clothe in fresh attire
>   The lily and rose, that neither sowed nor spun.
> What neat repast shall feast us, light and choice,
>   Of Attic taste, with wine, whence we may rise
>   To hear the lute well touched, or artful voice
> Warble immortal notes and Tuscan air?
>   He who of those delights can judge, and spare
>   To interpose them oft, is not unwise.

Favonius is the west wind and Pattison suggested that there is an allusion to Horace *Odes* I iv i: *Solvitur acris hiems grata vice veris et Favoni* (Keen winter is melting at the welcome change to spring and Favonius). There is no agreement about the ambiguous 'spare' which can mean 'refrain from interposing them oft' or 'spare time (in a busy life) to interpose them oft'. The first interpretation fits too neatly with the traditional picture of Milton the sour Puritan: he had shown, after all, his Christian belief in the reference to the flowers that neither toiled nor spun 'yet Solomon in all his glory was not arrayed like one of these'. The idea that harmless pleasure, of a refined sort, is not wicked fits in with the interpretation 'spare time'. Lawrence was a political colleague of Milton's under the Commonwealth (made permanent chairman of the Council of State in January, 1654) and no doubt both men would have been sensible in snatching at such harmless leisure enjoyments as they could.

These two sonnets are not among Milton's greatest work, but I quote them because one shows a tenderness, and the other a charm, which we do not find directly expressed in him elsewhere. The last published of his works were *Paradise Regained* and *Samson Agonistes*, of which the first is a debate poem rather than an epic. It has a peculiar delicacy of diction which might have been out of place in *Paradise Lost* itself. The setting is the temptation in the wilderness. Satan, sly, insinuating, and always foiled by the better arguments of the Messiah has a kind of abjectness that makes him more like many people's picture of the Devil than the Satan of *Paradise Lost*: I quote the end of Book One:

> He added not; and Satan, bowing low
> His grey dissimulation, disappeared,
> Into thin air diffused: for now began
> Night with her sullen wing to double-shade
> The desert; fowls in their clay nests were couched;
> And now wild beasts came forth the woods to roam.

Readers may or may not feel the felicity with which Satan's 'grey dissimulation' diffused into the air seems to identify itself with the 'sullen wing' that we somehow associate with the desert birds in their 'clay nests', while the last line of apparently simple monosyllables (but none echoing the vowel or diphthong of another) – 'And now wild beasts came forth the woods to roam' – reminds us that, under his false humility, Satan's fierce enmity is still on the prowl. The thought seems at first transparent, but our feeling of a kind of subdued interconnectedness turns our attention back to the wonderful felicity of the words used to express it.

It has been a complaint of some critics of Milton (like the early Eliot) that his words, however effective individually, somehow do not mutually interfuse new life into each other. Eliot felt this for instance even about the magnificent 'Hid in her vacant interlunar cave' of *Samson Agonistes*. He can hardly, when he committed himself to this hostile view, have studied the interrelations of words in *Paradise Regained*. F. W. Bateson has said that *Paradise Regained* responds admirably to what he calls the Oxford tradition of criticism: instead of a use of the words to explore the ideas, a use of the ideas to display the aptness and felicity of the words.

Samson Agonistes was published alongside *Paradise Regained* and there has been a tendency to take it as partly autobiographical, Samson representing the blind Milton among his triumphant foes at the Restoration, still trusting in God and the restoration of the just Hebraic (Commonwealth) order. A quite different interpretation sees the play as a Christian allegory in which Samson's death prefigures the sacrifice of Christ: it is typical of the kind of interpretation that might appeal to Milton's contemporaries (one remembers the Covenanters' war cry of 'Jesus and no quarter!'), but for a modern reader it is very difficult indeed to take Samson with this stoic courage and obdurate, unforgiving hatred as a prefiguration of Christ, however hesitant our exegesis of the nature of the Trinity and however uncertain our notion of the historical Jesus may now be. Yet such an interpretation might still appeal, perhaps, to the Papists and Protestants of Northern Ireland.

Dalila has been identified with Mary Powell and Harapha with Milton's controversial opponent Salmasius but Dalila seems rather to embody Milton's mixture of sensual delight and fear of subjugation when he thought of beautiful women, and Harapha's boasts are merely to exhibit Samson's undefeated spirit. Neither episode (Dr Johnson thought this was true of all the episodes) hastens or retards the catastrophe. The modern theory is that the play was written before the Restoration, when Milton was deep in bitter controversy and already blind. The entrance of Dalila, and her vain appeal to Samson's softer nature has been seen as the hinge of the drama, when Dalila sweeps in like a 'stately ship of Tarsus' only to find Samson's hate still as cruel as the sea. But apart from the sea imagery she is a snake and a 'flower', which implies her beauty, but cool with 'dew'. Samson associates her with old sores and wounds. Perhaps she represents Milton's rejection, finally, for himself if not for Samson, of sexual love: his third wife was a mere cook-housekeeper and, without giving his daughters any proper education, he used them as amanuenses for his post-Restoration works. Like many republicans abroad, he was a tyrant at home.

In its rhythms, *Samson Agonistes* has a strange contorted strength which Hopkins saw as anticipating his own 'common rhythm counterpointed'. The play which has shown us Milton's mind, and Samson's, raging like the sea, and is in its morality typically Old Testament, a tribal revenge tragedy of a very bloody sort, ends in strange serenity:

> Oft he seems to hide his face,
> But unexpectedly returns,
> And to his faithful champion hath in place
> Bore witness gloriously; whence Gaza mourns
> And all that band them to resist
> His uncontrollable intent:
> His servants he, with new acquist
> Of true experience from this great event,
> With peace and consolation hath dismissed,
> And calm of mind all passion spent.

Nothing could be more noble. Yet God's 'uncontrollable intent' might suggest to us, irreverently, not merely an irresistible force but an uncontrollable bad temper, like Milton's own: the reason why Milton is our most learned but not our wisest poet, our greatest artist in verse, but except in places an artist without an inner being, all glittering outside. Yet that grand and sometimes also supremely delicate style silences criticism in awe and sweeps all before it.

In a sense, it seems to me, Milton was born at the wrong time. He was a man of high and stern, though sometimes relaxed and genial, humanist morality. In an age in which most poets aimed at ingenuity, he aimed, going back to older models like Spenser, at high art, and achieved it. In an age in which religion was the dominant concern, he was not naturally at all a religious man (there is little sign, in any of his writings of a sense of sin and compunction and *Paradise Lost*, with all its splendour, lacks the sense of the *mysterium tremendum*). People complain of small verbal difficulties but from another point of view *Paradise Lost* – compare the endless depths and heights of Dante – is all too straightforward. But religion was there: and Milton made the best of what, at some deep unconscious level of his being, was a bad job. As a humble Anglican layman myself, I read *Paradise Lost* as a great poem in which different characters have similar names. It is the only successful classical Christian epic, because of the cool distance at which Milton found it so easy to keep his subject matter. It was fitted, for the same reason, to become the one acknowledged English classic of the latitudinarian free-thinking eighteenth century. From one point of view, Milton is refreshingly free from 'enthusiasm' or religious fervour.

John Dryden is less so. His excellent satires are only part of his production (and of these *Absalom and Achitophel* is an epic satire and *Mac Flecknoe* a burlesque epic satire) and he was a great master of all verse forms, rivalled only, according to an expert on both of them, the editor of both, Kinsley, by Dunbar. Ode, song, elegy, complimentary or familiar epistle were all at his command. Though of too shy and phlegmatic a temperament, too little able to enter into the emotions of either his characters or his audience, to be a dramatist of the very first rank his classical treatment of Anthony and Cleopatra in *All For Love* and the gaiety of *Marriage à la Mode* can still, on their occasional revivals, hold the stage. His version of Virgil is in its own right an English classic; but even more surprising is the zest with which in the *Fables*, whose preface is his critical masterpiece, he discovers Chaucer and translates *The Knight's Tale*. His masterly use of the couplet, in its mixture of ease and energy, left Waller and Denham standing and prepared the way for Pope and the Augustan tradition. Yet, when he writes about either religion or politics, he seems very much a poet of his own century not the next. The magnificent opening of *Religio Laici, or a Layman's Faith* suggests the Metaphysical style at its highest: the simile has the intellectual precision that the true conceit demands but also – like 'A bracelet of bright hair about the bone' – its own grandeur as a visual image:

> Dim as the borrow'd beams of moon and stars
> To lonely, weary, wand'ring travellers
> Is Reason to the soul . . .

The simile is sustained:

> And as those nightly tapers disappear,
> When day's bright lord ascends our hemisphere;
> So pale grows Reason at Religion's sight;
> So dies, and so dissolves in supernatural light.

The Hind and the Panther begins with a passage whose beauty is unquestionable (though Matthew Arnold, who hated the poetry of the Augustans, hints uneasily that it feels like great poetry but somehow isn't):

> A milk-white Hind, immortal and unchang'd,
> Fed on the lawns, and in the forest rang'd;
> Without unspotted, innocent within,
> She fear'd no danger, for she knew no sin.
> Yet she had oft been chas'd with horns and hounds,
> And Scythian shafts; and many winged wounds
> Aim'd at her heart: was often forced to fly,
> And doom'd to death, tho' fated not to die.

The Hind is the Roman Catholic Church and the poem is a theological debate in the form of a beast fable, in which the main other debater is the Church of England:

> The Panther, sure the noblest, next the Hind,
> And fairest creature of the spotted kind . . .

Surely, apart from the neatness of the couplets, this medieval allegory looks back to the whole history of the Church rather than forward to the soothing simplifications, equating reason with religion, and self-love properly developed with social love, of Pope's *Essay on Man*. Dryden also in discussing his own beliefs (and his not very saintly early life) has an earnestness and agony that look backward, not forward:

> What weight of ancient witness can prevail,
> If private reason hold the public scale?
> But, gracious God, how well dost thou provide

For erring judgments an unerring guide!
Thy throne is darkness in th'abyss of light,
A blaze of glory that forbids the sight.
O teach me to believe thee thus conceal'd,
And search no farther than thyself reveal'd:
But her alone for my director take,
Whom thou hast promis'd never to forsake!
My thoughtless youth was wing'd with vain desires,
My manhood, long misled by wand'ring fires,
Follow'd false lights; and, when their glimpse was gone,
My pride struck out new sparkles of her own.
Such was I, such by nature still I am;
Be thine the glory, and be mine the shame.
Good life be now my task: my doubts are done
(What more could fright my faith, than three in one?)
Can I believe eternal God could lie
Disguis'd in mortal mold and infancy?
That the great Maker of the world could die?
And after that trust my imperfect sense,
Which calls in question his omnipotence?
Can I my reason to my faith compel,
And shall my sight, and touch, and taste rebel?
Superior faculties are set aside:
Shall their subservient organs be my guide?
Then let the moon usurp the rule of day,
And winking tapers show the sun his way:
For what my senses can themselves perceive,
I need no revelation to believe.
Can they who say the host should be descried
By sense, define a body glorified?
Impassible, and penetrating parts?
Let them declare by what mysterious arts
He shot that body thro' th'opposing might
Of bolts and bars impervious to the light,
And stood before his train confess'd in open sight?

This is the strongest piece of religious argument in verse in Dryden, remarkable for its personal honesty, and for the coherence of its argument. (To put it with a coarseness and directness which Dryden would not object to: the arguments against Roman Catholicism are either arguments, like the lack of evidence in a world of violence and sorrow where bad men flourish and good men suffer unjustly under an all-loving God's omnipotence, against Christianity as such: or if they have swallowed the camels of the Trinity, the

Incarnation, the death upon the Cross, and the Resurrection, why should other Christians strain at the gnat of Transubstantiation?)

Dryden convinces us all the more of his sincerity because he admits to a wordly youth and a pride in his own ingenuity, and confronts here a mystery which he admits even his very powerful mind cannot comprehend. Of eighteenth century critics, I think only Dr Johnson – good theologians were thin on the ground in his time – would have understood, and wholly entered into the spirit of, this passage. Anglicans in fact, though they believe that God is in a real and spiritual sense present in the Bread and Wine, reject Transubstantion not for the lack of visible evidence but because they believe that Christ's sacrifice on the Cross was a single, complete, and final act of Atonement and that, though the taking of Communion is not merely commemorative but properly sacramental, the presence of Christ in the elements does not imply a repetition of his sufferings on the Cross.

An Anglican nevertheless feels that with Dryden's poetry he is in familiar country, whereas with *Paradise Lost* he is in a more strange though more splendid one. I offer this long passage, however, rather than something from the more familiar satires, as incontestable evidence of Dryden's greatness, at his best, as a poet: a greatness based, apart from his energy and skill in versification, on what he called the 'sequaciousness' of his mind (it follows the clue of a leading thought as a hound follows a scent) and his honesty. Nobody could say of him, as Johnson with noble generosity said of Milton, that his 'life was a continual prayer'. But he remains one of the last great poetic spokesmen of a God-intoxicated century.

Dryden, whose marriage was a prosaic one, wrote no love poems, except for plays. He was, in this at least, anticipating the next century, and it is hard to read unmoved the end of *To my Dear Friend, Mr Congreve* (whom, like many young writers, he had encouraged). The circumstances in which this was written were as follows. Under William and Mary, Dryden had lost his laureateship, though he was still allowed a small pension. But the new political world of Dutch alliances and government stock to finance wars at reliable interest was alien to him. He saw the Roman Catholics,

excluded from the army and the learned professions, supposed to live at a safe distance from the Court, hampered
even in their right to buy land or fine houses, as at least
under threat of a persecution, which was never in fact
(except in Ireland) seriously brought to bear.

Literature and the friendship of the brilliant new young
writers alone kept the old man happy: he was not wrong to
see in Congreve, the greatest English master of artificial
comedy, and a loyal and good friend to him, the symbol of
something he could still trust:

> Unprofitably kept at Heav'n's expense,
> I live a rent-charge on his providence:
> But you, whom ev'ry Muse and Grace adorn,
> Whom I foresee to better fortune born,
> Be kind to my remains; and O defend,
> Against your judgement, your departed friend!
> Let not the insulting foe my fame pursue,
> But shade those laurels which descend to you;
> And take for tribute what these lines express:
> You merit more: nor could my love do less.

This was written in 1694, and printed as a preface to
Congreve's *Double-Dealer*.

Dryden was born of a gentleman's family in 1631 (he had
been a minor civil servant under Cromwell and welcomed
the restored Charles II with an eulogy; he earned his living
as a poet and playwright). He died in 1700 looking back
sadly on the past century, the century of genius, which had
promised so much in that stability and legitimacy of government and religion which he valued so highly, and achieved
so little. There had been the simple days of James I, whose
favourite hobby was hunting, but who was ruled by his male
favourites; there had been Charles I, the Civil Wars, the rule
of Parliament, all ending in the Protectorate; and the
restored Charles II, who had wasted his opportunities in
sensual pleasures, in which the love, on either side, was not
even sincere. All the plans of James II for religious toleration and the rights of Roman Catholics had come to nothing;
and James, for all his dogged loyalty to his religion, had
been as eager an amorist as his brother, and his lack of tact
and foresight had set back till 1829 the Catholic emancipa-
tion and delayed also the general toleration he honestly, but

too hastily, aimed at. It was unlikely that English Roman Catholics, would succeed in their aim of making the unfortunate king (who, in his latter days, seems to have lost the once undoubted military courage that had made him a favourite of the great Turenne) a saint. Dryden has the tact and loyalty to leave James out of his picture, but he is bitter:

> All, all of a piece throughout:
> Thy chase had a beast in view:
> Thy wars brought nothing about:
> Thy lovers were all untrue.
> 'Tis well an old age is out:
> And time to begin a new.
> (The end of *The Secular Masque*)

I spoke of the seventeenth century, in English poetry, as the age of strength. Despair has never been expressed so strongly in the English language. The next century will offer us its own kinds of strength, strengths of social sanity; but one may well end this chapter with Rochester who expresses so passionately the worst that a naturally religious man (as Rochester, even and strikingly at his worst, clearly was) can fear:

> Books bear him up awhile, and make him try,
> To swim with Bladders of Philosophy;
> In hopes still t'oretake th'escaping light,
> The *Vapor* dances in his dazling sight,
> Till, spent, it leaves him to eternal Night,
> Then Old Age, and experience, hand in hand,
> Lead him to death, and make him understand,
> After a search so painful, and so long,
> That all his life he has been in the wrong;
> Hudled in dirt, the reas'ning *Engine* lyes,
> That was so proud, so witty, and so wise.

8

The Eighteenth Century

I The Strict Augustan Tradition

From Alexander Pope (1688–1744) to George Crabbe
(1754–1832) we can trace, in many of the leading poets of
the eighteenth century, notably Goldsmith (c.1730–74) and
Johnson (1709–84) the Augustan tradition, one of the long-
est-lived traditions in the history of English poetry, and
immediately recognisable both by its typical form (the
anthithetic closed heroic couplet) and its subject matter
(man as a social animal, with particular reference to his
moral and social duties). It is wrong to suppose that poetry
in this tradition, because it is predominantly concerned with
man's social nature is mainly satirical. Pope, generally
regarded as the master of the school, had in his first
collected volume, which came out in 1717, only one poem
that could be called satirical, and its satire is of a very
light-hearted and indulgent sort, pointing out the frivolity of
high society and the triviality of its concerns, but depicting
its gaiety and glitter with enjoyment. (Pope gave so little
offence by this poem, even to its targets, that he was able to
dedicate the second and elaborated version, with its mock-
heroic 'machinery' of protective sylphs and sinister gnomes,
to Miss Arabella Fermor, the model of his heroine, Belinda,
though it should be added that his dedication was heavily
ironic in tone.) The poem came to be written under the
following circumstances. The Fermors and the Petres were
two old Roman Catholic families; they had quarrelled
because Lord Petre had, in a frolic which was taken badly,
snipped off a lock of Miss Fermor's beautiful hair. Pope

himself was a Roman Catholic and a friend of the same persuasion, Caryll, had persuaded him to laugh the two families into a good mood again. The other poems in this brilliant volume of 1717 were descriptive or discursive. It began with some elegant but very artificial pastorals, because Virgil, the greatest poet of Augustus's court, had begun with pastorals. We talk of the English Augustan age, having in mind the grandeur of Virgil, which Pope in his version of *The Iliad* and his assisted version of *The Odyssey*, was to imitate; he worked hard on this between 1715 and 1726. Pope's invalid constitution had been conquered in his youth by high spirits but worsened under the pressure of his long labours on Homer. The attacks of envious critics and bad poets in 1728 induced a tetchiness of temper, which led him to write the first version of the ferocious but brilliantly energetic *Dunciad*. His most widely praised original poem in his own life time, however, was the sincere and moving (if not very intellectually profound) *Essay on Man*, an attempt to 'vindicate the ways of God to man' or an apology for natural religion. His *Moral Essays* and his *Imitations of Horace* contain savage attacks on those he hated but also warm tributes to his friends; the greatest of them, *Epistle to Dr Arbuthnot* is, for all the ferocity of the attack on Sporus, as a whole a self-portrait, an invalid poet's appeal for the reader's indulgence and sympathy, rather than a satire in the severest sense. In a rather parallel way, in the early poems of 1717, apart from *The Rape of the Lock*, one is struck by the musicality and Keatsian vividness of the *Pastorals* and *Windsor Forest* (a celebration of the prospects of lasting peace and world-wide trade opened out by the Treaty of Utrecht), the wit and aptness of the precepts in the didactic *Essay on Criticism* and the unexpected romantic fervour of two hitherto unpublished poems that wind up the volume – the mysterious, impenetrable, yet strangely powerful *Elegy to the Memory of an Unfortunate Lady*, and the clearer but more artificial *Eloisa to Abelard*, skilfully modelled on Ovid's *Heroides*, or imaginary letters to, or soliloquies about, their absent lovers or husbands by the heroines of classical mythology. Both these poems anticipate in many ways the romantic mood of poetry a hundred years later and the *Unfortunate Lady* looks back, also, to the Metaphysicals:

Most souls, 'tis true, but peep out once an age,
Dull sullen pris'ners in the body's cage
Dim lights of life that burn a length of years,
Useless, unseen, as lamps in sepulchres;
Like Eastern Kings a lazy state they keep,
And close confin'd to their own palace sleep.

In variety and swift modulation from one mood to another, Pope is one of the greatest of English poets and *too* various perhaps to be typically Augustan (though at the same time the greatest of all Augustan poets, and the model of his followers). We read him ultimately for his long revelation of his own strange and fascinating character. His versions of Homer, once one gets used to the deliberate artifice of the style – elsewhere his style is often a model of polite conversational ease – are among the great narrative poems in the English language. But if one were attempting to derive a definition of the Augustan mode from Pope's work as a whole, one would say that it is not primarily satirical but discursive. Augustan poetry is the poetry of speech not song, of reflection rather than the direct expression of emotion for its own sake, of description pointing a moral rather than what Pope called 'mere description'.

Pope sought fame but did not seek to found a tradition. The classical description of what the mid-Augustan poet was aiming at is to be found in Dr Johnson's *Rasselas, Prince of Abissinia*, in the words of the sage and poet Imlac in Chapter X:

'The business of the poet', said Imlac, 'is to examine, not the individual, but the species; to remark general properties and large appearances: he does not number the streaks of the tulip, or describe the different shades in the verdure of the forest. He is to exhibit in his portraits of nature such prominent and striking features, as recall the original to every mind; and must neglect the minuter discriminations, which one may have remarked, and another neglected', for those characteristics which are alike obvious to vigilance and carelessness.

Johnson was very short-sighted and he probably did not even see these 'minute discriminations'. I do not remember any general descriptions of natural scenery, of the sort he commends, in his verses though there are some magnificent ones in prose, like the general conspectus of the Highlands in *A Journey to the Western Isles*:

> What is not heath is nakedness, a little diversified by now and then a stream rushing down the steep. An eye accustomed to flowery pastures and waving harvests is astonished and repelled by this wide extent of hopeless sterility. The appearance is that of matter incapable of form or usefulness, dismissed by nature from her care, and disinherited of her favours, left in its original elemental state, or quickened only with one sullen power of useless vegetation.

This great passage has something of the power of poetry, and corresponds exactly to Imlac's prescriptions for generalised natural description. But how very different it is with Johnson's master in versification, Pope, who delights to number the streaks of the tulip.

Here, for instance, is Pope on varieties of fresh water fish:

> Our plenteous Streams a various Race supply;
> The bright-ey'd Perch with Fins of *Tyrian* Dye,
> The silver Eel, in shining Volumes roll'd,
> The yellow Carp, in Scales bedrop'd with Gold,
> Swift Trouts diversify'd with Crimson Stains,
> And Pykes, the Tyrants of the watry Plains.

Just as in Johnson's passage on the Highlands we can see that Johnson is an extremely intelligent man, making intelligence supply the duties of a sharp, discriminating sense of sight, so we can see in the passage above that Pope's hobby was painting, and that he delighted in colour. Johnson's sympathy for Pope was limited in other ways. In his *Life of Pope*, he confesses that he did not understand why Pope considered the following two lines as the most musical of all his couplets (the music comes partly, of course, from the use of hiatus – 'Mae-o-tis', 'Tan-a-is', 'thro' a' – which gives a stately slowness to the lines like the motion of the freezing rivers). There are many passages with a music like that of this couplet which puzzled Johnson:

> Lo! where Maeotis sleeps, and hardly flows
> The freezing Tanais thro' a waste of snows.

It is doubtful, to say the least, whether Johnson would have been awed and enchanted, as modern readers are, by these lines which precede the final triumph of Dulness in the Fourth Book of *The Dunciad*:

> As one by one, at dread Medea's strain,
> The sick'ning stars fade off th'ethereal plain;
> As Argus' eyes, by Hermes' wand opprest,
> Clos'd one by one to everlasting rest . . .

But Johnson was a great critic, and for the many commentators who have found an easy target in his remarks on the streaks of the tulip, few or none have noted the magnificence (one passage anticipates, even verbally, Shelley's *Defence of Poetry*) of his remarks on the Augustan poet's attitude to human nature: Imlac continues:

> 'But the knowledge of nature is only half the task of a poet; he must be acquainted likewise with all the modes of life. His character requires that he estimate the happiness and misery of every condition; observe the power of all the passions in their combinations, and trace the changes of the human mind as they are modified by various institutions and accidental influences of climate or custom, from the spriteliness of infancy to the despondence of decrepitude . . .'

Here, in 1759, Johnson seems to be thinking not merely of his own Augustan tradition, but of Shakespeare, of whom he was to publish the first really great edition in 1765. But he, in the voice of Imlac, continues in a vein that is more typically Augustan, a vein which also anticipates Shelley's lofty conception of the social function of the poet:

> 'He must divest himself of the prejudices of his age and country; he must consider right and wrong in their abstracted and invariable state; he must disregard present laws and opinions, and rise to general and transcendental truths, which will always be the same: he must therefore content himself with the slow progress of his name; contemn the applause of his own time, and commit his claims to the justice of posterity. He must write as the interpreter of nature, and the legislator of mankind . . .'

Johnson, among all English men of letters, has perhaps

the greatest moral sanity and the most powerfully concentrated mind. Both are to be seen in all his poetry, but at their height in his masterpiece, an adaptation from Juvenal which is best seen as a sad meditation rather than a satire in the ordinary sense (if it is one, a tragical rather than a comical satire): *The Vanity of Human Wishes*. Pope with his volatile acute sensibility and extraordinary power of modulating his tone and manipulating, with the most tactful skill, the reader's sympathies, was a much greater poet in the strict sense than Johnson, one of the eight or nine very great poets in our language. Because he depended so much, as an invalid always in pain, on friendship and resented slights, insults, and snubs so bitterly, he lacks Johnson's moral sanity: and, a poet of sensibility rather than intellect, he would never have had Johnson's power of mind. But it is fair to compare them in two passages in which they are both aiming at 'general and transcendental truths'. In his most popular poem in his lifetime, *An Essay on Man*, Pope set out to 'vindicate the ways of God to man'. He saw the world we live in as the best that God could have created, and suggested that where it seems unjust, cruel, or inexplicable it is so for reasons which it is impious for us to enquire into. God wants us to worship Him but to study our own natures and purposes. He has given each of us a ruling passion because reason, though it should guide our actions, is not itself a motive to action ('Reason', the great Scottish philosopher David Hume was to write later in the century, 'is, and should be, the slave of the passions').

We follow our passions because we seek 'Happiness, our Being's end and aim'. We shall satisfy our ruling passion through benevolence and virtue, for happiness cannot be found in solitude, and in that happiness among our fellows we shall find a new awareness of, a new closeness to, God. Maynard Mack, whose introduction to *An Essay on Man* in the great modern Twickenham edition is the best critical study of the poem, praises particularly these lines from the fourth and final Epistle, for their lofty and thrilling evocation of cosmic harmony:

> God loves from Whole to Parts; but human soul
> Must rise from Individual to the Whole:
> Self-love but serves the virtuous mind to wake,
> As the small pebble stirs the peaceful lake;

The centre mov'd, a circle strait succeeds,
Another still, and still another spreads,
Friend, parent, neighbour, first it will embrace,
His country next, and next all human race,
Wide and more wide, th'o'erflowings of the mind
Take ev'ry creature in, of ev'ry kind;
Earth smiles around, with boundless bounty blest,
And Heav'n beholds its image in his breast.

If one can believe in cosmic harmony, as something clearly evident to the pious and candid man in this world, one will agree with Mack that this is not only a sublime but mystical passage, with its image of the fusion of human love outwards and upwards and of divine love downwards and inwards, till Heaven is reflected in the human breast. There is no doubt of the sincerity of Pope's religion though it was a religion oddly untouched by a sense of man's fallen state and also, in spite of the pain which Pope endured with growing intensity during his comparatively short life, not much concerned with the problems of sufferings or evil. We must trust God, not enquire into what we cannot understand, and believe that crimes and disasters mysteriously serve a general scheme of Divine beneficence, whose details are beyond our knowledge and should be beyond our curiosity. What gives Pope's satire its sharpness and its personality (too often, for a true satirist, he attacks the man rather than the vice) is his sincere belief that if we will only let our passions be guided by reason and piety we can live in a happy world. If he saw vice and folly in the world around him, he also saw civilisation and improvement, social gaiety, improvements in taste and manners.

Wide and more wide, th'o'erflowing of the mind
Takes ev'ry creature in, of ev'ry kind;
Earth smiles around, with boundless bounty blest,
And heav'n beholds its image in his breast.

Johnson thought *An Essay on Man* a shallow poem, with nothing new in it, and raising more problems than it solved. Both *Rasselas* and *The Vanity of Human Wishes* preach an opposite doctrine to Pope's, the doctrine that happiness is not to be found in this world and that occasional appearances of what seems to be happiness are either illusory or at the best transitory. He was acutely aware, in a way that Pope never was, of the fact that the rewards of effort ('Slow rises worth by poverty depress'd') never, in the end, seem commensurate with the effort, that lives of brilliant achievement have petty endings, that however we occupy ourselves we are likely to be struck at some point with feelings of weariness and boredom. There is an impatient restlessness in human nature, a recurrent sense of disappointment, both of which suggest that happiness is not our being's end and aim here. Johnson was far from despising innocent enjoyment, and thought that a book served no purpose unless it helped us to enjoy life or endure it; reading should also make us better men (it is a trite but always relevant truth that in everything he wrote Johnson was primarily a moralist).

But our point was to contrast a passage of Johnson's, in which he pleads for the efficacy of prayer in a world that, of necessity, as a place of probation for a better world, cannot offer us lasting happiness, with the cosmic optimism of Pope. The passage, deservedly famous, is at the end of *The Vanity of Human Wishes*:

> Where then shall Hope and Fear their Objects find?
> Must dull Suspence corrupt the stagnant Mind !
> Must helpless Man, in Ignorance sedate,
> Swim darkling down the Current of his Fate?
> Must no Dislike alarm, no Wishes rise,
> No Cries attempt the Mercies of the Skies?
> Enquirer, cease, Petitions yet remain,
> Which Heav'n may hear, nor deem Religion vain.
> Still raise for Good the supplicating Voice,
> But leave to Heav'n the Measure and the Choice.
> Safe in his Pow'r, whose Eyes discern afar
> The secret Ambush of a specious Pray'r.
> Implore his Aid, in his Decisions rest,
> Secure whate'er he gives, he gives the best.
> Yet with the Sense of sacred Presence prest,
> When strong Devotion fills thy glowing Breast,
> Pour forth thy Fervours for a healthful Mind,
> Obedient Passions, and a Will resign'd;
> For Love, which scarce collective Man can fill;
> For Patience, sov'reign o'er transmuted Ill:
> For Faith, that panting for a happier Seat,
> Thinks Death kind Nature's Signal of Retreat:

These Goods for Man the Laws of Heav'n ordain,
These Goods he grants, who grants the Pow'r to gain;
With these celestial Wisdom calms the Mind,
And makes the Happiness she does not find.

If we compare this with the equivalent passage in Pope, we would praise Johnson for weight, Pope for a light exultant buoyancy. Johnson has not Pope's ear: a line like

Mu*st* dull Suspe*n*ce corru*p*t the Stagna*n*t M*i*nd!

is, in a phrase that Johnson himself used oddly of Collins, 'clogged with consonants'. The echo in

No *Cries* attempt the Mercies of the *Skies*,

grates on the ear. For all his weight, also, Johnson lacks Pope's concision; and if Johnson is the profounder thinker and the greater man, Pope in spite of his volatility and inconsistency – perhaps because of these, since they help to make him the liveliest and most various poet of his century – remains far and away the greater poet. What may surprise, perhaps, readers who still accept Matthew Arnold's definition of Augustan verse as failing to be poetry but succeeding only in being the versified conventional wisdom of an 'age of prose and reason', is the deep and genuine religious piety of both Johnson and Pope. The mood of the French *philosophes*, though it had a certain effect on English and Scottish thinkers from the flashy Bolingbroke to the profound Hume, never affected any of the greater poets. Some, like William Cowper, combined a loveable ease and humour (more genuinely like Horace, Sir Herbert Grierson thought, than Pope's imitations of that poet) and a fresh delight in country scenery with a religious melancholia, verging on madness, the result of the influence on him of a former Captain of a slave-ship turned Calvinist evangelist, John Newton. Other poets in a new style, sometimes called 'the sublime style' and sometimes the style of sensibility, a style which greatly influenced Keats, Thomas Gray (1716–71) and William Collins (1721–59) suffered, the first and greater from constitutional melancholy the latter, towards the end of his life, from actual madness. Arnold, whose essay on Gray is still a classic, may have been right in supposing that there was something in the subdued, reasonable atmosphere of the eighteenth century that prevented a poet like Gray (though Johnson, who disliked his more experimental poems, was right in finding the famous *Elegy Written in a Country Churchyard*, the only really great eighteenth-century poem written in quatrains) from ever properly 'speaking out'. (And yet it would be difficult to find a bad, and impossible to find a clumsy poem or even line or phrase in Gray.) But a case can certainly be made that a sad and subdued tone that marks much eighteenth-century poetry of the meditative sort springs rather from a sincere but joyless religiousness than from a shallow cult of rationalism. Virgil had created pious Aeneas to symbolise the virtues of the Roman Augustan age, and Aeneas's piety is marked by a perpetual spirit of renunciation.

Various as he is, that spirit is to be found in some of Pope's most moving moments: in these lines from an imitation of the first poem in Horace's first book of epistles:

> Long, as to him who works for debt, the Day;
> Long as the Night to her whose love's away;
> Long as the Year's dull circle seems to run,
> When the brisk Minor pants for twenty-one;
> So slow th'unprofitable Moments roll,
> That lock up all the Functions of my soul;
> That keep me from Myself; and still delay
> Life's instant business to a future day:
> That task, which as we follow, or despise,
> The eldest is a fool, the youngest wise;
> Which done, the poorest can no wants endure,
> And which not done, the richest must be poor . . .

The mood could be called a Christian Stoicism, mingled (as Aeneas mourns in Virgil for Dido) with a wistfulness for some kind of high delight which has been renounced. Goldsmith, who had the sweetest voice of all these poets (sweeter though less various than Pope's), mourns thus for the poetic gift which earning his living as a brilliant London hack-essayist, biographer, author of an unreal but delightful prose pastoral *The Vicar of Wakefield* and of at least one comedy, *She Stoops to Conquer*, which has something of the

innocent delight of Shakespeare's golden period – has
forced him to renounce:

> And thou, sweet Poetry, thou loveliest maid,
> Still first to fly where sensual joys invade;
> Unfit, in these degenerate times of shame,
> To catch the heart or strike for honest fame;
> Dear charming nymph, neglected and decried,
> My shame in crowds, my solitary pride;
> Thou source of all my bliss and all my woe,
> That found'st me poor at first and keep'st me so;
> Thou guide by which the nobler arts excel,
> Thou nurse of every virtue, fare thee well.

Something of the same spirit of resignation is to be found
in the epitaph which ends Gray's great *Elegy*:

> Here rests his head upon the lap of Earth
> A Youth to Fortune, and to Fame unknown.
> Fair Science frown'd not on his humble birth,
> And Melancholy mark'd him for her own.
>
> Large was his bounty, and his soul sincere,
> Heaven did a recompence as largely send:
> He gave to Mis'ry all he had, a tear,
> He gained from Heav'n ('twas all he wished) a friend.
> No farther seek his merits to disclose,
> Or draw his frailties from their dread abode,
> (There they alike in trembling hope repose)
> The bosom of his Father and his God.

Not everybody shares my own taste for this tone, and it is
certainly not characteristic of contemporary poetry. A poet
and critic of distinction said to me recently: 'Do you not *hate*
piety?' On the contrary, I think it is this quality (more than
satiric wit) which makes the deepest appeal to the few genuine
lovers of eighteenth-century poetry.

In the last great Augustan poet, George Crabbe, who made
his reputation as a grim and realistic poet of rural poverty
(which had marked his own youth at Aldeburgh), and whose
later experiences, first as a clergyman in his native borough,
where his unexpected success and elevation aroused the
hatred of his congregation, and later as a humble chaplain to
the Duke of Rutland at Belvoir castle, still further sharpened
his eyes but did not mellow his mood, the tone is less Christian

Stoicism than subduedly eloquent bitterness. The late Cyril
Connolly rightly admired the following passage in which a grim
precision of natural description (Crabbe, whose hobby was
botany, ignores the precepts of Imlac) stands as a symbol for
the vice and misery which beset the life of the poor:

> Lo! where the heath, with withering brake grown o'er,
> Lends the light turf that warms the neighbouring poor;
> From thence a length of burning sand appears,
> Where the thin harvest waves its wither'd ears;
> Rank weeds, that every art and care defy,
> Reign o'er the land, and rob the blighted rye:
> There thistles spread their prickly arms afar,
> And to the ragged infants threaten war;
> There poppies nodding, mock the hope of toil;
> There the blue bugloss paints the sterile soil;
> Hardy and high, above the slender sheaf,
> The slimy mallow waves her silky leaf;
> O'er the young shoot the charlock throws a shade,
> And clasping tares cling round the sickly blade;
> With mingled tints the rocky coasts abound,
> And a sad splendour vainly shines around.

That 'sad splendour' reminds us that Crabbe was a friend of
Wordsworth's, and there seems to me to be just a touch of
the more melancholy kind of romantic in him. I do not mean
merely that he describes natural scenery with more colour
than Wordsworth – who, living in his grey northern fells,
and his lakes reflecting grey skies, is remarkably lacking in
painterly qualities (try counting the colour-adjectives in the
first book of *The Prelude*), but that he has a sense (like
Coleridge in *Dejection: An Ode*) of the kind of desolate
beauty which, in outer nature, echoes an inner mood of
constitutional melancholy. But certainly Crabbe (though
this is also true, as Donald Davie has pointed out, of the
early Wordsworth) feels the Augustan need, even if he is
often a romantic without knowing it, to point a moral. The
passage I have quoted continues:

> So looks the nymph whom wretched arts adorn,
> Betrayed by man, then left for man to scorn;
> Whose cheek in vain assumes the mimic rose,
> While her sad eyes the troubled breast disclose;

Whose outward splendour is but folly's dress,
Exposing most, when most it gilds distress.

This is a heavy and trite conclusion to a great passage. This poem of Crabbe's *The Village* was intended as an answer to Goldsmith's *The Deserted Village*, with what Crabbe thought its wholly idealistic picture of country life. But how much better Goldsmith deals with the same topic of the pretty country girl who has fled, or been lured, to the great city to find her ruin:

Tumultuous grandeur crowds the blazing square,
The rattling chariots clash, the torches glare.
Sure scenes like these no troubles e'er annoy!
Sure these denote one universal joy!
Are these thy serious thoughts? – Ah, turn thine eyes
Where the poor, houseless, shivering female lies.
She once, perhaps, in village plenty blest,
Has wept at tales of innocence distrest;
Her modest looks the cottage might adorn,
Sweet as the primrose peeps beneath the thorn;
Now lost to all; her friends, her virtue fled,
Near her betrayer's door she lays her head,
And, pinch'd with cold, and shrinking from the shower,
With heavy heart deplores that luckless hour,
When idly first, ambitious of the town,
She left her wheel and robes of country brown.

George Crabbe, though a great poet, is also, as the beginning and end of the above quotation from *The Village* show, a very uneven poet. Edward Fitzgerald, the translator of Omar Khayyam, perhaps had it right when he said that there were times when any poetaster could write as well as the old fellow but other times when you could compare him with Shakespeare. Fitzgerald was no doubt thinking of a tale like *Peter Grimes*, which shows a gift for telling a grim and yet pitiful tale, a tale of crime and madness, in verse, and a depth of psychological intuition that is not shown by any of the earlier Augustans. Crabbe's gift here of entering into the lonely heart and nearly insane mind of a man who, to the earlier Augustans, would have been merely a repulsive villain shows, again, an inwardness of feeling that links him unconsciously with the great romantic. He had the curiosity and exactness, at a lower social level, of his great contemporary Jane Austen, as well as a sense of the frightening expressiveness of nature which she quite lacked. Wordsworth was a friend of Crabbe, admired him, and commemorates him in a late and moving poem, *An Extempore Effusion on the Death of James Hogg*:

> Our haughty life is crowned with darkness,
> Like London with its own black wreath,
> On which with thee, O Crabbe! forth-looking,
> I gazed from Hampstead's breezy heath.

Wordsworth saw and felt the true poet under the late Augustan manner; nor, indeed, as he himself was both one of our greatest poets and, as his friend Coleridge pointed out, one of our most uneven, would Crabbe's unevenness much worry him. Wordsworth's unevenness, of a different type from Crabbe's, is shown in the last two lines of that quatrain, of which the first two are so much in the grand style:

> On which with thee, O Crabbe, forth-looking,
> I gazed from Hampstead's breezy heath.

Nobody would quote these two lines to illustrate Wordsworth's greatness: yet, in their setting, they place and specify what would otherwise be a lofty but too vague expression of feeling. Crabbe's flatnesses and awkwardnesses, which led to his being sneered at as 'Pope in worsted stockings', are not so fortunate. Yet it is interesting that Wordsworth, so ready to accept Crabbe with all his unevenness, rejected one of the perfect artists of his time, Jane Austen: he saw the skill and art and perfect observation of her fiction: but he felt a lack of poetic feeling in it, and much preferred the rambling wizardry of his friend Sir Walter Scott. (I do not know if he ever read her one intense love story, with its pictures of the autumn fields, *Persuasion*, or had studied the pages in which Emma, miserable in her consciousness of folly, looks through her window at the rain among the trees.)

I have painted the strict Augustan tradition from an unfamiliar angle. But, of course, satire, both serious and light, and pure comedy, played a larger part in it than in any other English tradition of such long life: and I shall deal now, but more briefly, with that too familiar topic.

II The Strict Augustan Tradition: Serious and Light Satire

The literary form known as satire is the only major form to be invited by the Romans rather than the Greeks and has nothing to do (though a number of seventeenth-century poets, like Rochester, by their spelling of the word seemed to think it had) with the comic Greek satyr plays, which were acted as interludes between tragedies. It comes from the Latin noun *satura*, a medley of mixed foods, something like the Spanish *olla podrida*, and connected with *satis*, enough, and *saturare*, from which we get our verb to saturate. It was a chatty, conversational poem, in a light tone, on a variety of topics, and in Horace, its first master, its satire, in our English sense, was good-natured, aimed at the mild absurdities of life, rather than fierce. The much more ferocious satire of the later Roman writer, Juvenal, which aimed at denouncing the corruptions of the later Roman Empire, is sometimes called tragical satire in contrast with Horace's comical satire. The purpose of satire was supposed to be to correct the milder follies and vices of the day by mild ridicule; it should be aimed at the fault rather than the man, so nobody ought to resent a form which did not attack him personally but merely pointed out faults he could easily correct, and thus ought to arouse his gratitude. Swift, often thought of as the most ferocious of Augustan satirists, was born in 1667 and died of senile decay a year after his friend Pope in 1745. He was the longest lived (unhappily for him) of the early Augustan poets – in many ways the gayest and most good-natured of Augustan satirists. He was from his adolescence a sufferer from Ménière's syndrome, a combination of giddiness, deafness, and occasional fits of nausea. He was, unlike his friend Pope, whose invalidism was of a more painfully continuous sort (Pott's disease, or curvature and growing weakness of the spine), a profoundly ambitious man and useful to the Tory chiefs, Harley and Bolingbroke, in writing political pamphlets, particularly the pamphlet *The Conduct of the Allies*, which strengthened the Tories in bringing about the downfall of Marlborough and ultimately the signing of the Treaty of

Utrecht. But the best his friends could do for him (Queen Anne, a genuinely religious woman, felt that his brilliant early prose satire, *The Tale of a Tub*, though aimed particularly against the Roman Catholics and the Nonconformists, was irreverent in its attitude towards Christianity generally) was to get him the Deanery of St Patrick's in Dublin; he had wanted an English Bishopric and, though born in Ireland, felt living in Dublin a kind of exile. Yet, though he hated Papistry and despised the native Irish, he fought for elementary justice for them in *The Drapier's Letters* and *A Modest Proposal*. His poems, often light and trifling, evince his determination to make the best of a bad job and live up to his new motto, '*Vive la Bagatelle!*' His most famous poem, *Verses on the Death of Dr Swift, D.S.P.D.* is an enlargement and improvement of a shorter and possibly earlier version published in 1733 and a correction of a version published in England in 1738, with omissions and with inclusions from the earlier version approved by Pope, in Twickenham, but not by Swift in Dublin. The version he approved came out in Dublin in 1739 and he may be said to have been working on it, and its predecessor, since 1731. The remarkable ease of the concluding lines, with their excellent account of the proper function of satire, is not therefore a mark of easy writing (which, as has been often said, does not make for easy reading) but of very patient care and labour. This is how Swift would like to be remembered: a detached and just observer is supposed to be describing the dead Dean:

> 'Perhaps I may allow, the Dean
> Had too much Satyr in his Vein;
> And seem'd determin'd not to starve it,
> Because no Age could more deserve it.
> Yet, Malice never was his Aim;
> He lash'd the Vice, but spar'd the Name.
> No Individual could resent,
> Where Thousands equally were meant:
> His Satyr points at no Defect,
> But what all Mortals may correct;
> For, he abhorr'd that senseless Tribe
> Who call it Humour when they jibe:
> He spar'd a Hump or crooked Nose,
> Whose owners set not up for Beaux.

> True genuine Dulness mov'd his Pity,
> Unless it offer'd to be witty.
> Those, who their Ignorance confess'd,
> He ne'er offended with a Jest;
> But, laughed to hear an Idiot quote
> A verse from *Horace*, learn'd by Rote.
>
> 'He knew an hundred pleasant Stories,
> With all the Turns of *Whigs* and *Tories*:
> Was chearful to his dying Day,
> And Friends would let him have his Way.
>
> 'He gave the little Wealth he had,
> To build a House for Fools and Mad:
> And shew'd by one satyric Touch,
> No Nation wanted it so much;
> That Kingdom he hath left his Debtor,
> I wish it soon may have a Better.'

The proper function of satire and the proper mood of a good-natured satirist have never been better described. Perhaps, in being forced into exile among kindly but commonplace companions, in becoming through *The Drapier's Letters* an Irish national hero, Swift had learned sociability while forgetting, except in occasional bitter moments, ambition. But alas, we may feel, for the most decent and modest human ambition when we read the line 'Was chearful to his dying day'. Swift connected Ménière's syndrome with madness and was once reported to have said, 'I shall die like a tree at the top'. Unpleasant as it is, it does not lead to madness. Swift died, as many old people do to-day, of senile dementia: to which was added the pain of a horrible inflammation of one eye. He had to be tied to his bed to prevent him from attempting to tear the eye out. His wretched attendants showed off the great dying man to visitors for sixpence a head. Johnson, who disapproved of Swift, nevertheless in *The Vanity of Human Wishes* describes him with pity as an example of how age torments greatness:

> From *Marlb'rough*'s Eyes the Streams of Dotage flow,
> And *Swift* expires a Driv'ler and a Show.

Alexander Pope's gifts as a satirist were so various (and he so often attacked the man rather than the vice) that his genius in satire can hardly be illustrated here. He has, however, an unusual but effective set piece (on Philip Duke of Wharton, who was not among his acquaintances) which makes an interesting comparison with Dr Johnson's set piece (adapted from Juvenal on Hannibal) on Charles XII of Sweden in *The Vanity of Human Wishes*. Both have a similar subject matter: a great talent, tasting early triumph, and then, through rashness, ending in disaster. Pope uses Wharton to illustrate his favourite, and over simple, psychological theory of the ruling passion; Johnson uses Charles to illustrate, as in *Rasselas*, the uncertainty of happiness and the vicissitudes of human fortune. Johnson's skill in the condensed presentation of character, his gift for the precise choice of an epithet, make the comparison between Pope's passage and his a more even one than our last similar comparison; Pope has still more liveliness and variety, but Johnson is more gravely, and pityingly, severe. Here is Pope on the wild young Wharton:

> Wharton, the scorn and wonder of our days,
> Whose ruling Passion was the lust of Praise;
> Born with whate'er could win it from the Wise,
> Women and Fools must like him or he dies;
> Tho' wond'ring Senates hung on all he spoke,
> The Club must hail him master of the joke,
> Shall parts so various aim at nothing new?
> He'll shine a Tully and a Wilmot too.
> Then turns repentant, and his God adores
> With the same spirit that he drinks and whores;
> Enough if all around him but admire,
> And now the Punk applaud, and now the Fryer.
> Thus with each gift of nature and of art,
> And wanting nothing but an honest heart;
> Grown all to all, from no one vice exempt,
> And most contemptible, to shun contempt;
> His Passion still, to covet gen'ral praise,
> His Life, to forfeit it a thousand ways;
> A constant Bounty which no friend has made;
> An angel Tongue, which no man can persuade;
> A Fool, with more of Wit than half mankind,
> Too quick for Thought, for Action too refin'd;
> A Tyrant to the wife his heart approves;
> A Rebel to the very king he loves;
> He dies, sad out-cast of each church and state,

And (harder still) flagitious, yet not great!
Ask you why Wharton broke thro' ev'ry rule
'Twas all for fear the Knaves should call him Fool.

Here is Johnson's portrait, more deeply in the vein of
'tragical satire', of Charles XII of Sweden:

On what foundation stands the Warrior's Pride?
How just his Hopes let *Swedish Charles* decide;
A Frame of Adamant, a Soul of Fire,
No Dangers fright him, and no Labours tire;
O'er Love, o'er Fear, extends his wide Domain,
Unconquer'd Lord of Pleasure and of Pain;
No Joys to him pacific Scepters yield,
War sounds the Trump, he rushes to the Field;
Behold surrounding Kings their Pow'r combine,
And One capitulate, and One resign;
Peace courts his Hand, but spread her Charms in vain;
'Think Nothing gain'd', he cries, 'till nought remain,
On *Moscow*'s Walls till *Gothic* Standards fly,
And all is Mine beneath the Polar Sky.'
The March begins in Military State,
And Nations on his Eye suspended wait;
Stern Famine guards the solitary Coast,
And Winter barricades the Realms of Frost;
He comes, nor Want nor Cold his Course delay; –
Hide, blushing Glory, hide *Pultowa*'s Day:
The vanquish'd Hero leaves his broken Bands,
And shews his Miseries in distant Lands;
Condemn'd a needy Supplicant to wait,
While Ladies interpose, and Slaves debate.
But did not Chance at length her Error mend?
Did no subverted Empire mark his End?
Did rival Monarchs give the fatal Wound?
Or hostile Millions press him to the Ground?
His Fall was destin'd to a barren Strand,
A petty Fortress, and a dubious Hand;
He left the Name, at which the World grew pale,
To point a Moral, or adorn a Tale.

T. S. Eliot wrote an introduction to a small edition of
London and *The Vanity of Human Wishes*; his essay, which
he never collected, is to be found easily only in the first
volume of the World's Classic's *Twentieth Century Critical
Essays*. Eliot, whose taste in diction was impeccable, calls

attention not to the last couplet (which has, of course, particularly the last line, become a proverb) but to the wonderful inevitability of the sequence of *barren*, *petty*, and *dubious*. One thinks of Johnson as exhibiting, in poetry, a heavy strength but here he astonishes us with a forceful and condensed delicacy.

Augustan satire could be light and delicate as in *The Rape of the Lock* as well as grave or fierce. William Cowper, more famous as a poet of sensibility and natural description, and occasionally, very terribly, of religious despair, in *Conversation* makes light and excellent, but not angry or self-righteous, fun of various kinds of conversational bore. His own writing, deliberately avoiding the emphatic and the striking, exhibits quiet conversational charm:

> The emphatic speaker dearly loves to oppose
> In contact inconvenient, nose to nose;
> As if the gnomon on his neighbour's phiz,
> Touched with the magnet, had attracted his.
> His whispered theme, dilated and at large,
> Proves after all a wind-gun's airy charge,
> An extract of his diary – no more,
> A tasteless journal of the day before.
> He walked abroad, o'ertaken in the rain
> Called on a friend, drank tea, stepped home again;
> Resumed his purpose, had a world of talk
> With one he stumbled on, and lost his walk.
> I interrupt him with a sudden bow,
> 'Adieu, dear Sir! lest you should lose it now.'

Cowper's quiet and gentle humour can be compared and contrasted with Goldsmith's equally good-natured but pointed farcical portraits of his friends in *Retaliation*. Goldsmith's choice of a metre, anapaestic tetrameters instead of iambic pentameters, indicates that he is not to be taken too seriously, that his tone is that of farce: though farce with a sting. His bookseller (which then also meant his publisher), Kearsley of Fleet Street, explains the circumstances: 'Dr Goldsmith belonged to a club of *beaux esprits*, where wit sparkled sometimes at the expense of good nature. It was proposed to write epitaphs on the Doctor; his country [*Ireland*], dialect and person furnished subjects of witticism. The Doctor was called on for *retaliation*, and at their next meeting produced the following poem, which I think adds one wreath to his immortal wreath.' It is hard to choose among these epitaphs, of which the best are those on Garrick (which has vinegar as well as oil in its dressing) and the wholly friendly, and shorter, epitaph on the great Edmund Burke. I choose the Burke:

> Here lies our good Edmund, whose genius was such,
> We scarcely can praise it or blame it too much;
> Who, born for the universe, narrowed his mind
> And to party gave up what was meant for mankind;
> Though fraught with all learning, yet straining his throat
> To persuade Tommy Townshend to lend him a vote;
> Who, too deep for his hearers, still went on refining,
> And thought of convincing, while they thought of dining;
> Though equal to all things, for all things unfit;
> Too nice for a statesman, too proud for a wit;
> For a patriot too cool; for a drudge, disobedient;
> And too fond of the *right* to pursue the *expedient*.
> In short, 'twas his fate, unemployed or in place, sir,
> To eat mutton cold and cut blocks with a razor.

One has to imagine old-fashioned cut-throat razors and blocks of wood. The Oxford English Dictionary, defines the phrase as 'a metaphor describing absurdly incongruous and futile application of abilities or means'. Cold mutton, which we now relish with mint sauce and salad, was so despised as a dish, as we can learn from Thackeray and early Dickens, that footmen would refuse to eat it. Tommy Townshend was a professional politician whom Goldsmith disliked because he had attacked the grant of a pension to Dr Johnson. Burke is the only man of intellectual genius who ever lent himself to English politics, and whose speeches are still a delight to read. But his Irish accent, his ungraceful posture and delivery, and his tendency to turn a speech into a philosophical lecture earned him the nickname of 'the dinner-bell of the House of Commons' (though there were, in fact, great occasions when he could hold the House). It was one of the felicities of Augustan satire that it could be used, as here, to disguise high and deserved compliment. It could also be used, as in Gray's *On Lord Holland's seat near Margate*, to express an almost savage fury, too grand and too furious to fit in easily with one's ordinary idea of satire. (Henry Fox,

Lord Holland, was a skilful and very good-natured politician, the father of the great gambler and radical Whig,
Charles James Fox, but after he became Paymaster General
in 1757 he used his post to amass a great fortune; and in 1762
as Leader of the House of Commons under Bute he used
bribery lavishly to assure the acceptance of the Peace of
Paris in 1763. Modern historians have defended him as no
more corrupt than most politicians of his time, including Sir
Robert Walpole, later Earl of Orford, the father of Gray's
dear friend Horace Walpole. But Horace and Henry Fox
were at daggers drawn politically and Gray, the loyalest of
friends, adopted Horace's hatreds.)

On Lord Holland's seat near Margate

Old and abandoned by each venal friend,
    Here Holland took the pious resolution
To smuggle some few years, and strive to mend
    A broken character and constitution.

On this congenial spot he fixed his choice,
    Earl Goodwin trembled for his neighbouring sand;
Here sea-gulls scream and cormorants rejoice,
    And mariners, though shipwrecked, dread to land.

Here reign the blustering North and blighting East,
    No tree is heard to whisper, bird to sing,
Yet Nature cannot furnish out the feast,
    Art he invokes new horrors still to bring.

Now moldering fanes and battlements arise,
    Arches and turrets nodding to their fall,
Unpeopled palaces delude his eyes,
    And mimic desolation covers all.

'Ah,' said the sighing peer, 'had Bute been true,
    Nor Shelburne's, Rigby's, Calcraft's friendship vain,
Far other scenes than these had blessed our view,
    And realised the ruins that we feign.

Purged by the sword and beautified by fire,
    Then had we seen proud London's hated walls;
Owls might have hooted in St Peter's choir,
    And foxes stunk and littered in St Paul's.'

'Fox', of course, was Holland's family surname and,
strangely enough, his famous son Charles was notorious for
his carelessness about personal cleanliness (as well as for

gambling madly till he had got rid of exactly the sum his father had appropriated as Paymaster, after which he gave up gambling for ever).

Any good anthology of Augustan poetry will give a wider representation of satire and cite more poets. In the few pages the reader has just finished it has been my wish, choosing (with the exception of Cowper) acknowledgely major poets for examples, to demonstrate how Augustan satire, like the wider Augustan mode of discursive poetry, does not fall into a single mechanical mould. It expresses, certainly, a socially and morally critical mood which was typical of the Augustan age and a readiness to make critical points with witty sharpness. Yet the different personalities of Swift, Pope, Johnson, Goldsmith, Gray dominate, and give in each case a quite individual turn, to the common mode they are using. The greatest critical mistake that can be made about the Augustan age (Matthew Arnold made it most memorably) is to suppose that its greater poets are very like each other and that their poetry, discursive or satirical, has a monotonous sameness.

III Shifts in the Augustan Tradition: Nature, the Past, Sensibility, the Sublime Style

There is no rigid line of division between the Augustan and the Romantic poets, Wordsworth attacked the gaudy and inane phraseology of contemporary writers in his famous *Preface to the Lyrical Ballads*, yet the most distinguished poem in that volume, *Lines Written a Few Miles Above Tintern Abbey*, though free of gaudiness and inanity, is in its tone and dignity typical of the late Augustan period. There are Augustan echoes too in the high conversational diction of poems like Shelley's *Julian and Maddalo* and in Byron's rapid modulation of wit and feeling in *Don Juan*, not unlike Pope's. The Romantic preoccupation with feeling was not new; during the Augustan period the poetry of sensibility and of escape into dream, fantasy and brooding contemplation was enjoying an independent development.

Pope, as a young man, and Swift too, in middle age, had a slight acquaintance with Anne Finch, Countess of Winchilsea (1661–1720) who is perhaps the first English poet, as in her *Petition for an Absolute Retreat*, to be concerned not with the action and situation of the garden retreat she glorifies but with the feeling of peace and serenity that attends that solitude:

> Give me, Oh indulgent fate!
> Give me yet, before I die,
> A sweet, but absolute retreat,
> 'Mongst paths so lost, and trees so high,
> That the world may ne'er invade
> Through such windings and such shade
> My unshaken liberty.
>
> No intruders thither come,
> Who visit but to be from home!
> None who their vain moments pass
> Only studious of their glass;
> News, that charm to list'ning ears,
> That false alarm to hopes and fears,
> That common theme of every fop,
> From the statesmen to the shop,
> In those converts ne'er be spread
> Of who's deceas'd, or who's to wed;
> Be no tidings thither brought
> But silent as a midnight thought:
> Where the world may ne'er invade
> Be those windings and that shade.

It was a period when women were beginning to publish poems and to bring to poetry their own special delicacy: in one poem, *A Circuit of Apollo*, a variation of the old *Sessions of the Poets* theme, in which Apollo has to judge the best living poet, Lady Winchilsea applies the same technique. Apollo laments the death of Aphra Behn,

> And said, amongst females, was not on the earth
> Her superior in fancy, in language, or wit,
> Yet own'd that a little too loosely she writ:
> Since the art of the Muse is to stir up soft thoughts,
> Yet to make all hearts beat without blushes or faults.

Laura attracts Apollo's attention with an elegy for another famous woman poet of the Restoration period, Katherine Philips, 'the matchless Orinda'. He also expresses admiration for Alinda, Valeria, and Ardelia (whom we know from another poem to be Lady Winchilsea herself) but tactfully refuses to give a special crown to any of the four ladies. It was still odd for a woman to write verses and Lady Winchilsea's peculiar delicacy, and her delight in a garden's evening solitude in *A Nocturnal Reverie*:

> When a sedate Content the Spirit feels,
> And no fierce Light disturbs, while it reveals;
> But silent Musings urge the Mind to seek
> Something too high for Syllables to speak,

though they seem to us to anticipate the age of sensibility has very little, if any, direct effect on subsequent poets. Some critics, however, have noted the contrast between the quiet delicate loveliness of her refusal to busy herself with pointless embroidery,

> Nor will in fading silks compose
> Faintly the inimitable rose,

and Pope's condensed and dramatic line, perhaps suggested by that couplet,

> Die of a rose in aromatic pain.

The poet of nature who was widely read in Pope's time, the Scotsman James Thomson (1700–48), lacked her *finesse* but had much more energy. His *The Seasons*, Hazlitt tells us, was still a century later the book likely to be lying by the ingle-nook of an inn. The ordinary reader would appreciate at once the innocent sensuousness of the tale of Damon and Musidora from *Summer*:

> She felt his flame; but deep within her breast,
> In bashful coyness, or in maiden pride,
> The soft return concealed; save when it stole
> In side-long glances from her downcast eye,
> Or from her swelling soul in stifled sighs.
> Touched by the scene, no stranger to his vows,
> He framed a melting lay, to try her heart;
> And, if an infant passion struggled there,
> To call that passion forth. Thrice-happy swain!
> A lucky chance, that oft decides the fate
> Of mighty monarchs, then decided thine.

For lo! conducted by the laughing Loves,
This cool retreat his Musidora sought;
Warm in her cheek the sultry season glowed;
And, robed in loose array, she came to bathe
Her fervent limbs in the refreshing stream.
What shall he do? In sweet confusion lost,
And dubious flutterings, he a while remained,
A pure ingenuous elegance of soul,
A delicate refinement known to few,
Perplexed his breast and urged him to retire.
But love forbade. Ye prudes in virtue, say,
Say, ye severest what would you have done?

What Damon does is to stay, concealed by the 'bending willows' and watch Musidora, described with formal propriety of language but with relishing detail, strip and swim. But sheer embarrassment overcomes him and he leaves a modest message on the bank, and retreats:

> . . . 'Bathe on, my fair,
> Yet unbeheld save by the sacred eye
> Of faithful love. I go to guard thy haunt;
> To keep from thy recess each vagrant foot,
> And each licentious eye.'

Musidora, emerges from the water, and clutches the 'alarming paper' but her feelings, at first mixed, are at least favourable. She inscribes on the 'spreading beech' that hangs over the stream:

> 'Dear youth! sole judge of what these verses mean,
> By Fortune too much favoured, but by Love
> Alas! not favoured less, be still as now
> Discreet; the time may come you need not fly.'

Thomson is little read to-day: his blank verse, though, as Johnson noted, original and quite unMiltonic robs his rural scenes both of Pope's bright-coloured artificial vividness and Crabbe's harsh realism. Though he can be considered in some ways a precursor of the Romantics, his very generalised descriptions of natural scenery corresponded to Imlac's advice about making one's depiction of nature broad and obvious. Yet there is a certain warmth and eagerness of feeling, a broad simplicity, about the Damon-Musidora passage which a good-natured reader of catholic tastes may still find attractive. His comic imitation of Spenser, *The Castle of Indolence*, shows a humour and a power of individual portraiture not found in *The Seasons*. It looks forward, also, to the Gothic taste for the Middle Ages which became so important in the second half of the century. His early and unpoetic death in 1748 (of a violent purgative which he took, against the advice of his doctor, to cure a colic brought on by a surfeit of summer fruit) robbed us perhaps of a deeper development of his talent.

When one turns to Cowper one is aware of a far deeper and finer strain of feeling. This passage, about his conversion by John Newton, is deservedly famous for its religious authenticity though it is impossible to read these lines from *The Task* without reflecting that the naturally timid Cowper lost the assurance of salvation which Newton had helped to give and spent his latter days, civil and cheerful in their outward appearance, tormented every night by the horrors of religious despair. Religious melancholy and even madness are so common among the poets of the latter half of the eighteenth century that one sometimes wishes that Arnold's fatuous picture of a cheerful and shallow 'age of prose and reason' had more truth in it:

> I was a stricken deer that left the herd
> Long since; with many an arrow deep infixed
> My panting side was charged, when I withdrew
> To seek a tranquil death in distant shades.
> There was I found by One who had Himself
> Been hurt by the archers. In His side He bore,
> And in His hands and feet, the cruel scars,
> With gentle force soliciting the darts,
> He drew them forth, and healed and bade me live.

The situation and event, the sense of hopeless dereliction and of rescue by a Saviour who is the mirror image of one's own suffering, are dramatic enough: but we read the passage more deeply if we concentrate, as Wordsworth prescribes for the sort of poetry he approves of, with our attention primarily fixed on Cowper's feelings: the horror of pain and the joy of salvation, through Christ's pain, both under such extraordinary strict control.

The contrast with Thomson (who would have been incap-

able of these feelings) is more obvious in the first book of
The Task, where, in a diction that has still here and there
something of Thomson's Latinate dignity, Cowper shows a
precision of observation (and conveys a sense of personal
delight of the scene) of which Thomson was incapable:

> Here the grey smooth trunks
> Of ash, or lime, or beech, distinctly shine,
> Within the twilight of their distant shades;
> There lost behind a rising ground, the wood
> Seems sunk, and shortened to its topmost boughs.
> No tree in all the grove but has its charms,
> Though each its hue peculiar; paler some,
> And of a wannish grey; the willows such,
> And poplar that with silver lines his leaf,
> And ash far stretching his umbrageous arm;
> Of deeper green the elm; and deeper still,
> Lord of the woods, the long-surviving oak,
> Some glossy-leaved, and shining in the sun,
> The maple, and the beech of oily nuts
> Prolific, and the lime at dewy eve
> Diffusing odours: nor unnoted pass
> The sycamore, capricious in attire,
> Now green, now tawny, and ere autumn yet
> Have changed the woods, in scarlet honours bright
> O'er these, but far beyond (a spacious map
> Of hill and valley interposed between).
> The Ouse, dividing the well-watered land,
> Now glitters in the sun, and now retires,
> As bashful, yet impatient to be seen.

No critic would number Cowper among our greatest poets:
yet, in such a passage as this, especially with a reader who
has a taste and eye for the fine shades of a country
landscape, he may seem among our most comforting, or
comfortable, poets. But such a critic might then remember
the frightening early *Lines Written Under the Influence of
Delirium*,

> Hatred and vengeance, – my eternal portion
> Scarce can endure delay of execution, –
> Wait with impatient readiness to seize my
> Soul in a moment,

and the more frightening (because in tone calm and re-

signed) last two stanzas of the late *The Castaway*: I give also
the third-last stanza, to indicate the example (a worthy sailor
washed overboard on an Atlantic voyage with the heroic
Anson) from which Cowper took his theme:

> No poet wept him; but the page
>   Of narrative sincere,
> That tells his name, his worth, his age
>   Is wet with Anson's tear:
> And tears by bards or heroes shed
> Alike immortalize the dead.
>
> I therefore purpose not, or dream,
>   Descanting on his fate,
> To give the melancholy theme
>   A more enduring date;
> But misery still delights to trace
> Its semblance in another's case.
>
> No voice divine the storm allay'd,
>   No light propitious shone;
> When, snatched from all effectual aid,
>   We perish'd, each alone:
> But I beneath a rougher sea,
> And whelmed in deeper gulfs than he.

Again, the intensity of the feeling is Romantic; yet the quiet
courtesy, the lack of any hysteria, with which Cowper in the
last two lines refers to his calm conviction of his own eternal
damnation exemplifies the strict Augustan tradition at its
noblest. In the history of poetry one prevailing mood almost
insensibly modulates towards its opposite. It is not a case of
a sudden starting pistol in 1798, Wordsworth and Coleridge
at the starting line poised for the race: and, lo and behold,
with *Lyrical Ballads*, Augustan poetry vanishes and the
Romantic movement is in full swing. Change is in the air
before it is noticed or defined; and old conventions (as in
Crabbe's case), when their day is supposed to be over, show
a remarkable continuity of toughness.

Romanticism, however, is not a concept that even the
greatest of our Romantic poets, Wordsworth, has been able
fully to define. He has nothing to say about what I will call
word-magic, though, for instance, in the strange and mysterious Lucy poems, he sometimes exemplifies it himself. I

mean by word-magic a use of language in which the shaping of the lines and stanzas, the choice of words, the vividness of the images which the words call up in us, move us much more than the mere sense, and suggest, indeed, a deeper sense than is expressed. We find this word-magic among the poets in a different mode who follow Pope, notably in Gray and Collins. William Empson has referred to Gray's *Elegy* as a plea for leaving things socially as they are, seeking to persuade both the poor themselves, if they could read him, and the more comfortably off, who may be occasionally troubled by the rough life and sparse comfort of the rural labourer, that the poor are, on the whole, lucky, for if genius expires among them, neither is it exposed to the temptations of the world. Gray, like all the better minds of his century, whether Whig, like himself, or Tory, was socially a conservative and quite untainted with 'democracy': a word which was used by Dryden as we use 'anarchy', and in the time of the French Revolution by George Canning as old-fashioned Tories once used 'Bolshevik'. Before we denounce conservatism in the Augustan age, certainly reflected in its poetry, we should notice that it saved us from the equivalents of the French Revolution and the revolutions of 1830 and 1848: and that, unlike the countries of Europe which enjoyed these experiences, we can boast of a steady progress, without internal violence, towards greater individual and social liberty.

Gray, in any case, was not a man without pity or feeling for thwarted opportunity; it was by scholarship and charm that, from a very humble background, he made his way to Eton, to the friendship of Horace Walpole (a friendship which, largely because of his own touchy pride, was broken off for several years), and to what amounted to a sinecure at Cambridge (as Professor of History, he never gave a lecture, and, though he accumulated some rough notes for a history of English poetry, never began to write this work). All this success could not cure his natural loneliness and constitutional melancholy, but it certainly prevents the *Elegy Written in a Country Churchyard* from seeming smug. One can feel that he is almost guilty about his own success compared to what he feels about his imaginary obscure rustic genius:

But Knowledge to their eyes her ample page

> Rich with the spoils of time did ne'er unroll;
> Chill Penury repress'd their noble rage,
> And froze the genial current of the soul.
>
> Full many a gem of purest ray serene,
> The dark unfathom'd caves of ocean bear;
> Full many a flower is born to blush unseen,
> And waste its sweetness on the desert air.

Excellent as the Augustan moral weight of that first stanza is, it is the second stanza which startles us with its word-magic. It is, of course, a metaphor, of which the tenor is the existence of much obscure, hidden genius: but it is the vehicle of the metaphor, the shining gem hidden in the deep, dark ocean cave, the flower squandering its sweetness in the desert, that haunts us with its beauty. We remember the stanza, after a single reading, when we have forgotten what the metaphor refers to. It becomes more than a metaphor, it becomes a symbol, embodying all that we feel about beauty hidden and wasted and yet deriving, from that very fact, a greater preciousness. The word-magic of Romantic poetry, which Gray anticipates here, is a magic that conveys a kind of profound meaning to the inner feelings, a meaning that cannot be expressed in abstract words. The meaning, too, seems to be crystallised in the very shape of the poem (like the meaning of one of the great triumphs of this kind of language in our poetry, Coleridge's *Kubla Khan*) rather than to refer to any tangible or actual world outside the strange suggestiveness of the words.

In Gray's most famous poems, the Pindaric odes, *The Progress of Poesy* and *The Bard*, a modern reader, while admiring their experimental skill, might reluctantly agree with Dr Johnson in finding a certain stilted artificiality. I find more of the quality that really attracts me to Gray in earlier poems like *Ode on the Spring*,

> Lo! where the rosy-bosomed Hours,
> Fair Venus' train, appear,
> Disclose the long-expecting flowers,
> And wake the purple year!
> The Attic warbler pours her throat,
> Responsive to the cuckoo's note,
> The untaught harmony of spring:

> While whispering pleasure as they fly,
> Cool zephyrs through the clear blue sky
> Their gathered fragrance fling . . .

or the unfinished late *Ode on the Pleasure Arising from Vicissitude* (the title is that of Gray's friend Mason who also, with the aid of four lines from a commonplace book of Gray's, and with the advice of Gray's friends, attempted to expand and complete the poem: but the lines printed here are Gray's own):

> Now the golden Morn aloft
> Waves her dew-bespangled wing;
> With vermeil cheek and whisper soft
> She wooes the tardy spring,
> Till April starts, and calls around
> The sleeping fragrance from the ground;
> And lightly o'er the living scene
> Scatters his freshest, tenderest green.
>
> New-born flocks in rustic dance
> Frisking ply their feeble feet;
> Forgetful of their wintry trance
> The birds his presence greet:
> But chief the sky-lark warbles high
> His trembling thrilling ecstasy
> And, lessening from the dazzled sight,
> Melts into air and liquid light.
>
> Yesterday the sullen year
> Saw the snowy whirlwind fly;
> Mute was the music of the air,
> The herd stood drooping by:
> Their raptures now that wildly flow,
> No yesterday nor morrow know;
> 'Tis man alone that joy descries
> With forward or reverted eyes.

It is interesting that, as in the quotation from *Spring* we found Keat's nightingale and Wordsworth's cuckoo, here we find Shelley's skylark. For Wordsworth, of course, Gray, a poet writing for poets (he is full of echoes of Milton and Dryden), was the opposite of Wordsworth's ideal of a man writing for men. Quoting in his famous Preface, Gray's

Sonnet on the Death of Mr Richard West, Wordsworth speaks of Gray as being 'at the head of those who by their reasonings have attempted to widen the space of separation betwixt Prose and Metrical Composition, and was more than any other man curiously elaborate in the structure of his own poetic diction.' He then quotes the West sonnet, finding its only merit in these five lines, which 'except in the rhyme, and in the use of the single word "fruitless" for "fruitlessly", which is so far a defect,' in their language 'in no respect differ from that of prose':

> A different object do these eyes require.
> My lonely anguish melts no heart but mine;
> And in my breast the imperfect joys expire . . .
>
> I fruitless mourn to him that cannot hear,
> And weep the more because I weep in vain.

Roger Lonsdale in his excellent annotated edition of Gray, Collins, and Goldsmith suggests that Gray was inspired by a sad poem of West's, written shortly before his early death, in which West, assured that nature will be indifferent to his death, hopes that a friend at least will remember him. The description of nature is therefore deliberately ornate and artificial, though I am surprised that Wordsworth did not find the third last line,

> 'To warm their little loves the birds complain'

beautiful. And both the syntactical order, object before subject, of

> 'A different object do these eyes require,'

and the antitheses of the last two lines are unprosaic:

> I fruitless mourn to him that cannot hear,
> And weep the more because I weep in vain.

'Fruitless' was a permissible Latinism but I would be willing to take it as 'Fruitless I' – 'I in my barrenness can produce nothing to nourish my dead friend', in a direct adjectival sense. What is very interesting is that the same archaic diction that was rejected by the greatest of Augustan critics, Dr Johnson,

> Wheresoe'er I turn my View,
> All is strange, yet nothing new;
> Endless Labour all along,
> Endless Labour to be wrong;
> Phrase that Time has flung away,
> Uncouth Words in Disarray:
> Trickt in Antique Ruff and Bonnet,
> Ode and Elegy and Sonnet,

should be rejected by the greatest theorist (Coleridge was the greatest critic) among the Romantics, Wordsworth.

Johnson was a personal friend of William Collins (1721–59) whose life was a particularly sad one. Collins, after inheriting from an uncle a sum that assured him of a modest independence, fell into a habitual melancholy which became madness, but of a violent sort; his younger sister Anne removed him in 1754 from a private madhouse at Chelsea, and looked after him lovingly. Between 1751 and 1754 he travelled in France, in a vain attempt to restore his strength and spirits; Johnson met him at Islington on his return and found that the only book this learned man now possessed was an English New Testament: '*I have but one book*, said Collins, *but that is the best.*' Collins's poetry was not of a kind that Johnson could take much pleasure in, but he tries to be fair:

> He had employed his mind chiefly upon works of fiction, and subjects of fancy . . . He loved fairies, genii, giants, and monsters; he delighted to rove through the meanders of enchantment, to gaze on the magnificence of golden palaces, to repose by the water-falls of Elysian gardens. This was, however, the character rather of his inclination than his genius; the grandeur of wildness, and the novelty of extravagance, were always desired by him, but were not always attained. Yet as diligence is never wholly lost, if his efforts sometimes caused harshness and obscurity, they likewise produced in happier moments sublimity and splendour.

It is not Collins's exercises in fancy, like the *Persian Eclogues*, that are most admired now. Perhaps his most famous and most beautiful poem is the *Ode to Evening*, one of the finest unrhymed lyrical poems (only Tennyson, perhaps, has excelled Collins in this mode) in the English language, metrically modelled on Milton's version of Horace's 'Pyrrha' ode, and in diction and feeling owing something to Milton's *Il Penseroso*. I quote a fragment:

> Now air is hush'd, save where the weak-ey'd bat
> With short shrill Shriek flits by on leathern Wing,
>   Or where the Beetle winds
>   His small but sullen Horn,
> As oft he rises mid the twilight Path,
> Against the pilgrim borne in heedless Hum:
>   Now teach me, Maid composed,
>   To breathe some softened Strain,
> Whose numbers stealing through thy dark'ning vale,
> May not unseemly with its stillness suit,
>   As musing slow, I hail
>   Thy genial lov'd Return.

Collins's odes tend to be more abstract and more difficult than Gray's, and Lonsdale describes the *Ode on the Poetical Character*, particularly its second section, as the most 'controversial' of all Collins's poems. The following section in particular has been taken by Northrop Frye and Harold Bloom as anticipating Blake's mythology – God as begetting the Poet, by a sexual act, on a Fancy who in the first section has already been personified as female:

> The Band, as Fairy Legends say,
> Was wove on that creating Day
> When He, who called with Thought to Birth
> Yon tented Sky, this laughing Earth,
> And dressed with Springs and Forests tall,
> And pour'd the Main engirting all,
> Long by the loved *Enthusiast* woo'd,
> Himself, in some Diviner Mood,
> Retiring, sat with her alone,
> And placed her on his Sapphire Throne,
> The whiles, the vaulted Shrine around,
> Seraphic Wires were heard to sound,
> Now sublimest Triumph swelling,
> Now on love and mercy dwelling;
> And she, from out the veiling Cloud,
> Breathed her magic Notes aloud:

And Thou, Thou rich-haired Youth of Morn,
And all thy subject life was born!
The dangerous Passions kept aloof,
Far from the sainted growing Woof,
But near it sate ecstatic *Wonder*,
List'ning the deep applauding Thunder;
And *Truth*, in sunny Vest array'd,
By whose the Tarsel's eyes were made;   *male*
All the shad'wy tribes of *Mind*   *hawk's*
In braided Dance their Murmurs joined,
And all the bright uncounted *Pow'rs*,
Who feed on Heav'n's ambrosial Flow'rs.
Where is the Bard, whose Soul can now
Its high presuming Hopes avow?
Where He who thinks, with rapture blind,
This hallowed Work for Him designed?

Lonsdale dislikes the idea of a sexual union between God (even a God surely pagan rather than Christian, capable of some 'diviner mood') and sees Collins as describing 'the imaginative act of creation by which God, through the embodiment of his "Fancy", himself became the supreme type of the poet'. He does not seem to me to strengthen this argument by seeing – one would say correctly – the 'rich-haired youth of morn' as the Sun or Apollo, also the god and type of poetry. This is a difficult passage but it becomes more difficult still if one tries to make it feel Christian: it may have been remorse for dallying with such 'false surmise' that led Collins, later, to melancholy and madness.

It seems to me to have been Collins even more than Gray who led the self-educated young genius, William Blake (1757–1827) to the delicate imitation of the styles and themes of the sixteenth and seventeenth century in his first collection, *Poetical Sketches* (1783). The only volume of Blake's to be printed rather than engraved, it came out in a tiny edition, for distribution privately among friends, of fifty copies. In its imitations, it demonstrates more strikingly than anything else of Blake's the range of his skill and the delicacy of his lyric sense. Either Collins or Gray would have admired it and seen in the young Blake (mistakenly) a successor of their own elaborately literary and deliberately reminiscent, styles. But even while he was learning from them, the young Blake (who will be dealt with in more detail in the next chapter) was aware that they were cultivating delicacy at the expense of vigour. The lovely poem that follows, *To the Muses*, is at once like a tribute to Gray and Collins for what they did and a lament for what they failed to do:

To the Muses

Whether on Ida's shady brow,
  Or in the chambers of the east,
The chambers of the sun, that now
  From ancient melody have ceased;

Whether in heaven ye wander fair,
  Or the green corners of the earth,
Or the blue regions of the air,
  Where the melodious winds have birth;

Whether on crystal rocks ye rove,
  Beneath the bosom of the sea
Wandering in many a coral grove,
  Fair Nine, forsaking poetry!

How have you left the ancient love
  That bards of old enjoyed in you!
The languid strings do scarcely move,
  The sound is forced, the notes are few.

Ida, of course, is the mountain in Greece which was the home of the Muses, and the reference to the 'chamber of the east' may refer to Persian and Indian poetry, which Sir William Jones's translations were popularising in the late eighteenth century.

But though the last quarter of the century saw several masterpieces – the completion of Gibbon's *Decline and Fall of the Roman Empire* and the beginning of the several sketches of his posthumously published autiobiography; Boswell's book on his jaunt to the Western isles with Johnson and his great *Life*; and Burke's *Reflections on the French Revolution* – the two modes for which the century is most famous, the novel and poetry, seemed to be decaying. Wordsworth (1770–1850) and Coleridge (1772–1834) were seeking new forms and themes well before the turn of the century, but did not find their voice till the *Lyrical Ballads* of 1798 and 1800. Blake's revolution was more complete but, owing to his humble and private social station, almost

(except for a few disciples like Samuel Palmer, more influenced by his art than his poetry) hardly known. It was
Wordsworth and Coleridge, to be dealt with in the next
chapter, who are to be considered the real founding fathers
of English nineteenth-century poetry. Their triumph led to a
general critical rejection of the eighteenth century, which I
hope the brief treatment of that century in this chapter has
proved unjust. Yet, for a poet, the eighteenth century was
possibly an excessively sedate century; and it was the
promise of change, offered first by the French Revolution,
then by the philosophy of Godwin, and then both by the
sense of something 'far more deeply interfused' in nature,
the immanence of the divine, and the sense of the dignity
not only of the speech but of the lives of the shepherds and
farmers of the Lake District that enabled Wordsworth to
bring into English poetry the ring of change and the voice of
'a man speaking to men'. The more wildly imaginative and
more melancholy and inward-turned Coleridge was to make
a grand imaginative use of fantasy and legend, and to
explore the depths and miseries of the inner self, in another
way that was new in English poetry. Conservatives who
precede a great and successful literary revolution (and such
were the strict Augustans compared to the Romantics) have
to wait sometimes for a century or two till justice begins to
be done to them.

IV The Scottish Vernacular Tradition, Till Burns

In 1603, King James VI of Scotland became also King James
I of England. Though Dunbar and Henryson had not been
succeeded by any poets of similar greatness, lyrical poetry in
Scots had continued to flourish throughout the sixteenth
century and broad Scots was still the language of the court
and the law. But James's most notable courtiers followed
him to England, and even country gentlemen who stayed at
home, like Ben Jonson's host, Drummond of Hawthornden, wrote in English, in a slightly old-fashioned Elizabethan style. English was also the language of the great
soldier, first for the Covenant and then for the King, the
Marquis of Montrose. Scots, in so far as it survived, became
a vernacular language, for comic pastoral, as by Robert
Sempill, Laird of Beltrees, in his famous *The Life and Death*

of Habbie Simson, the Piper of Kilbarchan, the first really popular Scots poem in what was to become known as the Burns stanza (and in Burn's own time would have been called 'standard Habbie'):

> Kilbarchan now may say alas!
> For she hath lost her game and grace,
> Both *Trixie* and *The Maiden Trace*;   *names of tunes*
>   But what remead?
> For no man can supply his place:
>   Hab Simson's deid.

Sempill (1590–1660) was long-lived but is little known but for this one poem. He founded a style, however, and William Hamilton, Laird of Gilbertfield (1665–1751), though a couple of generations younger, seems exactly to echo him in the tone as well as the stanza of *The Last Dying Words of Bonnie Heck, a famous Grey-hound in the Shire of Fife*:

> Alas, alas, quo' bonnie Heck,
> On former days when I reflec';
> I was a dog much in respec'
>   For doughty deed:
> But now I must hing by the neck
>   Without remeid.

The regret which both poems echo is for a lusty, rustic, traditional way of life, a life of pipe-playing, hunting, greyhound racing, which the social, political, and religious changes of a century have put out of fashion. The two lairds look back sadly on a heartier, simpler way of life.

It was a man of humbler origins, Allan Ramsay the Edinburgh bookseller and publisher (1686–1758) who was to do more, by his own poems, and by publishing editions (modernised and inaccurate) of some of the older Scottish poets who was to put Scottish poetry, at least in Edinburgh, back on the map. (The gentry, of course, now on the whole avoided broad Scots, and King James's Bible had made standard Southern English understandable from every pulpit.) He tried to adapt, not wholly unsuccessfully, the traditions of the more idealistic kind of English pastoral to the rough climate of the north:

The lass of Patie's Mill,
So bonny, blyth, and gay,
In spite of all my skill,
She stole my heart away.
When tedding of the hay
Bare-headed on the green,
Love 'midst her locks did play,
And wanton'd in her een.

Her arms white, round and smooth,
Breasts rising in their dawn,
To age it wou'd give youth,
To press 'em with his hand.
Thro' all my spirits ran
An extasy of bliss,
When I such sweetness fand
Wrapt in a balmy kiss.

Robert Fergusson (1750–74) was a far more realistic, piercing, and intelligent poet. Born in Edinburgh of Aberdeenshire parents, he has a sophisticated, satirical sense of town life which his greater successor, Burns, never acquired: and, unlike Burns, he has no pose of rustic simplicity. He had a good education, at Edinburgh High School where he won a bursary which took him first to Dundee Grammar School and then to St Andrews University, which he left without taking a degree, becoming a copying clerk in Edinburgh to support his widowed mother. Edinburgh, where he made congenial friends, inspired his best poems; but he had a mental breakdown in 1774 and died in the same year, his promise suggested but not fulfilled, in Edinburgh Bedlam. As an urban rather than a rustic poet he might have founded a tradition in a way that Burns, for all his greatness, failed to do. Fergusson was, at least, as David Daiches has put it 'the only Scots poet of his century to be able to look contemporary civilisation in the eye'. One can see his sophistication in *Braid Claith*, a poem on the theme that clothes make the man:

For thof ye had as wise a snout on
As *Shakespeare* or *Sir Isaac Newton*,
Your judgment fouk wou'd hae a doubt on,   *folk*
  I'll tak my aith.
Till they could see ye wi' a suit on
  O' gude Braid Claith.   *Broad Cloth*

In *The Daft Days*, Fergusson deals splendidly with an old Scots theme, the sharpness of a Scottish winter and the sociability in which Scotsmen find consolation for that:

Now mirk December's dowie face	*dark gloomy*
Glours our the rigs wi' sour grimace,	*glowers, ridges*
While, thro' his *minimum* of space,	
The bleer-eyed sun,	
Wi' blinkin light and stealing pace,	
His race doth run.	

From naked groves nae birdie sings,
To shepherd's pipe nae hillock rings,
The breeze nae od'rous flavour brings
   From *Borean* cave,
And dwyning nature droops her wings,
   Wi' visage grave,

Mankind but scanty pleasure glean	
Fraw snawy hill or barren plain,	
Whan Winter, 'midst his nipping train,	
Wi' frozen spear,	
Sends drift ower a' his bleak domain,	
And guides the weir.	*war*

Auld Reikie! thou'rt the canty hole,	*comfortable*
A bield for mony a caldrife soul,	*shelter, shivering*
Wha snugly at thine ingle loll,	
Baith warm and couth;	*at ease*
While round they gar the bicker roll	*beaker*
To weet their mouth.	*wet*

The contrast of cold and comfort is delightful (Auld Reekie, Old Smokie, is of course Edinburgh).

    Fergusson and Burns have this in common at least, that they have a kind of plain, earthy directness that is not to be found in any of the English poets of the eighteenth century. Scotland was a poorer and simpler country than England, the manners of the poor and the local lairds who (by Scottish rather than English standards) were the rich was not so very different. They mixed socially and easily in taverns in a way that was not common in England, and were not so very different in education. Burns tells us in a long letter to Dr

John Moore (a London-Scots literary exile) how when he was fifteen the pretty girl who worked alongside him in the harvest field used to sing at her work and how one of her songs

> was said to be composed by a small country laird's son, on one of his father's maids, with whom he was in love; and I saw no reason why I might not rhyme as well as he, for excepting smearing sheep and casting peats, his father living in the moors, he has no more Scholarcraft than I.

Burns therefore was, by breeding and observation, unlike any English poet of his time, a believer in human equality. His life, as a boy, had been a life of toil on his father's small Ayrshire farm and later, unsuccessfully, on a small farm of his own at Mossgiel. He decided to go to the West Indies as an overseer of slaves, but first published at Kilmarnock his early poems; they were very well received indeed and he enjoyed a short period of lionising in Edinburgh. But his marriage to his early love, Jean Armour (her father, thinking him a wild young man, had made her destroy her marriage lines) set him to work again, first combining the tasks of a small farmer and an exciseman, and then solely as an exciseman. Like many Scotsmen of his time he was a heavy drinker and he was rarely, if ever, out of love. Referring to his affair with an inn-keeper's daughter, Anna Park, whose illegitimate child she brought up with her own, Jean Armour, a patient woman, said: 'Our Robbie should hae twa wives'. It was not dissipation of any kind that killed him at thirty-nine; it was rather a constitution ruined by too much physical work from late childhood on and the folly of a doctor who recommended deep sea-bathing as a remedy for a weak heart. To the last, Burns was busy writing; his longer and more ambitious poems belong to the time before his Kilmarnock volume and to his period of comparative leisure in Edinburgh. His songs, written for two Edinburgh collections, were either adaptations of old Scots folk songs or new words for old tunes: he could have been well paid for this labour but he felt it his patriotic duty to offer this service to the Scottish folk-song tradition free. As Kinsley has said, he served Scottish poetry in two ways: as a great original poet,

particularly in a humorous and satirical vein, and as a kind
of living museum of the older Scots folk-song tradition.

His comic satirical gifts are brilliantly displayed in *Holy
Willie's Prayer* in which he satirises the 'Auld Lichts', the old
hard-line Calivinists of the Church of Scotland with their
detailed supervision of the morals and sexual habits of every
parish (Burns himself belonged to the more moderate
liberal wing of the Church.) *The Twa Dogs* and *The Cottar's
Saturday Night* assert the essential worth and decency of the
ordinary man. Burns's great strength as a lyric and comic
poet lay in his grasp of the plain and permanent things in
human nature; his was an earthiness of the best kind
drawing poetry from the life around him, handling words
with a flickering skill veering easily from comic to serious
and back again.

He was fearless in affirming frankly and fiercely his belief
in liberty; his sympathy with the French Revolution sprang
from his belief in the dignity of man, of all men, so boldly
expressed in the famous *A Man's a Man for a' That*. His
fiercely expressed approval of the executions of Louis XVI
and Marie Antoinette so offended his old friend, Mrs
Dunlop, that it almost cost him her friendship; he was
genuinely surprised when she cut short their correspon
dence. These are his words on that historic event in a letter
to her of 1795:

> What is there in the delivering over a perjured Blockhead &
> an unprincipled Prostitute to the hands of the hangman, that
> it should arrest for a moment, attention, in an eventful hour
> when, as my friend Roscoe in Liverpool gloriously expressed
> it –
> > When the welfare of Millions is hung in the scale
> > And the balance yet trembles with fate!

He was thought too radical for an exciseman but saved his
job by joining the Volunteers and writing a patriotic song for
them, in which, however, the radical still creeps in:

> Who will not sing, *God save the king*,
>   Shall hang as high's the steeple;
> But while we sing *God save the king*,
>   We'll ne'er forget the people.

Burns is at his best, however, in his lyrics which express the simple truths of the heart, as in one of his earliest songs, *Mary Morison* –

> Yestreen, when to the trembling string
>   The dance gaed thro' the light ha',
> To thee, my fancy took its wing,
>   I sat, but neither heard or saw:
> Tho' this was fair, and that was braw,   *handsome*
>   And yon the toast of a' the town,
> I sigh'd and said amang them a': –
>   'Ye are na Mary Morison!'

– and in his broad humour, as in his one tale (of almost Chaucerian excellence) *Tam o'Shanter*:

> When chapman billies leave the street   *pedlar fellows*
> And drouthy neebors neebors meet;   *thirsty*
> As market-days are wearing late,
> An' folk begin to tak the gate: *way home*
> While we sit bousing at the nappy,   *boozing, ale*
> An' getting fou and unco happy   *full (of drink): very*
> We think na on the lang Scots miles,
> The mosses, waters, slaps, and styles,   *breaches*
> That lie between us and our hame,
> Whare sits our sulky, sullen dame,
> Gathering her brows like gathering storm,
> Nursing her wrath to keep it warm . . .

Or in the shrewd practical advice of the verse epistles, like *Epistle to a Young Friend* (the epistles are Burn's nearest equivalent to the Augustan discursive style, but in their homely direct intimacy not in the least derived from that):

> The sacred lowe o' well-plac'd love,   *flame*
>   Luxuriantly indulge it;
> But never tempt th' illicit rove,
>   Tho'naething should divulge it:
> I waive the quantum o' the sin,
>   The hazard of concealing;
> But, och! it hardens a' within,
>   And petrifies the feeling! . . .
>
> The fear o' Hell's a hangman's whip
>   To haud the wretch in order;

> But where ye feel your honour grip,
>   Let that ay be your border:
> Its slightest touches, instant pause –
>   Debar a' side-pretences;
> And resolutely keep its laws,
>   Uncaring consequences.

The last stanza shows that Burns, unlike any important English poet of his time, was essentially a Deist. His great satire *Holy Willie's Prayer* shows his intellectual and moral contempt for the Scots Calvinism of his time. He was not, however, an atheist: perhaps a touch of caution held him back:

> An atheist laugh's a puir exchange
>   For Deity offended!

Of all the poets of this island, of his century, Burns has been most widely praised, and translated. Wordsworth, who shared none of his weaknesses, nevertheless adored him, perhaps for his plainness, honesty, and directness, another 'man speaking to men'. Yet with his realistic and direct view of life nobody would call him a pre-Romantic.

9

The Nineteenth Century

I The Founding Fathers of Romanticism: Wordsworth, Coleridge, Blake

The Romantic movement in English poetry resists easy definition. Perhaps what enables us to distinguish English Romantic poetry, so various in itself, from both the pure Augustan and the Victorian modes is a mark noted by Wordsworth in his famous *Preface to the Lyrical Ballads*, and applying, I think, not only to his own poems:

> . . . but it is proper that I should mention one other circumstance which distinguishes these poems from the popular poetry of the day; it is this, that the feeling therein developed gives importance to the action and situation, and not the action and situation to the feeling.

I think this neglected sentence is the most important of many important sentences in Wordsworth's *Preface*, though it is the least often quoted. What all the English Romantic poets have in common (one would except Sir Walter Scott who is essentially a storyteller in verse) is a preoccupation with feeling rather than action. It seems to me also to be the case that the Romantic poets, especially if one contrasts them with the Augustans, are extremely subjective, more preoccupied, in a way that is new in poetry, with the growth of the inner sensibility than with outer social observation. This is true even of a narrative poem like Coleridge's *The Ancient Mariner*. The mariner, struck into a fit of deadness by his arbitrary act in killing the albatross, is particularly

205

appalled by the contrast between his fellow mariners who lie
dead beside him and the horrible living water snakes crawl-
ing on the sea:

> The many men, so beautiful!
> And they all dead did lie:
> And a thousand thousand slimy things
> Lived on; and so did I.
>
> I looked upon the rotting sea,
> And drew my eyes away;
> I looked upon the rotting deck,
> And there the dead men lay.

Yet the mariner begins to find his salvation when he begins
to look on the 'slimy things' as creatures of strange beauty:

> Beyond the shadow of the ship,
> I watched the water-snakes:
> They moved in tracks of shining white,
> And when they reared, the elfish light
> Fell off in hoary flakes.
>
> Within the shadow of the ship
> I watched their rich attire:
> Blue, glossy green, and velvet black,
> They coiled and swam; and every track
> Was a flash of golden fire.
>
> O happy living things! no tongue
> Their beauty might declare:
> A spring of love gushed from my heart,
> And I blessed them unaware:
> Sure my kind saint took pity on me,
> And I blessed them unaware.
>
> The self-same moment I could pray;
> And from my neck so free
> The Albatross fell off, and sank
> Like lead into the sea.

The intense action is interior (the albatross around the
mariner's neck is an emblem of an inner state, like Christian's burden in Bunyan's *The Pilgrim's Progress*).

If a story-poem like *The Ancient Mariner* is most deeply the expression of a subjective state, a great personal poem, *Dejection: An Ode*, is not merely 'lyrical' but also in a sense a 'ballad'. Under the guise of meditative discourse, it tells a story, of a painfully intimate sort. In 1795, under the influence of his friend Southey, Coleridge had married a milliner from Bath, Sarah Fricker; she was not a bad woman, but of limited education and conventional views, anxious that her husband should have regular employment. His friendship with Wordsworth becamse intense in 1797, when Wordsworth was living near his home at Nether Stowey, Somerset, and through Wordsworth he met Sarah Hutchinson (the sister of Wordsworth's future wife, Mary) and fell hopelessly in love with her. *The Ancient Mariner* was written in 1797, *Dejection: An Ode* (of which there is also a more intimate version in the form of a verse epistle) in 1802. It is almost like *The Ancient Mariner* in reverse. Coleridge sees beauty but he cannot bless it:

> . . . All this long eve, so balmy and serene,
> Have I been gazing on the western sky,
> 　And its peculiar tint of yellow green:
> And still I gaze – and with how blank an eye!
> And those thin clouds above, in flakes and bars,
> That give away their motion to the stars . . .
> Yon crescent Moon, as fixed as if it grew
> In its own cloudless, starless lake of blue;
> I see them all so excellently fair,
> I see, not feel, how beautiful they are!

The failure of feeling, the seeking for a refuge in 'abstruse research', in German metaphysics, are all due to his need to love – a need the proper outlet for which was stifled in Coleridge. He was not able to console himself with Wordsworth's sense of the divine immanence, 'something far more deeply interfused', in nature. He saw this as being a projection:

> I may not hope from outward forms to win
> The passion and the life, whose fountains are within . . .
>
> O Lady! we receive but what we give,
> And in our life alone does Nature live:
> Ours is her wedding garment, ours her shroud!
> 　　　　　　　　　　　　　(*Dejection: an Ode*)

Melancholy as such lines are, and though Coleridge in a
fairly long life wrote perhaps only a dozen important poems
(he was born in 1772, died in 1834: born in 1770, his friend
and inspirer, Wordsworth, died in 1850), there is a sense in
which Coleridge though weaker is yet more sensitive and
more wildly imaginative than Wordsworth, a more hesitant
yet more penetrating and acutely analytic critic. (*Biographia
Literaria*, especially its chapters on Wordsworth's strengths
and weaknesses as a poet, and on Wordsworth's theories
about poetic diction, is in a sense the first 'modern' work of
criticism in our language, demonstrating strikingly the ur
bane Victorian limitations of Matthew Arnold.) And in
some of his poems, like *Kubla Khan*, he continues to at once
baffle and overwhelm all his critics.

I do not believe a word about *Kubla Khan* being partly
composed (verbally, at least) in sleep, or about the poem's
continuation being interrupted by the untimely intrusion of
a 'person from Porlock'. It is complete in itself, it is today
what we might call a 'symbolist' poem, and what it embodies
is the combination of fierce subconscious, or unconscious
impulse and the element of deliberate and extravagant
artifice that combine, mysteriously, to form one kind of true
poem:

> The shadow of the dome of pleasure
> Floated midway on the waves;
> Where was heard the mingled measure
> From the fountain and the caves.
> It was a miracle of rare device,
> A sunny pleasure-dome with caves of ice!

The important things in these lines are the combination of
'miracle' and 'device' (the element of inspiration, the ele
ment of contrivance, in all true poetry) and the contrast of
'sunny' and 'ice'. Important also is the end of the poem, in
which for Coleridge the poet is not a 'man speaking to men'
but a sort of shaman, as in Plato's *Republic*, a speaker
possessed by powers he does not understand, but magically
moving others because supernatural voices speak through
him:

> . . . with music loud and long,
> I would build that dome in air,

> That sunny dome! those caves of ice!
> And all who heard should see them there,
> And all should cry, Beware! Beware!
> His flashing eyes, his floating hair!
> Weave a circle round him thrice,
> And close your eyes with holy dread,
> For he on honey-dew hath fed,
> And drunk the milk of Paradise.

There are excellent poems like *This Lime-tree Bower my Prison* (1797) and *Frost at Midnight* (1798) in what one might call a subdued Wordsworthian tone, less calm and assured but more self-questioning and sensitive; and a strange poem *The Eolian Harp*, composed in 1795, the year of his marriage, in which he anticipates the sense of divine immanence, of 'something far more deeply interfused', which was to be the theme, in *The Lyrical Ballads*, of Wordsworth's *Tintern Abbey*: (these particular lines were added as errata in 1817.)

> O! the one Life within us and abroad,
> Which meets all motion and becomes its soul,
> A light in sound, a sound-like power in light,
> Rhythm in all thought, and joyance every where . . .

But, alas, he flings it all away in the last paragraph to placate the timid Biblical orthodoxy of his stupid and unsympathetic wife:

> But thy more serious eye a mild reproof
> Darts, O belovéd Woman! nor such thoughts
> Dim and unhallow'd dost thou not reject,
> And biddest me walk humbly with my God.
> Meek Daughter in the family of Christ!

Wordsworth was in his time a Girondin, a Godwinian anarchist, a panentheist (one who believes that God is *in* everything, not a pantheist, who believes that everything is God), and in his later years a staunch Church-and-State Tory.

He had, as a boy, a profoundly mystical experience of nature, as a source of joy and a moral instructor through pain, combined with a sense of nature's visionariness – he would touch a tree to prove to himself that it was tangibly there. These early experiences faded away, as we are told in the Immortality Ode, but the memory of these early 'spots of time' remained the 'master-light of all (his) seeing' and the association of places with memories of people and affections gave them a new kind of consoling magic. In his great poem *The Prelude* something entirely subjective, the growth of a poet's mind, is treated as an epic subject, in Miltonic blank verse. (The first version was completed by 1805, the second by 1834. The second version, in which Wordsworth tried to cut out prosaic and perhaps irrelevant details and to aim at a more sustained dignity of style is different in feeling, but by no means generally inferior, to the first.) When one compares Wordsworth with Coleridge one is struck by the older man's sheer stamina and persistence; and the odd unevenness of Wordsworth's style, which Coleridge in *Biographia Literaria* was the first to notice, becomes to those who love him one of his endearing characteristics.

He dominated his century with his 'healing power': Coleridge with his brilliant vulnerability looks far more to our own century. (There are touches of him both in Yeats and Eliot: *Kubla Khan* and *Byzantium* have strong family resemblances; Eliot, in his *Notes Towards a Definition of Culture*, is attracted by the idea of a role once played by churchmen now being played by civilised minds (who may even be atheists), 'the clerisy'.)

Wordsworth does not look forward in this sense; his progress is a slow one from a rebellion against much in his world to a Tory acceptance of it, shown in *Ecclesiastical Sonnets* and in the *Sonnets Upon the Punishment of Death* (written in 1839 and 1840, ten years before Wordsworth's own death):

> Is *Death*, when evil against good has fought
> With such fell mastery that a man may dare
> By deeds the blackest purpose to lay bare –
> Is Death, for one to that condition brought, –
> For him, or any one, – the thing that ought
> To be *most* dreaded? Lawgivers, beware,
> Lest, capital pains remitting till ye spare
> The murderer, ye, by sanction to that thought,
> Seemingly given, debase the general mind;
> Tempt the vague will tried standards to disown;

Nor only palpable restraints unbind,
But upon Honour's head disturb the crown,
Whose absolute rule permits not to withstand
In the weak love of life his least command.

Few readers today will share the sentiments; but the sonnet
has that painstaking honesty and consistency which marks
Wordsworth from beginning to end, and which is not to be
found in Coleridge, in whose brilliant prose arguments on
religion and politics one has a sense of puzzlement ('A letter
from Mr Coleridge', wrote the Tory Prime Minister, Lord
Liverpool, 'I do not understand it.') and of Coleridge
struggling over-ingeniously to convince himself.

Yet Wordsworth was not simple. Blake, often thought of
as the most revolutionary of all Romantic poets, was profoundly shocked and distressed by the fragment from the
first book of the relinquished long poem *The Recluse*, with
its cavalier treatment of Jehovah:

All strength – all terror, single or in bands,
That ever was put forth in personal form –
Jehovah – with his thunder, and the choir
Of shouting Angels, and the empyreal thrones –
I pass them unalarmed. Not Chaos, not
The darkest pit of lowest Erebus,
Nor aught of blinder vacancy, scooped out
By help of dreams – can breed such fear and awe
As fall upon us often when we look
Into our Minds, into the Mind of Man –
My haunt, and the main region of my song.

Blake's mind was, unlike Wordsworth's, essentially mytho-
poeic; he could not, like Wordsworth here, see a myth for a
grand symbol, or cluster of symbols, leading us back to a
deeper understanding of familiar experiences, but only as
something literal: Blake could distort myth, or make his own
myths as substitutes for the accepted ones, but Wordsworth
shocked him here:

Solomon, when he Married Pharoah's daughter & became a
convert to the Heathen Mythology, Talked exactly in this way
of Jehovah as a Very inferior object of Man's Contemplation;
he also pass'd him by unalarm'd and was permitted. Jehovah
dropped a tear and follow'd him by his Spirit into the

Abstract Void; it is called the Divine Mercy. Satan dwells in it, but Mercy does not dwell in him; he knows not how to Forgive.

Strange and striking as Blake's imagination is, it is impossible here not to feel that, of the two, Wordsworth has by far the deeper and saner poetic mind. He knows that the poetic mind shapes the strength of form and is not shaped by it; he knows that our images of the divine or the demonic are *our* images, though there is a divine mystery in the power that enables us to shape them. Blake was equally shocked by the following wise perception:

> . . . while my voice proclaims
> How exquisitely the individual Mind
> (And the progressive powers perhaps no less
> Of the whole species) to the external World
> Is fitted: – and how exquisitely, too –
> Theme this but little heard of among men –
> The external World is fitted to the Mind . . .

For Blake, the actual external world was always an enemy to the true and eternal world of Imagination. The body was evil, something veiling us from eternity. He quotes a few more lines of Wordsworth's, in which this sense of fittingness consoles the great poet even for the violence and anguish in life:

> – Such grateful haunts foregoing, if I oft
> Must turn elsewhere – to travel near the tribes
> And fellowships of men, and see ill sights
> Of madding passions mutually inflamed;
> Must hear Humanity in fields and groves
> Pipe solitary anguish; or must hang
> Brooding above the fierce confederate storm
> Of sorrow, barricadoed evermore
> Within the walls of cities – may these sounds
> Have their authentic comment; that even these
> Hearing, I be not downcast or forlorn! . . .

Blake is fretted by these two passages almost to a foaming madness:

You shall not bring me down to believe such fitting & fitted. I know better & please your Lordship . . .

He then quotes the second passage and thunders:

> Does not this Fit, & is it not Fitting most Exquisitely, too, but to what? – not to Mind, but to the Vile Body only & to its Laws of Good and Evil its enmities against Mind.

Blake's cry of rage seems to be a cry against the real and actual world we live in, though his poems often show a profound sense (especially *Songs of Experience*) of the actual 'Laws of Good and Evil' of our world. But the true world for him was the world of *Songs of Innocence* and of his prophetic books (many of which can be read as attempts to reconstruct the Old Testament in accordance with his own very personal myth-system): the World of Imagination, or Eternity. Both as a poet and as a graphic artist, he found the natural world which Wordsworth rested on, and Coleridge gazed on with a wistful longing for joy, an obstruction. Some weaknesses of his bias can be seen in his graphic art, in the decorative drawings and emblems, for instance, with which he surrounded his self-engraved poems; the tyger, in the terrifying poem of that name, looks oddly like a pussy cat. His tall figures, with their heads crouched between their knees, would, so rudimentary is his sense of anatomy, fall to pieces if they attempted to stand up. This does not prevent him from being a very great visual artist, any more than the fact that, technically, many of his poems owe something to hymns and simple poems for children prevents him from being a very great poet. Nor does the fact that unlike Wordsworth he makes no attempt to reconcile the joy with the sadness of life, that he sees all progression as by contraries, make him a weaker poet than Wordsworth. For sheer strength of impact neither Wordsworth nor any other poet of the Romantic period in England perhaps wrote anything to equal Blake's *London*.

> I wander thro' each charter'd street,
> Near where the charter'd Thames does flow,
> And mark in every face I meet
> Marks of weakness, marks of woe.

In every cry of every Man,
In every Infant's cry of fear,
In every voice, in every ban,
The mind-forg'd manacles I hear.

How the Chimney-sweeper's cry
Every black'ning Church appalls;
And the hapless Soldier's sigh
Runs in blood down Palace walls.

But most thro' midnight streets I hear
How the youthful Harlot's curse
Blasts the new born Infant's tear
And blights with plagues the Marriage hearse.

This has the quality in Blake which T. S. Eliot called 'the naked vision'. We connect at once the 'Chimney-sweeper's sigh' with the 'blackening' Church: the 'Soldier's sigh' (breathing out his blood as he lies on his face dying, perhaps, on the field of battle) runs directly down the palace walls. This is the literalism of symbolism (as we find it in the hymns by Watts or Charles Wesley which were one of Blake's sources), totally objective, not the subjective groping of Romanticism. The most terrible stanza is the last:

But most thro' midnight streets I hear
How the youthful Harlot's curse
Blasts the new born Infant's tear,
And blights with plagues the Marriage hearse.

The young aristocrat ('a chartered libertine', as the streets, the river itself are 'chartered', protected by special laws of privilege from the poor) comes from the ball where he has been flirting politely and chastely with young unmarried women of his own class to make free with a teenage prostitute; she infects him with the diseases that will kill off his children and bring his wife to an early grave. Blake's symbols do not derive from the French or American Revolutions: they are other literal symbols of what surged up from inside him. His vision anticipated Nietszche's and Freud's. For example in *The Marriage of Heaven and Hell*: 'Sooner murder an infant in its cradle than nurse unacted desires.' 'Without contraries is no progression. Attraction and Repulsion, Reason and Energy, Love and Hate, are necessary to Human existence . . .' Then, in spite of Blake's talk about 'Vile Bodies' in his animadversions on Wordsworth, we have the very persuasive *Voice of the Devil*:

> 1. Man has no Body distinct from his Soul; for that call'd Body is a portion of Soul discern'd by the five Senses, the chief inlets of Soul in this age.
> 2. Energy is the only life, and is from the Body: and Reason is the bound or outward circumference of Energy.
> 3. Energy is Eternal Delight.

This is the same poet who wrote among his miscellaneous poems and fragments:

> Abstinence sows sand all over
> The ruddy limbs & flaming hair,
> But Desire Gratified
> Plants fruits of life and beauty there.

And:

> In a wife I would desire
> What in whores is always found –
> The lineaments of Gratified desire.

Among modern English poets, Blake is perhaps the ancestor of D. H. Lawrence; Yeats is too much of a conscious artificer and too much a wearer of masks to be very like him in either substance or surface. Yeats of course was not really a mystic, but I doubt if in the deeper sense (Wordsworth's sense) Blake was either: both were something else, mythmakers. One can only, I think, in this brief and awkward way indicate Blake's peculiar greatness. He had admirers, like Rossetti, among both poets and artists in his own century: but his myths were (and still are) too idiosyncratic for any other poet to use; his explosive morality, his 'naked vision', was hard for the moralising High Victorians and the Aesthetes who succeeded them to take. There is no agreement about him now: there are those (I am among them) who believe that it is better to nurse unacted desires than to strangle a baby in his cradle and that the horses of instruction are wiser than the tigers of wrath. But there is a prophetic grandeur, like that of an Old Testament Prophet, that seems to make that cold rational approach impertinent:

> The roaring of lions, the howling of wolves, the raging of the stormy sea, and the destructive sword are portions of eternity, too great for the eye of man.

In a sense Blake in his completeness is such a 'portion of eternity' himself.

But one comes back, in discussing the founder figures of Romanticism, to Wordsworth's 'healing power'. He is perhaps, as John Stuart Mill, whom his poetry helped to cure of a nervous break-down, the poet of unpoetical natures: there are many noble and unpoetical natures, like Mill himself, and they deserve their healer. In the properly experimental poems, the two volumes of *Lyrical Ballads*, one is struck again and again by the piercing originality of Wordsworth's thought and insight, though it often lies under a mask of seeming obtuseness. In one of the conversation poems, for instance, with old Matthew, Matthew has this stanza:

> 'My days, my Friend, are almost gone,
> My life has been approv'd,
> And many love me; but by none
> Am I enough beloved.'

This is something we all feel as we grow older, but only Wordsworth has had the intuition, the courage, to say it and set it down. Only he, at the end of *The Idiot Boy* – the boy riding out alone at night has frantically alarmed his mother – has evoked the strange, innocent, one might almost say Blakean paradise in which a very limited consciousness can find joys from which we are cut off: the moon is a kind of sun to him, owls a sort of tree-perching barnyard cock:

> Now Johnny all night long had heard
> The Owls in tuneful concert strive;
> No doubt too he the Moon had seen;
> For in the moonlight he had been
> From eight o'clock till five.
>
> And thus, to Betty's question, he
> Made answer, like a Traveller bold,
> (His very words I give to you,)

'The Cocks did crow to-whoo, to-whoo,
And the Sun did shine so cold.'
– Thus answered Johnny in his glory,
And that was all his travel's story.

These ballad poems are often amusing as well as touching.
But above all they rouse sympathy. Johnny's brain does not
work but his senses and imagination do; out of his very
muddles he makes discovery and delight.

Less strange than either Coleridge or Blake, less interesting as a mind and personality than the one, less of an utter
unpredictable 'sport' than the other, Wordsworth somehow
is larger, saner, more central to the English tradition than
either. One looks in him, also, not merely for 'healing
thoughts' (a phrase of his own, towards the end of *Tintern
Abbey*) but also for the mysterious strange beauty of the
Lucy poems. *Lucy Gray*, based on a true account of a lost
girl, contains in a more scattered form the fused ideas of
solitariness and of a sweetness which belong alike to natural
things and to a young girl lost:

> Oft I had heard of Lucy Gray:
> And when I crossed the Wild,
> I chanc'd to see at break of day
> The solitary Child.
>
> No Mate, no comrade Lucy knew;
> She dwelt on a wide Moor,
> The sweetest thing that ever grew
> Beside a human door! . . .
>
> Not blither is the mountain roe:
> With many a wanton stroke
> Her feet disperse the powd'ry snow,
> That rises up like smoke . . .

Lucy had disappeared when sent by her foolish parents on
an errand to the nearest village on a stormy night. Her
footsteps ended in the middle of a plank of a bridge:

> . . . Yet some maintain that to this day
> She is living child;
> That you may see sweet Lucy Gray
> Upon the lonesome Wild.

> O'er rough and smooth she trips along,
> And never looks behind;
> And sings a solitary song
> That whistles in the wind.

Lucy Gray was earlier than the other Lucy poems and, unlike them, is a true lyrical ballad (its attractions are lyrical rather than narrative, but it tells a story). The later and more famous Lucy poems are like lyrical fragments of ballads; a story lies behind them but is not told. For Wordsworth a fusion of the ideas of solitariness, preciousness, a resemblance to a natural thing (something that 'grows' beside a cottage door, a violet by a mossy stone, a mountain roe kicking up the powdery snow), death or disappearance, and yet a kind of permanent elusive presence, symbolised (and only here is he a symbolic poet) the sources of his elusive, intermittent inspiration.

II Younger Romantics and the Beginnings of Victorianism

John Keats wrote in 1819 and published in July 1820 (a haemorrhage in February of that year had already made it clear to this former surgeon's apprentice that he was fatally ill with that consumption of the lungs that had carried off his brother Tom in December of 1818) the volume *Lamia, Isabella, The Eve of St Agnes, and other Poems* on which his fame mainly rests. He admits in his letters that *To Psyche*, one of the great odes which are the crowning glory of that volume, was the first poem on which he had taken any care in the way of artistic revision. His first volume of *Poems* published in 1817 contains some very bad poems, though also some fresh and delightful pieces of descriptive verse:

> Here are sweet peas, on tip-toe for a flight:
> With wings of gentle flush o'er delicate white,
> And taper fingers catching at all things,
> To bind them all about with tiny rings.

It would have been found pleasant enough, by a kindly critic, but without the promise of greatness. His second poem, *Endymion*, did not satisfy himself. It is an account of the love of Peona for the shepherd-king Endymion and though it is a quest poem, working on a kind of myth which also fascinated Shelley, it is also too clearly a kind of substitute, or imaginary, satisfaction for the sexual desires which tormented, vainly, this very full-blooded and sensuous young poet. As a narrative, if it is the business of a narrative to tell a story straightforwardly, it is hopeless; what Keats is doing, however, is turning a frustrated sexual adolescent urge into poetry, postponing again and again the climax, because the climax is something that the written word cannot provide. Keats is the most sensual of English poets which is why Byron, who is passionate but not sensual, disliked him, speaking of his poetry as a sort of 'self-soliciting', even of 'Mr Keats's piss-a-bed poetry'. It was only in this volume when the erotic urge was expanded to include the whole sensuous universe, that he became a very great poet. He broadly agreed with Croker's harsh, but not wholly uncivil, review of *Endymion* in the Tory *Quarterly Review*: Croker felt that *Endymion* lacked construction, that the rhyme led the thought rather than the thought the rhyme; he found it very difficult to read through, and I am not, I think, alone among modern readers in sharing his difficulties. Keats himself in his preface of April 10th, 1818, saw what was most deeply wrong:

> The imagination of a boy is healthy, and the mature imagination of a man is healthy; but there is a space of life between, in which the soul is in a ferment, the character undecided, the way of life uncertain, the ambition thick-sighted: thence proceeds mawkishness, and all the thousand bitters which those men I speak of /men who are competent to look, and who do look with a zealous eye, to the honour of English Literature/ must necessarily taste in going over the following pages.

Keats largely agreed therefore with Croker's harsh but not malicious criticism: perhaps some words of Endymion's in the poem itself echo Keats's feeling about it:

> I have clung
> To nothing, lov'd a nothing, nothing seen
> Or felt but a great dream!

Endymion, however, though it is a failure as a whole (it *is* immature, Keats was born in 1795 and this long poem was published in 1818, in his twenty-third year) has its splendours. The lyrical and pictorial passages are among its occasional triumphs, like this processional stanza about Bacchus which reminds one a little of Rubens:

> Within his car aloft, young Bacchus stood,
> Trifling his ivy-dart, in dancing mood,
>   With sidelong laughing;
> And little rills of crimson wine imbrued
> His plump white arms, and shoulders, enough white
>   For Venus' pearly bite:
> And near him rode Silenus on his ass,
> Pelted with flowers as he on did pass
>   Tipsily quaffing . . .

Even more splendid is the slightly later stanza in Book 4 about the Satyrs who follow Bacchus:

> Whence came ye, jolly Satyrs! whence came ye?
> So many, and so many, and such glee?
> Why have ye left your forest haunts, why left
>   Your nuts in oak-tree cleft? –
> 'For wine, for wine we left our kernel tree;
> For wine we left our heath, and yellow brooms,
>   And cold mushrooms;
> For wine we follow Bacchus through the earth . . .'

Yet scattered felicities like this do not make a great or even a good poem, when the central controlling idea is not given a dramatic unifying interest; and Keats's central controlling idea has probably less to do with indulging a vicarious sensuality in the story of Endymion and Cynthia than the excitement of writing a long poem full of these classical images which he knew less from reading (he had no Greek) than from Renaissance pictures. The poem fails to embody an adequate object for its groping power to grasp at. It moves back on the frustrated Keats:

> Straight he seiz'd her wrist;
> It melted from his grasp: her hand he kiss'd,
> And, horror! kiss'd his own – he was alone.

Apart from the heavy petting which was as much, apparently, as his beloved Fanny Brawne would indulge him in (and the effect on an excitable young man incubating consumption was that of arousal and frustration, not satisfaction: hence his strange lines in *Ode on a Grecian Urn*:

> All breathing human passion far above,
> That leaves a heart high-sorrowful and cloy'd,
> A burning forehead, and a parching tongue),

Keats, apart from little party flirtations, an Oxford escapade for which he required treatment with mercury, and a friendly but as far as the record goes not quite sexual encounter with the mistress of an elderly M.P., though no poet was ever more beloved by his friends and his family, 'was alone' in Endymion's sense till the end. He was what Jungians call an introverted sensualist, dwelling with more delight on anticipation and memory than in the 'brief benefit of a bewildering minute' just as he was emotionally extroverted, identifying himself with the problems of his friends, sharing with delight the being of the sparrow pecking on the window sill. He sought no doctrine, though in his last important attempt at a long poem, *The Fall of Hyperion: A Dream*, he seems to be reproaching himself (he was, like Shelley and Byron a radical in a period of triumphant reaction, but less absorbed than either of the other two in politics) for not being 'committed':

> . . . 'High Prophetess,' said I, 'Purge off,
> Benign, if so it please, thee, my mind's film.' –
> 'None can usurp this height,' returned that shade,
> 'But those to whom the miseries of the world,
> 'Are misery, and will not let them rest.
> 'All else who find a haven in the world,
> 'Where they may thoughtless sleep away their days,
> 'If by a chance into this fane they come,
> 'Rot on the pavement where thou rottedst half. –'

The Fall of Hyperion, Keats's reaction against its predecessor, the unfinished Miltonic epic, *Hyperion*, which his publishers included in his last volume rather against his wishes, might have been the first step in a new and more, at least morally, ambitious kind of poetry. But such a poetry could have hardly, as art, have excelled his unsurpassable odes. Keats all his life had been attempting to write sonnets, and he has a few good and one perhaps great sonnet, *Bright star, would I were stedfast as thou art . . . .* As a writer of sonnets he does not begin to rank with Shakespeare, Sidney, Milton, or Wordsworth. Except for the first of the odes, the irregular *To Psyche*, the great odes, *To a Nightingale*, *On a Grecian Urn*, *On Melancholy*, and *To Autumn*, are composed in a ten- or eleven-line stanza in which the first quatrain is that of a Shakespearian sonnet and the final sestet that of a Petrarchan sonnet, a little disguised in *Nightingale* by a third last line which is an iambic trimeter and in *To Autumn* by an extra line turning the sestet into a septet. This stanza at once gives Keats's thought room to turn, as the sonnet does, but does not have the static quality which makes the sonnet an unsuitable form for a stanza. Keats's great gift is the modulation of feeling from stanza to stanza, a pattern of what one might call escape and return, and for this he had in all the great odes except *Psyche* found the ideal form. *To Psyche* remains important as the first poem on which he took, as he puts it, any reasonable pains; a sense of continual and unrevised and uncriticised improvisation is one of the things that weakens *Endymion*, for instance. But the odes he revised and polished. The theme of all of them, except perhaps *Psyche*, and except in a transcended form in *To Autumn*, is the desire to escape from finitude, to a kind of absolute of experience in nature, in art, in the fusion of pain and delight, into an emotion more intense and complete than either. The sensuality is not now embarrassing. It works in terms of symbolism, as in these two stanzas of *Ode to a Nightingale*:

> Away! away! for I will fly to thee,
>   Not charioted by Bacchus and his pards,
> But on the viewless wings of Poesy,
>   Though the dull brain perplexes and retards:
> Already with thee! tender is the night,
>   And haply the Queen-Moon is on her throne,
>   Cluster'd around by all her starry Fays;
>   But here there is no light,
> Save what from heaven is with the breezes blown
>   Through verdurous glooms and winding mossy ways.
>
> I cannot see what flowers are at my feet,
>   Nor what soft incense hangs upon the boughs,

But, in embalmed darkness, guess each sweet
 Wherewith the seasonable month endows
The grass, the thicket, and the fruit-tree wild;
 White hawthorn and the pastoral eglantine;
  Fast fading violets cover'd up in leaves;
   And mid-May's eldest child,
 The coming musk-rose, full of dewy wine,
  The murmurous haunt of flies on summer eves.

The first of these stanzas shows us clearly that – and the
contrast with the Augustans is clear – there is no accepted
romantic *style*. Keats is not writing as a 'man writing to
men', but as a poet, creating a poetic object, interested in
the literary association of words and their emotional impact
on each other. The allusion to Bacchus and his attendant
leopards, personification in the style of Gray and Collins
('Viewless wings of Poesy'), 'Queen-Moon', 'starry Fays',
such diction and such metaphors would have appalled
Wordsworth like the allusion to Phoebus in Gray's sonnet to
West. He would have been infuriated both with the artificial, dramatic punctuation and the reversed word order of

 Already with thee! tender is the night,

and with 'haply' for 'perhaps'. He would not have noticed,
perhaps, the expressive felicity of the word 'cluster' and
how the spendid last line

 Through verdurous glooms and winding mossy ways

reinforces itself through the similar shaping of the last line of
the next stanza:

 The murmurous haunt of flies on summer eves,

where 'murmurous' seems to both enrich, and be enriched,
by the preceding 'verdurous' and the 'summer eves' make
the same metrical pattern as the preceding 'mossy ways'.
One sense in which the Keats of the *Odes* is the first of the
moderns is in the way he fingers words for the right
combination of concentrated sensuous expressiveness and
musical surprise, is aware of the poem as moods modulating

through words, through verbal juxtapositions at once felicitous and surprising.

For instance, in the second stanza quoted above Keats sets himself the almost impossible task of evoking the flowers of a woodland thicket without the use of a single word alluding to colour (in 'embalmed darkness', 'white hawthorn' darkness and white mark the limits of colour, are not themselves colours, and the 'fast-fading violets' might be as easily white instead of violet – just as we do not assume the 'musk-rose' to be pink). Instead, Keats appeals to our senses of smell ('incense', 'embalmed'), of taste or smell and taste combined ('sweets', 'dewy wine'), of touch (the suggestion of slight stickiness in 'incense' and 'embalmed', of exploratory touching in 'cover'd up in leaves'), of hearing ('murmurous haunt'), even of atmosphere and temperature ('summer eves'). We are *inside* his thicket, as nowhere else in English poetry. In his best romantic narrative poem, *The Eve of St Agnes*, he frames the poem in coldness, distance, and death:

> St Agnes Eve – Ah, bitter chill it was!

at the beginning, and at the end

> And they are gone: aye, ages long ago
> These lovers fled away into the storm

(and are themselves dead and 'bitter chill' *now*, of course). But at the centre of the poem there is warmth and erotic delight, though threatened still by the sleet pattering on the windows of Madeline's boudoir:

> Into her dream he melted, as the rose
> Blendeth its odour with the violet, –
>   Solution sweet. Meantime the frost-wind blows
>   Like Love's alarum pattering the sharp sleet
> Against the window-panes; St Agnes' moon hath set.

Keats differs from the other romantics in that, for all his sensuous delight in the detail of nature (this Cockney who wrote 'sea-spry' when he meant 'sea-spray' was a far closer examiner of flowers, for instance, and weather than the countryman Wordsworth) he did not seem to seek in nature

for a living spirit. He sought everywhere for the projection
of a symbol adequate to his own emotional needs, for a rich
fusion of experience in which the nagging nearness of death,
the hungry generations that tread us down, are conquered,
but it is achieved, if at all, in the nightingale's song, as
something momentary, which may be a hallucination ('Fade
far away, dissolve and quite forget') though it may also be
the timeless moment of illumination experienced in the
nightingale's song against which the film of custom blinds us.
Keats, the least dogmatic of great English poets, leaves the
reader to make up his own mind:

> Was it a vision, or a waking dream?
> Fled is that music: – Do I wake or sleep?

Keats and Shelley (1792–1822) are often classed together.
Both died very young, Keats of consumption in Severn's
arms in Rome in February 1821, at the beginning of his
twenty-sixth year; Shelley in July 1822, drowned in the Gulf
of Spezia, just a month before his thirtieth birthday.
Shelley's friend Byron was to live to the comparative
maturity, for this group, of his thirty-sixth birthday, on
which he wrote a noble poem; and he was to have time to lay
the foundations of the liberation of Greece and leave at least
a noble sketch of himself as a man of action, a role which he
had always considered more interesting (as he had perhaps
considered even the role of the man of fashion, or dandy)
than the mere poet's. He was a heroic cynic, Shelley a
growingly pessimistic idealist, searching for a fusion of pure
souls the world did not seem to offer him; Keats a man in
love with poetry and with everything delightful in love, and
at last, in the forty or so pages of his really great poems, in
love with poetry as an art: but Keats was haunted by death,
as Byron was by guilt, and Shelley by the increasing failure
of reality to correspond to the ideal.

All three (but Keats the least, perhaps largely from lack of
adequate temptation or opportunity) were much freer than
Coleridge, Wordsworth, and Blake in their sexual ethics
('What a set!' said Matthew Arnold). All three were more
interested in art, in history, in the romance of foreign places
and, at least in the case of Shelley and Keats, in the romance
of classical mythology than Blake, Coleridge, or Words-

worth. None went through a period of naive hopefulness
about the world but none relinquished a radical attitude to
politics. They are not so great as the founding fathers: but
we feel today closer to them, more their contemporaries.
One might add for what it is worth that the more one knows
of Byron the more this Don Giovanni seems a man pursued
by women, and politely and sometimes reluctantly obliging,
rather than a woman-chaser; and if Shelley seems in his
thought less (to use Matthew Arnold's term) 'ineffectual' he
also seems, the more one knows about *his* conduct with
women, less an 'angel'. When Mary Shelley ironically described *Epipsychidion* as 'Shelley's *Italian* Platonics' – it is a
poem which as it develops becomes more and more desperately excited, addressed to Emilia Viviani, an Italian girl of
some literary pretensions whom the Shelleys met at a
convent school where she was being kept by her family till a
suitable husband could be found for her – she may have
given 'Italian' a very special stress. She may not have
relished such famous lines as these:

> I never was attached to that great sect,
> Whose doctrine is, that each one should select
> Out of the crowd a mistress or a friend,
> And all the rest, though fair and wise, commend
> To cold oblivion, though it is the code
> Of modern morals, and the beaten road
> Which those poor slaves with weary footsteps tread,
> Who travel to their home among the dead
> By the broad highway of the world, and so
> With one chained friend, perhaps a jealous foe,
> The dreariest and the longest journey go.
>
> True Love in this differs from gold and clay,
> That to divide is not to take away.
> Love is like understanding, that grows bright,
> Gazing on many truths; 'tis like thy light,
> Imagination! which from earth and sky,
> And from the depths of human fantasy,
> As from a thousand prisms and mirrors, fills
> The Universe with glorious beams, and kills
> Error, the worm, with many a sun-like arrow
> Of its reverberated lightning. Narrow
> The heart that loves, the brain that contemplates,
> The life that wears, the spirit that creates

One object, and one form, and builds thereby
A sepulchre for its eternity.

Matthew Arnold reproached Shelley with what one might call a lack of subject matter; T. S. Eliot, in some lectures delivered in America as *The Use of Poetry and the Use of Criticism*, with possessing a philosophy which not only differed from Eliot's own Christian philosophy (Eliot had no objection to Lucretius's use in poetry of an atheistic materialism) but was so vague and immature and incoherent in itself as seriously to damage Shelley's use of his undeniably splendid poetic gift. Both great critics seem to me mistaken; the quality of his intellect was a powerful one, and he had purchased, as it were, both by intensity of experience and intellectual struggle (that of a man whose reading ranged from Plato – he had written a prose version of the *Symposium* – to Dante) the right to the originality of his speculations. The passage I have just quoted is extremely coherent. As an argument against monophilia (the belief of Lawrence's character, Birkin, that besides a wife a man needs one, and only one, male friend) it is unanswerable; as an argument against monogamy in the Christian sacramental sense, or in the sense of a life-long contract sanctioned and protected by the state, it is still very strong. I know in fact very few young people, though I know some, who follow the beaten road of 'modern morals' in Shelley's sense. He owed some of these ideas to his very unpleasant father-in-law, Mary Godwin's father and the dead Mary Wollstonecraft's former husband, and Godwin has worked out the best arguments I know against either observing contracts or keeping promises, if to do so conflicts with one's own feelings or interests. Godwin worked out the most coherent system of non-violent anarchism of any British philosopher. Individual freedom for him had primacy over everything else and he thought it wrong, for instance, to become a member of an orchestra since one subjected oneself to the will of a conductor and became a temporary member of a sort of Fascist state, wrong, perhaps, even to play a piece of music that one has not composed oneself (one is not to become the mere instrument for another's self-expression). One reason why his anarchism is non-violent is that in a violent revolution one submits oneself unreasoningly to the orders of those above one and to an enforced co-operation with those of one's own rank. For the slow transformation of the world one must wait for the gradual spread of a perception of the truths perceived by Godwin: and clearly the man who could so deeply influence the young Wordsworth as well as the young Shelley, through his arguments alone (he was a tedious conversationalist and an unattractive personality), was not negligible as a thinker.

A deeper influence working on Shelley, however, was Plato and perhaps not so much Plato in himself but the mystical religion made out of him by the neo-Platonists. *Adonais*, Shelley's pastoral elegy for Keats, shows no understanding of the human character, the greatness, or the 'flint and iron' of his subject: Keats died of a physical illness, consumption, which would have killed him anyway, not from a few snobbish sneers in *Blackwood's* at the 'Cockney school of poetry' or Croker's harsh but not wholly unfair review of *Endymion* in *The Quarterly*. He was not a weakling; his third and greatest volume was in fact favourably reviewed, with a particularly sympathetic notice in *The London Magazine* by Charles Lamb. But, as a dying man, deprived for ever of the hope of a lasting and fulfilled relationship with Fanny Brawne, Keats was indifferent to praise, as he had been indifferent to vituperation. Shelley's sensitive weakling who had something in common with his picture of himself as a beautiful but vulnerable spirit, suited his poetic purposes better: Shelley, in fact, in *Adonais*, deals with himself in far more loving detail, among the mourners of Keats, than he deals with Byron ('The Pilgrim of Eternity') or Tom Moore,

> . . . from her wilds Ierne sent
> The sweetest lyrist of her saddest wrong,
> And Love taught grief to fall like music from his tongue.

But when he comes to himself all the stops are out: this is Shelley's Shelley:

> Midst others of less note, came one frail Form,
> A phantom among men; companionless
> As the last cloud of an expiring storm
> Whose thunder is its knell; he, as I guess,
> Had gazed on Nature's naked loveliness,
> Actaeon-like, and now he fled astray

With feeble steps o'er the world's wilderness,
  And his own thoughts, along that rugged way,
Pursued, like raging hounds, their father and their prey.

  A pardlike Spirit beautiful and swift –
  A love in desolation masked; – a Power
  Girt round with weakness; – it can scarce uplift
  The weight of the superincumbent hour;
  It is a dying lamp, a falling shower,
  A breaking billow; – even while we speak
  Is it not broken? On the withering flower
  The killing sun shines brightly: on a cheek
  The life can burn in blood, even while the heart may break.

There are still two more stanzas about this mythic version of
Shelley, at the end of one of which he adapts Cowper's
famous line about the stricken deer –

  A herd-abandoned deer struck by the hunter's dart –

and in the last of which he makes a dramatic self-revelation
which, in a way, might better suit Byron:

  . . . sad Urania scanned
  The Stranger's mien, and murmured: 'Who art thou?'
  He answered not, but with a sudden hand
  Made bare his branded and ensanguined brow
  Which was like Cain's or Christ's – oh! that it should be so.

There was a need, perhaps, in Shelley both to turn himself
into a mythic figure (more usually engaged in a quest for
ideal love) and to emphasise both his weakness and the
strength that spoke through him; as in the *Ode to the West
Wind* written in 1819:

  I fall upon the thorns of life! I bleed!

followed by

  Make me thy lyre, even as the forest is:
  What if my leaves are falling like its own!
  The tumult of thy mighty harmonies

  Will take from both a deep autumnal tone,

Sweet though in sadness. Be thou, Spirit fierce,
My spirit! Be thou me, impetuous one.

Shelley was in fact anything but the lonely, guilty or sacrificial stranger of *Adonais*: from Peacock and Hogg to Trelawney and Byron, from Harriet Westbrooke and Mary Godwin to Claire Clairmont and Emilia Viviani and Jane Williams, men and women loved this strange, graceful self-absorbed creature. But their love was not enough and time and life were a burden. What Shelley wanted, and in the nature of things could never have, was what he evokes wonderfully in *Epipsychidion*: a state of mind in which ideas assume the force of sensations (or sensations the clarity of ideas) through the fusion, or confusion, of thought with the objects of thought. It would be impossible to say whether the following passage is a great piece of erotic writing or of philosophic allegorising. It is probably both.

> . . . the brief fathom-line of thought or sense.
> The glory of her being, issuing thence,
> Stains the dead, blank, cold air with a warm shade
> Of unentangled intermixture, made
> By Love, of light and motion: One intense
> Diffusion, one serene Omnipresence,
> Whose flowing outlines mingle in their flowing,
> Around her cheeks and utmost fingers glowing
> With the unintermitted blood, which there
> Quivers (as in a fleece of snow-like air
> The crimson pulse of living morning quiver,)
> Continuously prolonged, and ending never,
> Till they are lost, and in that Beauty furled
> Which penetrates and clasps and fills the world;
> Scarce visible from extreme loveliness.
> Warm fragrance seems to fall from her light dress
> And her loose hair; and where some heavy tress
> The air of her own speed has disentwined,
> The sweetness seems to satiate the faint wind;
> And in the soul a wild odour is felt,
> Beyond the sense, like fiery dews that melt
> Into the bosom of a frozen bud . . .
> Spouse! Sister! Angel! Pilot of the Fate
> Whose course has been so starless! O too late
> Belovèd. O too soon adored, by me!
> For in the fields of immortality
> My spirit should at first have worshipped thine . . .

And in the greatest stanza of *Adonais* time and life, anything other than the 'fields of immortality', are rejected:

> The one remains, the many change and pass;
> Heaven's light forever shines, Earth's shadows fly;
> Life, like a dome of many-coloured glass,
> Stains the white radiance of Eternity,
> Until Death tramples it to fragments. – Die,
> If thou woulds't be with that which thou dost seek!
> Follow where all is fled! – Rome's azure sky,
> Flowers, ruins, statues, music, words, are weak
> The glory they transfuse with fitting truth to speak.

He had given up, when he wrote that, the image of fusion with the ideal soul-mate (though, shortly before his death by drowning, he was writing exquisite love lyrics to a new arrival in the Shelley circle, Jane Williams), and his latest, unfinished (but if it had been finished possibly greatest) long poem, *The Triumph of Life*, is a Dantesque exercise (T. S. Eliot, in a late essay on Dante, and as an attempt to appease Shelley's insulted shade for his earlier condescension, rightly judges this poem to be the greatest use of *terza rima* in the English language) in seeing physical and historical life as a triumphal chariot that leads the soul captive in a sort of hell on earth:

> Yet ere I can say *where* – the chariot hath
> Passed over them – nor other trace I find
> But as of foam after the ocean's wrath
>
> Is spent upon the desert shore; – behind,
> Old men and women foully disarrayed,
> Shake their gray hairs in the insulting wind,
>
> And follow in the dance, with limbs decayed,
> Seeking to reach the light which leaves them still
> Further behind and deeper in the shade.

The last terzet there has a weight and tragic concision which we do not associate with the earlier Shelley; we feel about them as not about Keats or Byron (who had achieved what they had to achieve) that he died too soon. The great fragment of *The Triumph of Life* ends on an agonised question asked by the spirit of Rousseau, transformed, with

a memory of Dante's wood of the suicides, into a rotting
tree:

> '. . . After brief space,
> From every form the beauty slowly waned;
>
> 'From every firmest limb and fairest face
> The strength and freshness fell like dust, and left
> The action and the shape without the grace
>
> 'Of life. The marble brow of youth was cleft
> With care; and in those eyes where once hope shone,
> Desire, like a lioness bereft
>
> Of her last cub, glared ere it died . . .
>
> '. . . and long before the day
>
> 'Was old, the joy which waked like heaven's glance
> The sleepers in the oblivious valley, died;
> And some grew weary of the ghastly dance,
>
> 'And fell, as I have fallen, by the wayside;
> Those soonest from whose forms most shadows passed,
> And least of strength and beauty did abide.
>
> "Then, what is life?" I cried.' –

Shelley's answer, of which the beginning only was managed
before it was smothered for ever by the waters of the Gulf of
Spezia, would have been worth waiting for. As it is he
remains the most fragmentary and uneven of our great
poets, but unmatched for sweetness in the short poem, and
for icy and starry glitter and incredible rapidity of movement
in the longer one. He lacked Wordsworth's humanity,
Coleridge's power of self-analysis, Keats's warm awareness
of the world's richness-in-sadness, Byron's direct pure passion and flippant glancing wit; but in his visionary quality,
though utterly unlike in temperament, he is to be classed
only with Blake.

Byron was born rather earlier than Keats and Shelley, in
1788, in London, and died of fever among the marshes and
bullfrogs of Missolonghi (still one of the most unattractive
little towns in Greece) in 1824, having shown surprising

patience and tact in working to unite the mutually hostile and suspicious factions of the Greek resistance against the Turks. He had achieved great personal triumphs out of a background that would have crushed the resistance of any other man. He hardly saw his father who, after marrying one rich wife, whose lands, when she died, were entailed away from him, desperately wooed a rather plain Miss Gordon of Hight, of the great Aberdeenshire family of the Gordons, of whose fortune he had an exaggerated idea. Byron's father squeezed what he could out of his wife's fortune but even then fled overseas to escape imprisonment for debt; abroad he may have committed suicide. Mrs Byron had still hung on to some house property in Aberdeen and with her small son, who had been born with one weakened or deformed foot – the evidence is not certain whether it was a club foot or a weakened ankle – she went back to live in Aberdeen, sending her son to Aberdeen Grammar School, a very old foundation but not in any sense an aristocratic English public school. Byron, while still a boy in Aberdeen, was seduced by a drunken nursemaid; he was also taught by another servant the terrifying Calvinist doctrine of supralapsarian predestination – God had arbitrarily ordained our salvation or damnation *before* the Fall, so the sense in which the Crucifixion was our Redemption was doubtful: the example of Christ's obedience unto death saved only those who would in any case, by God's eternal decree, have been saved without it. This experience, this doctrine, explain the fastidiousness which mingled itself with Byron's Libertinism, and the sense of unexplained guilt that hangs around *Childe Harold's Pilgrimage* and his early verse romances like *The Corsair*. Remnants of Calvinist antinomianism lingered with him (if one is to be saved anyway nothing that one does can alter God's decree, and if one is to damned one might as well be hung for a sheep as a lamb) and explain his recklessness. He was noted for his fondness for young men as well as young women, and his passionate fondness for his half-sister, Augusta, his father's daughter by his first marriage and married to a neglectful husband. His bitter and nagging mother had never shown any love for him, and though it was no doubt a relief to her when two successive deaths gave Byron the family peerage and the decrepit Newstead Abbey near Nottingham, his inheritance was

encumbered with debts. Augusta gave him, when they me
for the first time, the affection that his mother never had an
his feelings for her were more tender than for any othe
woman. No doubt their relationship became incestuous; she
may well have taken the lead as did other women like th
Countess of Oxford, Caroline Lamb, Claire Clairmont
Teresa Guiccoli. As he was always kind and courteous to
Teresa he had also a very special tenderness for Augusta
and showed the greatest tact and kindness (unreciprocated
in dealing with Caroline Lamb. He could not manage hi
wife, a rich bluestocking to whom he had earlier proposed
and been refused, but was shocked when, after a visit to he
parents, she arranged her legal separation and secured
custody of their daughter. All sorts of rumours went round
London and Byron was driven abroad, pursued by Mary
Godwin's step-sister (the daughter of Godwin's second wife
by a former marriage) Claire Clairmont. He, the Shelleys
and Claire lingered a while in Switzerland, and Claire
became pregnant and the mother of his daughter, Allegra
He had always disliked Claire and her opinions and, thinking his own wild Venetian household an unsuitable setting
for Allegra, sent her to a convent school, the equivalent in
these days of a good boarding school, where later the child
fell ill and died. There is no reason to suppose that Byron,
who had real reasons to distrust Miss Clairmont (a recent
biography of Shelley makes it clear that in sending Mary
ahead of him with a sick child to see a doctor in Venice,
Shelley was assuring himself of privacy to make love to
Claire) did not love Allegra or was not acting for her good.
His last attachment to a married woman, with a complaisant
husband, Countess Guiccoli, was a mostly peaceful one.
Under her gentle and refined manners Teresa was, as her
later English lover Henry Fox was to discover, almost
savagely passionate; she was also very romantic and several
times almost persuaded Byron to drop his masterpiece, *Don
Juan*, which she considered horrid and cynical. He became a
little bored and that, no doubt, was one of his motives for
undertaking the Greek enterprise. His last love, unreciprocated, was for one of his Greek pages at Missolonghi: he
tells about it in one of his most dramatic and noble poems,
On This Day I Complete My Thirty-Sixth Year (Missolonghi,
Jan. 22, 1824):

'Tis time this heart should be unmoved,
   Since others it hath ceased to move:
Yet, though I cannot be beloved,
   Still let me love!

My days are in the yellow leaf;
   The flowers and fruits of love are gone;
The worm, the canker, and the grief
   Are mine alone!

The fire that on my bosom preys
   Is lone as some volcanic isle;
No torch is kindled at its blaze –
   A funeral pile.

The hope, the fear, the jealous care,
   The exalted portion of the pain
And power of love, I cannot share,
   But wear the chain.

But 'tis not *thus* – and 'tis not *here* –
   Such thoughts should shake my soul, nor *now*,
Where glory decks the hero's bier,
   Or binds his brow.

The sword, the banner, and the field,
   Glory and Greece, around me see!
The Spartan, borne upon his shield,
   Was not more free.

Awake! (not Greece – she *is* awake!)
   Awake, my spirit! Think through *whom*
Thy life-blood strikes its parent lake,
   And then strike home.

Tread those reviving passions down,
   Unworthy manhood! – unto thee
Indifferent should the smile or frown
   Of beauty be.

If thou regrett'st thy youth, *why live?*
   The land of honourable death
Is here: – up to the field, and give
   Away thy breath!

Seek out – less often sought than found –

A soldier's grave, for thee the best;
Then look around, and choose thy ground,
   And take thy rest.

Byron's death *was* heroic, but even as one admires the strength and sincerity of this piece, written so shortly before his fever killed him, one notices in it an element of theatricality, especially in the rhetoric. Byron's enormous popularity in Europe (like the later popularity of Poe in France) rested largely on the fact that foreign readers can never or rarely appreciate the delicacy of language in a poet from another country but can appreciate the spirit of the poem, especially if the poet has something of the gifts of self-projection of a great actor. In his choice of words, even such a rapid and often careless writer as Sir Walter Scott noted that Byron 'wielded his pen with the easy negligence of a nobleman'. The most famous example of these accumulating small infelicities is the second line of the first stanza of the Fourth Canto of *Childe Harold*:

I stood in Venice on the Bridge of Sighs;
A palace and a prison on each hand . . .

One sees these elegant, but when Byron let his weight go, rather podgy hands each balancing on itself a miniature Doge's Palace *and* a miniature State prison; what Byron means is that, on the Bridge of Sighs, if he was facing towards the canal one way or the other, the palace lay to his right (or left) hand and the prison towards his left (or right). There are other famous blunders, as in *The Dying Gladiator* – 'There let him *lay*!'

Byron was, half by ancestry, and in the most formative years of his childhood, a Scotsman and, unlike the Irish, the Scots have rarely handled the English language with casual mastery. David Hume's clarity of thought, frankness, good nature, and lack of cumbrous technicalities, make him one of the best writers among English philosophers; but he was not a *great* stylist like the Irish Bishop Berkeley, whose *Alciphron: or The Minute Philosopher*, a philosophically very vulnerable attack on deists and on the theory that the attraction of a virtuous action is its beauty not any reward it brings, can still be read with delight by readers who do not begin to be convinced by it. Byron, oddly, *did* handle English prose with mastery: Ruskin, in *Praeterita*, was the first to notice the ease, speed, vivacity of his letters and journals. Byron felt it appropriate that his history should make him melancholy, but his temperament was volatile and sanguine, his mind quizzically questioning. His poetic genius found proper expression in volatility, in poems that strike attitudes and question them: *Beppo, The Vision of Judgment, Don Juan*; and in a handful of lyrics where the truth of feeling conquers the wish to pose.

Byron escapes from the stagey, for instance, in such a song as this poem, *Stanzas for Music*, addressed to a choirboy he met and made friends with at Cambridge. This piece of information has no importance, except that it explains the first line, and explains the preoccupation of the whole poem with evoking a vague, sweet, and dreamy musicality: strictly speaking, it *says* nothing:

> There be none of Beauty's daughters
>   With a magic like thee;
> And like music on the waters
>   Is thy sweet voice to me:
> When, as if its sound were causing
> The charmed ocean's pausing,
> The waves lie still and gleaming
> And the lull'd winds seem dreaming:
> And the midnight moon is weaving
>   Her bright chain o'er the deep;
> Whose breast is gently heaving,
>   As an infant's asleep:
> So the spirit bows before thee
> To listen and adore thee;
> With a full but soft emotion,
> Like the swell of Summer's ocean.

The 'full but soft emotion' is evoked perfectly: Byron himself, playing any of his parts, is invisible for once. On the other hand, in *Don Juan*, he is present with the natural, easy off-hand charm that made him perhaps the only poet (though one should remember he was also a lord) to be wholly at home in the London world of fashion and flirtation – a world where even wit had to be careless and off-hand:

I perch upon a humbler promontory,
   Amidst life's infinite variety;
With no great care for what is nicknamed glory,
   But speculating as I cast mine eye,
On what may suit or may not suit my story,
   And never straining hard to versify,
I rattle on exactly as I'd talk
   With anybody on a ride or walk.

It is this easy tone, this sense that one is in the world with its vicissitudes, where there is much to delight in, much to make the heart sad, but also much to laugh at in appreciative amusement or light scorn that makes Byron such a good companion in *Don Juan*: a book as easy to read as a novel, the lightest and most unpretentious of great long poems in our language, but a great poem nevertheless.

Though Browning and Tennyson learned much from the young romantics and were publishing before Victoria's reign (Browning *Pauline* in 1833, Tennyson *Poems by Two Brothers* in 1827, *Poems Chiefly Lyrical*, 1830, *Poems*, 1833) their chief preoccupations, about science and religion and the possibility of making poetry (in the dramatic monologue) out of attitudes one could imagine but did not share, were more typical of the High Victorian age than of the romantic age in its decline. Roughly contemporary with the young romantics, George Darley (1795–1846) in *Nepenthe* showed a Keatsian touch, but with a rather chill and tinkling difference, a taste for prettiness rather than a passion for the beautiful, as in *The Mermaiden's Vesper-Hymn*:

Troop home to silent grots and caves!
   Troop home! and mimic as you go
The mournful winding of the waves
   Which to their dark abysses flow.

At this sweet hour, all things beside
   In amorous pairs to covert creep;
The swans that brush the evening tide
   Homeward in snowy couples keep.

In his green den the murmuring seal
   Close by his sleek companion lies;
While singly we to bedward steal,
   And close in fruitless sleep our eyes.

In bowers of love men take their rest,
  In loveless bowers we sigh alone,
With bosom-friends are others blest,–
  But we have none! but we have none!

This *is* exquisitely pretty but we do not 'warm' to it, any more than we do to the unfortunate lonely mermaids. Darley has none of Keats's faults of taste, his embarrassing moments, or his carelessness, but he could never have conceived the great odes.

A similar debt to Keats can be seen in Thomas Hood, mainly known as a joke poet with a mania for puns, but his *Ode: Autumn* could not have been written without the inspiration of Keats's *To Autumn*. One should read that again before judging whether Hood's poem was really necessary (Hood used *Ode to a Nightingale*, too):

Where are the songs of Summer? – With the sun,
Oping the dusky eyelids of the south,
Till shade and silence waken up as one,
And Morning sings with a warm odorous mouth.
Where are the merry birds? – Away, away,
On panting wings through the inclement skies,
  Lest owls should prey
  Undazzled at noon-day,
And tear with horny beak their lustrous eyes.

One thinks of 'Where are the songs of Spring? Ay, where are they?' And from *Nightingale*, 'Where Beauty cannot keep her lustrous eyes', 'O for a beaker full of the warm South', 'Away! Away! for I will fly to thee', and (for 'warm odorous mouth') of Keats's 'purple-stained mouth', and for Hood's use of 'odorous' one of Keats's 'verdurous' and 'murmurous'. But the early impact of a greater poet on a lesser one is always interesting, and greater men than Hood were to find Keats good to steal from. Browning remarks on this ironically (the murex is a now extinct shellfish from which the ancients got their richest purple dye: a poor man might keep himself cheaply alive on oatmeal porridge):

Who fished the murex up?
What porridge had John Keats?

One should add that Hood's inclement skies and his owl
with its horny beak are very much his own, though 'the
dusky eyelid's owe something to Collins's *Ode to Evening*.
We are reaching that very awkward stage of literary history
where the imagination tries to breed from the imaginary,
where real poems beget chimerical ones. I quote Hood
largely to indicate why, in the rest of this book, it will be
necessary drastically to omit many minor figures.

Thomas Beddoes, a more original and striking figure than
either Darley or Hood was born in 1803 and killed himself,
for love of a young man, and also from constitutional
melancholy, in 1849. He had been trained as a doctor and
his plays, in the Elizabethan manner, are obsessed excessively, though their versification is often striking, with the
dead and with ghosts. He is original metrically, reminding
us, if of anybody, more of Shelley than Keats. But the effect
of repeated rhyme-words here is all his own:

Dirge

The swallow leaves her nest,
The soul my weary breast;
But therefore let the rain
   On my grave
Fall pure; for why complain?
Since both will come again
   O'er the wave.

The wind dead leaves and snow
Doth hurry to and fro;
And, once, a day shall break
   O'er the wave,
When a storm of ghosts shall shake
The dead, until they wake
   In the grave.

The most important poet whom we have not yet considered, Walter Savage Landor, was born in 1775 and lived till
1864, to be a friend of Dickens (who put him into *Bleak
House*) and to greet the young Browning as a new Chaucer.
He was not, in the ordinary sense, a romantic but neither
was he an Augustan. He might be described as a romantic
classic whose pleasure it was to express an intensely passionate nature through words that are fit to chisel in stone. For

the single quality not of suggestiveness or depth or self-revelation (it was his pride to reveal little of himself) but of *perfection* over a limited range of themes he ranks with A. E. Housman. He cannot be read without admiration; but he cannot be read long, for one wearies of the same exact stroke again and again repeated. Yet one's sense of what is *not* expressed makes the poems sometimes paradoxically moving. This late one, for instance, called *Separation*:

> There is a mountain and a wood between us,
> Where the lone shepherd and late bird have seen us
> Morning and noon and even-tide repass.
> Between us now the mountain and the wood
> Seem standing darker than last year they stood,
> And say we must not cross, alas, alas!

III The High Victorian Age

Both the older and younger romantics lived through a time of revolution, of the isolation of Great Britain from Europe, and, after 1815, of the triumph of the Holy Alliance and of conservative, or even reactionary principles. Wordsworth and Coleridge had a strong streak of revolutionary, or renovatory, enthusiasm in their youth; they considered seriously Southey's proposal for founding a small Utopian community on the banks of the Susquehannah. Keats, Shelley, Byron were all second-generation radicals, free in conscience to hate kings and Tories since the defeat of Napoleon made such a hatred once more possible to a patriot. Unlike the older romantics they were uninfluenced by their fathers, who either died when they were very young or were not dominating characters. Most sons either model themselves on their fathers, or rebelliously try to turn themselves into their fathers' opposites. The Romantic poets had to create their own personalities, and the lack of disguise shows itself in their clean-shaven faces. The great Victorians were much influenced by their fathers. Tennyson's was a melancholic, hard-drinking Lincolnshire clergyman and the Tennysons had been disinherited of expected inheritances in favour of cousins from a younger branch of the family, who later called themselves Tennyson d'Eyncourt. A constitutional melancholy ran through the Tennyson brothers, of whom one other, Charles, also showed real poetic gifts. Browning, Tennyson's rival for poetic fame, lived at home supported by his father (a bank clerk) until in his early thirties he eloped with Elizabeth Barrett, then turned forty, and lived with her in Italy till her death in 1861. Arnold's father was the famous headmaster, Dr Arnold of Rugby, a clergyman, but a great success, as Tennyson's father was a great failure. Clough's father emigrated to America but sent the boy back to England. Clough was educated at Rugby School, found in Thomas Arnold a substitute father, and after early success resigned his fellow-ship at Oriel for religious reasons (he could not swallow the Thirty-Nine Articles) and became head of the non-sectarian University Hall in London. The wish to show gratitude to fathers, to live up to their success or ideals, to compensate for their failures, explains the liberal-conservative tone of Victorian poetry. The fathers had all been men of simple faith, and the sons were aware of the strength of German textual criticism against any theory of the Bible as a reliable historical document, and the arguments of Lyell's geology (and the theory of evolution, which was in the air well before Darwin) against any attempt to take the conflated creation myths at the beginning of Genesis as literally true. The question of what could be salvaged of Christian belief and morality troubled them all, even Arnold, whose greatest short poem *Dover Beach* (unlike his prose books *Literature and Dogma* and *St Paul and Protestantism*) is the expression of a melancholy atheism. Compared to the Romantics, the high Victorians seem to us a little localised in their interests: consider, for example, the point most frankly expressed by Tennyson in his sonnet to Gladstone on the Second Reform Bill,

> Steersman, be not precipitate in thine course,

and by Matthew Arnold in *Friendship's Garland* and *Culture and Anarchy*, that we want more democracy, but not yet: we must educate our masters, our coming masters, the popu-lace; we must teach ourselves, the middle-class philistines and the aristocratic barbarians, a respect for the things of the mind, for 'the best that has been thought and said'. Matthew Arnold's fairly humble profession, that of an inspector of schools who was also asked to prepare a report on the far more efficient schools of France and Germany, gave him a realistic sense of the dangers of too much indifference to the State and a sense, also, of the need to extend the State's influence to cultural matters. These are historically interesting questions, but they lack the universality of the problems, raised by the French Revolution and then Napoleon, that troubled the Romantics. They are also questions not easy to answer. The beards, the whiskers, that encumber the faces of so many great Victorians, including poets, show how the new role of public moralist (and the new duty of not saying anything that would have hurt father) robbed serious, thoughtful, and honest men of directness. It is often very difficult to decide whether a Victorian poet is saying what he thinks, or what he thinks he ought to think. (The Victorian age is also, of course, the great period of the English novel, but there is no novelist with the firm and unstressed assurance of rightness that marks Jane Austen: the time of change, of shifting social and intellectual boundaries, of growing prosperity and growing ugliness and squalor, combined, however, with gigantic sanitary reforms and innovations in medicine and nursing, of moral stuffiness and furtive licence, did not make an unstressed assurance of rightness possible.)

Tennyson (1809–92) was certainly the greatest poet of that age. He has been described by Auden as a very great technician, wonderfully fitted to express his own unappeasable inner melancholy, but the stupidest of all the great English poets. I deny the stupidity, though Tennyson did enjoy baffling younger men of letters who met him, like the young Henry James, with a pose, which became in later years habitual to him, of bluff bardic simplicity. But *In Memoriam*, a poem of doubt and faith, as T. S. Eliot remarked, but greater as a poem of doubt, is not the work of a stupid man. Unlike Wordsworth, Tennyson knew that the 'everlasting hills', the hills to which we are to lift our eyes, for thence doth come our aid, are not everlasting:

> The hills are shadows, and they flow
> > From form to form, and nothing stands;
> > They melt like mist, the solid lands,
> Like clouds they shape themselves and go.   (cxxiii)

Very clearly, Tennyson saw the strength of all the new

arguments against traditional Christian belief, the weakness
of all the arguments (like the argument from design) for it.
The deepest argument was in his own emotional need:

> I found Him not in world or sun,
>   Or eagle's wing, or insect's eye;
>   Not thro' the questions men may try,
> The petty cobwebs we have spun:
>
> If e'er when faith had fall'n asleep,
>   I heard a voice 'believe no more'
>   And heard an ever-breaking shore
> That tumbled in the Godless deep;
>
> A warmth within the breast would melt
>   The freezing reason's colder part,
>   And like a man in wrath the heart
> Stood up and answered 'I have felt.'
>
> No, like a child in doubt and fear:
>   But that blind clamour made me wise;
>   Then was I as a child that cries,
> But crying, knows his father near . . .   (cxxiv)

A poet who counts so delicately his own pulse beats, and
who knows also that strong emotion is not an argument, but
is more telling than arguments, cannot be called stupid.

In Memoriam, like most great poems, is about love and
death: the early death of Arthur Henry Hallam, Tennyson's
closest friend at Cambridge, and held to him by a love like
that of Saul and Jonathan, 'surpassing the love of women':
though we have no reason to think that there was anything
consciously sexual in the love. Hallam was engaged, with
Tennyson's delight and approval, to Tennyson's sister, and
his other Cambridge friends shared Tennyson's love and
admiration for him, as the most brilliant and inspiring young
man they had known. He died in 1833 and *In Memoriam*,
composed in sections over at least fifteen years, was not
published till 1850, the year of Wordsworth's death and
Tennyson's appointment as Poet Laureate. It tells us more,
not about Tennyson's art, his deep passions, his visionary
gift, but about the surprising complexity of his personality
than any other poem of his. Hallam for him was something

like a Christ-figure; the point in Christianity he could never
forego was the hope of personal immortality and being
united again with Hallam and all those he loved. The
introductory stanzas to the poem which he wrote in 1849
ring with a firmer belief than anything in the body of it:

> Strong Son of God, immortal Love,
>   Whom we, that have not seen thy face,
>   By faith, and faith alone, embrace,
> Believing where we cannot prove . . .

Yet even in that stanza after the ringing first line there seems
to be a diminuendo, a steady lessening of confidence:
'Believing where we cannot prove' has anything but the
positive ring of 'Strong Son of God, immortal Love'. Yet
these two stanzas express eloquently the piety and humility
that so often accompanies Victorian 'honest doubt':

> Let knowledge grow from more to more,
>   But more of reverence in us dwell;
>   That mind and soul, according well,
> May make one music as before,
>
> But vaster. We are fools and slight;
>   We mock Thee when we do not fear:
>   But help thy foolish ones to bear;
> Help Thy vain worlds to bear thy light.

Three Biblical quotations, coming from 'fools' and 'foolish',
the verb 'fear', the adjective 'vain'. The fool hath said in his
heart, There is no God, from Psalm XIV. The fear of the
Lord is the beginning of wisdom from Psalm III. Vanity of
vanities, saith the Preacher, vanity of vanities: all is vanity.
Tennyson was not a clergyman's son for nothing and ancient
Hebrew literature echoes what he calls in the first section, a
section organic to the poem, its 'divers tones'. We are to
believe, or we are fools, for the way to wisdom is fear: yet
we are to fear the creator of worlds where all is vanity.

In Memoriam, then, is both about the impossibility of
defining a faith, and yet the impossibility of living without
one while being aware all the time that one *may* be wishfully
deceiving oneself. This mood was central to the 'high
seriousness' of the Victorian age. But Auden is right in

suggesting that it is Tennyson's rich and melancholy voice, deep and strong, that draws us. It is one of the unforgettable voices in English poetry and especially suited to conveying a fused sense of richness and loss. There is Tithonus who asked the goddess of dawn, Aurora, for eternal life but forgot to ask her for eternal youth (Aurora, in the end, but later than the story told in Tennyson's poem, turned him into a grasshopper). The fusion of utter exhaustion and utter adoration has never been better expressed than at the end of this poem:

> Ay me! ay me! with what another heart
> In days far-off, and with what other eyes
> I used to watch – if I be he that watched –
> The lucid outline forming round thee; saw
> The dim curls kindle into sunny rings;
> Changed with thy mystic change, and felt my blood
> Glow with the glow that slowly crimson'd all
> Thy presence and thy portals, while I lay,
> Mouth, forehead, eyelids, growing dewy-warm
> With kisses balmier than half-opening buds
> Of April, and could hear the lips that kissed
> Like that strange song I heard Apollo sing,
> While Ilion like a mist rose into towers.

> Yet hold me not for ever in thine East:
> How can my nature longer mix with thine?
> Coldly thy rosy shadows bathe me, cold
> Are all thy lights, and cold my wrinkled feet
> Upon thy glimmering thresholds, when the steam
> Floats up from those dim fields about the homes
> Of happy men that have the power to die,
> And grassy barrows of the happier dead.
> Release me, and restore me to the ground;
> Thou seest all things, thou wilt see my grave:
> I earth in earth forget these empty courts,
> And thee returning on thy silver wheels.

The sound is marvellous everywhere but attains a special magic, I think, in the last two lines of each passage (and the imagery, of course, is haunting too):

> Like that strange song I heard Apollo sing,
> While Ilion like a mist rose into towers.

I earth in earth forget these empty courts,
And thee returning on thy silver wheels.

In the repeated long 'ee' vowel ('thee', 'wheels') and in the slightly smoother and easier movement of 'silver' one seems to see and hear the rotation of Aurora's chariot wheels: an effect reinforced by an undersense of 'returning' – turning over and over like chariot wheels. Tennyson perpetually demands this slow, lingering appreciation. It is enough, however, to make the point that his perfect ear, his truth to feeling, and his unmatched artistry in versification would make him a very great poet even if here not so centrally the representative voice of his age.

He may, perhaps, for some tastes require too much fingering, be too lingeringly ornate. Walter Bagehot, the editor of *The Economist* but also an excellent literary critic, wrote a striking essay on the pure, the ornate, and the grotesque styles in poetry as exemplified by Wordsworth, Tennyson, and Browning. He took as an example of Tennyson's tendency to prettify things this account of Enoch Arden's trade, before he is apparently lost at sea, so that his wife, when he returns, has married an old suitor, Philip, supposing Enoch dead:

> . . . for in truth
> Enoch's white horse, and Enoch's ocean-spoil
> In ocean-smelling osier, and his face,
> Rough-reddened with a thousand winter gales,
> Not only to the market-cross were known,
> But in the leafy lanes behind the down,
> Far as the portal-warding lion-whelp,
> And peacock-yewtree of the lonely Hall,
> Whose Friday fare was Enoch's ministering.

So much, as Bagehot notes sardonically, has never before been made of selling fish. And yet the very fanciness of the language makes Tennyson look as if he were desperately disguising from himself the unpoetic nature of his subject matter. Enoch took his fishcart to sell fresh fish from baskets not only to the market but to neighbouring grand houses. Fish is just fish: and ocean-spoil and ocean-smelling osier and portal-warding lion-whelp and peacock-yewtree cannot draw a veil over that, but rather draw a disporportionate attention to what is a humble, unpoetical, but honest trade.

Except, perhaps, in the *Northern Farmer* poems in Lincolnshire dialect Tennyson has nothing of the understanding of humble joys, trades, and sorrows that Wordsworth shows in a tragic pastoral like *Michael*. He could do almost everything in poetry: but it is a very typical exception that he cannot be plain, direct, and bare. The distance between his poetic language and the language of men is much greater than in Wordsworth; and where he is greatest as a poet he is so by working feelings to an intensity which, for the common reader, they perhaps rarely have: as in *Mariana* suggested by Mariana in the moated grange in *Measure for Measure*:

> All day within the dreamy house,
>   The doors upon their hinges creaked;
> The blue fly sung in the pane; the mouse
>   Behind the mouldering wainscot shrieked,
> Or from the crevice peered about.
>   Old faces glimmered through the doors,
>   Old footsteps trod the upper floors,
> Old voices called her from without.
>   'She only said, 'My life is dreary,
>   He cometh not,' she said;
>   She said, 'I am aweary, aweary,
>   I would that I were dead!'

Tennyson's friend Edward Fitzgerald thought that these earliest lyrics had a 'champagne flavour' never quite caught again. There are certainly touches of mawkishness in *Enoch Arden* and elsewhere, and there are other places where Tennyson is writing in what Hopkins called Parnassian or Castalian – keeping up his style, but with nothing much to say. But considering his long life, his Victorian copiousness and the fact that some of his best poems belong to the later years, one must commend his general standard. He deserved his peerage (which put his cousins the Tennyson d'Eyncourts in their places) and his very special place in the heart of his age.

Yet, though Tennyson was the central figure, there were those, the founders of the Browning Society, which has branches all over England, who found Browning deeper and more thoughtful, with a more interesting though more

puzzling 'message'. He has quite recently become an intellectual fashion again, especially among academics. I think
that as a creator of character, of intriguing situations, a
dramatist of personalities, a sketcher of foreign places, of
odd and sometimes sinister types and moods he beats
Tennyson. He was a natural story-teller in verse and one can
see why Landor compared him with Chaucer and why he
was, far and away, Henry James's favourite Victorian poet.
He shared the religious puzzledness of his age but felt he
could get round it. For Browning faith was something real
but profoundly subjective. In his long narrative poem, *The
Ring and the Book*, the final judgment of death against the
murderer of his innocent wife is given by an aged Pope
whose divine authority rests not on his apostolic succession
from St Peter (he is perfectly aware how much that has been
tangled by the medieval quarrels of Popes and anti-Popes,
each excommunicating the other) but on his wisdom, goodness, and the fact that his judgment is respected. In the
Epistle of Karshish a learned physician, an Arab, has heard
of the story of the apparent raising of Lazarus from the dead
(the man must have had a fit, been in a learned trance or
coma). As a doctor, Karshish knows that the cured patient
can regard his healer not as God's instrument but as God
himself. He has heard rumours of the Nazarene's strange
gospel and execution. It is probably all a foolish rumour,
probably the crowd killed the Nazarene out of fear of his
skill and because his skill could not prevail everywhere: yet
it raises a strange and interesting speculation:

> The very God! think, Abib; dost thou think?
> So, the All-Great, were the All-Loving too –
> So, through the thunder comes a human voice
> Saying, 'O heart I made, a heart beats here!
> Face, my hands fashioned, see it in myself.
> Thou hast no power nor mayst conceive of mine,
> But love I gave thee, with myself to love,
> And thou must love me who have died for thee!'
> The madman saith He said so: It is strange.

We are to think of Karshish with his openness of mind and
heart as saved; we are to think of Cerinthus in the companion piece *A Death in the Desert*, as damned, but Brown-

ing leaves it uncertain whether this is because he refuses to
take all the beliefs of all the early Christians literally, or
because he forces himself to do so. The passage Cerinthus
reads is an addition to a narrative of St Paul's (to-morrow he
goes to fight the beasts in Ephesus) after he has witnessed the
death of the aged St John in the desert. For the dying John it
is the spirit not the letter that matters: the letter is true or
false as it touches the spirit to true life:

> 'The statuary ere he mould a shape
> Boasts a like gift, the shape's idea, and next
> The aspiration to produce the same;
> So, taking clay, he calls his shape thereout,
> Cried ever "Now I have the thing I see":
> Yet all the while goes changing what was wrought,
> From falsehood like the truth, to truth itself.
> How were it had he cried, "I see no face,
> No breast, no feet i'the ineffectual clay"?
> Rather commend him that he clapped his hands,
> And laughed "It is my shape and lives again!"
> Enjoyed the falsehood, touched it on to truth,
> Until yourselves applaud the flesh indeed
> In what is still flesh-imitating clay.'

Cerinthus muses over the appendix to St Paul's letter, in
another hand, an appendix that insists on the literal truth of
all the promises and, in doing so, perhaps traps the soul of
Cerinthus into dishonesty:

Cerinthus read and mused; one added this:

> 'If Christ, as thou affirmest, be of men
> Mere man, the first and best but nothing more, –
> Account Him, for reward of what He was,
> Now and for ever, wretchedest of all.
> For see; Himself conceived of life as love,
> Conceived of love as what must enter in,
> Fill up, make one with His each soul He loved:
> Thus much for man's joy, all men's joy for Him.
> Well, He is gone, thou sayest, to fit reward.
> But by this time are many souls set free,
> And very many still retained alive:
> Nay, should His coming be delayed awhile,
> Say, ten years longer (twelve years, some compute)
> See if, for every finger of thy hands,
> There be not found, that day the world shall end,

Hundreds of souls, each holding by Christ's word,
That he will grow incorporate with all,
With me as Pamphylax, with him as John,
Groom for each bride! Can a mere man do this?
Yet Christ saith, this He lived and died to do.
Call Christ, then, the illimitable God,
Or lost!'

'But 't was Cerinthus that is lost.' Is Cerinthus lost because he is impressed by this, and thinks that he must after all believe in the imminent end of the world if he is to believe in the Incarnation? Or is he lost because he believes Christ is lost, and not being the God of wonders and miracles, at least from now on, is not God? Or because, in his puzzlement, he turns away from the difficult path of enlightenment? In such poems Browning certainly does set the mind trickier puzzles than Tennyson in *In Memoriam* and shows a religious optimism that is in practice invulnerable since, for all his elaborations of syntax and nuance, the grounds of the religion are never made quite clear nor its scope circumscribed by a definition. One might call it the religion of a strenuous and sanguine Victorian earnestness. It is true to Browning's temperament; but there is something in it (if we compare the doubt and personal agony of *In Memoriam*) a little dodgy, if not merely windy and facile. Browning is a little too much at ease in Zion.

'The proper study of Mankind is Man.' Browning is infinitely better as an explorer of human mood and character than as a religious or metaphysical thinker. His strange tolerance not only of human oddity but of some kinds of human wickedness, and his genuine if often grotesque sense of humour, makes him at least understand Porphyria's lover who strangles his loved one with her own beautiful hair and then sits with her head cradled in his lap till morning: Caliban, and his god Setebos who is like Caliban cruel, unpredictable, and frightened, and therefore must have his own God to be frightened of: the Duke who had caused his last Duchess to be put to death not because she was polite, charming, warmly grateful to himself, but because she was the same to everybody else: the delightfully irreverent old man who is not going to pretend on his death-bed that life has been misery or that its fun has not been naughty:

> What is he buzzing in my ears?
>   'Now that I come to die
> Do I view this world as a vale of tears?
>   Ah, reverend sir, not I!'

The impression of place, like eighteenth-century Venice in the tinkling of *A Toccata of Gallupi's*, is again always masterly:

> As for Venice and her people, merely born to
> bloom and drop,
> Here on earth they bore their fruitage, mirth and
> folly were the crop:
> What of soul was left, I wonder, when the kissing had
> to stop?
>
> 'Dust and ashes!' so you creak it, and I want the heart
> to scold.
> Dear dead women, with such hair, too – what's
> become of all the gold
> Used to hang and brush their bosoms? I feel chilly
> and grown old.

Or a very different landscape (and Browning's most beautiful single stanza, I think) in *Two in the Campagna*:

> The champaign with its endless fleece
>   Of feathery grasses everywhere!
> Silence and passion, joy and peace;
>   An everlasting wash of air –
> Rome's ghost since her decease.

As a poet of sudden, surprising evocation, as there, Browning is unsurpassed in the language and few poets have surpassed him in a range of human sympathy which embraced, one might say, everything but the ordinary. He can be grand and terrible, too, as at the end of *Childe Roland to the Dark Tower Came*, a kind of riddle poem but with no clear answer. I am not sure whether the dark tower is death, judgment, or the dreadful hidden knowledge of oneself in one's own heart, or whether the pilgrimage towards it is suicidal, vainglorious, or heroic: it may, in fact, often be Browning's genius to present his topics with such extraordinary vividness that the reader is forced to invent, or

imagine, a shape and meaning in the whole, worthy of the
compulsive power of the detail:

> Not hear? when noise was everywhere! it tolled
>   Increasing like a bell. Names in my ears
>   Of all the lost adventurers my peers, –
> How such a one was strong, and such was bold,
> And such was fortunate, yet each of old
>   Lost, lost! one moment knelled the woe of years.
>
> There they stood, ranged along the hill-sides, met
>   To view the last of me, a living frame
>   For one more picture! in a sheet of flame
> I saw them and I knew them all. And yet
> Dauntless the slug-horn to my lips I set,
>   And blew.
> '*Childe Roland to the Dark Tower came.*'

Browning puzzles elderly critics; with his gift for exciting
stories he remains the best way into English poetry for
children.

Matthew Arnold (1822–88) was the most fastidious and
subtle English critic of poetry of his time, and had an
extremely witty and eloquent prose style whose only fault is
a tendency to excessive repetition of his favourite phrases
('What I tell you three times', a mocking contemporary
commented, 'is true'.) Though he wrote an excellent appreciative essay about Wordsworth as poet rather than thinker,
and made amends in late years to Keats in whom he had
seen a mere stream of images but in whom he now discovered a 'vein of flint and iron', Arnold on the whole deplored
the effects of the Romantic movement. He would not have
agreed that it is the feeling, in modern poetry, that should
lend interest to the action, and attempted two narrative
poems in a traditional epic style, *Sohrab and Rustum* and
Balder Dead (from Persian and from Scandinavian mythology) which have splendid passages, but a little too much of
the air of being composed according to a recipe. In prose,
his attitude to religion was the opposite of Browning's: for
Browning faith was everything, the changing forms in which
it embodied itself nothing: Arnold loved the services of the
Anglican *Book of Common Prayer* and would not have had
them tampered with; he saw Jesus as a sage who conveyed

his 'secret' to his true disciples and God Himself (the concept of the Trinity he saw as nonsense rather than as a mystery) as 'something not ourselves that makes for righteousness'. F. H. Bradley pointed out that this minimal theism was about as inspiring as the conception of soap as 'something not ourselves that makes for cleanliness', and as poor nourishment for the worshipping spirit. But Arnold believed that poetry was likely gradually to take the place of conventional religion as a *magister vitae* (master or ruler of life) and his greatest short poem, *Dover Beach* is frankly atheistic. There is love between persons and the world appears beautiful; but there is no God to turn to in our despair and there is not even any clear direction of history in a meaningless universe:

> Ah, love, let us be true
> To one another! for the world, which seems
> To lie before us like a land of dreams,
> So various, so beautiful, so new,
> Hath really neither joy, nor love, nor light,
> Nor certitude, nor peace, nor help for pain;
> And we are here as on a darkling plain
> Swept with confused alarms of struggle and flight,
> Where ignorant armies clash by night.

If Arnold's life as an inspector of schools, Professor of Poetry at Oxford, lecturer in America, writer of sharply satirical books on English philistinism, had not been such a busy one, he would have been able to give all his poems the finish that only perhaps the half-a-dozen best ones have. His gift was for elegy, as in *Thyrsis*, on his friend Clough, or *The Scholar Gypsy*, on the lost graces of the seventeenth century, rather than for the heroic. One of the poems that moves me most is *A Southern Night*, about his brother, an Indian civil servant, who died exhausted on the way home at Gibraltar, having left his young wife buried in the foothills of the Himalayas:

> In cities should we English lie,
>   Where cries are rising ever new,
> And men's incessant stream goes by –
>   We who pursue

Our business with unslackening stride,
  Traverse in troops, with care-filled breast
The soft Mediterranean side,
  The Nile, the East,

And see all sights from pole to pole,
  And glance, and nod, and bustle by,
And never once possess our soul
  Before we die.

Not by those hoary Indian hills,
  Nor by this gracious Midland sea
Whose floor to-night sweet moonshine fills
  Should our graves be.

Arnold was himself a great public servant, and I am not sure
whether the description of the hurrying cares of the English
who hold the Empire together is without a stoic pride. One
side of him hated the modern world, as is shown in his
warning to the scholar gypsy not to stray, in his eternal
wanderings, into modern times:

O born in days when wits were fresh and clear,
  And life ran gaily as the sparkling Thames;
    Before this strange disease of modern life,
With its sick hurry, its divided aims,
  Its heads o'ertax'd, its palsied hearts, was rife –
    Fly hence, our contact fear!
Still fly, plunge deeper in the bowering wood!
  Averse, as Dido did with gesture stern
  From her false friend's approach in Hades turn,
Wave us away, and keep thy solitude!

Dido suggests the lonely Tyrian trader in the great Homeric
simile at the end (Carthage was a Tyrian colony) and the
Greeks suggest British trade and sea-power: but there is an
odd shift in tone between the gloom of 'With its sick hurry,
its divided aims' and the buoyancy of 'The young light-
hearted masters of the waves':

Then fly our greetings, fly our speech and smiles!
– As some grave Tyrian trader, from the sea,
  Descried at sunrise an emerging prow
Lifting the cool-hair'd creepers stealthily,
  The fringes of a southward-facing brow

> Among the Aegean isles;
> And saw the merry Grecian coaster come,
>   Freighted with amber grapes, and Chian wine,
>   Green, bursting figs, and tunnies steeped in brine,
> And knew the intruders on his ancient home,
>
> The young light-hearted masters of the waves . . .

I feel that here, against the current of his own argument, Arnold moves our sympathies towards the Greeks; and along with an awareness of sick hurries and divided aims had, perhaps unknowingly, an awareness of British wealth and power. He remained a strenuous Victorian to the last in many ways, dying in his mid-sixties of a sudden heart-attack after leaping over a fence to greet his married daughter, returning from America, at Liverpool station. He would be a greater, if not necessarily a more attractive poet, if more of the wit of his prose had got into the fading, graceful moonlit greys of his poetry. He does not lack pathos or flexibility but a little, perhaps, bite, colour and passion. Yet even where the versification is clumsy as (because of haste, perhaps) it too often is, we are aware, behind an awkward presentation, of a graceful soul. He cared very deeply for a kind of serious beauty, and sometimes achieved it.

Nobody, I think, would go to Arthur Hugh Clough for grace or beauty but they might possibly go for a wit like that of a more earnest and intellectual Byron and for a more strenuous self-questioning, and a harsher probing of the problems of doubt or faith, than they can find among his more famous and successful contemporaries. (Arnold, his one close friend among the poets, felt that Clough made poetry do work of close thinking that prose was better equipped to do; and that he was blankly indifferent to beauty.) His life, like his poetry during his lifetime (and indeed largely after it), was, after a deceptive start at Rugby where he was headboy and Dr Arnold's favourite pupil, a long study in honourable failure. He gave up his Oxford fellowship for honourable but growingly inessential reasons, found his headship of University Hall dull, sought in vain for a congenial post in America, and married a pious wife who, though a bluestocking herself, deplored his religious probings. In her (anonymous) introduction to his posthumous collected poems his wife suggests that the happiness of marriage and fatherhood quieted an unnecessarily restless mind (it certainly put paid to his poetry). He was one of the many willing slaves at the beck and call of Florence Nightingale. This worrying history, so full of problems and so empty of satisfactory solutions, perhaps accounts for Clough's comparatively short life (1819–65). He never had the sense of achievement and recognition that was to sustain Tennyson, Browning, and Arnold in their later years.

Clough's masterpiece of ironic hesitation, over commitment either in politics or love, *Amours de Voyage* – a technical triumph also in its use of the accentual hexameter with a natural and conversational ring – is too long to quote here. His humour can perhaps best be suggested by a stanza or two from *Spectator Ab Extra*, an intelligent soliloquy by a *nouveau riche* who is getting on in society but who wants to learn the manners of the old aristocracy before his class ousts them from power. (Clough underestimated the toughness of the English aristocracy, who clung on to their share of power, married the new rich, and learned the ways of the City of London.)

> There's something undoubtedly in a fine air,
> To know how to smile and be able to stare.
> High breeding is something, but well bred or not,
> So needful it is to have money, heigh-ho!
> So needful it is to have money.
>
> And the angels in pink and the angels in blue,
> In muslins and moirés so lovely and new,
> What is it they want, and so wish you to guess,
> But if you have money, the answer is Yes.
> So needful, they tell you, is money, heigh-ho!
> So needful it is to have money.

One should contrast with the neatness of those stanzas, these clumsy but sincere stanzas in which Clough wonders if pride of intellect has led him from the patience that waits for spiritual vision:

> Come back again, my olden heart! –
>   With incrustations of the years
> Uncased as yet, – as then thou wert,
>   Full-filled with shame and coward fears:
> Wherewith, amidst a jostling throng
> Of deeds, that each and all were wrong,

The doubting soul, from day to day,
Uneasy paralytic lay . . .

Come back again, old heart! Ah me!
  Methinks in those thy coward fears
There might, perchance, a courage be,
  That fails in these the manlier years;
Courage to let the courage sink,
Itself a coward base to think,
Rather than not for heavenly light
Wait on to show the truly right.

One admires the extraordinary honesty of these lines but, with the admiration, there goes a wish that Clough had been able to take a standpoint and stick to it, a feeling that his thinking seems to veer or hobble, and that the vision he half hopes for never seems to fully alight in his verse. One can see why this permanently but uncomfortably open mind made a deep impression, and still does, on academics; one can see also what Clough meant when, in a witty prose dialogue, he suggested that Dr Arnold's strenuous moral and intellectual training at Rugby robbed his best pupils of their youth. When they came to Oxford or Cambridge their first freshness was already gone. (The young Matthew saved himself perhaps by his dandy ways and mockery, by his savouring of the more urbane and dashing civilization of France.) Clough is no doubt an improving writer and an indispensable companion to the intellectual and spiritual uncertainties of the high Victorian age; but no poet of his stature is more completely lacking in what Matthew Arnold called 'natural magic'.

For that, Clough's contemporaries, Tennyson, Browning, Arnold had in the end to look beyond the immediate problems of the age and their own adjustments to these problems. They escape from themselves in the power and delight of the possession and exercise of the poetic gift, and in life's daily satisfactions; such an escape was never to be Arthur Hugh Clough's. He has not been as popular with his fellow poets as with academics. Swinburne wrote in a famous prose limerick: 'There was a dull poet called Clough, whom his friends found it useless to puff; for the public, though dull, has not such a skull as belongs to believers in Clough.' More quietly, in our own time, Auden simply left

Clough out of the appropriate volume, *Tennyson to Yeats*,
of the excellent anthology, *Poets of the English Language*,
which he compiled with Norman Holmes Pearson.

IV Rustic and Light Verse

There are two nineteenth-century traditions, which the
solemnity of our subject matter so far has made us ignore,
those of rustic and light verse. At the very beginning of the
century, Robert Bloomfield (1766–1823) won a real and
undeservedly transient reputation with his poem in late
Augustan descriptive couplets, *The Farmer's Boy*. Young
Bloomfield knew something of country life and sometimes
lived with a benefactor in the country, had a little schooling
and much self-education by reading, and was by trade a
lady's shoemaker not a farmer's boy. But if a town boy, he
was observant, and we can still enjoy this account of wrong
and right ways to make cheese: and of the excessive
demands of London on country food:

> Thou, like a whirlpool, drain'st the countries round,
> Till London market, London price, resound
> Through every town, round every passing load,
> And dairy produce throngs the eastern road:
> Delicious veal, and butter, every hour,
> From Essex lowlands, and the banks of Stour;
> And further far, where numerous herds repose,
> From Orwell's brink, from Waveny, or Ouse.
> Hence Suffolk dairy-wives run mad for cream,
> And leave their milk with nothing but its name;
> Its name derision and reproach pursue,
> And strangers tell of 'three times skimm'd sky-blue'.
> To cheese converted, what can be its boast?
> What, but the common virtues of a post!
> If drought o'ertake it faster than the knife,
> Most fair it bids for stubborn length of life,
> And, like the oaken shelf whereon 'tis laid,
> Mocks the weak efforts of the bending blade;
> Or in the hog-trough rests in perfect spite,
> Too big to swallow, and too hard to bite.
> Inglorious victory! Ye Cheshire meads,
> Or Severn's flow'ry dales, where Plenty treads,
> Was your rich milk to suffer wrongs like these,
> Farewell your pride! farewell renowned cheese!

The skimmer dread, whose ravages alone
Thus turn the mead's sweet nectar into stone.

I do not know whether this poem, or the competition of the market, was the cause, but I have never seen or tasted this hard, unappetising Suffolk skimmed-milk cheese. It is interesting when good minor poems remind us of vanished everyday things.

John Clare, born in 1793, was a genuine farmer's boy, but the fame of his early poems uprooted him from his old position and did not give him a new one. He sought in his poems a girl whom he had loved and whose death his imagination could not accept. The later part of his life was spent in the county asylum at Northampton, where he was allowed a great deal of freedom, wandering the town and scribbling verses in public houses in return for free drinks: he was encouraged to write verses, also, but unfortunately the kindly but critically obtuse asylum doctor copied the poems, in his own versions with the spelling, punctuation, and diction corrected, in a large notebook and Clare's original manuscripts have vanished. His best poems are those like *Secret Love* in which his sharp and exact countryman's observation are mingled with tenderness for a not wholly real, but all the more intensely desired, loved one:

> I met her in the greenest dells,
> Where dewdrops pearl the wood bluebells;
> The lost breeze kissed her bright blue eye,
> The bee kissed and went singing by,
> A sunbeam found a passage there,
> A gold chain round her neck so fair;
> As secret as the wild bee's song
> She lay there all the summer long.

The last line makes a climax of beautiful intensity and pathos.

William Barnes (1801–86) was a Dorset man of a similar humble background who did not go mad but became a schoolmaster and then a parson. His memory is still as much loved in Dorset as that of Hardy (who, like Hopkins, admired him and learned very much from him) is distrusted. (Hardy, I learned from an expert in Dorset traditions, is remembered for his evasiveness, his mean and ungenerous nature, and the sly flirtations which persisted into his extreme old age.) Barnes certainly demands attention as the only modern English poet to use a local dialect, and one without a literary tradition, as expertly as Burns, almost a century before, used a wide vernacular with a long literary tradition behind it. Geoffrey Grigson calls attention to the 'pictorial exquisiteness', one of Barnes's 'colour contrasts', of this stanza from 'The Sky a-Clearèn':

> Below the hill's an ash; below
> The ash, white elder-flow'rs do blow;
> Below the elder is a bed
> O' robinhoods o' blushèn red;
> An' there, wi' nunches all a-spread,
> The haÿ-meäkers, wi' each a cup
> O' drink, do smile to zee hold up
> The raïn, an' sky a-cleärèn . . .

Much more would bear quotation: poets like Clare and Barnes are wholesome to bear in mind when we are plunged into the hothouse world of the aesthetes and decadents of the end of the century.

The writers of light verse and nonsense verse are worth bearing in mind also. Winthrop Mackworth Praed in his light verse is like a miniature version of the Byron of *Beppo* and *Don Juan*, often neater in his versification, certainly free of guilt in his life. Born in 1801, dead in 1839, in Parliament first as a moderate Whig supporting the Reform Bill in 1830, then as a moderate Tory (or, to use Peel's new word, Conservative) supporting Peel, he died, like Keats, of consumption, though he was active in Parliament till a month before his death. He left a sorrowing wife, two small children, and a devoted but too dilatory or too conscientious friend, the Reverend Derwent Coleridge, who took twenty-four years to bring out a first edition which included all Praed's slightest pieces and juvenilia: poor Mrs Praed was then herself dead. Praed had married Helen in 1835, at the height of his Parliamentary success, but only four years before his death.

He was capable of a well-bred passion, as in *My First Folly*:

> Pretty Coquette, the ceaseless play
> Of thine unstudied wit,

And thy dark eye's remembered ray
  By buoyant fancy lit,
And thy young forehead's clear expanse,
Where the locks slept, as through the dance,
  Dreamlike, I saw thee flit,
Are far too warm and far too fair,
To mix with aught of earthly care,
But the vision shall come when my day is done,
A frail, and a fair, and a fleeting one!

Not too shallow, not too deep: his light and quizzing attention to the pleasures of fashionable life – quizzing, not mocking – was perhaps that of a man who knew instinctively that his artificial paradise was to be a short one. No matter, as in *Good-Night to the Season* he bows himself politely off stage:

Good-night to the Season! – the splendour
  That beamed in the Spanish Bazaar;
Where I purchased – my heart was so tender –
  A card-case, a pasteboard guitar,
A bottle of perfume, a girdle,
  A lithographed Riego, full grown,
Whom bigotry drew on a hurdle
  That artists might draw him on stone; –
A small panorama of Seville, –
  A trap for demolishing flies, –
A caricature of the Devil, –
  And a look from Miss Sheridan's eyes . . .

Good-night to the Season! – another
  Will come, with its trifles and toys,
And hurry away, like its brother,
  In sunshine, and odour, and noise.
Will it come with a rose or a briar?
  Will it come with a blessing or curse?
Will its bonnets be lower or higher?
  Will its morals be better or worse?
Will it find me grown thinner or fatter,
  Or fonder of wrong or of right,
Or married – or buried? – no matter,
  Good-night to the Season – good-night!

The London season of fashionable routs and balls and bazaars and dinners would find him married, and then buried, soon enough. He would retain to the last that wistful love of the surface of things, which he knew to be deceptive; those deeper and sadder feelings which, in polite society, must be passed off as a whimsy. He remains our master poet of *vers de société*.

William Makepeace Thackeray (1811–63), whose fame rests on two great novels *Vanity Fair* and *Esmond*, lived, unlike Praed, in a bohemian rather than a fashionable world, though he was as conscious as Praed of his status as a gentleman and had a similar flicking, dismissive wit. With a little too much Victorian sentiment for our taste, he had also – as in his imitation of Béranger's *Le Grenier* – an unVictorian frankness. Here is the original:

> Lisette ici doit apparaître,
> Vive, jolie, avec un frais chapeau;
> Déjà sa main a l'étroite fenêtre
> Suspend son schal, en guise de rideau.
> Sa robe aussi va parer ma couchette;
> Respecte, Amour, ses plis longs et flottans.
> J'ai su depuis qui payait sa toilette.
> Dans un grenier qu'on est bien a vingt ans!

And Thackeray's version:

> And see my little Jessy, first of all;
>   She comes with pouting lips and sparkling eyes:
> Behold, how roguishly she pins her shawl
>   Across the narrow casement, curtain-wise;
> Now by the bed her petticoat glides down,
>   And when did woman look the worse in none?
> I have heard since who paid for many a gown,
>   In the brave days when I was twenty-one.

Light verse at its best has always a touch of sadness, and one might quote a clergyman, the Reverend Richard Harris Barham (1788–1845), whose racy and irreverent *Ingoldsby Legends* came out near his death, in 1840. He has a funny but sad allusion to Horace's most melancholy ode,

> Eheu fugaces, Postume, Postume,
> Labuntur anni . . .

(Alas, Postumus, Postumus, swift glide away the years . . .)

Barham's odd but unforgettable little allusion (he alters, Maurice Baring thinks, the Latin order of the words to run with the English metre) runs thus:

> What Horace says is –
> Eheu fugaces
> Anni labuntur, Postume, Postume!
> Years glide away and are lost to me, lost to me!
> Now, when the folks in the dance sport their merry toes,
> Taglionis and Ellslers; Duvernays and Ceritos,
> Sighing, I murmur, 'O mihi praeteritos!'

The names are those of famous Victorian dancers: 'O mihi praeteritos', 'Lost, past to me: gone beyond me'. In both Thackeray and Barham there is a sighing for a past world.

Somehow in the mid-Victorian age this kind of light verse changed into nonsense verse. Its great master, Edward Lear (1812–88), used nonsense to express a deep inner loneliness of a rather Tennysonian sort. He was a water-colour landscape artist of considerable talent, taught his art to the children of noble families like the Stanleys who treated him as a household pet, was loved by children for whom his first *Book of Nonsense* (revised in 1861, and enlarged or enriched with supplementary volumes till 1877) was written in 1846; but underneath the nonsense (he was an ugly, awkward, shy though very attractive man, who aroused protective and amused feelings, but never romantic love) there is a plangent sense of loss: it is an interesting critical question, for instance, whether *How Pleasant to Know Mr Lear!* is *really* a nonsense poem:

> How pleasant to know Mr Lear,
>   Who has written such volumes of stuff!
> Some think him ill-tempered and queer,
>   But a few think him pleasant enough . . .
>
> When he walks in a waterproof white,
>   The children run after him so!
> Calling out, 'He's come out in his night-
>   Gown, that crazy old Englishman, oh!'
>
> He weeps by the side of the ocean,
>   He weeps on the top of the hill;
> He purchases pancakes and lotion,
>   And chocolate shrimps from the mill.

He reads but he cannot speak Spanish,
He cannot abide ginger-beer:
Ere the days of his pilgrimage vanish,
How pleasant to know Mr Lear!

Lewis Carroll (The Reverend Charles Lutwidge Dodgson, 1832–94) created in the White Knight an endearing and inept figure, like the figure of Lear in this self-portrait; but in such poems as *Jabberwocky* (a game with words which relies on the tendency of readers, like Carroll's illustrator Sir John Tenniel, to make vague concepts and precise pictures of creatures like 'mimsy borogroves' and 'mome raths' in a narrative and descriptive poem about non-existents) we are more aware of the sharpness of Carroll's logical gift, or elsewhere of his gift for parody, than of the romantic agony of an isolated man. In his close, but delicately innocent, friendships with young girls Carroll had found a kind of sublimated happiness. With his fondness for taking photographs of little girls posed almost in the nude he would have had a miserable life today; his fellow Oxford dons realised, however, that their children, who delighted in his stories, were safe with him. I find his true poetry in the prose of *Alice in Wonderland*, *Through the Looking Glass and What Alice Found There*, and *Silvie and Bruno*. In the verse (including the long *Hunting of the Snark*, a sort of nonsense version of a combination of *Moby Dick* and the *Ancient Mariner*) I find cleverness, fun, and a gift for parody.

Late Victorian parodists like J. S. Calverley and J. K. Stephen are 'merely literature'. One writer of *vers de société*, who joins Praed before him and Betjeman after him by a thin but exquisite thread, is Frederick Locker-Lampson (1821–95), also editor of the best English anthology of light verse except Auden's, *Lyra Elegantiarum*. Lady Dorothy Nevill sketches this survivor from a less earnest age:

... I used to see a great deal of Mr Frederick Locker [*he changed his surname to Locker-Lampson in later life, GSF*], whose delicate verse had an especial charm for me, and I still treasure a copy of *London Lyrics*, which he presented to me, inscribed with the too flattering dedication:

The Muse I woo'd was fair and true,
And all her charms I find in you.

Mr Locker was fond of owls, and always kept some of these solemn birds at his house at Rowfant in Sussex, to which I have paid many pleasant visits. Often would we talk over old days and Lord Cantilupe, mentioned in *Rotton Row*:

> But where is now the courtly troop
>   That once rode laughing by?
> I miss the curls of Cantilupe,
>   The laugh of Lady Di.

I well remember the curls in question and their owner at Florence many, many years ago, in the early forties. Lord Cantilupe was, indeed, one of the very last of that race, now passed away, whose recognised mission in life was to be dandies.

The 1890s would, as we shall see, produce its own dandyism in literature; but attended by tragedy, rather than dandyism, in life.

V Aesthetes, Decadents, Isolated Greatness

The particular problems that worried the high Victorian poets, the problems about religion and science, about the poet as the spokesman of a noble but generous morality in personal life and of a sane liberal-conservatism in politics – the poet as a combination of teacher and preacher – had less effect, less importance, for the chief poets of the second half of the century. They were beginning to become a little bored with the earnest game of hide and seek between doubt and belief. Their political views were either more reactionary or more revolutionary than those of the high Victorians, and religion was becoming for them, at least in its Christian version, something accepted on authority (as by Christina Rossetti, Coventry Patmore, Gerard Manley Hopkins, Alice Meynell) or something fiercely or regretfully denied (as by Swinburne, Hardy, A. E. Housman). There were others, like Dante Gabriel Rossetti and William Morris, poets of the pre-Raphaelite movement, much influenced by Ruskin, to whom the Middle Ages were an inspiration and who could use their version of medieval religion for brilliant poetic colouring, like Rossetti in *The Blessed Damosel*. For William Morris, on the other hand, in his best volume, *The*

Defence of Guenevere, it was the mingling of fierceness and chivalry, gallantry and cruelty, the roses and the tapestry and the blood on the sword, that fascinated him. He was an early Socialist whose burly courage in demonstrations brought him at times within risk of imprisonment (it was the age of chivalry of early Socialism). But for Morris true Socialism, as he described in his prose utopia, *News from Nowhere*, was a turning back from the industrial revolution towards guilds of handicraftsmen; and it was, in fact, not to the town workers but to the cultivated middle classes that his wall-paper, the furniture and the plain, decent houses made by his disciples, brought an escape from ugliness. He was sometimes (like the poetry of some pre-Raphaelites) over-elaborate: his Kelmscott Chaucer is a striking print *pastiche* of medieval script, but with its heavy gothic lettering not a text in which anybody could study Chaucer or read him for pleasure. It is an *object*, and it is a criticism of later nineteenth-century poetry that too many of its masters were content to create ornate objects rather than to express thought or passion. Morris, after *The Defence of Guenevere*, produced too many long volumes of medieval tales on which he himself pronounced the just verdict: 'The idle singer of an empty day'.

Algernon Charles Swinburne, never strictly a pre-Raphaelite, for all the shrillness of his voice and the uncontrolled abundance of his self-soliciting self-expression, had gifts for expressing passion which Morris lacked. Queen Victoria, always widely informed even about matters outside her central interests, was right in 1892, on Tennyson's death, to assume that she could not choose Swinburne as the new laureate (because of the scandal caused by his early *Poems and Ballads*, with their sadistic sexual fantasies, and because of the equal wildness of his alcoholic and – he could get sexual arousal only from being flagellated – masochistic life, till Watts-Dunton lured him into protective custody at Putney): but also to 'understand that Mr Swinburne was the best poet in Her Majesty's dominions'.

We are much more forgiving about Swinburne's drink problem and his confused sexual fantasies than about his habit of running on the spot, his sheer inability to halt the engine.

He was the only Victorian poet who could be described as an aristocrat, the son of an Admiral of an old Northumberland family. In spite of his wild sexual fantasies the one physical exercise into which he flung himself with daring and delight was swimming, and his verse at its best often contains images of and imitates the swell of the sea. In spite of his heavy drinking in youth, he lived from 1837 to 1909, though his later poems – boosting Italian nationalism, attacking Napoleon III and the Boers, and showing an old man's sentimental fondness for babies in perambulators – are less interesting than those of his early wildness. He was a fine scholar (Jowett of Balliol consulted him on his translation of Plato, and was ready to accept Swinburne's amendments) and at times a remarkably acute literary critic (the first to see the pre-eminent importance in Keats's work, of the odes). But his criticism is liable to explode in hysterical outbursts of rage; and his metrical virtuosity has not enough of the real experience of human passion to fasten on. If I were asked to choose his greatest lines (though this is not how to judge Swinburne) I would choose the last six lines of this second stanza of *Ave Atque Vale*, Swinburne's memorial tribute to Charles Baudelaire. I quote the whole stanza, italicising the lines I have in mind:

> For always thee the fervid languid glories
> 　Allured of heavier suns in mightier skies;
> 　Thine ears knew all the wandering watery sighs
> Where the sea sobs round Lesbian promontories,
> 　The barren kiss of piteous wave to wave
> 　That knows not where is that *Leucadian grave*
> *Which hides too deep the supreme head of song.*
> *　Ah, salt and sterile as her kisses were,*
> *　The wild sea winds her and the green gulfs bear*
> *Hither and thither, and vex and work her wrong,*
> *　Blind gods that cannot spare.*

The allusion is of course to Sappho of Mytilene or Lesbos, a lover of her own sex, who is said to have hurled herself from a promontory because her love for a man had been rejected. The six lines I have italicised move me because, apart from seeing and hearing the sea in them, one finds also a concise agony of feeling and longing –

> Ah, salt and sterile as her kisses were . . .
> 　Blind gods that cannot spare . . .,

which Swinburne usually does not consciously aim at and certainly seldom achieves. His more typical kind of achievement is to be found in one of his greatest sustained poems, *The Triumph of Time*, inspired by what can hardly have been an unforeseen rejection of the shrill and impotent little man's love. The poem works by expanding away from the unbearable humiliation at its centre with an extraordinary rebounding energy:

> There lived a singer in France of old
>   By the tideless dolorous midland sea.
> In a land of sand and ruin and gold
>   There shone one woman, and none but she.
> And finding life for her love's sake fail,
> Being fain to see her, he bade set sail,
> Touched land, and saw her as life grew cold,
>   And praised God, seeing; and so died he.

Swinburne was a very learned poet, and one has to know about the troubadour Geoffroi de Rudel and his love for the unattainable *princesse lointane*, in far away Syria, before one fully construes this passage. But what leaves Swinburne just on the wrong side of being a great poet (he is a major figure in the history of poetry, which is something different) is that construing the references adds little to what we can get from the vague and general connotations of the words and the movement of the rhythm. As we are being bounced along on 'A land of sand and ruin and gold' it is irritating, rather then helpful, if a reader over our shoulder murmurs: 'Syria, in the time of the Crusaders . . .'

William Morris (1834–96), unlike Swinburne, lived a sane and healthy life and enjoyed ten years less of it. And in his best poems, like *The Haystack in the Floods*, he gives us not primarily sound or subjective feeling but object and action:

> Had she come all the way for this,
> To part at last without a kiss?
> Yea, had she borne the dirt and rain
> That her own eyes might see him slain
> Beside the haystack in the floods?
>
> Along the dripping leafless woods,
> The stirrup touching either shoe,
> She rode astride as troopers do;

With kirtle kilted to her knee,
To which the mud splash'd wretchedly;
And the wet dripp'd from every tree
Upon her head and heavy hair,
And on her eyelids broad and fair;
The tears and rain ran down her face.

I read that first as a schoolboy and it still haunts me. If only Morris could have stayed in that vein!

Both as a painter and as a poet, Dante Gabriel Rossetti, much more than the early Morris or than Swinburne at his most intense, seems to belong to another world than ours. One of the best collections of pre-Raphaelite paintings is in Manchester, and I remember noticing there how bilious are the complexions of his tall, gaunt, bony beauties and how exophthalmic their eyes. He created an image of the beautiful woman which one begins, unless one makes an effort of appreciation, to find grotesque; but one knows also from photographs that the great beauties of the pre-Raphaelite circle, like Jane Morris, Morris's wife, on whom Rossetti doted, *were* like the pictures. And Janey's photographs do suggest that she was what Rossetti called a 'stunner': one would have admired the original, whatever one thinks of the representation.

Rossetti's life (1828–82) was for a Victorian poet a short and, at the end, a sad one. Remorse for the death of his model, and later his wife, Elizabeth Siddall, which he felt had been hastened by his infidelities, made him bury his unpublished poems with her; poetic pride later made him get permission for a friend to dig them up again (the rather sinister friend who dug them up died from a knife attack in Soho with a guinea clenched in his teeth). His love for Janey must later, however Platonic, have involved remorse about his hero-worshipped friend Morris. He died a melancholy solitary, daily dowsing his creative fire with chloral.

As with his paintings of women, one feels that the emotions behind Rossetti's poems are true but have been stylised and worked upon till the style questions the emotions. Rossetti, for instance, the son of an Italian radical free-thinker, was not a practising Christian and what he looked for in women was not a virginal quality. He did, however, love the painted paradises of Italian medieval painting. Is that all *The Blessed Damosel* is about?

The blessed damozel leaned out
  From the gold bar of Heaven;
Her eyes were deeper than the depth
  Of waters stilled at even;
She had three lilies in her hand,
  And the stars in her hair were seven.

Has Rossetti chosen 'three' and 'seven' because they are traditional symbolic numbers (the three supernatural virtues: the seven sorrows of Our Lady, for instance) or do they symbolise something for him? Does his richly pictorial poetry have, for instance, the profound personal symbolism that the moon shining gules through Madeline's window, the bitter chill at the beginning, the storm at the end, long, long ago these lovers fled away, have for Keats? Take even a poem famed for the precision with which it images its emotion, *The Woodspurge*:

Between my knees my forehead was, –
My lips, drawn in, said not Alas!
My hair was over in the grass,
My naked ears heard the day pass.

My eyes, wide open, had the run
Of some ten weeds to fix upon;
Among those few, out of the sun,
The woodspurge flowered, three cups in one.

From perfect grief there need not be
Wisdom or even memory:
One thing then learnt remains to me, –
The woodspurge has a cup of three.

The woodspurge is one of several plants belonging to the genus *euphorbia*, which when squeezed give out a peculiar acrid milk with healing properties; the flower, like the obsolete verb to spurge or purify, with its triple cup might suggest the Trinity and the resemblance in sound of *spurge* to *asperge* might suggest the opening words of the Roman

Mass, 'Asperges me, Domine, hyssopo . . .', 'Sprinkle me, Lord, with hyssop . . .' In Biblical use, the hyssop was probably the thorny caper (*capparis spinosa*) whose branches were used for sprinkling; but in Kings iv, 33, it has become any lowly plant: 'And hee spake of trees, from the Cedar tree that is in Lebanon even unto the hyssop that springeth out of the wall.' This was the usual Middle English sense and in its vague spread would cover Rossetti's woodspurge. The words of Psalm li, 7, and of the opening of the mass would be appropriate to his grief: 'Purge me with hyssop, and I shall be clean.' But we have no means of knowing whether he had all this in mind, or is not merely contented with the vaguely suggestive, precise but opaque image, as in the 'three' and 'seven' of *The Blessed Damozel*. All Rossetti's verse has an Italianate sweetness and he is at his best, probably, in English versions of Dante and Cavalcanti where his originals, whose rhythmical movement he follows without effort, provide a hard foundation of thought for him. In his original poems the question is always whether seeming to see much, in a glass darkly, he sees merely the pretty frame and flashing lights and colours reflected on the surface of the glass.

His sister Christina, who had a firm and definite Christian faith to which she was willing in the end sadly to sacrifice the love of a man who did not share it, is a less ambitious but spiritually truer poet. Nor is she merely a pious poet but, as in the poem which I. A. Richards chose for his pupils to examine in *Practical Criticism*, one aware of natural delight of a world beyond (though the natural here is unaffectedly a symbol) in a way her brother could not have managed – the supernatural was merely a poetic convention to him:

Spring Quiet

> Gone were but the Winter,
>   Come were but the Spring,
> I would go to a covert
>   Where the birds sing;
>
> Where in the white-thorn
>   Singeth a thrush,
> And a robin sings
>   In the holly-bush.

Full of fresh scents
 Are the budding boughs,
Arching high over
 A cool green house:

Full of fresh scents
 And whispering air
Which sayeth softly:
 'We spread no snare;

Here dwell in safety,
 Here dwell alone,
With a clear stream
 And a mossy stone.

Here the sun shineth
 Most shadily;
Here is heard an echo
 Of the far sea,
Though far off it be.'

It is in the last three lines of that last stanza –

 'Here is heard an echo
  Of the far sea,
 Though far off it be.' –

that we feel in Christina a buoyant assurance in the handling of symbolism, and a freshness, which Dante Gabriel's too rich and cloying manner lacks. Perhaps in his lust for greatness, Dante lost the chance of becoming like his sister merely a good human being, merely a good poet.

One poet stands out among the later Victorian poets for fierce power, grief and delight, and for a metrical and verbal inventiveness so surprising that many critics have seen him (wrongly, for he was formed by Ruskin and Newman, and not untouched by the aesthetic creed of Pater) as a 'modern' poet born out of due time: the Roman Catholic convert and Jesuit priest, Father Gerard Manley Hopkins (1844–89). In choosing the Jesuits, Hopkins found the iron discipline he wanted (becoming to his superiors, according to the code of the order, like a stick in a blind man's hand) but found also the order which has always furthered in its ranks talent of worldly use but been most afraid of originality and thinkers.

Hopkins was original, not only in his poetry; he was alone among his order, in his time, in preferring Scotism, with its emphasis on God's will and his love for the species, to Aquinas with his emphasis on God's reason or justice. The difference between the two great schoolmen is shown in their sharply contrasting theories of individuation. God, for Aquinas, thought of the species, Man: and the difference between individual men is like the difference, an accidental difference due to the firing of the oven or the mixture of the dough, between different loaves from the same batch. According to Scotus, and this was what attracted the poet in Hopkins to him, God loved the *haecceitas*, the 'thisness', what Hopkins was to call the selving, the saking, the inscape, of every man on earth, of every peculiar distinguishing mark of every man, of every leaf on every tree, of every pattern made by the growth along a river bank, of every group of trees. One saw God at work not in the dull general similarity of the formative ideas behind every species but in the dazzling variety of the actual:

> Glory be to God for dappled things –
>   For skies of couple-colour as a brinded cow;
>   For rose-moles all in stipple upon trout that swim;
> Fresh-firecoal chestnut-falls; finches' wings;
>   Landscape plotted and pieced – fold, fallow, and plough;
>   And all trades, their gear and tackle and trim.
>
> All things counter, original, spare, strange;
>   Whatever is fickle, freckled (who knows how?)
>   With swift, slow; sweet, sour; adazzle, dim;
> He fathers-forth whose beauty is past change:
>   Praise him.

Hopkins in a way is the last of the Romantics; but instead of 'something far more deeply interfused' in Nature, he saw Christ, in his role of the second person of the Trinity, as the instrument and the sustainer, through the individuating love which moved him towards it, of the creation of the physical universe. Thus in his very vivid awareness of particularised beauty he was aware of Christ: but Christ was also the figure whom he followed in self-sacrifice, was his Muse also, and was the lover whom he could reproach for neglect: one might say that he saw Christ everywhere at work in the outward world, almost in a sense directly, but was growingly aware of Christ's not speaking to him in his derelict inner heart. That side of Hopkins comes out in a sonnet like the following: ('fell' is like 'felt', the rough hairy skin of an animal, such as Jacob wore when cheating Esau of his birthright. The night descends on Hopkins smotheringly, as if he were being stifled by such a hide).

> I wake and feel the fell of dark, not day.
> What hours, O what black hours we have spent
> This night! what sights you, heart, saw; ways you went!
> And more must, in yet longer light's delay.
>
> With witness I speak this. But where I say
> Hours I mean years, mean life. Any my lament
> Is cries countless, cries like dead letters sent
> To dearest him that lives alas! away.
>
> I am gall, I am heartburn. God's most deep decree
> Bitter would have me taste: my taste was me;
> Bones built in me, flesh filled, blood brimmed the curse.
>
> Selfyeast of spirit a dull dough sours. I see
> The lost are like this, and their scourge to be
> As I am mine, their sweating selves; but worse.

The dead letter office in the post-office collects letters sent to non-existent addresses where the sender has written no clue to his own address either (in the most passionate faith there is the cruellest doubt). In the third last line it is the self yeast of the spirit that sours not the dull dough of the body. It is a poem of desperation, not despair: Hopkins is not damned, and the state of the damned is worse than his. It is eternal and his tribulations are both a gift and a warning. Hopkins is stirred by the glory and terror of the storm in *The Wreck of the Deutschland* and by the suffering of the nuns delivered from their pain through Christ's passion. Sometimes the awareness of death almost overwhelms his faith as in the following passage from *That Nature is a Heraclitean Fire and of the Comfort of the Resurrection*:

> Million-fuelèd,ʹ nature's bonfire burns on.

But quench her bonniest, dearest' to her, her
clearest-selvèd spark
Man, how fast his firedint,' his mark on mind, is gone!
Both are in an unfathomable, all is in an enormous
dark
Drowned. O pity and indig' nation! Manshape, that
shone
Sheer off, disseveral, a star,' death blots black out; nor
mark
      Is any of him at all so stark
But vastness blurs and time' beats level. Enough! the
Resurrection . . .

'Enough the Resurrection . . .' is not poetically quite enough, but the fiercely triumphant 'In a flash at a trumpet crash/I am all at once what Christ is' in the last stanza seems to annihilate doubt. The possible finality of death, something which haunted all Victorian poets, was a worry to Hopkins too: as in his lovely sonnet to a young child, in short four-stress, four-foot lines in 'sprung rhythm' *Spring and Fall* (a sprung rhythm foot can be of one to five syllables, and is counted from the first stressed syllable: one knows which this is – or Hopkins puts an accent in to guide one – because it is the syllable naturally emphasised, in ordinary speech, for sense):

> Márgarét, are you griéving
> Over Goldengrove unleaving?
> Léaves, like the things of man, you
> With your fresh thoughts care for, can you?
> Áh! ás the heart grows older
> It will come to such sights colder
> By and by, nor spare a sigh
> Though worlds of wanwood leafmeal lie;
> And yet you *will* weep and know why.
> Now no matter, child, the name:
> Sorrow's springs are the same,
> Nor mouth had, no nor mind, expressed
> What heart heard of, ghost guessed:
> It is the blight man was born for,
> It is Margaret you mourn for.

From this still centre of the certainty of death he reaches out beautifully to the divine glory speaking to him in every detail of nature: (from *Binsey Poplars*)

> My aspens dear, whose airy cages quelled,
> Quelled or quenched in leaves the leaping sun,
> All felled, felled, are all felled;
>   Of a fresh and following folded rank
>   Not spared, not one
>   That dandled a sandalled
>   Shadow that swam or sank
> On meadow and river and wind-wandering
>   weed-winding bank.

And it is with a prophet's indignation that he at last confronts a God unresponsive, apparently, to his need for creative renewal:

> Wert thou my enemy, O thou my friend,
> How wouldst thou worse, I wonder, than thou dost
> Defeat, thwart me? Oh, the sots and thralls of lust
> Do in spare hours more thrive than I that spend,
>
> Sir, life upon thy cause. See, banks and brakes
> Now, leavèd how thick! lacèd they are again
> With fretty chervil, look, and fresh wind shakes
>
> Them; birds build – but not I build; no, but strain,
> Time's eunuch, and not breed one work that wakes.
> Mine, O thou lord of life, send my roots rain.

There are the great themes of all poetry: love, death, the true, the good, the beautiful. But for a truly great poet, like Hopkins, they are never havens to rest in, premature ultimates, but points of departure for new explorations. Lack means search.

Hopkins is sometimes seen as a 'modern' poet, born before his due time. It is better to see him as a late Victorian of genius, owing much to Ruskin (as the sketches in his notebook bear witness) in his detailed vision of nature, with a personal feeling for Christ (and for the image of manly beauty) not unlike Tennyson's feeling for Hallam. He was Victorian in his use of a very elaborately contrived and muscular metrics and a deliberately surprising diction (which, when one thinks it is a coinage, as in the word 'burl', often turns out to have dialect justification) to put over a vision of life and a set of emotional problems which are moving and dignified but not deeply intellectually puzzling. Auden's generation, the poets of the 1930s, saw what he was after; from what they write about him, both Yeats and Eliot were unable properly to hear his rhythms, and found his strong, battering simplicity unsympathetic. When Bridges published the first edition of Hopkins, of about one thousand copies in 1918, Yeats was developing his own new style and Eliot was moving towards *Gerontion* and *The Waste Land*. They felt that the eccentric Jesuit who died in 1889 had nothing to teach them. By 1930, when Charles Williams edited the second edition, with a much more enthusiastic preface than Bridges's, Auden and his generation wanted strength, direction, and simplicity, and greeted Hopkins warmly. Yet even on them, except on very minor members of that loosely-knit 'Auden generation' like Rex Warner, it is difficult to see that Hopkins had a very direct technical influence. The young Auden owed much more, for instance, to Hardy, as he admits, to Laura Riding and Robert Graves (about whose influence he was more reticent), medieval and Anglo-Saxon poetry, Icelandic blood-feud themes, English folk-songs and ballads, and any influence he could absorb as he went along from West Indian calypsos to Byron's *Don Juan*. It is as a great and moving poet in himself, not as an influence, that Hopkins matters.

After Hopkins, the nineteenth century is notable for the beginnings of two great poets, Yeats and Hardy, and the early publications of two good ones, A. E. Housman and Robert Bridges. There are interesting oddities like Coventry Patmore who combined and wished to fuse a repetitive uxoriousness (his wives kept dying, and he kept remarrying) with a Roman Catholic mysticism: Hopkins, whom he knew slightly, was repelled by his attempt in a prose book, *The Root, The Rod, and The Flower* to use sexual imagery to express the sense of mystical union of the soul as the Bride with Christ as the Bridegroom. But, of course, Hopkins's own deep personal devotion to the humanity of Christ had a homosexual tinge, so he was biassed against Patmore's enthusiastic heterosexuality. Mysticism very often expresses itself in sexual metaphors, just as the expression of an intense sexuality can take on a religious tinge. In which way s Patmore going, for instance, in a poem like *To the Unknown Eros*?

> What rumour'd heavens are these
> Which not a poet sings,
> O, Unknown Eros? What this breeze
> Of sudden wings
> Speeding at far returns of time from interstellar space
> To fan my very face,
> And gone as fleet,
> Through delicatest ether feathering soft their solitary beat,
> With ne'er a light plume dropp'd, nor any trace
> To speak of whence they came, or whither they depart?

The answer is, at the end of the free ode, still an exciting enigma:

> And might some note of thy renown
> And high behest
> Thus in enigma be expressed:
> 'There lies the crown
> Which all thy longing cures.
> Refuse it, Mortal, that it may be yours!
> It is a Spirit, though it seems red gold;
> And such may no man, but by shunning, hold.
> Refuse it, till refusing be despair,
> And thou shalt feel the phantom in thy hair.'

This long poem, which gives the impression of being made up of two or three prolonged and suspensive sentences, shows a remarkable metrical skill, one which no doubt drew Hopkins to Patmore: but read too much of Patmore and one has a hot, cloying sensation, a feeling of an excitement that creates itself by caressing itself, and turns back with relief to Hopkins for the open and various world, the shock of reality.

James Thomson ('B.V.' or Bysshe Vanolis, with a memory of Shelley and the German Romantic aphorist, Novalis) in *The City of Dreadful Night* creates out of atheism a dense, foggy gloom, grimly and monotonously expressive of an even worse claustrophobia than Patmore's. He had a tragic life, dismissed for drunkenness from an army schoolmaster's post, losing an early sweetheart who might have made his life happy, earning a precarious living as a journalist reporting the second Carlist war and making contributions to Bradlaugh's rationalist weekly. The protection of a Leicester family who sheltered and cared for him gave him a few months of happiness in his last years but he could not keep away from drink and was driven back to his lonely and self-destructive life in London again. In spite of very humble origins, he was a man of some culture who translated the prose works of the great Italian pessimist poet, Leopardi. And it is only fair to his sincerity and strength in this dark and stifling poem to say that his self-destructive life sprang from his pessimism, rather than the pessimism from his life. Most early atheists, like Bradlaugh himself, saw their atheism as a liberation from all the old chains; few took James Thomson's view that it created a grey and gloomy world in which death was man's only final goal and hope: his City of Night is less like the slums of London, which he knew well than like what he himself called 'some necropolis':

> The City is of Night, but not of Sleep;
>   There sweet sleep is not for the weary brain;
> The pitiless hours like years and ages creep,
>   A night seems termless hell. This dreadful strain
> Of thought and consciousness which never ceases,
> Or which some moments' stupor but increases,
>   This, worse than woe, makes wretches there insane.
> They leave all hope behind who enter there:
>   One certitude while sane they cannot leave,
> One anodyne for torture and despair;
>   The certitude of Death, which no reprieve
> Can put off long; and which, divinely tender,
> But waits the outstretched hand to promptly render
>   That draught whose slumber nothing can bereave.

It is almost impossible to *enjoy* the monotonous dead march of Thomson's verse or the strong, repeated gloom of his insistence that a sane and sober awareness of life is agony but it is impossible not to respect him.

That respect was felt by one of the greatest poets of our own century, T. S. Eliot – and perhaps it is impossible now to read *The City of Dreadful Night* without a certain sense of a fore-shadowing of *The Waste Land* – as he felt respect for another Scotsman of low birth, John Davidson (1857–1908) an elementary schoolmaster, who came to London to make a living by writing poetry and, for a wonder, just managed to do so. His poems were long narrative poems, in loose and rather undistinguished blank verse, in which he expressed a Lucretian materialism and the Nietzschean view of life which was then (it also greatly affected Bernard Shaw) beginning to become fashionable. As his sales dropped, he was given a Civil List pension of £100 a year and in the year before he drowned himself Shaw gave him £250 to complete a long poem, *God and Mammon* on which he was then working, under great financial difficulties and living a life of melancholy solitude. He got through the £250 quicker than he intended (though, unlike James Thomson, he was not a drinker, and lived a prudent and meagre life) and rather than ask Shaw for another loan he drowned himself in 1908, leaving the last part of his trilogy incomplete. Eliot writes, combating a misleading idea that he was indebted to Davidson only for technical hints:

> Certainly, *Thirty Bob a Week* seems to me the only poem in which Davidson freed himself completely from the poetic diction of the English verse of his time (just as *Non Sum Qualis Eram* seems to me the only poem in which, by a slight shift of rhythm, Ernest Dowson freed himself). But I am sure that I found inspiration in the content of the poem, and in the complete fitness of content and idiom; for I also had a good many dingy urban images to reveal.

Maurice Lindsay in his selection from Davidson quotes in the preface two stanzas which show what Eliot admired; the controlled bitterness of the poor clerk (even in the 1890s, thirty shillings a week was just enough to keep alive on, no more) who will not seek escape in crime or blame his own natural inferiority on bad luck, though swallowing the sense of it is as bitter as hell could be:

> I couldn't touch a step and turn a screw,
> And set the blooming world a-work for me,
> Like such as cut their teeth – I hope, like you –
> On the handle of a skeleton gold key;
> I cut mine on a leek, which I eat it every week:
> I'm a clerk at thirty bob as you can see.
>
> But I don't allow it's luck and all a toss;
> There's no such thing as being starred and crossed;

It's just the power of some to be a boss,
And the bally power of others to be bossed;
I face the music, sir; you bet I ain't a cur;
Strike me lucky if I don't believe I'm lost!

It is dangerous to disagree with such a great poet and critic as Eliot but I confess there is just a little too much in this poem for me of the old serio-comic 'character' recitation of the music halls. I prefer *A Runnable Stag*:

When the pods went pop on the broom, green broom,
    And apples began to be golden-skinn'd,
We harbour'd a stag in the Priory coomb,
    And we feather'd his trail up-wind, up-wind,
    We feather'd his tail up-wind –
        A stag of warrant, a stag, a stag,
        A runnable stag, a kingly crop,
        Brow, bay and tray and three on top,
        A stag, a runnable stag,

or even *In Romney Marsh*:

As I went down to Dymchurch Wall,
    I heard the South sing o'er the land;
I saw the yellow sunlight fall
    On knolls where Norman churches stand.

And ringing shrilly, taut and lithe,
    Within the wind a core of sound,
The wire from Romney town to Hythe
    Alone its airy journey wound . . .

But one can see that these pleasanter and more musical verses had not the touch of raw newness which in *Thirty Bob a Week* attracted the young Eliot. They do illustrate the difference between Davidson, whose natural tendency was to enjoy life (the fear that he had cancer, not money worries, drove him to suicide) and the hell of grey dull melancholia, the torment of sober insomniac consciousness in which, unless he could drug himself for a little with alcohol, James Thomson lived.

Another Thompson, Francis Thompson, had a life mostly of miserable failure. Enlisted by his father, a doctor, at Owens College, Manchester, he was too shy to attend lectures and failed his examinations three times. Drifting to London, he was like the similarly homeless and penniless De Quincey befriended by a prostitute and given shelter and food in her room; but at the same time became an opium addict. The Meynells, Wilfred and Alice, were impressed by two or three poems sent to their magazine *Merrie England*, arranged for the publication of his *Poems* at the age of thirty-four and for the last nineteen years of his life (1859–1907) he was more or less weaned of the opium habit and lived for a time as the guest of Franciscan monks. The poem that remains in many readers' minds is less the once famous *Hound of Heaven* than the posthumous one, *The Kingdom of God*, of which these are the last three stanzas:

> The angels keep their ancient places; –
> Turn but a stone, and start a wing!
> 'Tis ye, 'tis your estrangèd faces,
> That miss the many-splendoured thing.

> But (when so sad thou canst not sadder)
> Cry; – and upon thy so sore loss
> Shall shine the traffic of Jacob's ladder
> Pitched betwixt Heaven and Charing Cross.

> Yea, in the night, my Soul, my daughter,
> Cry, – clinging Heaven by the hems;
> And lo, Christ walking on the water
> Not of Gennesareth, but Thames!

As one lays these almost too abundant poets of the later nineteenth century alongside each other, in their unquestioned belief, or unquestioned disbelief, does one not have a feeling of wistfulness for the moral and intellectual strenuousness of the high Victorian age? They are somehow, as people, less interesting than Tennyson, Browning, Clough, Arnold.

Strangely some of the 'decadent' poets of the 1890s like Ernest Dowson (1867–1900) and Lionel Johnson (1867–1902) and Arthur Symons (1865–1945), whose *The Symbolist Movement in Literature* of 1899 was of the utmost importance to his friend Yeats and ten years later, quite independently, to the young T. S. Eliot in his Harvard days, made positive capital out of this lack of intellectual content. They were, like the younger Keats himself, though none of them equalled the rich embroidery of his coat, poets of mood, impression, of music and suggestiveness, not of argument and statement. It is, as Eliot said, a subtle shift in metre that rescued Dowson's *Non sum qualis eram bonae sub regno Cynares* (*I am not such as I was under the rule of the benign Cynara*) from the commonplace. In this poem the thought is busy about the form rather than the substance of the poem:

> Last night, ah, yesternight, betwixt her lips and mine
> There fell thy shadow, Cynara! thy breath was shed
> Upon my soul between the kisses and the wine;
> And I was desolate and sick of an old passion,
>   Yea, I was desolate and bowed my head:
> I have been faithful to thee, Cynara! in my fashion . . .

Johnson, a learned man (who 'loved his learning better than mankind/though courteous to the worst. . .', Yeats was to say) could not be quite so vague, but for all his theological learning and rigour (Yeats says he detested the vulgarity of those who would not believe in eternal damnation) his *Dark Angel* seems a projection of solitary broodings:

> I fight thee, in the Holy Name!
> Yet, what thou dost, is what God saith:
> Tempter! should I escape thy flame,
> Thou wilt have helped my soul from Death:
>
> The second Death, that never dies,
> That cannot die, when time is dead:
> Live Death, wherein the lost soul cries,
> Eternally uncomforted.
>
> Dark Angel, with thine aching lust!
> Of two defeats, of two despairs:
> Less dread, a change to drifting dust,
> Than thine eternity of cares.
>
> Do what thou wilt, thou shalt not so,
> Dark Angel! triumph over me:
> *Lonely, unto the Lone I go,*
> *Divine, to the Divinity.*

The movement is so sad and compelling that one does not notice that in four stanzas Johnson has drifted from the idea of Satan as God's messenger and tester (as in the *Book of Job*), to the idea of Satan (as in Milton) as a rebel against God and man's enemy and eternal tormenter if he can be ('Eternally uncomforted'), to the idea of Satan as somehow a personification of one's own terrors ('lust', 'despairs', 'eternity of cares' – the lost soul *becomes* Satan). In the course of this intellectual voyage the poet also moves from the comparative bearability of materialism ('a change to drifting dust') to an evasion of these torments that arise because man is a soul animating immortal body (or body which is to be resurrected to eternal bliss or torment), and on to a complete separation of the invulnerable divine spark of the soul *from* the drifting dust of the body: the soul, impregnable to any Dark Angel, is to be reabsorbed in the Neo-Platonic One. The passage moves us precisely *because* of its inconsistency of doctrine, because of the struggle of the tormented spirit of the poet from images of eternal fear, perhaps imaginary, to equally imaginary eternal bliss.

Symons, an impressionist, interested in streets in the fog, in glimpses of sordid rooms, anticipated aspects of Eliot. But what moved Eliot more than his poems was his famous essay on Laforgue in which he translates some lines of Laforgue's famous prose poem on Hamlet. We feel what we think of as the modern mood, in Eliot, of intelligent dislocation, strangely anticipated: because it was from Jules Laforgue, as he found him in Symons, that the young Eliot learned his trade:

> Perhaps I have still twenty or thirty years to live, and I shall pass that way like the others. Like the others? O Totality, the misery of being there no longer! Ah! I should like to set out to-morrow, and search all through the world for the most adamantine processes of embalming. They, too, were, the little people of History, learning to read, trimming their nails, lighting the dirty lamp every evening, in love, gluttonous, vain, fond of compliments, hand-shakes and kisses, living on bell-tower gossip, saying, 'What sort of weather shall we have to-morrow? Winter has really come . . . We have had no plums this year.' Ah! everything is good, if it would not come to an end. And thou, Silence, pardon the Earth; the little madcap hardly knows what she is doing; on the day of the

great summing-up of consciousness before the Ideal, she will be labelled with a pitiful *idem* in the column of the miniature evolutions of the Unique Evolution, in the column of negligible quantities . . . To die! Evidently, one dies without knowing it, as, every night, one enters upon sleep. One has no consciousness of the passing of the last lucid thought into sleep, into swooning, into death. Evidently. But to be no more, to be here no more, to be ours no more! Not even to be able, any more, to press against one's human heart, some idle afternoon, the ancient sadness contained in one little chord on the piano!'

Born in Paris in 1860, Laforgue died in 1887, a few months after his marriage, and had never at any time in his short adult life 'twenty or thirty years to live'. From his twentieth to his twenty-sixth year he had the post of reader to the Empress Augusta in Berlin. He has influenced English-speaking poets (Eliot and Pound) more than any other Frenchmen: he was, from what his friend Gustave Kahn tells us, like a French cartoon version of a correct young Englishman, 'very correct, high stiff collars, sober neckties, English-looking garments, an Anglican clergyman's overcoat, and, should it to be needed, a rolled up umbrella stiffly stuck under his arm'. He foretold, even in appearance, the young Eliot; and Symons, neither a major critic, nor a major poet, showed genius here as a translator and as the bringer of a new kind of mask into English poetry. (He also translated, at sight, into English, other French symbolists, for the benefit of Yeats who knew little French, and took Yeats to Paris to see Alfred Jarry's *Ubu Roi*. 'After us', Yeats commented, 'the Savage God!')

Yeats was happy enough to meet these 'decadent' poets at the Cheshire Cheese and to say, in the first poem in his *Collected Poems*, 'Words alone are certain good'. Yeats is a great modern poet who, in the 1890s, partly imitating his friends of the Rhymers' Club, partly drawing on the example of the pre-Raphaelites and attempting to make an Irish or Celtic tradition out of minor nineteenth-century poets who had drawn on Irish mythology, could not even at the beginning (born in 1865, he died in 1939) wholly hide his greatness. The new mood of the 1890s, the sense of transience all around and sudden and inexplicable changes even in what he had thought the eternal pattern of things, was never better expressed than in *The Moods*:

Time drops in decay,
Like a candle burnt out,
And the mountains and woods
Have their day, have their day;
What one in the rout
Of the fire-born moods
Has fallen away?

Underneath all the ornateness of his early verse he was from the first capable of bitterness, as in *The Fish*,

Although you hide in the ebb and flow
Of the pale tide when the moon has set,
The people of coming days will know
About the casting out of my net,
And now you have leaped times out of mind
Over the little silver cords.
And think that you were hard and unkind,
And blame you with many bitter words.

Does one blame a little fish for refusing to be caught in one's most subtly spread nets? Though the bitterness is real so, I think, is the young Irishman's awareness of its moral absurdity. Maud Gonne, was the daughter of an Ascendancy Colonel, with a post at Dublin Castle; she had an illegitimate daughter by a French anarchist journalist, and later married a drunken soldier of fortune, Major John MacBride. Though Yeats was her friend whom she also saw as a useful instrument for Irish nationalist propaganda, he did not attract her erotically: though they may have come together briefly in 1907 or 1908, when both had lost their first bloom. Yeats loved Maud but hated her fanaticism and opinionated hatred, and briefly in the 1890s found a more suitable mistress, the gentle Olivia Shakespeare, a much sweeter woman who broke off the affair when she realised that the image of Maud still haunted him:

Pale brows, still hands and dim hair,
I had a beautiful friend
And dreamed that the old despair
Would end in love in the end:
She looked in my heart one day
And saw your image was there;
She has gone weeping away.
(*The Lover Mourns for the Loss of His Love*)

Even in the long wistful hesitation and growingly hopeless expectation which lasted in Yeats till Lady Gregory took him back to Ireland and brought out, in his management of the Abbey Theatre, his latent masterfulness, he *lived* his poetry in a way that sets him quite aside from his friends Johnson, Symons, and Dowson.

Yeats is one of the seven or eight very great English poets. In the 1890s, an essentially modest man, he disguised himself as well as he could as one of the minor poets of the Rhymers' Club. His father was an extremely good but commercially unsuccessful portrait painter. On both his father's and mother's side he belonged to the minor Irish Protestant gentry. A grandfather had been rector of the Church of Ireland church at Drumcliffe where he is buried, his mother's family, the Pollexfens, were flax-merchants and sea-captains in Sligo. Nineteenth-century Ireland was like eighteenth-century Ireland in accepting a gentry (wider and more inclusive than the English concept of a gentry) and a peasantry or in the towns a shopkeeper class (what Yeats called 'hucksters'). Being a member of the Church of Ireland, the Church of the Ascendancy, was a class-marker rather than a spiritual experience; it would have been as impossible for Yeats to become a Roman Catholic as to align himself with the Dublin shop-keeping class for whom he felt a passionate contempt:

> For men were born to pray and save . . .

But being, as he says, 'a very religious' man he invented his own religion, made out of what he calls a 'fardel' of old images or tales: true religion was something subjective or antithetical, springing out of the spontaneous 'self-affrighting, self-delighting' nature of the self: false religion, or the religion that did not attract Yeats, was primary or objective: the exposure of the self to an alien judging mirror. This is expressed in his most profound poem of the 1890s, certainly, I would think, a poem beyond judgment or appreciation by his 'companions of the Cheshire Cheese', who were much more irregular in their lives than Yeats but were both bored and disconcerted by the power of his intellect. The strength of an Oxford education of that time was that it obviated the necessity of further thinking: any new problem that cropped up would be a variation of something one knew already. I wonder what they made of this, which comes obliquely, of course, out of the Genesis folktale about the Creation, the Temptation, the Fall. For Yeats these three concepts are symbols for a process that is inner and eternal:

The Two Trees

Beloved, gaze in thine own heart,
The holy tree is growing there;
From joy the holy branches start,
And all the trembling flowers they bear.
The changing colours of its fruit
Have dowered the stars with merry light;
The surety of its hidden root
Has planted quiet in the night;
The shaking of its leafy head
Has given the waves their melody,
And made my lips and music wed,
Murmuring a wizard song for thee.
There the loves a circle go,
The flaming circle of our days,
Gyring, spiring to and fro
In those great ignorant leafy ways;
Remembering all that shaken hair
And how the wingèd sandals dart,
Thine eyes grow full of tender care:
Beloved, gaze in thine own heart.

Gaze no more in the bitter glass,
The demons, with their subtle guile,
Lift up before us when they pass,
Or only gaze a little while;
For there a fatal image grows
That the stormy night receives,
Roots half hidden under snows,
Broken boughs and blackened leaves.
For all things turn to barrenness
In the dim glass the demons hold,
The glass of outer weariness
Made when God slept in times of old.
There, through the broken branches, go
The ravens of unresting thought;
Flying, crying, to and fro,
Cruel claw and hungry throat,

Or else they stand and sniff the wind,
And shake their ragged wings: alas!
Thy tender eyes grow all unkind:
Gaze no more in the bitter glass.

He might have been understood by A. E. Housman who published his *A Shropshire Lad* in 1895 and who is still for us a very contemporary poet; his great skill in verse and his diction have not dated; or, just possibly, by as great a poet but a very rootedly English one, Thomas Hardy, to whom I shall turn in the next chapter.

10

The Twentieth Century

I Places and Periods

With British accession to the Common Market and, even more, with the growing influence of American poets like Allen Tate, John Crowe Ransom, Laura Riding, Ezra Pound, H.D., William Carlos Williams, Robert Frost, Sylvia Plath, John Berryman, Robert Lowell, it might be said that English poetry has not come to an end, but has become a comparatively minor part of poetry in English, whether written in England (or in English or Lowland Scots in Scotland, in Anglo-Welsh in Wales, or Anglo-Irish in Ulster and the Republic) or in America or elsewhere in the world. Philip Larkin is probably justly the most famous of living English poets and his reputation rests on four slim volumes published roughly between his early twenties and his early fifties at intervals of ten years. There should be a fifth volume in his sixties, a sixth in his seventies, and, if he shows the stamina of Robert Graves, a seventh in his eighties. Nobody seeks to compete with him and, if one compares his work with Lowell's very large production before his death at sixty, one is reminded of General Forrest and his wish to be 'fustest with the mostest'. A talented American poet wants to be top poet; the old country is still a more civilised place, and most English poets (even in very grand periods, like the seventeenth century) have been content to be good poets. They do not stretch their vocal chords.

Of strictly English poets in this century Thomas Hardy (1840–1929) is one of the two greatest, and the most uneven,

291

but extraordinary in his mastery of shifts of rhythm, and in his gift of transferring to poetry the sense of mood, atmosphere, and character that distinguish him as a great Victorian pastoral novelist. He is happiest, as in the novels, with a country setting and a wistful backwards look. He is also one of the most felicitous of English poets in his diction, coining words very freely, ('outleant', 'wistlessness'). In some of his work there is a touch of his own Jude's pedantry of the self-educated man; elsewhere he displays a touch of the ballad-singer and country story-teller, reminding one at times of a poet in the corner of a country newspaper. The poems in which he struggles with abstract ideas – he called himself a poet of 'unadjusted impressions', and in his attitude to life a 'meliorist' – are confused and bewildered. The unadjusted impressions convince, yet his confusion moves us. An atheist, he still had a wistful longing for the village churches of his childhood and his sad poem on the turn of the century, *The Darkling Thrush*, suggests a hymn:

> So little cause for carolings
>   Of such esctatic sound
> Was written on terrestrial things
>   Afar or nigh around,
> That I could think there trembled through
>   His happy good-night air
> Some blessed Hope, whereof he knew
>   And I was unaware.

The retrospective love poems, looking back to early meetings with his wife, written in his early seventies after his first wife died and after they had been estranged for many years, are among the few great love poems in the language. It had not been a happy marriage (his first wife, Emma, the sister of a clergyman at St Juliot's in Cornwall thought herself socially his superior), yet Hardy's early deep feelings for her were movingly expressed in these late love poems.

Hardy created for many poets of this century an alternative tradition, purely English, to that of Pound and Eliot. Yet at times he writes almost as an Imagist, not tied to a theory. Here is one of his finest short poems:

Snow in the Suburbs

Every branch big with it,
Bent every twig with it;
Every fork like a white web-foot;
Every street and pavement mute:
Some flakes have lost their way, and grope back upward, when
Meeting those meandering down they turn and descend again.
The palings are glued together like a wall,
And there is no waft of wind with the fleecy fall.

A sparrow enters the tree,
Whereon immediately
A snow-lump thrice his own slight size
Descends on him and showers his head and eyes,
And overturns him
And near inurns him,
And lights on a nether twig, when its brush
Starts off a volley of other lodging lumps with a rush.

The steps are a blanched slope,
Up which, with feeble hope,
A black cat comes, wide-eyed and thin;
And we take him in.

Hardy was copious, sometimes careless, but there are enough great poems to make him deserve G. M. Young's salutation: *Ultimus Anglorum*.

It is interesting that Eliot disliked Hardy intensely (the poems seemed to him typically a novelist's poems and in prose Hardy seemed to him to move from strikingly bad to sublime writing without ever going through the intermediate stage of writing merely well). Eliot's slightly older mentor, Ezra Pound, however, greatly admired Hardy. It would be difficult to find another short poem in English as vivid, concentrated, and exact in its evocation of a physical scene as *Snow in the Suburbs*, or another writer who, having made a great reputation as a tragic, pastoral novelist, from his fifty-fifth to his eighty-eighth year slowly built up a still grander reputation as a poet.

Eliot himself was a great English poet in almost exactly the sense that Henry James was a great English novelist – they had similar American backgrounds. Like James, Eliot could have gone back to America to take a

Ph.D. on F. H. Bradley, and to become an assistant professor of philosophy. But after his scholarly visits to the Sorbonne, Marburg, and Merton College, Oxford, his interests had shifted. Indeed they had begun to shift at Harvard where, after writing a number of early poems only to be published at the end of his life, he had worked out the earliest draft of *The Love-Song of J. Alfred Prufrock*. I remember hearing Leavis lecturing on Eliot, saying how wonderful to write such a poem in 1917, the date of *Prufrock and Other Observations*. I reflected that some knowledge of history and biography does not misbecome even a major critic. Eliot's first marriage was very unhappy. There was a sense in which women, even the *odor di femina* ('female smells in shuttered rooms') disgusted him; a sense in which physical desire for his wife Vivien was thwarted by disgust: certainly she ended up mad, after Eliot had left her, and there were no children. One imagines a series of fiascos, which was probably why Eliot did not resent Bertrand Russell's taking Vivien away for a week-end to teach her to enjoy love-making. Alas, it was probably he who needed the lessons. And there may have been other complications. The dedication of *Prufrock and Other Observations* is to a young Paris friend of Eliot's, Jean Verdenal, recently dead in the First World War, whom Eliot described (in a prose note much later in *The Criterion*) as once greeting him in a Paris park clutching a branch of lilac. The Dante passage that follows might read thus in English:

> Now you can understand the quantity
> Of that love which warms me towards you
> When I put out of mind our vanity
> Treating the shadow as a solid thing.

The Verdenal family have asserted that this was a perfectly normal relationship and that indeed Verdenal was too busy with his medical studies to have seen much of Eliot. It is Eliot's feelings that matter, however, and it seems clear from his poems that he thought of women as whores, victims, or madonnas and, less from his poems than from what biographical information is available, that he was capable of warm and frank friendship with men. Mrs Valerie Eliot quotes a letter which Eliot sent to his friend in

Harvard, Professor Theodore Spencer, about *The Waste Land*, and which Spencer later quoted in a lecture: 'Various critics have done me the honour to interpret the poem in terms of the contemporary world, have considered it, indeed, as an important piece of social criticism. To me it was only the relief of a personal and wholly insignificant grouse against life; it is just a piece of rhythmical grumbling.' Perhaps an awareness of how much a reading of *The Waste Land*, and of the poems before it, 'gave him away' was responsible for Eliot's belief that the important poem adds to and alters the tradition (all great works are eternally contemporary, but the new great work, like a mountain arising out of a receding sea, alters our whole perspective on the landscape) and for his insistence on the impersonality of great poetry. In fact, he is the most uncomfortably intimate of all great English poets and his world is the one contemporary poetic world in which – no poet of English birth, for instance, has 'done' London as well – we find ourselves hauntingly immersed, as in an actual dream or nightmare.

It is a mistake, however, to see Eliot as engaged in writing a single poem with an inevitable Christian spiritual ending. Though there are Christian allusions in two sections, 'The Fire Sermon' and 'What the Thunder Said', in *The Waste Land*, the allusions to the Buddhistic Fire Sermon and to the ancient Sanskrit fable about the message of the Thunder, 'Give, Sympathise, Control', seem strong also and more sympathetic than the discovery, or achievement of the quest, of the Chapel Perilous. The shifts and tesselations – of syntax as well as languages, of high and low style, of compassion and disgust – seem today a little too conscious, and explain a remark of Auden's in a short memorial address on Eliot's death that a writer like Eliot must in his originality have had a great influence on subsequent poets but that it is remarkably difficult to track this down in any detail.

There were those who from the first disliked *The Waste Land* (and Eliot himself) like Robert Bridges, the Poet Laureate, who, in his brilliant parody, *Poor Poll*, compared Eliot to a parrot who mimics with extraordinary precision but does not understand what he is saying. At the same time, rather contradictorily, Bridges saw *The Waste Land* as a first step in a painstaking job of social climbing:

'Tis all that doth your silly thoughts so busy keep
The while you sit moping like Patience on a perch
– *Wie viele Tag' und Nachte bist du geblieben!*
La possa delle gamba posta in tregue –
the impeccable spruceness of your grey-feathcr'd poll
a model in hairdressing for the dandiest old Duke
enough to qualify you for the House of Lords
Or the Athenaeum Club, to poke among the nobs
great intellectual nobs and literary nobs
scientific nobs and Bishops *ex officio* . . .

Eliot was, indeed, headed this way; but he was in his last and
greatest poem, *Four Quartets*, to show the true nature o
worldly success:

O dark dark dark. They all go into the dark,
The vacant interstellar spaces, the vacant into the vacant,
The captains, merchant bankers, eminent men of letters.
The generous patrons of art, the statesmen and the rulers,
Distinguished civil servants, chairmen of many committees,
Industrial lords and petty contractors, all go into the dark,
And dark the Sun and Moon, and the Almanach de Gotha,
And the Stock Exchange Gazette, the Directory of Directors,
And cold the sense and lost the motive of action.

His Christianity in *Four Quartets* is still very bleak (behind
the Unitarian tradition was still the old dead Puritan tradi
tion) and in Eliot's greatest sustained piece of writing (he
tended to tesselate short passages, each directly inspired
and linked by congruities or contrasts of mood, not by logic
at the climax of 'Little Gidding', modelled on Canto XV o
the Inferno, the hell of the sodomites, where Dante greets
his old teacher of rhetoric, Brunetto Latini, sadly, 'And you
here, Ser Brunetto?', Eliot greets the 'baked brown fea
tures' of the 'familiar compound ghost' he creates for
himself. Eliot gives the greeting to the ghost, who is in a
sense unreal, unlike his model, Ser Brunetto, and for Eliot a
kind of ventriloquist's doll (Eliot conjures the figure out o
the dusk of dawn, as he walks home from a night's stint as an
air-raid warden in the Second World War). The ghost's
account of the gifts reserved for age and the purifying fire in
which the soul on the purgatorial road must dance reminds
one of Yeats's *Byzantium* and his late poem, 'You think i

horrible that lust and rage . . .' about which Eliot frankly
and honestly said that Yeats was only being honest:

> 'Since our concern was speech, and speech impelled us
>   To purify the dialect of the tribe
>   And urge the mind to aftersight and foresight,
> Let me disclose the gifts reserved for age
>   To set a crown upon your lifetime's effort.
>   First, the cold friction of expiring sense
> Without enchantment, offering no promise
>   But bitter tastelessness of shadow fruit
>   As body and soul begin to fall asunder.
> Second, the conscious impotence of rage
>   At human folly, and the laceration
>   Of laughter at what ceases to amuse.
> And last, the rending pain of re-enactment
>   Of all that you have done, and been; the shame
>   Of motives late revealed, and the awareness
> Of things ill done and done to others' harm
>   Which once you took for exercise of virtue.
>   Then fools' approval stings, and honour stains.
> From wrong to wrong the exasperated spirit
>   Proceeds, unless restored by that refining fire
>   Where you must move in measure, like a dancer.'
> The day was breaking, In the disfigured street
>   He left me, with a kind of valediction,
>   And faded on the blowing of the horn.

The horn would be the morning 'all clear' signal. The
'exasperated spirit' of which the Bruno figure speaks is
clearly Eliot's own, but to the end of 'Little Gidding' he goes
on struggling for serenity, though the key words of this
passage, for instance, are those of the medieval mystic
Dame Julian of Norwich, who was tormented by the image
of the eternity of Hell:

> And all shall be well and
> All manner of thing shall be well
> By the purification of the motive
> In the ground of our beseeching.

Let us hope that Eliot found, before the end, that purity in
prayer of which Dame Julian speaks. He seems to have been
happy after his second marriage and reached a popular

audience with at least two of his verse plays of modern life, *The Cocktail Party* and *The Confidential Clerk*: dilutions of his proper poetry, the tiger in the tiger-pit with his teeth drawn. For, like Dante and Pascal, Eliot was a great Christian visionary and apologist without having anything like a naturally Christian temperament.

I treat Yeats, whom I see as a greater poet than Eliot or Hardy, under Anglo-Irish poets. There are a number of poets, Kipling, Graves, Housman for instance, who have classical status without being great; Philip Larkin, our most notable living poet, who has certainly written five or six great poems (mostly about death) or John Betjeman, I would call very good poets who because of some limitations of interest or sympathy – not through lack of extraordinary metrical skill, lexical tact, or emotional sincerity – are very good without being great. C. H. Sisson and Basil Bunting, brought to general critical attention late in life, seem to me, if one claims greatness for them, to have major energy but to lack a sort of balance. Sisson's continual grouse is surprising after an unusually successful life, even if the frustration of early love is something never forgotten. Basil Bunting's wonderful musicality makes one aware, sometimes, of the lack of any coherent 'philosophy' behind it, or interwoven with it, at least one expressible in words. I happen to be one of the very few readers who take Wordsworth's 'something far more deeply interfused' seriously: Bunting gives me a sense of groping for something like that, but not grasping it. But these are two belated arrivals on the scene whom I do not know familiarly enough for it to be fair for me to judge them.

One other poet for whom I would claim not greatness, but something more than goodness, let us say extraordinary individual distinction, is William Empson. But it is clear to me that the third unarguably great poet, who in spite of his adoption of American nationality is essentially English, is W. H. Auden. A master of every kind of metrical device and tone of speech, Auden has the powerful discursive range of mind of Dryden: Landor's famous couplet which is almost right for Dryden, is similarly almost right for Auden:

> Though never tender or sublime,
> He wrestles with and conquers Time.

It is only *almost* right because both poets are capable of the tender and sublime on occasion: Dryden to Congreve:

> And oh! defend,
> Against your judgment, your departed friend,

Auden in the early, profoundly mysterious *This Lunar Beauty* (which no doubt owes something, like many of his earlier poems, to Laura Riding's manner: which is why Graves, who also learned from her – a discipular relationship abruptly and bitterly ended when Miss Riding returned to the United States – called the young Auden 'a synthetic poet'. The master to whom Auden admitted was Hardy, a sufficiently uneven poet for young writers to imitate without despair):

> This lunar beauty
> Has no history,
> Is complete and early;
> If beauty later
> Bear any feature,
> It had a lover
> And is another.
>
> This like a dream
> Keeps other time,
> And daytime is
> The loss of this;
> For time is inches
> And the heart's changes,
> Where ghost has haunted
> Lost and wanted.
>
> But this was never
> A ghost's endeavour
> Nor, finished this,
> Was ghost at ease;
> And till it pass
> Love shall not near
> The sweetness here,
> Nor sorrow take
> His endless look.

I can construe this poem, but in prose which would seem to

readers more complex, and less haunting, than Auden's verses.

Yet Auden, who was, outside a possible amorous relationship, curiously uninterested in himself and other people except as social, psychological, or cultural specimens, is essentially, like Dryden, a discursive poet. He writes great poems about love (*Lay your sleeping head, my love*) rather than great love poems; great poems about pagan and Christian versions of religion and the religions of power and envious despair, and the soils and the seas that foster them (*In Praise of Limestone*) rather than devotional poems. He disliked devotional poems; himself a devout Anglican, though one whom a profound trust in God's free Grace prevented from attempting to lead a sober or chaste life, he felt that one is either devoting oneself with as little distraction as possible to God in prayer, or perfecting a pattern of words on the page, and that it is insincere to attempt to do both simultaneously. Similarly a poem like *The Fall of Rome* is about the horror, comedy, and awesomeness of historical change rather than being a political poem. After a flirtation with Marxism in the 1930s (a much less deeply engaged flirtation than careless generalisers suppose, and, I am afraid, indulged in partly for the purpose of building up his reputation) Auden confessed to Isherwood, and Isherwood to Auden, on their voyage to America in early 1939 that all that political stuff no longer interested either of them. The one world in which Auden spoke from the inside, not as the acute outside observer, was the world of culture: as in *Musée des Beaux Arts*, or in one of his very greatest poems, *In Memory of W. B. Yeats*.

> For poetry makes nothing happen; it survives
> In the valley of its saying where executives
> Would never want to tamper; flows on south
> From ranches of isolation and the busy griefs,
> Raw towns that we believe and die in; it survives,
> A way of happening, a mouth.

Yeats would not have agreed; poetry may make things happen that the poet would not have wanted to happen, if he could have foretold:

> Did that play of mine send out
> Certain men the English shot?

It was a factor anyway. And in fact Auden did believe that

poetry makes things happen in the soul. The conclusion of his great poem, inscribed on Auden's memorial stone in Westminster Abbey, shows that in his heart he took poetry as more than 'a serious game' (though it was that too, and he meant by the phrase that it could never belong to the same order of importance as Christian assent):

> Follow, poet, follow right
> To the bottom of the night,
> With your unconstraining voice
> Still persuade us to rejoice;
>
> With the farming of a verse
> Make a vineyard of the curse,
> Sing of human unsuccess
> In a rapture of distress;
>
> In the deserts of the heart
> Let the healing fountain start,
> In the prison of his days
> Teach the free man how to praise.

Chester Kallman, Auden's life-long companion in America and during their vacations first in Ischia and then in Austria, took to spending half the year away in Greece. Auden, who had earlier been a very successful Professor of Poetry in Oxford, oppressed by a fear of the loneliness and violence of New York for a man living alone, took up in 1972 residence at Christ Church, of which he was an honorary fellow. The second visit was less successful. Undergraduates pride themselves on an indifference to the superior qualities of their elders; life and poetry started yesterday; they paid little attention to him. Auden was lonely and often expressed his wish not to see out man's span of seventy years. A poem, tender and sublime, in his posthumous volume *Thank You, Fog* expresses tenderly this wish and his gratitude for all the life he had been given. He was always granted his wishes and died peacefully in his hotel bedroom, in his sleep, in the autumn of 1973 (at sixty-five) after a very successful lecture in Austria. The grief-stricken Chester Kallman died a little later.

Some good critics, including A. Alvarez, would claim greatness for D. H. Lawrence as poet as well as storyteller.

He certainly wrote some great poems like *Snake, Bavarian Gentians*, and *The Ship of Death*, and has at his best in verse the same extraordinary pouncing vividness of perception that belongs to his best prose. But it was typical of him always to start a new version (as with *Bavarian Gentians* and *The Ship of Death*) rather than perfect an old. His spontaneity has a price to be paid for it (including preachiness) and in his poetry he is good at birds, beasts, and flowers but less so, except very occasionally, at human beings. In an age in which hard work and scrupulous self-examination characterise the great poets, he does not quite make their grade. He is also perhaps too uneven a poet for one to claim classical status for him; what one is left to say is that Lawrence's poems are a part, but not a major part, of an achievement that is great as a whole. His poems do not begin to compare with Thomas Hardy's, the English novelist from whom, as his long early critical study shows, he learned most, while profoundly disagreeing with Hardy's basic attitudes.

So much for the greater English poets. Now it is the turn of the Anglo-Irish, headed by Yeats, the one indubitably great Irish poet, writing English, of this century. Englishmen tended to think of him as the *only* Irish poet, and he has tended (till the recent troubles, which as always in Ireland, and for Yeats himself in *Easter 1916, Nineteen Hundred and Nineteen*, and *Meditations in Time of Civil War*, have been fruitful times for poets) to overshadow poets who in another country and another time would have won much praise, and who have carefully avoided imitating Yeats's style. Yeats himself was so great and abundant a poet that it would take too much space in a chapter like this to sketch, however thinly, his development. His style showed a steady development from the dreamy, romantic poems of the 1880s and 1890s to the tougher, more direct style of this poem, *Adam's Curse*, written at the beginning of the century:

> We sat together at one summer's end,
> That beautiful mild woman, your close friend,
> And you and I, and talked of poetry.
> I said, 'A line will take us hours maybe;
> Yet if it does not seem a moment's thought,
> Our stitching and unstitching has been naught.
> Better go down upon your marrow-bones

And scrub the kitchen pavement, or break stones
Like an old pauper, in all kinds of weather;
For to articulate sweet sounds together
Is to work harder than all these, and yet
Be thought an idler by the noisy set
Of bankers, schoolmasters, and clergymen
The martyrs call the world . . .' –

His poetry, right up to his posthumous *Last Poems* of 1939, showed a growing sobriety and precision of diction, a discursive gift for argument and satire, and a true and real bitterness of passion lacking in the early work. I indicate these qualities by two poems, one a fragment of a long poem, *Meditations in Time of Civil War*, written not about the Black and Tans but about the civil war between De Valera's Republicans and Cosgrave's Free Staters. Yeats was saddened because the new Irish community he had helped to call into existence was bloodier, crueller, and less rational than the older Ireland of his time had been. The Ireland of Queen Elizabeth, when Spenser advocated the extermination of the Irish, of Cromwell and his murderous crew, of the Anglo-Irish Castlereagh's crushing of the rebellion of 1798, was another story. Nineteenth-century Ireland before Yeats's time had its minor rebellions, its assassinations and dynamiters, and the central tragedy, which halved the Irish population, the great famine. Yeats in this section of *Meditations in Time of Civil War*, 'The Stare's Nest by my Window' (it is a window in Thoor Ballylee, the old half-broken-down tower, which was procured for him by Lady Gregory after his marriage to George Hyde-Lees) broods on the savagery and destructiveness of the fighting. 'Stare' is Anglo-Irish for a starling; the bees are to make us think of Shakespeare's 'singing masons' that build the harmony of a state:

> The bees build in the crevices
> Of loosening masonry, and there
> The mother-birds bring grubs and flies.
> My wall is loosening; honey-bees,
> Come build in the empty house of the stare.
>
> We are closed in, and the key is turned
> On our uncertainty; somewhere

A man is killed, or a house burned,
Yet no clear fact to be discerned:
Come build in the empty house of the stare.

A barricade of stone or of wood;
Some fourteen days of civil war;
Last night they trundled down the road
That dead young soldier in his blood:
Come build in the empty house of the stare.

We had fed the heart on fantasies,
The heart's grown brutal from the fare;
More substance in our enmities
Than in our love; O honey-bees,
Come build in the empty house of the stare.

Yeats could describe violence vividly and see, as in *Easter 1916*
the heroism involved in it; but essentially his ideal Ireland was
something like that of Grattan's Parliament of the time of the
American Revolution, in which the Irish militia, theoretically
defending Ireland against a possible French invasion, was able
to bring pressure to bear on England to achieve complete
independence. English policies even now still prevailed but at
the cost of lavish bribery. Nevertheless, with Swift, Bishop
Berkeley, Goldsmith, Burke, the eighteenth century became
for Yeats the ideal century of Anglo-Irish civilisation. He
dreamt, vainly, of a hierarchical society, with an Anglo-Irish
Protestant ascendancy and a loyal Catholic peasantry. But in
fact the peasantry hated the Irish Protestant ascendancy even
more bitterly than it hated the English.

Growing disillusionment with the new Ireland turned Yeats
to what was to become a central theme, the combined growth
of physical passion, and understanding of its nature, with an
elderly man's weakness or impotence. Yeats sought to solve
this problem by a Steinach operation, which revives an elderly
man's powers of erection but makes emission impossible. The
Dublin wits quoted, with a new and coarse application, a
famous line from Milton's sonnet on his blindness:

They also serve who only stand and wait.

Sometimes no doubt there was no physical fulfilment. In
1929 Yeats wrote this touchingly beautiful poem for Olivia

Shakespeare, who had been briefly his lover in the 1890s and remained his dear friend and 'the centre of my London life', he says, ever after.

After Long Silence

Speech after long silence; it is right,
All other lovers being estranged or dead,
Unfriendly lamplight hid under its shade,
The curtains drawn upon unfriendly night,
That we descant and yet again descant
Upon the supreme theme of Art and Song:
Bodily decrepitude is wisdom; young
We loved each other and were ignorant.

'. . . the supreme theme of Art and Song' was, of course, love. There have in fact been good judges, like the late Frank O'Connor in a memorial lecture, who thought that Yeats was a greater poet of friendship than of love: as at the end of *The Municipal Gallery Revisited*:

Think where man's glory most begins and ends,
And say my glory was I had such friends.

His supreme theme, whether love or friendship, was certainly not Homeric violence, and he loathed the violence and gossiping spite of his own country:

Out of Ireland have I come,
Great hatred, little room . . .

He could, of course, like all Irishmen, hate; he had to wait till George Moore's death to punish him, in *Autobiographies*, for *Hail and Farewell*: the punishment is adequate, leaving Moore as the eternal embodiment of loutishness.

One of his most distinguished younger contemporaries was Austin Clarke. Clarke was a Roman Catholic who, deserted by his wife, could have no recourse to divorce. Like a number of intelligent Roman Catholics (in France as well as in Ireland) be believed in the dogmas and sacraments of the Roman Church but hated and despised its priests. His peculiarly bitter contempt for Irish Roman Catholic bigotry comes out in a poem on the burial of the first President of

Ireland, Dr Douglas Hyde who was a great scholar and translator of Gaelic poetry, but unfortunately, from the point of view of the majority, a Protestant. The cabinet, at once bigots and cowards as far as their religion was concerned, would have dodged the simple Protestant service:

Burial of an Irish President

> At the last bench
> Two Catholics, the French
> Ambassador and I, knelt down.
> The vergers waited. Outside.
> The hush of Dublin town,
> Professors of cap and gown,
> Costello, his Cabinet,
> In Government cars, hiding
> Around the corner, ready
> Tall hat in hand, dreading
> *Our Father* in English. Better
> Not hear that 'which' for 'who'
> And risk eternal doom.

Strangely, Hyde's own translations were sometimes Christian enough in feeling to be equally inoffensive to Catholics and Protestants:

> O King of the Friday
> Whose limbs were stretched on the cross,
> O Lord who didst suffer
> The bruises, the wounds, the loss,
>
> We stretch ourselves
> Beneath the shield of thy might.
> May some fruit from the tree of thy passion
> Fall on us this night!

Patrick Kavanagh is another Roman Catholic poet, whose satires are weak, and whose long poem *The Great Hunger*, set in his native Donegal, one of the barrenest regions of Ireland, is about how marriage is delayed among the peasantry till the father is too old to run the farm (this is one reason why the Irish population remained stable after the depredations of the famine); it made him famous. He went to Dublin, where he was very unhappy. But his last volume

Come Dance With Kitty Stobling shows him to be a genuine mystic in a way in which Yeats and A.E. never were, and Austin Clarke never sought to be. He finds the glory of God as he sits on a shabby seat by a canal bank. He does not need obvious beauty:

Lines written on a seat on the Grand Canal

O commemorate me where there is water,
Canal water preferably, so stilly
Greeny at the heart of summer. Brother
Commemorate me thus beautifully,
Where by a lock Niagariously roars
The falls for those who sit in the tremendous silence
Of mid-July. No one will speak in prose
Who finds his way to these Parnassian islands.
A swan goes by head low with many apologies,
Fantastic light looks through the eyes of bridges –
And look! a barge comes bringing from Athy
And other far-flung towns mythologies.
O commemorate me with no hero-courageous
Tomb – just a canal-bank seat for the passer-by.

Samuel Beckett is famous chiefly as a playwright, but this poem, one of a group set in Dieppe, and written first in French, has an agonising desolation (just as Patrick Kavanagh has an unaffected mysticism not to be found in any other modern Irish poet) that is not equalled by any other Irish poet and would be masked by irony in Beckett's prose. The English version, Beckett's own, is:

I would like my love to die
and the rain to be falling on the graveyard
and on me walking the streets
mourning she who sought to love me.

The novelist, James Joyce's most perfect poem, in my opinion, is *Ecce Puer*. The father-figure here makes a strange contrast with the Simon Dedalus of *Portrait of the Artist as a Young Man* and *Ulysses*. We are reminded also of the remark of a Roman Catholic priest who said that for all the wildness of his youth, his denial of the authority of the Church, James might return to the Church at any time. In contrast, Stanislaus, who had no vices, who could not, however, think of his father without contempt, who helped James but perhaps less from brotherly love than from admiration of James's genius and a dry sense of duty, would be an atheist till his dying day. Here is James's poem; the death of his father had coincided with the birth of his son:

Ecce Puer

Of the dark past
A child is born;
With joy and grief
My heart is torn.

Calm in his cradle
The living lies.
May love and mercy
Unclose his eyes!

Young life is breathed
On the glass;
The world that was not
Comes to pass.

A child is sleeping:
An old man gone.
O, father forsaken,
Forgive your son!

It is Irish Roman Catholics rather than Protestants who have this special feeling about their fathers. Yeats's father, though never strikingly successful as an artist, was, to judge from examples of his work in private hands I have been lucky enough to see, a man of sensitive talent; it could be claimed that his letters are more brilliant than his son's, which are to a remarkable degree concerned in a business-like way with details about the design and production of his books. In the poems, so far as I can remember, J. B. Yeats gets one mention from his son, a tribute to his wit in confronting a hostile audience protesting against *The Play-boy of the Western World* – 'A land of saints – of plaster saints!'

In Irish novels and poems the figure of the father carries an emotional weight which in English, and Anglo-Irish

Protestant writing, he does not. Jane Austen, for instance, was a devout Anglican, but Mr Bennett, Mr Woodhouse, Sir Walter Elliot, are two of them fools (one innocent, the last a model of selfish and inane vanity) and Mr Bennett's wit does not compensate for his inadequacy (and to Mary positive cruelty) as a father. In English fiction and poetry, even before the Reformation, fathers play no central part; and later Milton's God the Father is generally agreed by critics to be an unlikeable figure; he spends too much time stating that he is not responsible for what he cannot help foreseeing. *Qui s'excuse, s'accuse.*

The Irish attitude of profound personal love for the living father, combined with the Irish love of the rich local soil, is found in a beautiful poem by F. R. Higgins (1896–1941) whose death in his middle forties was a great loss to Irish poetry. He came from the rich pasture land of Meath, the opposite of the stubborn, harsh soil of Patrick Kavanagh's Donegal:

Father and Son

Only last week, walking the hushed fields
Of our most lovely Meath, now thinned by November,
I came to where the road from Laracor leads
To the Boyne river – that seemed more lake than river,
Stretched in uneasy light and stript of reeds.

And walking longside an old weir
Of my people's, where nothing stirs – only the shadowed
Leaden flight of a heron up the lean air –
I went unmanly with grief, knowing how my father,
Happy though captive in years, walked last with me there.

Yes, happy in Meath with me for a day
He walked, taking stock of herds hid in their own breathing;
And naming colts, gusty as wind, once steered by his hand,
Lightnings winked in the eyes that were half shy in greeting
Old friends – the wild blades, when he gallivanted the land.

For that proud, wayward man now my heart breaks –
Breaks for that man whose mind was a secret eyrie,
Whose kind hand was sole signet of his race,
Who curbed me, scorned my green ways, yet increasingly loved me
Till Death drew its grey blind down his face.

And yet I am pleased that even my reckless ways
Are living shades of his rich calms and passions –
Witnesses for him and for those faint namesakes
With whom now he is one, under yew branches,
Yes, one in a graven silence no bird breaks.

Notice that the music of Anglo-Irish poetry is quite different
from that of English. The first line of this five-line stanza
need not rhyme but we will when it seems intended take
'fields' with 'leads' and 'reeds', 'weir' with 'air' and 'there'.
More elaborately the second and third lines must not rhyme
fully but must either be near-echoes or, if less near, metrical
echoes: November, river; shadowed, father; breathing,
greeting; éyriė, lovéd mė; passions, branches. The trochee
(a long stressed syllable followed by a short unstressed
syllable), a foot which has become general for words like
'námesåke' in England still remains a spondee (two long
stressed syllables) in Irish: nāmesāke, and preceded by a
strong syllable towards the end of a line, can, by catching up
the strong syllable of the preceding iambic foot, become a
molossus or three-stress foot like 'deép heárt's córe' at the
end of Yeats's *The Lake Isle of Innisfree* or 'faińt náme-
sakés' or 'nó biŕd bŕeaks' here. As regards diction, or choice
of words, one can notice that Higgins can use words like
'lovely', 'wild blades', 'gallivanted', 'wayward' which a
roughly contemporary English poet would have avoided (or
a poet of Northern Irish blood, but English domicile and
habits of mind, like Louis MacNeice). One may say that
time does not kibe the heels of Irish poets as of English;
their world is more naturally timeless.

The price to be paid for timelessness is the substitution of
a dance of repeated myth for a rational sense of historical
change. In Ulster, William of Orange is still at war with King
James, Londonderry is still being defended by heroic Protestant 'prentice boys, though there is nobody as rational as
Patrick Sarsfield, the Catholic champion, to say (as he does
in Lady Gregory's play, at least), 'Let us change Kings, and
I will fight it again.' As Conor Cruise O'Brien has put it, the
inhabitants of Ulster are two sets of imaginary ancient
Hebrews at war with each other for an imaginary promised
land. The poets of course are aware of this, like Michael
Longley, a Protestant, and Seamus Heaney, a Catholic

(close personal friends), probably not sharing the ancestral faiths but tied to the tribal loyalties, Longley has written:

> I who have heard the waters break
> Claim this my country, though today
> *Timor mortis conturbat me,*

Heaney, born like Longley in 1939, and probably the best of the younger Irish poets, celebrating the savage self-defence and savage slaughter of the 'croppy boys' (the Roman Catholic peasantry) in 1798 wrote:

Requiem for the Croppies

> The pockets of our great coats full of barley –
> No kitchens on the run, no striking camp –
> We moved quick and sudden in our own country.
> The priest lay behind ditches with the tramp.
> A people, hardly marching – on the hike –
> We found new tactics happening each day:
> We'd cut through reins and rider with the pike
> And stampede cattle into infantry,
> Then retreat through hedges where cavalry must be thrown.
> Until on Vinegar Hill, the fatal conclave.
> Terraced thousands died, shaking scythes at cannon.
> The hillside blushed, soaked in our broken wave.
> They buried us without shroud or coffin
> And in August the barley grew up out of the grave.

In other poems Heaney shows an interest in the Tollund man totally preserved in the bog at Aarhus, thinking of dead Irish history as being preserved in the same way. He and his generation, mainly from the north, have slightly over-shadowed poets about ten years older, now in their fifties, like another Ulsterman, John Montague; and the Dubliner, Thomas Kinsella, skilled and melancholy in his personal poems and full of rough vigour in his version of the early heroic lay *The Tain*. Of the same generation as these, living in Connemara, Richard Murphy wrote, well before the present troubles, a long poem about the battle of Aughrim. In his more isolated setting, the isolation increased by his Protestantism and his largely English background, Murphy was able, looking back, to anticipate the present, continually recurring, situation in Ulster. John Montague now lives largely in Paris with a yearly term at Trinity College, Dublin; his early poems were about Ulster. He is unique among Irish poets (the years in Paris may have helped) in writing love poems free of either defiance or the sense of sin, with a certain cold sophistication:

The Same Gesture

There is a secret room
of golden light where
everything – love, violence,
hatred is possible;
and, again love.

Such intimacy of hand
and mind is achieved
under its healing light
that the shifting of
hands is a rite

like court music.
We barely know our
selves there though
it is what we always were
–most nakedly are –

and must remember
when we leave, re-
suming our habits
with our clothes:
work, 'phone, drive

through late traffic
changing gears with
the same gesture as
eased your snowbound
heart and flesh.

A poem like this shows that Irish poetry need not be caught for ever in its myth trap; one step forward, and it can assume the universality of the shockingly private.

Next to Irish poetry, Scots poetry has, outside the English tradition, had most distinction; I refer in both cases to

poems in Anglo-Irish and Anglo-Scots and broad Scots; I
cannot speak of poems in Irish or Scots Gaelic, though I
know that major claims have been made for the Scots Gaelic
poems of Sorley MacLean and George Campbell Hay. But
among a number of good poets in English and Scots, most
critics would probably claim greatness for, above all, Hugh
MacDiarmid, whose long life began in 1892 and, sadly,
ended before the appearance of a definitive edition of his
poems in 1979. Edwin Muir (1887–1959) was an Orcadian
exiled to Glasgow when his father's landlord refused to
renew his lease; in the Glasgow slums, the Muir family died
off very quickly. Muir was saved from utter misery when he
married his wife, Willa, a fine classical scholar, with whom
he earned a living in London partly by reviewing, and partly
by translating great new German writers like Kafka and
Broch. The Kafka interest took him for a time, under the
auspices of the British Council, to Prague; he felt a richness
and mellowness in central European culture that he had
never felt in Scotland. His work for the British Council
made him aware of the splendour of Christian religious art
of the Renaissance. His attitude, always unconsciously
Christian, became consciously so, though he never became a
member of any Church or attended any service. Perhaps the
Nietszchean creed by which he had, in Glasgow, protected
himself against the vulgarities of undiluted Socialism remained strong. Biblical imagery and Homeric imagery are
used to the last in his poems with the truth of fable, or myth,
rather than story. His happiest time in Scotland was during
the war, in Edinburgh, where he made cultural contacts with
Polish and Czech soldiers, and after the war, when he was
Warden of Newbattle Abbey. In his last years, he often
dreamt of revisiting not Scotland but the Orkneys; but his
health was never good enough for the long sea voyage. He
was a man almost universally loved where MacDiarmid, a
borderer with the borderers' traditional hatred of the
English was very widely disliked. MacDiarmid – combative,
jealous, uneven, and not like Muir a master of graceful
prose – was a great rambler in his later poems (he lost his
lyric gift during a disastrous year in England in his middle
life) and a certain stony fierceness went even into his
ramblings. Muir represented the civilized mind, MacDiarmid the passion of the fanatic. Yet the narrow, bitter,

half-educated man is in the end the greater poet. MacDiarmid is best briefly represented by one of his lovely early
Scots lyrics:

The Bonnie Broukit Bairn

Mars is braw in crammasy,	*fine, red velvet*
Venus in a green silk goun,	
The ault mune shak's her gowden feathers,	
Their starry talks a wheen o'blethers,	*lot of nonsense*
Nane for thee a thochtie sparin;	*little thought*
Earth, thou bonnie broukit bairn!	*handsome dusty child*
– *But greet, and in your tears ye'll droun*	*cry*
The haill clanjamfrie!	*the whole set of them*

Edwin Muir is well represented in his sad backward glance
at a vanished Scotland from the contemporary Scotland he
has come to hate:

Scotland's Winter

Now the ice lays its smooth claws on the sill,
The sun looks from the hill
Helmed in his winter casket,
And sweeps his arctic sword across the sky.
The water at the mill
Sounds more hoarse and dull.
The miller's daughter walking by
With frozen fingers soldered to her basket
Seems to be knocking
Upon a hundred leagues of floor
With her light heels, and mocking
Percy and Douglas dead,
And Bruce on his burial bed,
Where he lies white as may
With wars and leprosy,
And all the kings before
This land was kingless,
And all the singers before
This land was songless,
This land that with its dead and living waits
    the Judgment Day.
But they, the powerless dead,
Listening can hear no more
Than a hard tapping on the sounding floor

A little overhead
Of common heels that do not know
Whence they come or where they go
And are content
With their poor frozen life and shallow banishment.

Neither the Borderer nor the Orcadian is a typical Scot. In spite of his slogan, 'Not Burns, but Dunbar', MacDiarmid had little real feeling for the great dead kings or for Scottish medieval poetry. His little selection from Dunbar presents a very unscholarly text, it was about the Covenanters that he wrote with most enthusiasm, and there was a good deal of Burns in his nature. He was always denouncing his country, but in a fatherly scolding way; if they would follow him, they would be all right. The gentle Muir in these lines utters a hatred of contemporary Scotland (which *is* a singularly philistine country, on the whole) deeper and more killing than anything ever uttered, or felt, by MacDiarmid.

The third Scottish poet of this century for whom one would claim greatness would be Norman MacCaig, born 1910, and recently, after a life of teaching in Edinburgh, Reader in Poetry at Stirling University – very much admired by Muir and the life-long friend of MacDiarmid. This poem, *Byre*, recalls Muir's favourite Scots poet, Henryson, and the special Scottish comic tenderness for animals, expressed, for instance, in Burns's dialogue between the poor man's and the laird's dog and in his poem about the 'wee sleekit cowerin' timorous beastie':

Byre

The thatched roof rings like heaven where mice
Squeak small hosannahs all night long,
Scratching its golden pavements, skirting
The gutter's crystal river-song.

Wild kittens in the world below
Glare with one flaming eye through cracks,
Spurt in the straw, are tawny brooches
Splayed on the chests of drunken sacks.

The dimness becomes darkness as
Vast presences come mincing in,
Swagbellied Aphrodites, swinging
A silver slaver from each chin.

And all is milky, secret, female.
Angels are hushed and plain straws shine.
And kittens miaow in circles, stalking
With tail and hindleg one straight line.

MacCaig claims to have no invention or imagination, to work entirely from precise observation, to be unable to read any poet whose opinions he disagrees with. To read his poems carefully is, however, to find experiments on, alterations of, very many poets (Henryson, Muir, Empson) who do not fundamentally resemble each other or himself, though his most recent poems, written rapidly with the careless skill of much practice, like the drawings of a master, seem entirely his own.

There are many good Scots poets: George Bruce, Maurice Lindsay, Alexander Scott (a master of Scots), Ian Crichton Smith, Hamish Henderson (to be considered separately along with war poets of the two world wars), and Burns Singer.

Two other poets are worthy of more attention, Robert Garioch (Robert Sutherland, b. 1909) is, much more than MacDiarmid, a master of living, natural, spoken Scots, and treats all Scottish characteristics with a natural, sympathetic humour. This poem is about the strange Scottish passion (to be found as much in atheists like MacDiarmid as in believers) for endless discussion of theology:

And They Were Richt

I went to see 'Ane Tryall of Heretiks'
by Dionn MacColla, treated as a play;
a wycelike wark, but what I want to say   *wise-seeming*
is mair taen-up wi halie politics   *holy*

nor with the piece itsel: the kinna tricks   *than, kind of*
the unco-guid get up til when they hae   *over-good*
their way. Yon late-nicht ploy on Setturday
was thrang wi Protestants and Catholics   *crowded*

an eydent audience, wi fowth of bricht   *busy, plenty*
arguments wad hae kept them gaun till Monday.
It seemed discussion wad last out the nicht

hadna the poliss, sent by Mrs Grundy   *police*

pitten us out at twalve, And they were richt!   *put, twelve*
Wha daur debait religion on a Sunday?   *dare*

By way of contrast, W. S. Graham, born in Greenock but
settled for much of his life in Cornwall, is perhaps the only
Scots poet of his generation with a genius for technical
invention. Though certain images, based on his early experience as a fisherman, recur, Graham's infrequent but very
distinguished volumes are made out of words rather than
images and resist attempts at translation. When read aloud
in Graham's own renderings the poems have a strong
emotional movement; they are not poems *about* something.
His best friends in Cornwall have been painters rather than
poets and one could call his own work abstract poetry. He is
the first English poet (I call him so, leaving his Scots roots
aside), for instance, to make a poetic use of the preposition,
and the concluding adverb:

> Yes laugh then cloudily laugh
> Though he sat there as deaf
> And worn to a stop
> As the word had given him up.
> Stay still. That was the sounding
> Sea to be moved on burning
> His still unending cry,
> That night hammered and waved
> Its starry shipyard arms,
> And it came to inherit
> His death where these words merge.
> This is his night writ large.
> In Greenock the bright breath
> Of night's array shone forth
> On the nightshifting town.
> Thus younger burning in
> The best of his puny gear
> He early set out
> To write him to this death
> And to that great breath
> Taking of the sea,
> The graith of Poetry.

Such lines are abstract, untranslatable, but rich in implica-
tion. No other Scottish poet of this century is a formal
inventor of this sort.

The younger Scots poets of this century, those who came to notice in the 1970s, like Stewart Conn (b. 1936), Giles Gordon (b. 1940), Douglas Dunn (b. 1942), Alan Bold (b. 1943), Liz Lochhead (b. 1948) are, like the younger English poets of the same generation, refreshingly free from any single dominating style or attitude. One can salute promise and freshness and freedom in both cases, but cannot generalise usefully. But I see in this lack of conformity or dogmatism a welcome sign of renewal. (One should perhaps note in passing Canon Andrew Young, the author of many short poems combining exact botanical observation with metaphysical conceit, and one impressive long dream poem; Scots by origins and I would say very Scots by his tough character, but a Church of England clergyman in Southern England through most of his long life: generally recognised as a minor classic.)

Of poets with Welsh origins or connections I shall note Wilfred Owen and Alun Lewis in my consideration of war poems and shall leave out David Jones (whose graphic art, pencil-outlined water colours, and lettering, I prefer in any case to his writing) since the liturgical prose in which he wrote much of *The Anathemata* seems to me, like his more direct prose elsewhere, poetic in feeling but not in form. That leaves Edward Thomas (1878–1917), Dylan Thomas (1914–53), R. S. Thomas (b. 1913), a lonely and sometimes morose Episcopal clergyman in a largely Methodist country, and (breaking the row of Thomases) Vernon Watkins from the Gower peninsula, an old English enclave (as the name Watkins suggests) in Welsh Wales. In order to enjoy the waves and the view from Gower cliffs (there are great stretching rocks, one called – in an English medieval way – Worm's Head or Dragon's Head) Watkins (1906–67), who had a very good Cambridge degree in modern languages, was content to spend his life as a bank clerk, at the counter, in a bank in Swansea. Swimming and rock climbing kept him extraordinarily fit and when he had retired and was invited to give readings in American universities he died of a sudden, quite unpredictable heart-attack in the middle of a brisk set of tennis. He was the only poet whose advice Dylan Thomas genuinely respected.

Edward Thomas was one of the very few poets to whom the Great War was a blessing. He had earned a living by writing superior hack work in prose, in which there are nevertheless glimpses of the true poet. A commission and a period in England of training gave him leisure to write verse with a clear conscience and he got encouragement from, and gave encouragement to, Robert Frost. Though Edward Thomas lived most of his life apart from his war service in Oxfordshire and Gloucestershire, he was obviously Welsh by origin and there was a haunting 'Celtic magic' in his tone. One of his most beautiful poems, *Out in the Dark*, shows both nature's beauty and its alien quality, particularly in the last two lines:

> Out in the dark over the snow
> The fallow fawns invisible go
> With the fallow doe;
> And the winds blow
> Fast as the stars are slow.
>
> Stealthily the dark haunts round
> And, when the lamp goes, without sound
> At a swifter bound
> Than the swiftest hound,
> Arrives, and all else is drowned;
>
> And star and I and wind and deer,
> Are in the dark together, – near
> Yet far, – and fear
> Drums on my ear
> In that sage company drear.
>
> How weak and little is the light,
> All the universe of sight
> Love and delight,
> Before the might,
> If you love it not, of night.

The haunting feeling, of the night or winter, pursued him – as in the brief *Thaw*:

> Over the land freckled with snow half-thawed
> The speculating rooks at their nests cawed
> And saw from elm-tops, delicate as flower of grass,
> What we below could not see, Winter pass.

I have given a brief account of Vernon Watkins's background and his particular fascination with the sea-scape of the Gower peninsula. After the death of his young friend Dylan Thomas, he became rather more interested in poems on poetry and poets, and wrote a very moving poem, *A True Picture Restored*, on Dylan Thomas himself:

> And Wales, when shall you have again
> One so true as he,
> Whose hand was on the mountain's heart,
> The rising of the sea,
> And every praising bird that cries
> Above the estuary?
>
> He never let proud nature fall
> Out of its pristine state.
> The hunchback fed upon a love
> That made the crooked straight,
> No single promise broken
> On which the heart must wait.
>
> The heron poised above the glass
> With straight and stabbing bill,
> Among the water's moods that pass
> Choosing to strike and kill,
> Transfixed the sky with holiest eye
> When the whole heart was still.

One remembers Dylan Thomas's hunchback in the park and his 'heron-priested shore' and finds these called up (and other aspects of Thomas's genius) in a long poem in which Watkins cultivates a formal lucidity not typical of his pupil.

Literary criticism in verse does not sound an exciting genre, but it is almost the rarest of poetic gifts to be able to write it, and the following poem on Wordsworth says, and so briefly, more than all the prose critics have managed to say of this great, strange poet. It would have been written in 1950, on the anniversary of Wordsworth's death.

Wordsworth

> The barren mountains were his theme,
> Nature the force that made him strong.
> This day died one who, like a stone,
> Altered the course of English song.

A hundred years! The waters still
Murmur the truth he bent to glean
Where bird and sunset, copse and hill
Composed the grave, harmonious scene.

The humble and unknown became
His oracles. Infirm old age
Matching obscurity to fame
Taught, like a child, the listening sage.

About his melancholy mind
Thundered the waterfalls. How few
Have left on water, light and wind
So calm a print of all he knew.

How cold the waters, yet how clear:
How grave the voice, how fine the thread
That quickening the returning year
Restores his landscape and his dead!

Like Landor at his rare best, Watkins combines an extremely romantic temperament with a classical sense of form: a Christian, he deals most happily with pagan imagery, the Muse and her fountain of inspiration, Orpheus, Persephone, 'gloomy Dis'. Similarly, he speaks less of the resurrection than of the immortality a poet's agonies in life and death win for him. He writes of the sense of Lawrence's presence that the cottages which sheltered him in fear, rage, and isolation during the First World War at Zennor still bring him:

Zennor Cottages

Here is the landscape he
Knew bitterly; but now,
Where breaks the exterior sea,
I notice how

The fields he knew, though bleak,
Still nourish for their own
A strength which cannot speak
Till life is gone.

Vernon Watkins's son has recently complained that his

father, like many Anglo-Welsh poets, is ignored because he is Welsh. It would be truer to say of poets who can achieve a classic distance that one tends to forget their origins. By way of contrast, Dylan Thomas, who once said, 'Land of my fathers, and my fathers can have it!', is never out of Wales in his imagination, and even in a very early poem like *Before I knocked* is bitterly angry with a God the Father who, of his nature, cannot share his Son's sufferings on the Cross or give his Son's mother the natural delight (or the final delight in her Son's achievements) that every mother longs for:

> . . . I who was rich was made the richer
> By sipping at the vine of days.
>
> I, born of flesh and ghost, was neither
> A ghost nor man, but mortal ghost.
> And I was struck down by death's feather.
> And I was a mortal to the last
> Long breath that carried to my father
> The message of his dying christ.
>
> You who bow down at cross and altar
> Remember me and pity Him
> Who took my flesh and bones for armour
> And doublecrossed my mother's womb.

The sense in which Christ's manhood and Godhead are united into a single person of the Divine Substance lay behind all the early wrangles over the Creed. There are even Methodists like Lord Soper who disrupt the Trinity and deny Christ's Godhead. But, as one of the early fathers said, if he was not God, he was not even (like the Socrates of the death dialogues) an exceptionally good man.

Critics like Michael Schmidt allow for complexity in the early poems but feel that in the later ones everything is sacrificed to complex sound-patterning. In a true poet, it has to be sense-patterning too. Empson, in a brilliant analysis with which in the end I do not agree, has seen a *Refusal to Mourn the Death, by Fire, of a Child in London* – a refusal, in a sense, to write propaganda during the Second World War – as expressing a pessimistic pantheism. The urge to life is a persistent urge to pain and anybody is lucky to be dead for good. But it can be taken the other way round:

Deep with the first dead lies London's daughter,
Robed in the long friends,
The grains beyond age, the dark veins of her mother,
Secret by the unmourning water
Of the riding Thames.
After the first death, there is no other.

But can the riding Thames, riding triumphantly, be indifferent? Perhaps he is rejoicing that his daughter is at last at peace? Is her mother not the earth-mother who, in the second Theban play of Sophocles, opens her womb to the now purged Oedipus? And when he says, 'After the first death there is no other', he *may* be rejoicing in the finality of death but the associations of the words cannot help making us rejoice in Christian immortality. It is the ability to hold tensions between opposites that makes Thomas great. What *is* true is that in the more simply yet more ambitiously structured later poems like *A Winter's Tale* Thomas is readier to give himself to pure exultation and rejoicing:

> For the bird lay bedded
> In a choir of wings, as though she slept or died,
> And the wings glided wide and he was hymned and wedded,
> And through the thighs of the engulfing bride,
> The woman breasted and the heaven headed
>
> Bird, he was brought low,
> Burning in the bride bed of love, in the whirl-
> Pool at the wanting centre, in the folds
> Of paradise, in the spun bud of the world.
> And she rose with him flowering in her melting snow.

It is difficult to think, in other poetry, of a more splendid, exultant, and exact evocation of sexual consummation. The poet who wrote these lines was certainly not exhausted, but nearer the fountain of life, when he died, in New York, in squalid and agonising circumstances, in his thirty-ninth year. (I leave his life aside: he worked, for his family's sake, very hard at reading, acting, film-scripts, all sorts of decent hackwork, but neither he nor his wife could handle money: it was the tax-collector who drove him to these two humiliating American tours and to his death).

The Rev. R. S. Thomas (b. 1913), a priest of the Episcopal Church in Wales, is the most bitter of all modern Anglo-Welsh poets. He can feel not love but only a 'willed gentleness' towards his parishioners. He is a highly educated man preaching to clods, but before them he feels a strange humility:

They

I take their hands,
Hard hands. There is no love
For such, only a willed
Gentleness. Negligible men
From the village, from the small
Holdings, they bring their grief
Sullenly to my back door,
And are speechless. Seeing them
In the wind with the light's
Halo, watching their eyes
Blur, I know the reason
They cry, their worsting
By one whom they will fight.
Daily the sky mirrors
The water, the water the
Sky. Daily I take their side
In their quarrel, calling their faults
Mine. How do I serve so
This being they have shut out
Of their houses, their thoughts, their lives?

One remembers Kilvert and how idyllic the Welsh marches are in his diary. But that R. S. Thomas's self-reproaches may be just, that he cannot get to his parishioners' hearts or truly love them, does not destroy the deep, hopeless strength of his poems. He cannot reproach himself even with being pro-English; English tourist caravan settlements disgust him and are attacks on the true Wales. (Wales has little memorable architecture but its mountains, its coasts, its lakes, drained by the authorities into pipes for Birmingham business men to give their cars a Sunday washing, are its sacred places; the great medieval castles enabled the Plantagenets to hold off the angry natives with, for each castle, a garrison of as little as a hundred men.) The tourists with their Elsan water closets (open air, cleaned by chemicals)

are new and nastier Plantagenets (though castle sanitation
was pretty awful too):

Looking at Sheep

Yes, I know. They are like primroses;
Their ears are the colour of the stems
Of primroses; and their eyes –
Two halves of a nut.

           But images
Like this are for sheer fancy
To play with. Seeing how Wales fares
Now, I will attend rather
To things as they are: to green grass
That is not ours; to visitors
Buying us up. Thousands of mouths
Are emptying their waste speech
About us, and an Elsan culture
Threatens us.
              What would they say
Who bled here, warriors
Of a free people? Savagely
On castles they were the sole cause
Of the sun still goes down red.

The Welsh never conquered Edward III's impregnable
castles and when a Welsh Tudor dynasty ruled England for a
hundred years and more (with two unusually capable monarchs, Henry VII and Elizabeth) their rebellious instincts
were calmed. But the memory of these bloody and vain
sieges is still 'the sole cause/Of the sun still goes down red'.
Behind Welsh nationalism is pride in a language and culture
neglected or treated as comic by the English, not political
oppression; Welshmen of good professional qualifications
must find work in England (like Lloyd George), the country
can not possibly be self-subsistent, and nobody throws
bombs. But an injury to the soul (and a nation's language *is*
its soul) may be the most bitter of all injuries. R. S. Thomas
was born to speak out the grief and rage; like many
clergymen whose dedication is to God as love he is much
more lucky in the uncovenanted mercy of a gift for hate!

    Hate is perhaps an extreme of exasperated love. John
Betjeman, who in 1955 wrote an introduction to *Song at the*

Year's Turning said he did so not at Thomas's request but Thomas's publishers'. He pointed out that (singularly unlike himself) Thomas 'does not read nineteenth-century poets because he thinks that their obvious and jingly rhythms might insult his own sense of metre.' 'He thinks that poetry should be read to oneself not out loud and that it is heard by an inner ear.' He admits influence from only one recent writer, W. B. Yeats, which I, though something of a Yeats specialist, find it hard to detect; though one *can* think of some poems in which Yeats can be read aloud effectively only if the 'inner ear' has followed the shifts of feeling and thought (*The Man and the Echo, Cuchulain Comforted, The Circus Animals' Desertion*). Betjeman adds nobly: 'The "name" which has the honour to introduce this fine poet to a wider public will be forgotten long before that of R. S. Thomas.'

One bitter poem in this volume shows how for Thomas apparent hate is an expression of frustrated love. He hates the obstinate poverty bred by the Calvinist tradition, with its enmity to joy, and its destruction of the song of life:

The Welsh Hill Country

Too far for you to see
The fluke and the foot-rot and the fat maggot
Gnawing the skin from the small bones,
The sheep are grazing at Bwlch-y-Fedwen,
Arranged romantically in the usual manner
On a bleak background of bald stone.

Too far for you to see
The moss and the mould on the cold chimneys,
The nettles growing through the cracked doors,
The houses stand empty at Nant-yr-Eira,
There are holes in the roofs that are thatched with sunlight,
And the fields are reverting to the bare moor.

Too far, too far to see
The set of his eyes and the slow phthisis
Wasting his frame under the ripped coat,
There's a man still farming at Ty'n-y-Fawnog,
Contributing grimly to the accepted pattern,
The embryo music dead in his throat.

I would rank R. S. Thomas in his noble bleakness higher than

Dylan Thomas or Vernon Watkins and *as* high, anyway, as Edward Thomas. He may be the classic Anglo-Welsh poet of his century; he is the only one (except Edward Thomas, and in his playful place-name poems he is sometimes near it) who can never be accused of substituting seductive sound for hard sense. He is the only one who has expressed the deep caring bitterness of Wales.

I shall deal in the next two sections with poetry called 'war poetry' written in two wars; and with the anti-Nazi and anti-Fascist poetry of the years before 1939 (there is less of this, of a pure quality, than is thought). Then in the penultimate section I shall deal with the poets – remarkably frequent in this century, which is one of the richest periods in my book – who have 'classic' without necessarily having 'major' quality. In my final section I shall deal with the remarkable freedom of young poets since 1970, tied to no prevailing fashion. Joining Europe, living and writing where they please, tied to no great dead or living master, these young men have a new horizon.

When I leave anyone out, it is not for lack of space, but deliberately. I leave out the Liverpool Beats for instance and the Beatles, though one of their lines,

Lucy in the sky with diamonds,

has a haunting quality, even if the reference is to LSD or £ S. D., the ultimate fruit of their labours. Performance poems, that can be altered in peformance, like those of Brian Patten and Adrian Henri, are not poems in my sense.

I Poets of Two World Wars

In the first section of Cecil Torr's *Small Talk at Wreyland*, an informal notebook particularly rich in family history, there is this anecdote:

> As a lieutenant in the 15th Light Dragoons – now 15th Hussars – my great-uncle Edward Knight was in command of Sir John Moore's escort at Corunna. He was close by, when Moore was hit, and helped to bury him, 17 January 1809; and in after years he inveighed against the celebrated poem on the

Burial. It was not like that, he said, and 'had no damned poetry in it'.

Fighting soldiers have always been aware that there is 'no damned poetry' in actual warfare. The war poem in our century is an attempt to face the 'no damned poetry' and turn it into a poetry of damnation. Both wars were, in a sense, amateur wars, relying on volunteers and conscripts, men less hardened to the fact that it was 'not like that' and readier to protest against what seemed to them pointless horror. The war against the Kaiser seemed to poets like Siegfried Sassoon if not unnecessary, unnecessarily prolonged, and when the apparent chance of peace was turned down, Sassoon risked a court-martial and death by writing to *The Times* saying he was not going to fight. At Craiglockhart hospital, near Edinburgh, for mentally or nervously disturbed officers, he was persuaded to go back. As a hunting soldier, going under the wires alone to knife or bomb stray Germans, he had a cool, ferocious courage; the you-be-damned manner of his satirical poems did not offend all English readers, staff or civilian politicians. It was a relief that he should go back.

In the Second World War the destruction of Hitler would not seem a trivial aim and the mobile war of the Western Desert was for brave and competent soldiers like Hamish Henderson and Keith Douglas (Henderson, born 1919; Douglas, 1920–44) a rough and cruel game which they were good at playing; but what they had to say in verse about it was chilling, with the deep and wide pity under ice. Henry Reed's (b. 1914) witty and bitter poems, *Lessons of War*, make clear the contrast between life and its lovely growth and death's crude machinery. F. T. Prince's (b. 1912) *Soldiers Bathing* shows the naked, happy, and innocent bodies of young killers in an interval; the men are not what they do. Alun Lewis (1915–44) a disciple of Edward Thomas (he saw no action and was accidentally killed in India) was, like him, a poet of loneliness. Lewis's most anthologised poem, *All day it has rained* . . . gives his mood. There were poets like Drummond Allison (1921–43) dead at twenty-two worrying about not being up to the theme; others like the tough Gavin Ewart (b. 1916) for whom the theme was a bore. It takes all sorts to make a war.

The profoundest First World War poet was Isaac Rosenberg (1890–1918), a second generation immigrant East European Jew, who was at the Slade for some years till the possessive middle-class Jewish ladies who patronised him found the Slade School of Art style too modern. He drew well. The only considerable poet of the First World War not to be an officer he was not, in spite of a weak chest, given a relatively safe base posting but was killed in action in April 1918. He had gone to South Africa before the War for his health but came back to enlist largely for the sake of the grant to his mother; and a younger brother, equally impoverished, could use his civilian clothes. His war poems are not ones in which the poetry is in the pity (like Owen's) but sardonically rough. In *Break of Day in the Trenches* he sympathises with a rat:

> The darkness crumbles away –
> It is the same old druid Time as ever.
> Only a live thing leaps my hand –
> A queer sardonic rat –
> As I pull the parapet's poppy
> To stick behind my ear . . .
> Poppies whose roots are in man's veins
> Drop, and are ever dropping;
> But mine in my ear is safe,
> Just a little white with the dust.

Because he was not rooted in Great Britain, Rosenberg was able, with the Old Testament and Blake in mind, to write the one great prophetic poem of either war:

> *A Worm Fed on the Heart of Corinth*
>
> A worm fed on the heart of Corinth,
> Babylon and Rome:
> Not Paris raped tall Helen,
> But this incestuous worm,
> Who lured her vivid beauty
> To his amorphous sleep.
> England! famous as Helen
> Is thy betrothal sung
> To him the shadowless,
> More amorous than Solomon.

The worm is the 'invisible worm' of Blake's *O Rose thou art sick*, the Satan who is the 'lost traveller's dream under the hill' rather than the *Satan of The Marriage of Heaven and Hell* who embodies the eternal delight of energy.

But since the relationship of the worm to England and to many fallen powers is incestuous (from our birth, we have death close to us and part of us, like a twin), and amorphous (since life of any kind, including the natural self-shaping of crystals, is form, and death is the collapse of form), there is a remnant of hope; only the bethrothal stage has been reached, there is still the element of hope found, too, in Kipling's *Recessional*. Kipling thought of England as a chosen people like the Jews of the Old Testament and prayed that we may not become 'one with Nineveh and Tyre' by using 'such boastings as the Gentiles use'. In one of the great visionary poems of the Second World War, *Elegies for the Dead in Cyrenaica*, Hamish Henderson, who had been across the desert and on to Italy with the 51st Highland Division, a natural fighter as Rosenberg was not and as all Highlanders are, wrote a colder, but more piercing elegy for those of every nation whom the amorphous, incestuous dust of the desert holds for ever:

> There are many dead in the brutish desert
> > who lie uneasy
> among the scrub in this landscape of half-wit
> stunted ill-will. For the dead land is insatiate
> and necrophilous. The sand is blowing about still.
> Many, who for various reasons, or because of mere unan-
> > swerable compulsion, came here
> and fought among the clutching gravestones,
> > shivered and sweated,
> cried out, suffered thirst, were stoically silent, cursed
> the spittering machine-guns, were homesick for Europe
> and fast embedded in quicksand of Africa
> > agonised and died.
> And sleep now. Sleep here the sleep of the dust.

For Rosenberg and Kipling (though Rosenberg hated the Hebrew Father God and in his play *Moses* anticipated Freud's *Moses and Monotheism*; and Kipling, as his deadly poem on the Marconi scandals about Rufus Isaacs, later to be Lord Reading, Viceroy of India, shows, tended to hate actual Jews) there were chosen peoples; for Henderson with his larger, and only apparently colder, compassion, no

peoples are chosen, though all peoples are fated. The dead
of many wars sleep the sleep of the dust, not of the just.
Henderson's poem, *Elegies* was published in 1948, when
people were beginning to get tired of war poetry. Born in
1919, since producing this great poem Henderson has spent
his life recording what survives of song and ballad, Scots and
Gaelic, in the oral tradition.

Keith Douglas (1920–44) whose loyalty was to the remnants of the English hunting gentry who found themselves
riding tanks instead of horses, has a similar magnanimity in
one of his most famous poems, *Vergissmeinicht* (the German
for the flower Forget-me-not):

> . . . Look. Here in the gunpit spoil
> The dishonoured picture of his girl
> who has put: *Steffi. Vergissmeinicht*
> In a copybook gothic script.
>
> We see him almost with content
> abased, and seeming to have paid
> and mocked at by his own equipment
> that's hard and good when he's decayed.
>
> But she would weep to see to-day
> how on his skin the swart flies move;
> the dust upon the paper eye
> and the burst stomach like a cave.
>
> For here the lover and killer are mingled
> who had one body and one heart.
> And death who had the soldier singled
> has done the lover mortal hurt.

The tanks are on their way back to base and on the way out
the dead German had hit Douglas's tank with a hit like 'the
entry of a demon' though he had not stopped the tank.
Returning over 'the nightmare ground' from combat, Douglas and his crew are almost vindictively 'content' to see
their dangerous enemy decayed while his equipment remains hard and good. But the inscription on the picture of
the girl raises in Douglas the feeling that this was also a
fellow human being. He must be careful to avoid the
sentiment into which, in the First World War, even so
powerful a poet as Rosenberg had fallen. He uses both

lexical elements, 'the *swart* flies', the dust on 'the *paper* eye', 'the burst stomach like a cave', and the eighteenth century syntactical device of antithesis –

> And death who *had* the *soldier* singled
> *has* done the *lover* mortal hurt, –

to create, through distancing, an effect of icy pity: but the willed formality somehow makes us aware of all that lies beneath the tip of the iceberg.

In the First World War the poet who was up like a rocket and down like a stick was Rupert Brooke (1887–1915). His early war sonnets, notably *The Soldier*,

> If I should die think only this of me
> That there's some corner of a foreign field
> That is for ever England . . .

were first welcomed as a very eloquent expression (which they are) of the romantic idealism with which many young men of Brooke's class welcomed the war. (He was the son of a Rugby housemaster, with a very puritan mother; a pagan and an amorist in his Cambridge days, and already famous as a poet before the First World War began; the handsomest English poet since Byron, but like Byron uneasy, restless, sometimes irrationally jealous, bored or disgusted in his many love affairs.) The war simplified many things for him, for the short time it allowed him. He saw action only in Churchill's raid on Antwerp and died of fever on shipboard during Churchill's ill-planned and disastrous expedition to the Dardanelles. He could not have anticipated the horrors of trench warfare though phrases in his poems suggest that he would cope with it. *Heaven*, for instance, a skit on anthropomorphism, is ferociously funny:

> Unfading moths, immortal flies,
> And the worm that never dies.
> And in that Heaven of all their wish,
> There shall be no more land, say fish.

He anticipated Eliot's interest in Webster, in a still very readable book, and in seventeenth-century poetry (though of the emblematic rather than the metaphysical kind) in *The*

Funeral of Youth: Threnody. The mourners are enumerated
(and Brooke is talking of his own youth: he was twenty-eight
when he died, no longer young for a much wooed male
beauty):

> *Folly* went first.
> With muffled bells and coxcomb still revers'd;
> And after trod the bearers, hat in hand –
> *Laughter*, most hoarse, and Captain *Pride* with tanned
> And martial face all grim, and fussy *Joy*,
> Who had to catch a train, and *Lust*, poor, snivelling boy;
> These bore the dear departed.

In this witty parody, with its strong vein of self-contempt
and awareness of vain trivialities, one can see one of the
seeds that produced *The Soldier*. A notable critic once
reported to me a remark by one of the poet's friends:
'Rupert was not nearly so nice as people thought but he was
much cleverer.'

Brooke was not, of course, the only poet to greet the war
romantically. Julian Grenfell, a warrior by ancestry, a very
brave fighting soldier, also did so: so did Siegfried Sassoon
in his early *To Victory*. I prefer this to *The Soldier*, simply
because Sassoon was nice rather than clever, and is always
fresh and direct (for the same reason, I prefer him to
Wilfred Owen, about whom I rather agree with Yeats's
brutal verdict: 'blood and sucked sugar stick'.) Here is
Sassoon (1886–1967) in *To Victory*:

> Return to meet me, colours that were my joy,
> Not in the woeful crimson of men slain,
> But shining as a garden; come with the streaming
> Banners of dawn and sundown after rain . . .

It is an almost universal verdict that Wilfred Owen was
the greatest English poet of either world war, and that
Sassoon, a naturally minor poet, found only in the war a
proper expression for his limited gift. Let me indicate my
reservations about this, and my reasons. Let me take what I
think Owen's purest poem in diction and feeling, *Futility*:

> Move him into the sun –
> Gently its touch awoke him once,
> At home, whispering of fields unsown.

Always it woke him, even in France.
Until this morning and this snow.
If anything could rouse him now
The kind old sun will know.

Think how it wakes the seeds –
Woke, once, the clays of a cold star.
Are limbs, so dear-achieved, are sides
Full-nerved, – still warm, – too hard to stir?
Was it for this the clay grew tall?
– Oh, what made fatuous sunbeams toil
To break earth's sleep at all?

This is a great poem because, alone among Owen's poems, it has a diction which is exactly appropriate, neither over-sweet nor hysterically stretched. But even here the 'ead boy is a specimen not a person; just as all soldiers in Owen tend to be *they*, a mystically linked mass, rather than individuals. He and they in their mystical reunion re-enact, as one transcendent person, the sacrifice of Christ. Sassoon, as his brilliant prose memoirs show, was even in war intelligently observant of and emotionally interested in persons. Compare this poem of Sassoon's written at St Venant, July 1918. I am not sure that I can claim the same greatness for it, but it moves me more:

The Dug-out

Why do you lie with your legs ungainly huddled,
And one arm bent across your sullen, cold
Exhausted face? It hurts my heart to watch you,
Deep-shadow'd from the candle's guttering gold:
And you wonder why I shake you by the shoulder;
Drowsy, you mumble and sigh and turn your head . . .
You are too young to fall asleep for ever;
And when you sleep you remind me of the dead.

Sassoon had none of Owen's feelings about a mystical, merging, atoning death. As a fighting soldier, with his solitary night raids, he was at once daring, careful, and ruthless. As an officer, it was his duty to do what he could to see that his men survived. He had no patience with incompetence, as he shows in *The General*, which deserves its fame:

'Good morning; good morning!' the General said
When we met him last week on our way to the Line.
Now the soldiers he smiled at are most of 'em dead,
And we're cursing his staff for incompetent swine.
'He's a cheery old card', grunted Harry to Jack
As they slogged up to Arras with rifle and pack.

But he did for them both by his plan of attack.

He had always in his satires the 'you-be-damned' air of the English country gentleman totally sure of himself (he managed to black out the fact that on his father's side he was descended from rich Oriental Jewish merchants; he leaves his father right out of his later *Who's Who* entries). About the complacency of fathers about the deaths of their sons, he finds the one killing word:

'Yes,' wheezed the other, 'that's the luck!
My boy's quite broken-hearted, stuck
In England training all this year.
Still, if there's truth in what we hear,
The Huns intend to ask for more
      Before they bolt across the Rhine.'
I watched them toddle through the door –
      These impotent old friends of mine.

'Impotent' is the word that does it: the old men, despised in their fantasies of combative virility can have no answer. The ferocity about a music-hall show in *Blighters* shows both social contempt for vulgarians and the controlled ferocity that was one of Sassoon's qualities as a soldier:

The House is crammed: tier beyond tier they grin
And cackle at the Show, while prancing ranks
Of harlots shrill the chorus, drunk with din;
'We're sure the Kaiser loves our dear old Tanks!'

I'd like to see a Tank come down the stalls,
Lurching to rag-time tunes, or 'Home, sweet Home',
And there'd be no more jokes in Music-halls,
To mock the riddled corpses round Bapaume.

Wilfred Owen had not this confidence and could be described, perhaps, as upper-lower-middle-class' He was much the most original of English war poets of the First World War (except Rosenberg) but the originality has sometimes excruciating effects. Consider the rhymes in both these stanzas and the erotic-sadistic images in the second: I italicise the rhymes that jar on me:

> Red lips are not so red
>   As the stained stones kissed by the English dead.
> Kindness of wooed and *wooer*
> Seems shame to their love *pure*.
> O Love, your eyes lose *lure*
>   When I behold eyes blinded in my stead!

> Your slender atti*tude*
>   Trembles not exquisite like limbs knife-*skewed*,
> Rolling and rolling there
> Where God seems not to care;
> Till the fierce Love they bear
>   Cramps them in death's extreme decrepi*tude*.

I wonder if he said *woo-er, pyoo-er, loo-er*, twisting pronunciation, that is, rhyming a bisyllable with hiatus with a long dipthong better pronounced *peyoor* and a long vowel *poor*. Similarly, did he stretch the short rhymes royal of *attitude, decrepitude*, to match the long and emphatic final rhyme of *skewed*. His taste is never trustworthy. We should remember that the man himself was brave, gentle, and lovable, as Edmund Blunden notes in his long and fascinating memoir before his edition of 1931 (the standard and most scholarly edition is now Cecil Day-Lewis's). Blunden gives an extract from a letter on the exploit for which Owen won the M.C., and it is impossible not to like and admire Owen the man: 'I only shot one man with my revolver (at about thirty yards!); the others I took with a smile.' Perhaps like Keats whom he always admired passionately, and who wrote *salt sea-spry* for *salt sea-spray*, he was too grand for the restrictions of mere taste.

There are certainly passages of a grandeur far beyond Sassoon, for example in *Insensibility*, particularly the last stanza:

> But cursed are dullards whom no cannon stuns,
> That they should be as stones;
> wretched are they, and mean

With paucity that never was simplicity.
By choice they made themselves immune
To pity and whatever moans in man
Before the last sea and the hapless stars;
Whatever mourns when many leave these shores;
Whatever shares
The eternal reciprocity of tears.

There is his last great poem, *Strange Meeting*, with its
wonderful use of pararhyme (consonants at the beginning
and end of a rhyme word the same; internal vowel or
diphthong always different) and with a great vision – the
two enemies meeting underground, both potential poets and
healers; their reconciliation, but also sense of futility:

And of my weeping something had been left,
Which must die now. I mean the truth untold,
The pity of war, the pity war distilled.
Now men will go content with what we spoiled.
Or, discontent, boil bloody, and be spilled.
They will be swift with swiftness of the tigress,
None will break ranks, though nations trek from progress.
Courage was mine, and I had mystery,
Wisdom was mine, and I had mastery:
To miss the march of this retreating world
Into vain citadels that are not walled.
Then, when much blood had clogged their chariot-wheels,
I would go up and wash them from sweet wells,
Even with truths that lie too deep for taint.
I would have poured my spirit without stint
But not through wounds; not on the cess of war.
Foreheads of men have bled where no wounds were . . .

Even there, though, a pedantic critic might quibble at
details. 'Discontented' not 'discontent' is the negative form
of the adjective 'content'. The rhyme of 'tigress' and 'progress' verges on the comic (the story of the small menagerie
with its large notice, 'This way to the Egress'). 'Trek', with
its too local associations with the Boer War, is a word
lacking in dignity. If it is impossible for the healing poetic
spirit to heal the actual 'wounds', the 'cess' (cess-pool) of
war, what did Owen mean when in his famous gnomic
preface he wrote: 'Above all I am not concerned with
Poetry. My subject is War, and the pity of War. The Poetry

is in the pity'? Let us remember he was a young man, still twenty-nine when he was killed in November, 1918. He had a right to make mistakes and change.

What one can object to, legitimately, in a number of his most famous poems is no insincerity but a disproportion of tone. Perhaps the 'poetry' still did matter, not too much (it never can) but in a wrong way, as rhetorical exaggeration. For example it could be too sweet, as in the sestet of *Anthem for Doomed Youth*:

> What candles may be held to speed them all?
>   Not in the hands of boys, but in their eyes
> Shall shine the holy glimmers of good-byes.
>   The pallor of girls' brows shall be their pall;
> Their flowers the tenderness of patient minds,
> And each slow dusk a drawing-down of blinds . . .

Or it could be so hysterically and redundantly – that is, repeating the same concept unnecessarily in different phrases or images – as in these lines from *Dulce et Decorum Est*:

> If you could hear, at every jolt, the blood
> Come gargling from the froth corrupted lungs,
> Obscene as cancer, bitter as the cud
> Of vile, incurable sores on innocent tongues,

where, from 'Bitter as the cud . . .', Owen is simply rubbing in the agony of a point he has already made. The sestet is too vague and sweet, too Keatsian; many dead soldiers had no holy 'glimmer of good-byes', no perpetual still life of mourning from 'boys' and 'girls' to look forward to after their deaths. The later line, 'And each slow dusk of drawing-down of blinds' does not help. 'Pallor' at the beginning of the line and 'pall' at the end seems a sort of trickery (the vowels of 'pall' and 'pallor' are pronounced differently): and if a war, like the Second World War against Hitler, is generally recognised as just, its horrors can be endured. The logic of 'it is so nasty it cannot be right' is feeble; the war against the Kaiser was one we could possibly honourably have stood apart from, if we were not already committed to the *entente cordiale*; but the war against Hitler was one in which not to resist would have been to condone the triumph of the nastiness, of Auschwitzes in Britain, say, and would *not* have been 'dulce et decorum' . . . I find unsatisfactory the idealised sacrificial homosexuality of the poem I began with and of *Fragment; I saw his Round Mouth's Crimson*:

> I saw his round mouth's crimson deepen as it fell,
>   Like a Sun, in his last deep hour;
> Watched the magnificent recession of farewell,
>   Clouding, half gleam, half glower . . .

I could not fittingly judge so good, gentle, and brave a person as Owen as a man: as a poet I have the right to say that he strikes me as uneven, promising, and like Keats, whom he admired so much, great in patches.

Graves wrote no good war poems. Blunden's best war poems, in his prose and verse volume, *Undertones of War*, 1928 (just ten years after the armistice) and even more in *Near and Far*, 1929, are retrospective. *The Sunlit Vale* in a classical pastoral vein, from *Near and Far*, blends the pastoral dream and the grim fact with a thrilling balance:

> I saw the sunlit vale, and the pastoral fairy-tale;
> The sweet and bitter scent of the may drifted by;
> And never have I seen such a bright bewildering green,
>   But it looked like a lie,
>   Like a kindly meant lie.
>
> Where gods are in dispute, one a Sidney, one a brute,
> It would seem that human sense might not know, might not spy;
> But though nature smile and feign where foul play has stabbed and
>   slain,
>   There's a witness, an eye,
>   Nor will charms blind that eye.
>
> Nymph of the upland song and the sparkling leafage young,
> For your merciful desire with these charms to beguile,
> For ever be adored; muses yield you rich reward;
>   But you fail, though you smile –
>   The other does not smile.

III Waiting for Hitler

There has been a tendency to think of the 1930s in England

as a period when the young poets were warning us against the coming war with Hitler and begging us to seek an alliance with Stalin (one might have called this section, 'Waiting for Hitler and Lying to Oneself About Stalin'). Of what seem to me the two best warning poems of the decade, one was written by John Cornford, a young Cambridge man, the son of a great Greek scholar and an interesting Georgian woman poet, who died fighting in the International Brigade for a fusion of Communism and of Liberty, before he could realise how cynical the Russian exploitation of Spain was. The other good warning poem was by the realistic old Tory, Rudyard Kipling, who saw far more clearly than Auden, Spender, or MacNeice the exact nature of the threat we were facing: his illiberal prejudice against the Germans no doubt helped. Here is Cornford's poem, a love poem desperately asking his Muse (a living person, not the Marxian Dialectic) to give him courage and, if he dies, remember him kindly. I find it heart-rendingly moving, as I find few poems of the 1930s, that 'low, dishonest decade'.

Here is Cornford's poem: his dates are 1915–36, so, a poet of enormous promise, he died in his twenty-first year:

To Margot Heinemann

Heart of the heartless world,
Dear heart, the thought of you
Is the pain at my side,
The shadow that chills my view.

The wind rises in the evening,
Reminds that autumn is near.
I am afraid to lose you,
I am afraid of my fear.

On the last mile to Huesca,
The last fence for our pride,
Think so kindly, dear. that I
Sense you at my side.

And if bad luck should lay my strength
Into the shallow grave,
Remember all the good you can;
Don't forget my love.

Such a poem and such a death and such a love authenticate
Cornford, whatever he believed in.

Here is the Kipling poem:

The Storm Cone

This is the midnight – let no star
Delude us – dawn is very far.
This is the tempest long foretold –
Slow to make head but sure to hold.

Stand by! The lull 'twixt blast and blast
Signals the storm is near, not past;
And worse than present jeopardy
May our forlorn to-morrow be.

If we have cleared the expectant reef,
Let no man look for his relief.
Only the darkness hides the shape
Of further peril to escape.

It is decreed that we abide
The weight of gale against the tide
And those huge waves the outer main
Sends in to set us back again.

They fall and whelm. We strain to hear
The pulses of her labouring gear,
Till the deep throb beneath us proves,
After each shudder and check, she moves!

She moves, with all save purpose lost,
To make her offing from the coast;
But, till she fetches open sea,
Let no man deem that he is free.

At the time of publication critics may have objected to
touches of archaism in the vocabulary. (Similarly, Orwell
reproached Yeats for using emotive adjectives like 'mysterious, beautiful' instead of, like Day-Lewis, talking of 'arterial
roads' or like Spender describing pylons as resembling 'nude
giant girls that have no secrets'. It is the roads and the pylons
that seem dated and caught in the prison of a short period
now.)

Stephen Spender (b. 1909) was the most uneven but also the most tactlessly honest poet of his generation and in his excellent poem, *Two Armies*, on the Spanish Civil War, he would feel pity, not hate: I quote the two last stanzas, but the whole poem deserves studying:

> Clean silence drops at night, when a little walk
> Divides the sleeping armies, each
> Huddled in linen woven by remote hands.
> When the machines are stilled, a common suffering
> Whitens the air with breath and makes both one
> As though these enemies slept in each other's arms.
>
> Only the lucid friend to aerial raiders
> The brilliant pilot moon, stares down
> Upon this plain she makes a shining bone
> Cut by the shadows of many thousand bones.
>
> Where amber clouds scatter on No-Man's-Land
> She regards death and time throw up
> The furious words and minerals which destroy.

Auden deleted from his own collected poems, after attempting to amend it, his long eloquent poem, *Spain*, for which (so inclusive, so much a large tolerant family, is the English literary Establishment) he had received the King's Gold Medal for Poetry. In his Foreword to a collection of 1976 he says:

> I once wrote:
>
> > History to the defeated
> > May say alas but cannot help nor pardon.
>
> To say this is to equate goodness with success. It would have been bad enough if I had ever held this wicked doctrine, but that I should have stated it simply because it sounded to me rhetorically effective is quite inexcusable.

The poems of Auden's English period are a very grand achievement, but the ones directly about politics make a small proportion of them, many more being concerned with old Germanic feud and wander myths, guilty loving, analysis of social and psychological typology, and, in a very wide sense, culture. Never a member of the Communist Party he was at most a 'pink liberal', and Isherwood complained that in the plays on which they worked together he had always to prevent Auden from letting his characters fall on their knees, at the slightest excuse. They went different ways, one to New York, one to California, and both became American citizens.

The whole atmosphere of tension in the late 1930s is caught by Louis MacNeice in the best long poem of that decade, *Autumn Journal*. But notice that in these lines the atmosphere is left-of-centre, anti-Hitler but not pro-Stalin, and that there is a sardonic sense of what the war will cost in the amenities of life. A sensuous poet, the poet of 'Euston, the smell of soot and fish of petrol', of 'the moment cradled like a brandy glass', a scholar who notes how different and other the ancient Greeks are, MacNeice's interest in politics was by no means an exclusive one; rather it was forced on him by the times:

After the warm days the rain comes pimpling
    The paving stones with white
And with the rain the national conscience, creeping,
    Seeping through the night.
And in the sodden park on Sunday protest
    Meetings assemble not, as so often, now
Merely to advertise some patent panacea
    But simply to avow
The need to hold the ditch; a bare avowal
    That may perhaps imply
Death at the doors in a week but perhaps in the long run
    Exposure of the lie.
Think of a number, double it, treble it, square it,
    And sponge it out
And repeat *ad lib.* and mark the slate with crosses;
    There is no time to doubt
If the puzzle really has an answer. Hitler yells on the wireless,
    The night is damp and still
And I hear dull blows on wood outside my window;
    They are cutting down the trees on Primrose Hill.

I would read *Autumn Journal* frequently, if I were the reader, to get an honest, complex, and puzzling impression of what it all felt like. (I, the writer, am old enough to remember it myself.)

Cecil Day Lewis (1904–72) was a Communist for a longer time than any other of the better-known poets of the 1930s. In an epigrammatic poem of the year of the war's commencement he says sharply:

Where are the War Poets?

They who in folly or mere greed
Enslaved religion, markets, laws,
Borrow our language now and bid
Us to speak up in freedom's cause.

It is the logic of our times,
No subject for immortal verse –
That we who lived by honest dreams
Defend the bad against the worse.

But it is not for his pre-war Marxist poems, honest though their dreams are, that Day Lewis will be remembered. He became more and more attached to what, before the war, he would have taken for a dead past; he worked for years on one of the most living English versions of the whole of Virgil; in *An Italian Journey* he worked various parodies of Victorian poets into an amusing skit on Clough's *Amours de Voyage*. Then his sense of love and discipleship for authors rooted in the Victorian age especially for Hardy became serious. He also found a new lyrical vein all his own. He was an ideal choice for Poet Laureate when John Masefield died. His graceful memorial stone is in Stinsford churchyard in Dorset, alongside the two clumsier catafalques that enclose Emma Lavinia's body and Hardy's heart. He deserved that post as Laureate and that place in death. Nobody who knew him even very slightly, as I did, would think that this honourable man had betrayed his early beliefs; he had discovered his deeper roots. There is an amusing satirical poet, Edgell Rickword, who remained staunchly loyal to the Marxist gospel (born in 1898, he still survives, and is one of the poets whom the Carcanet Press deserves praise for reprinting). But it is possible for a good critic to admire the sincerity, as well as the skill, of both men.

Nothing can ever be proved, in criticism, or in history. But I hope that I have at least made a case that to tie long-lived and developing poets to *some* only of their poems in the 1930s is grossly to oversimplify both the literary atmosphere of the decade itself and the kind of various pressures (not all political) it put on poets.

IV Distinction and Possible Greatness

Like the seventeenth century, our own century has been a century of genius; but in both the periods the 'genius' is not confined to four or five obviously major poets, but offers, say, in Marvell or Charles Cotton charms and delicacies that are not to be found in Donne or Milton or Dryden. I want to indicate some instances of individuality: goodness, distinction, possible greatness, daring in experiment. I shall discuss at the end two poets, Basil Bunting and C. H. Sisson for whom, in their late years, claims of greatness have been made.

We have seen the Poet Laureate Robert Bridges (1884–1930) in a satirical vein. A stiffness, a distance, a rather unreal conventionality of thought, but suddenly a poem like Eros from *New Poems* will have strange lawless beauty: I quote the last lines,

> . . . Surely thy body is thy mind,
> For in thy face is nought to find,
> Only thy soft unchristen'd smile,
> That shadows neither love nor guile,
> But shameless will and power immense,
> In secret sensuous innocence.
>
> O king of joy, what is thy thought?
> I dream thou knowest it is nought,
> And wouldst in darkness come, but thou
> Makest the light where'er thou go.
> As yet no victim of thy grace,
> None who e'er longed for thy embrace,
> Hath dared to look upon thy face.

Perhaps a dozen poems of this directly sensuous or of a directly emotional quality,

> I never shall love the snow again
> Since Maurice died,

or

> I have loved flowers that fade,
> Within whose magic tents
> Rich hues have marriage made
> With sweet unmemoried scents:
>
> A honeymoon delight, –
> A joy of love at sight,
> That ages in an hour:
> My song be like a flower!

convince us that we are dealing with a classic English poet, passionate, sensuous, finding delight in the vividness and fading of beauty, not with a skilfully but pedantically experimental versifier. His late long poem *The Testament of Beauty* demonstrates both his metrical skill, comparable with that of Milton in *Paradise Lost*, and his failure in a chatty, reflective poem to achieve anything like Miltonic sublimity. Nevertheless, the young Auden found it oddly fascinating.

Robert Graves, born 1895, son of an Anglo-Irish father, Alfred Percival Graves, the author of *Father O'Flynn*, and a mother of German origin, of the family of the great historian Von Ranke, was a man tormented and ruled by dominating women. There was his first wife, Nancy Nicholson, a strong feminist, who came to her wedding in a land-girl's breeches; and then, as an instructor and companion, Laura Riding, who also left him and married an American journalist. His famous book, *The White Goddess* is a brilliant study of the mythical pagan goddess with many roles. Graves saw the White Goddess as the mother image (Lucina, the moon as the goddess of midwifery in the sky), the lover image who is elusive and cruel (Diana in the groves), and the image of death and torment. In middle age he married again, a much younger woman, Beryl Pritchard, took to happy domesticity mingled with flirtations with pretty young women who liked, briefly, to play the White Goddess in Majorca. He had been suffering from shell-shock till he got the war out of his system in *Good-Bye to All That* in 1928. When he had lost Laura Riding as well as Nancy Nicholson, and remembering also the nerve-racking years of the trenches, he wrote:

The Survivor

To die with a forlorn hope, but soon to be raised
By hags, the spoilers of the field, to elude their claws
And stand once more on a well-swept parade ground,
Scarred and bemedalled, sword upright in fist
At head of a new undaunted company:

Is this joy? – to be doubtless alive again,
And the others dead? Will your nostrils gladly savour
The fragrance, always new, of a first hedge-rose?
Will your ears be charmed by the thrush's melody
Sung as though he had himself devised it?

And is this joy: after the double suicide
(Heart against heart) to be restored entire,
To smooth your hair and wash away the life-blood,
And presently seek a young and innocent bride,
Whispering in the dark: 'for ever and ever'?

Full of doubt and bitterness as that is, it has not the eloquent
hopelessness of *Full Moon* (I quote the three last stanzas in
which two lovers are bewitched out of love by the moon):

> Your phantom wore the moon's cold mask,
>   My phantom wore the same;
> Forgetful of the feverish task
>   In hope of which they came,
> Each image held the other's eyes
> And watched the grey distraction rise
>   To cloud the eager flame –
>
> To cloud the eager flame of love,
>   To fog the shining gate;
> They held the tyrannous queen above,
>   Sole mover of their fate,
> They glared as marble statues glare
> Across the tesselated stair
>   Or down the halls of state.
>
> And now warm earth was Arctic sea,
>   Each breath came dagger-keen;
> Two bergs of glinting ice were we,
>   The broad moon sailed between;
> There swam the mermaids, tailed and finned,

> And love went by upon the wind
>   As though it had not been,

or the tragic ending of *Vanity*: the evil toad under the happy
lovers' hearth-stone knows

> . . . that certitude at last
> Must melt away in vanity –
> No gate is fast, no door is fast –
>
> That thunder bursts from the blue sky,
> That gardens of the mind fall waste,
> That fountains of the heart run dry.

Graves's greater grip as a poet owes much to Laura Riding
who was his companion and mentor (not his mistress) in
Majorca for several years. When she left him to join and
later marry a poet and *Time* journalist, Schuyler B. Jackson,
Laura (Riding) Jackson was angry that he continued to write
poetry after she had decided that it was almost (she herself
had almost done it) possible to write truth in poetry, but not
quite possible. Yet his later poetry written after their
separation has a moving and singing tone that (though he
occasionally, as Mrs Jackson and her disciples have noted,
lifts a line from her, in a way that some would call complimentary allusion and she plagiarism) is quite different
from his period under her influence and from his groping
and uncertain war-time and immediately post-war period. In
this lovely short poem there is, to use a word almost ruined
by D. H. Lawrence, 'tenderness':

She Tells Her Love While Half-Asleep

> She tells her love while half asleep,
>   In the dark hours,
>   With half-words whispered low:
> As Earth stirs in her winter sleep
>   And puts out grass and flowers,
>   Despite the snow,
>   Despite the falling snow.

I have given Graves so much space because he has seemed
to me since I first began to read him seriously (the little

selection *No More Ghosts* which I carried between Egypt, Eritrea, and Palestine, as it then was, during the Second World War) the best of our living poets, by which I mean the most consistently good one. He has never, since his early period, been clumsy or false in tone, nor has there been any Wordsworthian 'still sad music of senility'. His *Collected Poems* of 1975, published a little after his eightieth birthday, contained more new poems than any of his collections so far. It contained ten years of new poems, of which he writes 'I have written more new poems and discarded fewer than at any other time.' He is excellent not only in poems written for poets but in satires and grotesques written for wits. He has never aimed at 'greatness', which he sees as a way in which the poet blows himself up.

Norman Cameron (1905–53) was his most distinguished disciple. The short and extraordinarily haunting love poem, *Shepherdess*, is Graves with a difference:

All day my sheep have mingled with yours. They strayed
Into your valley seeking a change of ground.
Held and bemused with what they and I had found,
Pastures and wonders, heedlessly I delayed.

Now it is late. The tracks leading home are steep,
The stars and landmarks in your country are strange.
How can I take my sheep back over the range?
Shepherdess, show me now where I may sleep.

D. H. Lawrence has been mentioned already. Only a few of his poems are doubtfully good and even these show an uncertainty on the author's path. The two versions of *Bavarian Gentians* – in both of which the printers put 'Dio' for what is obviously 'Dis' and the three versions of *The Ship of Death* are not successive revisions but rewritings from scratch. Of course there are splendid poems of the *Birds, Beast and Flowers* type, like *Snake*, and some early, solidly realistic dialect poems: but I find it hard to get through Lawrence's most intimate and personal set of poems, about his struggling, difficult, and rewarding (in the end) relationship with Frieda, *Look! We Have Come Through*. It is something very private (where poetry should be personal and universal) and I do not want to look. I think that the crooked compliment one can pay to Lawrence's poems is that hasty and over-abundant though they are they do not clash with one's sense of Lawrence as a very great writer of prose.

Sir William Empson (b. 1906) (the well-deserved honour came late in life) is perhaps the only poet of this century, except Eliot, who is equally important as a critic. Both teach us to read poems in a new way, though Empson's way is more startling. Perhaps his poems are more startling too: 89 pages of *Collected Poems*, as poems, then pages 93 to 119 taken up with sometimes necessary and always useful and entertaining notes. He says of the notes: 'A claim is implied that the poem is worth publishing though the author knows it is imperfect, but this has a chance of being true. Also there is no longer a reasonably small field which may be taken as general knowledge. It is impertinent to suggest that the reader ought to possess already any odd bits of information one may have picked up in a field where one is oneself ignorant; such a point may be explained in a note without trouble to anybody; and it does not require much trouble to endure seeing what you already know in a note.'

One wonders if one catches him out in this note, and is not sure: 'The Roof of the World is, I believe, the Himalayas; the geography here is as dim as Mandevil's.' At least throughout the nineteenth century it was the High Pamir, perpetually frozen, first explored by a Scotsman who following the narrower fork of the river discovered one of the two sources of the Oxus; but I think Empson excuses himself by referring to his geography being as dim as Sir John Mandevil's in his *Travels*. He notes in passing that the best poems need the fewest notes, and indicates (though very indirectly) a kind of companionableness that gives the notes much of their charm: 'But it seems to me that there has been an unfortunate suggestion of writing for a clique about a great deal of recent poetry, and that very much of it might be avoided by a mere willingness to explain incidental difficulties.'

In the poems themselves one has the odd impression of a profound and passionate melancholy balanced by a very English blunt and dogged humour. Empson's background is various: a Yorkshire squirearchical family (the young Henry VIII's most popular act was to execute his father's too efficient tax-gatherers, Empson and Dudley), mathematics for the first part of the Cambridge tripos, English under an inspiring teacher, I. A. Richards, for the second, who urged him to turn a thesis into his first book, *Seven Types of Ambiguity*: a university teaching post in Japan, then, very differently, life as an itinerant teacher with Mao Tse-Tung's followers on their Long March: broadcasting on the Far Eastern section of the BBC during the war, post-war visits to Harvard, where he made a life-long friend of Robert Lowell, and to Peking (where I. A. Richards was also welcomed by the new *régime*): a Professorship at Sheffield, and visits to Canadian and United States universities after his retirement. Now in his seventies he has a happy marriage and two beloved sons, one of whom has done important experimental work, as a psychophysiologist, on dreams. In dreams, perhaps, begin Empson's unexpectednesses.

He leaves a unique 'taste in the head' (the phrase is my own) best illustrated, perhaps, by very brief random quotations:

> It is the pain, it is the pain, endures.
> Your chemic beauty burned my muscles through.
> Poise of my hands reminded me of yours. . . .

> Searching the cave gallery of your face
> My torch meets fresco after fresco ravishes
> Rebegets me; it crumbles each; no trace
> Stays to remind me what each heaven lavishes . . .

> Besides, I do not really like
>   The verses about 'Up the Boys',
> The revolutionary romp,
>   The hearty uproar that deploys
> A sit-down literary strike;
>   The other curly-headed toys
> The superrealistic comp.
>   By a good student who enjoys
> A nightmare handy as a bike.
>   You find a cluster of them cloys
> But all conventions have their pomp
>   And all styles can come down to noise . . .

(I underline the last three lines for their generosity of spirit;

his own convention may have its own pomp, his own style may come down to noise, and people are perfectly free to dislike him or find a cluster of them cloying. In the end there can be no valid critical argument about taste. One says 'I like this poem, and this and this are part of what I like, and so is the total pattern these build up.' People are still free to say, 'I still don't like it.')

I would like to quote the last personal poem in *Collected Poems*. The note says that Empson was trying to give the word 'pygmy' the impact of a contradiction when connected with the great word 'free': 'The pygmy method of singing (on the sound-track of an excellent travel film) sounded spontaneous though it was a gross and extreme example of collectivism.'

> Not wrongly moved by this dismaying scene
> 　　The thinkers like the nations getting caught
> 　　Joined in the organising that they fought
> To scorch all earth of all but one machine.
>
> It can be swung, is what these hopers mean,
> 　For all the loony hooters can be bought
> 　　On the small ball. It can then all be taught
> And reconverted to be kind and clean.
>
> A more heartening fact about the cultures of man
> 　　Is their appalling stubborness. The sea
> Is always calm ten fathoms down. The gigan-
>
> tic anthropolgical circus riotously
> Holds open all its booths. The pygmy plan
> 　　Is one note each and the tune goes out free.

It seems to me that Empson runs down this poem by failing to spot his own metaphorical meaning. The world will never be really at one because the separate cultures of human tribes are obstinate and deeply rooted, each, as it were, striking its own note. Yet when we listen to all the notes of our cultures (pygmies by metaphor, really tribes less simple than pygmy tribes) we hear a music. What is special about the pygmies as such, African pygmies or Australian aborigines, is the self-contained nature of their culture, related to its own structure and customs and not, except as something to be exploited, to the more evolved and various tribes around it. Why their unstructured singing (one man one note need not mean one man and *always the same* note) is 'a grotesque and extreme example of collectivism' I do not see, nor, I think, does the poem actually say this. What it does say in defence of deep, traditional cultural variety is interesting enough.

It is possible to read Empson understanding very little but perceiving that his ear, his sense of pace and pitch, of the noise that a style comes down to, is wonderfully acute. He loves poets with a similar sense, and unfashionable in his own time, like Edith Sitwell (1887–1964) and Roy Campbell (1901–57). He might like Dame Edith because she belonged to the aristocracy as he to the country gentry of the North. Her belated conversion to Roman Catholicism would not, in spite of his hatred of the Christian God, be something to be taken seriously. Similarly, though he thought Roy Campbell's support of the Francoists in the Spanish Civil War (though as a Carlist, Roy always insisted, not a member of the Fascist Falange) silly or wicked or both, the best poems thrilled him with their rhythmical mastery. He shared no opinions with, though he had a deep affection for, his Cambridge friend (b. 1908) Kathleen Raine, but delighted in her poems because 'her voice was ever soft, gentle and low, an excellent thing in woman'.

I shall quote these three briefly. Dame Edith's obituary in *The Times* had two or three brief quotations from her work, of which the opening of *The Sleeping Beauty*, a long poem, was perhaps the most striking:

> When we come to that dark house,
> Never sound of wave shall rouse
> The bird that sings within the blood,
> Of those who sleep in that dark wood.

Notice the consonantal off-rhyme, 'house', 'rouse' (*h:aus r:auz*) and the vocalic 'blood', 'wood' (*blud: wood*), and the echoes of 'house', 'sound', 'rouse': the chime of 'sings within' in the third line of short syllables; and the structural mirroring of 'dark house' and 'dark wood', both accentual iambics but quantitative spondees, 'dark house', 'dark wood.' There was a sense in which Edith Sitwell had very little to *say* (her later poems, inspired by the Second World War, attempt to say more, but their texture is less rich than that of *The Sleeping Beauty*). But it is hard to think of any woman poet with a stronger, richer more perfectly controlled voice. As a composer of poetry for the ear she had the physical equipment of a strong man. Some of the early poems, like *Façade*, are deliberate jokes with the possibilities of sound. If in the early poems there is very little meaning, in the abstract sense, there is a wonderful variety of mood, from the gallop of mockery to the dead march of despair. 'Thinking', in the sense of using verse as a vehicle for original thought, can be brought off by very few poets.

Roy Campbell, born in Africa, briefly at Oxford, taken up by Vita Sackville-West after his first success as a poet and later in *The Georgiad* savagely attacking the whole Bloomsbury culture, an itinerant journalist and propagandist rather than a soldier in Civil War Spain, a Sergeant in East Africa during the Hitler war (non-combatant because of an injured leg), a producer on the B.B.C. Home Service after the war, settling in Portugal, killed in a car accident, was one of these men whose lives seem a little more adventurous than they are. Even as an amateur bull-fighter in Spain (according to his friend the Afrikaans poet Uys Krige, who travelled with him as a professional footballer) he was gallant but inefficient. But as a poet his role of active defiance never fumbles. Consider these last two stanzas of a grand poem about the bleak island of Tristan da Cunha:

> Now in the eastern sky the fairest planet
> Pierces the dying wave with dangled spear,
> And in the whirring hollows of your granite
> That vaster sea to which you are a shell
> Sighs with a ghostly rumour, like the drear
> Moan of the nightwind in a hollow cell.
>
> We shall not meet again; over the wave
> Our ways divide, and yours is straight and endless,
> But mine is short and crooked to the grave:
> Yet what of these dark crowds amid whose flow
> I battle like a rock, aloof and friendless,
> Are not their generations vague and endless
> The waves, the strides, the feet on which I go?

One would not think that any poet could do the Byron of
Childe Harold over again, but there he is, and with a more
daunting energy!

Women poets, because they are individualists and never
get into groups, never are praised like men poets, who are
natural gangsters. Yet our century is so full of women poets
of quiet distinction that, on the whole, they exceed the
number of men of equal individual talent. Kathleen Raine
(b. 1908) has the hushed music Empson admires but also
darkly riddling thought: as in *In the Beck*, written for her
daughter:

> There is a fish, that quivers in the pool,
> Itself a shadow, but its shadow, clear.
> Catch it again and again, it still is there.
>
> Again the flowing stream, its life keeps pace
> with death – the impulse and the flash of grace
> hiding its stillness, moves, to be motionless.
>
> No net will hold it – always it will return
> when the ripples settle, and the sand –
> It lives unmoved, equated with the stream,
> as flowers are fit for air, man for his dream.

A younger poet, Elizabeth Jennings, b. 1926, has in *Song
at the Beginning of Autumn* a crisper and more dry music but
the same kind of riddle:

> But I am carried back against
> My will into a childhood where
> Autumn is bonfires, marbles, smoke;
> I lean against my window fenced
> From evocations in the air.
> When I said autumn, autumn broke.

Did autumn break into existence, real or remembered? Or
did it break as something that cracks in one's hand? The
marbles are, after a second of thought, marbles that a child
plays with not statues in a formal garden? Why is the poet
carried back 'into a childhood' against her will? The childhood, what we are given of it, seems pleasant. Was the
pleasantness unreal, or is the present so unhappy that

remembering happiness hurts? The reader feels in an odd way more satisfied with the richness of guessing than he could ever be with the flatness of knowing.

Sheila Wingfield, Dowager Countess Powerscourt, b. 1906, has been praised by Yeats, Walter de la Mare, and Herbert Read and, with a passion for travel, is a wonderful watcher of places, including English and Irish villages, and of creatures. But, a chronic but courageous invalid for many years, she can also express wonderfully a defiant persistence:

Poisoned in Search of the Medicine of Immortality

When Hsüang Tsung, great emperor,
Giddy and ill, carried in a litter,
Saw the stars sway,

His conquests and his arguments
And powers, falling into fever with him,
Pulsed their lives away.

Bow to his shade. To be at rest
Is but a dog that sighs and settles: better
The unrelenting day.

Charlotte Mew (1869–1928) was called by Hardy 'the best woman poet of our day', but after a long struggle with poverty, and the following of the grant of a Civil List Pension by the death of a sister whom she had long nursed, she took poison. Unlike Sylvia Plath's, perhaps like many English suicides as compared to American, her act was rational. So were her poems:

Sea Love

Tide be runnin' the great world over:
    'Twas only last June month I mind that we
Was thinkin' the toss and the call in the breast of the lover
    So everlastin' as the sea.

Heer's the same little fishes that sputter and swim,
    Wi' the moon's old glim on the grey, wet sand;
An' him no more to me nor me to him
    Than the wind goin' over my hand.

None of the poems by women I have quoted so far has that plain straightforwardness, for the riddle here needs no verbal trickery or play: it is a sad, familiar one to which we all know the answer.

Stevie Smith (1902–71), perhaps the most interesting person among all recent women poets seems straightforward and is often comical. She was a well-paid office worker till quite late in life. An aunt looked after her and it was only when the aunt fell ill that she learned to cook and house-keep. In her later years, she became a very popular reader on the poetry reading circuit. Her poems were often com-posed in the rhythm of hymn-tunes, and she chanted the hymn-poems in her readings, though she could not sing in tune. Her printed poems are illustrated by comic yet touch-ing drawings, a little, perhaps, like those of a more skilful and delicately minded Thurber. The liking for hymns came from a Protestant Ulster family background, from which also came her mixed attitude to Christianity.

> It is not interesting to see
> How the Christains continually
> Try to separate themselves in vain
> From the doctrine of eternal pain.
>
> They cannot do it,
> They are committed to it,
> Their Lord said it,
> They must believe it . . .

A poem called *Was He Married* argues acutely that a God incapable of suffering cannot either share or understand the feelings of man, though man has invented him to do just these things.

> All human beings should have a medal,
> A god cannot carry it, he is not able.
>
> A god is Man's doll, you ass,
> He makes him up like this on purpose.
>
> He might have made him up worse.
>
> He often has, in the past.

> To choose a god of love, as he did and does,
> Is a little move then?
>
> Yes, it is.
>
> A larger one will be when men
> Love love and hate hate but do not deify them?
>
> It will be a larger one.

As poetry of honest and direct statement, without music, without artifice, this would be hard to beat.

But for Stevie Smith, man, though like the god he invents he has often a passively comic role, suffers like that god (or let us say like Stevie Smith's notion of what a non-existent self-sufficiency would be like if it existed) from profound distance and loneliness. Stevie Smith knows that we can none of us bear the idea of eternal pain but knows also that the sense of loss and lack of purpose is a part of most human lives. What looks like comic clumsiness and social ineptness may be agony. In her cruel moods, the sad is funny: in her kind moods, the funny sad. One of the poems where her signature is firmest is *Not Waving But Drowning*:

> Nobody heard him, the dead man,
> But still he lay moaning:
> I was much further out than you thought
> And not waving but drowning.
>
> Poor chap, he always loved larking
> And now he's dead
> It must have been too cold for him his heart gave way,
> They said.
>
> Oh, no no no, it was too cold always
> (Still the dead one lay moaning)
> I was much too far out all my life
> And not waving but drowning.

I could have mentioned here other good women poets just as in the rest of this section there are some deservedly famous men poets like Walter de la Mare, Andrew Young, Donald Davie, Ted Hughes, Philip Hobsbaum, Thom Gunn, who invite statements of taste (liking or dislike, which good judges could share or disagree with) rather than interpretation. I am concentrating on poets, who seem to me to need a kind of *special* attention.

The sort of poet I have in mind is, for instance, I. A. Richards (1893–1979) who, after making a very distinguished reputation as a critical theorist (*Principles of Literary Criticism, Practical Criticism, Science and Poetry, How to Read A Page*, among others) and in what might be called philosophical semantics (*The Meaning of Meaning* with C. K. Ogden; *Mencius on the Mind*, based partly on a year's teaching in Peking), began in 1958 to publish his own poems. A copious collection, *Internal Colloquies* came out in 1971 and a small selection of new poems in *New and Selected Poems*, 1977.

Richards had been Empson's mentor at Cambridge but his own poems owed nothing to the example of his distinguished pupil. He believed that the poet is a kind of willing and passive medium through which the poem is able to shape itself. Its shape is often that of a riddle but one about its own nature. There is no intention to dazzle or puzzle the reader, but a wish, certainly, to make him aware of life's strangeness. As in *Talking to Himself*:

> 'Morning never tries you till the afternoon.'
>   So Kipling's 'Lullaby'. Not true for me.
>   My dayspring all bewilderment, so slow
>   Until moon toughened me to muddle through.
>
> You will not say you learnt much, late or soon.
>   That's not your way as even you'll agree,
>   Except that you no more pretend to know
>   What sort of ONE it is that talks to you.
>
> One with whom to sup, you need that longer spoon?
>   Or a celestial telling what to be?
>   Or both in one together counselling so
>   That you'll be less unready for what's due?
>   Thus questioned, I
>   May murmur in reply
>   Time was when sunsets hurt. But now
>   They hold my hand and tell me how.

That, ending in unexpected serenity, was published two

years before Richards's death. I quote another which, by its subject matter, was very recent. *Ecclesiastical Polity*, by Richard Hooker, was a late Elizabethan masterpiece which, among other purposes, sought to bring the Puritans into willing membership of the new Church of England, and yet to preserve the Catholic body built on the foundations of Cranmer's Prayer Book, too. Nobody reads it now, nor did it bring internal peace, and I think the seagull in this poem is not to mock Hooker, but to mock his mockers. Plato is quoted at the beginning.

Ecclesiastical Polity

Socrates: Be careful, Crito, and don't say anything you don't really believe . . . So reflect carefully. It is never right to return a wrong or to defend ourselves against a wrong by a threat of retaliation. You will agree to this or not?

> Ten Protestants, off a bus, lined up and shot;
>   Two days before, five Catholics much the same.
>   Poor Churches, dragged back so to former shame,
> Their lessons too well taught to be forgot.

> Pity these murderers, victims committedly
>   Of festering wrong. Before our world was built
>   Its man-trap had foreordained our guilt:
> That Accuser-Judge, that Heaven-Promising Tree.

> Eve's children still will need all 'forward wits',
>   Their utmost skill in spiritual surgery,
>   To clear these cankers, end this agony.

> Beneath the Towers of Exeter yet sits
>   Great Hooker on his throne, in gown and bonnet,
>   An agate-eyed, yellow-legged seagull perched upon it.

Hooker was born near Exeter but, leaving the high position of Master of the Temple, asked for a quiet small parish and was presented with the living of Bishopsbourne in Kent. His great book attacked the Puritan position that only Scripture had authority and asserted the authority, also, of reason and natural law. Attacking Richards's poems, Professor Frank Kermode has described Richards as a surviving Victorian poet archaically preoccupied with faith and doubt. Most readers will find his poem, about irrational violence in Ulster, uncomfortably topical. But if they honestly put themselves in Crito's place and try to answer Socrates's question they will find it very difficult to promise never to avenge an injury and never to protect themselves by threats. Virtue, Socrates is saying, must be heroically self-sacrificing.

Richards seems to me great because profoundly wise. But there are other kinds of greatness. Charles Tomlinson, b. 1927, Reader in Poetry at Bristol, writes poems which are the equivalent of a still life, or of a portrait by Cézanne. If it is not paradoxical, I would call him great at a distance or on a small scale. What one admires is a cool delight and a use of words so that one has the illusion that they are colours, movements, or shapes. Yet the words are not transparent: one admires their own patterns.

Paring the Apple

There are portraits and still-lifes.

And there is paring the apple.

And then? Paring it slowly,
From under cool-yellow
Cold-white emerging. And . . .?

The spring of concentric peel
Unwinding off white,
The blade hidden, dividing.

There are portraits and still-lifes
And the first, because 'human',
Does not excel the second, and
Neither is less weighted
With a human gesture, than paring the apple
With a human stillness.

The cool blade
Severs between coolness, apple-rind
Compelling a recognition.

Here are two of the best early poems of Ted Hughes (born 1930) and Thom Gunn (born 1929). One should note that

Gunn's smooth, erotic and ultimately very frightening poem is crueller than Hughes's poem about natural persistence. Here is Hughes's poem:

Snowdrop

Now is the globe shrunk tight
Round the mouse's dulled wintering heart.
Weasel and crow, as if moulded in brass,
Move through an outer darkness
Not in their right minds,
With the other deaths. She, too, pursues her ends,
Brutal as the stars of this month,
Her pale head heavy as metal.

Every word is right and the last line is startling and masterly.

Here is Gunn's. (It is one of Gunn's earliest experiments in syllabic verse, seven syllables to a line with no attempt either at regular feet or strong Old English or medieval stresses.) The total effect, as here, can be both quiet and very threatening.

The Feel of Hands

The hands explore tentatively,
two small live entities whose shapes
I have to guess at. They touch me
all, with the light of fingertips

testing each surface of each thing
found, timid as kittens with it.
I connect them with amusing
hands I have shaken by daylight.

There is a sudden transition:
They plunge together in a full
formed single fury; they are grown
to cats, hunting without scruple;

they are expert but desperate,
I am in the dark. I wonder
When they grew up. It strikes me that
I do not know whose hands they are.

There is no general agreement about recent poetry. Many

people dislike Ted Hughes's *Crow* poems and feel that there is an unwelcome softness in Thom Gunn's recent poems (he perhaps needed to be cruel, to himself as well as others).

I find the poems of Geoffrey Hill, especially *Mercian Hymns*, the prose poems with an Anglo-Saxon feeling and shape and an underlying autobiographical element, too deliberately baffling. (Hill was born in 1932 and is at present a Professor of English at Leeds.)

On the other hand I very much like *In Memory of Jane Fraser: An Attempted Reparation*, even though there are so many echoes of Wordsworth:

> When snow like sheep lay in the fold
> And winds went begging at each door
> And the far hills were blue with cold,
> And a cold shroud lay on the moor,
>
> She kept the siege. And every day
> We watched her brooding over death
> Like a strong bird above its prey.
> The room filled with the kettle's breath.
>
> Deep curtains glued against the pane
> Sealed time away. Her body froze
> As if to freeze us all and chain
> Creation to a stunned repose.
>
> She died before the world could stir.
> In March the ice unloosed the brook
> And water ruffled the sun's hair,
> And a few sprinkled leaves unshook.

One thinks at first of the Lucy poems:

> A slumber did my spirit heal;
>   I had no human fears;
> She seemed a thing that could not feel
>   The touch of earthly fears.
>
> No motion has she now, no force;
>   She neither hears nor sees;
> Rolled round in earth's diurnal course
>   With rocks and stones and trees.

There are a great many good poems today which have that quiet kind of dignity. Perhaps the poet most admired is Philip Larkin (b. 1922). He is a poet often witty and mocking but often verging, too, on the grand style. *An Arundel Tomb* is a moving poem about love and death, which is an exercise in style, a display of high-born dignity, and yet which somehow deeply moves and expresses profound feeling:

> Time has transfigured them into
> Untruth. The stone fidelity
> They hardly meant has come to be
> Their final blazon, and to prove
> Our almost-instinct almost true:
> What will survive of us is love.

I could go on quoting indefinitely but the quotations, from almost any poem, would express the mood of self-doubt contradicted by a sort of grandeur.

IV A Hesitant Summary

We have seen many styles in this chapter and in the very young poets, whom we have not covered, there is sometimes a strange mixture of plain and difficult styles. The grand style is avoided. But in recent poetry there is an honest plain style that gives one hope for the future.

I have made it clear that Larkin was not a model for poets of his own generation, but he is perhaps the model for a common idea of the poet. Today that means a deliberately phlegmatic writer, who would rather appear churlish than facile in his emotions; and it means also somebody intensely preoccupied with death. We shall nearly all of us, of course, unless we have the luck to be hit by a really serious stroke at home, die in hospital, and it is not a very agreeable prospect – like finding oneself back in barracks again, and knowing this time there is not any discharge. Still, it is a prospect everybody else faces too, and for an older generation like mine not something to fuss about. While one holds on to life, and is free, and reasonably well there are other things to engage one's emotions: ideas, people, weather, swimming as the waves buffet and the pebbles clash at

Aldeburgh: love, the special peace of certain places. I suppose death attracts the middle generation of poets as a limit, rounding up all lives in a democratic curve, the same one. The preoccupation is real but those really held by it do not, I notice, commit suicide.

Two poets of an older generation have recently attracted. or regained, attention partly, I think, because they are not phlegmatic or death-obsessed. C. H. Sisson had a most distinguished career in the Civil Service, and got special leave to do research on administration. What is interesting is that his poetry is not Horatian, the poetry of a good public servant retired to a country peace, but that of a man for whom success can never be consolation. As a young man, he fell hopelessly in love and nothing can ever make up for that loss:

> As my especial mode of thought
> Was finding where I had not sought,
> When Love at last possessed my mind
> It was exactly of that kind.
> There was no exercise of will:
> It came, I saw it and stood still.
> It was a blaze and I was dark.
> The grief that scorched me left the mark.
>
> No money and much time to spend.
> I walked the streets for hours on end
> Then lay upon my iron bed.
> Some have their youth. This was instead.

'This was instead': indeed, why should one ever forgive? Larkin, who shows no signs in his poetry, self-preoccupied as he is, of ever having felt the passion of love, would miss the point: and of this, the sense of that duty to be happy which an endlessly sulky heart prevents one from ever fulfilling:

> *Mortalia*
>
> In the leisurely days which precede my death
> There is nothing I shall not regret. Dorset my hills
> You have the shapes I have missed, the smile
> Of contentment that was never mine.
> Nothing but tears is hidden under your soil.

Basil Bunting, born in 1900, was brought up in a Quaker

public school and went on to the London School of Economics. He was born in Northumberland, whose dialect he uses in some of his poems. He was imprisoned during the First World War as a Conscientious Objector. He spent much of the 1930s in Italy, where he was influenced by Ezra Pound and was later in the United States, where Louis Zukofsky and his theory of Objectivism in poetry had a much deeper effect. He was Persian correspondent for *The Times* after the Second World War, and became an expert translator of classical Middle Eastern poetry. Learned and gifted though he was, England had nothing to offer him, nothing but twelve years of sub-editorship on *The Newcastle Evening Chronicle*. He had married, as his second wife, Sima Alladadian, whom he had met in Persia, and by her had two daughters. Cyril Connolly's praise of his poetry led to widespread reading in America, Presidency of the Poetry Society of London, and an Arts Council Poetry Bursary. The publication of his *Collected Poems* by the Oxford University Press was another mark of public recognition for a poet whose gifts had been recognised warmly by a few admirers but never had a wide public recognition.

He is still found difficult because he thinks of poetry as a kind of music. In the 29th Ode from his second book of odes, for instance, the feeling is intense and personal but conveyed wholly by pitch, pause, and rhythm that pulls back and at the same time intensifies loss and grief. (The date is 1935.)

> Southwind, tell her what
> wont sadden her,
> not how wretched
> I am.
>
> Do you sleep snug these
> long nights or
> know I am lying
> alone.

There are excellent longer poems which Bunting calls sonatas. The best is probably the last, *Briggflats*, which blends Northumbrian history and a man's personal love story. Bunting says it is autobiography but not a record of fact:

The truth of the poem is of another kind.' There is the same
direct mysteriousness as in *Southwind*:

> Fifty years a letter unanswered;
> A visit postponed for fifty years.
>
> She has been with me fifty years.
>
> Starlight quivers. I had day enough.
> For love uninterrupted night.

Contrast with this the following picture of a young and
unpostponed love. ('Girdle' is Northumbrian for the Southern 'griddle'. But the connection of the two words perhaps
emerges unconsciously in the linking of food and sex.)

> My love is young but wise. Oak, applewood,
> her fire is banked with ashes till day.
> The fells reek of her hearth's scent,
> Her girdle is greased with lard;
> hunger is stayed on her settle, lust in her bed.
> Light as spider floss her hair on my cheek which a puff scatters,
> light as a moth her fingers on my thigh.
> We have eaten and loved and the sun is up,
> We have only to sing before parting:
> Good-bye, dear love.
>
> Her scones are greased with fat of fried bacon,
> her blanket comforts my belly like the south.
> We have eaten and loved and the sun is up.
> Goodbye.
>
> Applewood, hard to rive,
> its knots smoulder all day.
> Cobweb hair on the morning,
> A puff would blow it away.
> Rime is crisp on the bent,
> ruts stone-hard, frost spangles fleece . . .

We have suddenly moved from the warm house to the frost
on the bent (the word comes in Scottish ballads, too, 'over
the bent sae broun'). The other kind of meaning is the
meaning of life in a northern setting, life in its historical
sense too (Harold Bloodaxe, King of the Orkneys, King of

Dublin, King of York, but killed in Northumberland). The kind of meaning Bunting is aiming at is not simple and primitive but the musical meaning of a total composition:

> As the player's breath warms the fipple the tone clears.
> It is time to consider how Domenico Scarlatti
> condensed so much music into so few bars
> with never a crabbed turn or congested cadence,
> never a boast or a see-here . . .

An achievement something like Scarlatti's is Bunting's imperfectly in the earlier sonatas, perfectly in *Briggflats* and in his adaptation from a Japanese classic, *Chomei a Toyama*:

> I am shifting rivermist, not to be trusted.
> I do not ask anything extraordinary of myself.
> I like a nap after dinner
> And to see the seasons come round in good order.
>
> Hankering, vexation and apathy,
> That's the run of the world.
> Hankering, vexation, and apathy,
> Keeping a carriage won't cure it.

Bunting responds to the total musical shape of life. His deep music will not translate into prose but his Northumberland, his Japan, his fertile crescent in *The Spoils* are tangible and real. He has no phlegm and no obsession with death.

V The Prospects for Poetry Today

The 1970s have been like the beginning of a new world. The modern period, in the older senses, is over. There are no religious or political preoccupations, but there are young men working seriously on poetry. Just so, in the arts today there is no dominant style, but one has a sense of people thinking and working. Veronica Forrest-Thomson, who died in 1975, was the first poet to exploit the unintendedly poetic side of Wittgenstein:

With the configuration of chess-pieces
limbs describe themselves in rooms
under the angle-poise.
'What is the opposite of brown?
– orange?
– another shade
of brown.'
Limbs of the angle alter,
poise, in rooms:
What is the opposite of me?
– you?
– another shade
of me. . . .

Or a contrasting poem by Robert Wells, and yet not wholly contrasting, since it seems to assert the poetic source by questioning it:

The Unnamed Pool

'Why have you left the path? What makes you stare?'

'This water, pale beneath the darkening air,
Haunts with a look that I must try to forget
Or to meet fully?'
'It's look cannot be met.
There is nothing there, neither a challenge nor a claim.'

'Tell me its name.'
'How can I? It has no name.'

The same sort of skill is to be found in the first volume of Andrew Motion, born in 1952, and so a poet of the second half of the century. In *Past Midnight* what one admires is a sense of the proportionate. That controlled dark feeling belonged also to the first poems, the old English ones, we discovered together. All English poetry has been from the start (it is one of the strong Anglo-Saxon words the Conquest lost for us) a poetry of *mood*; the sense of the discouraging weather of the heart, controlled:

Past midnight now, I look down
from an open window: mist rides
on the river, and streets away

the lights of late travellers
circle, then turn into darkness.

They are all that remain of home,
these familiar signs – although
they explain and confirm nothing,
since they depend on you, and you
ignore them by seeming to sleep.

Your breathing steadies behind me,
drawn in where soon we shall lie
in silence again, not touching,
with only the moon to show us
the lives we found, and cannot keep.

'Although they explain and confirm nothing'. 'Tell me its name.' 'How can I? It has no name.' 'What is the opposite to me. – you? – another shade of me . . . [?]' These young poets are teasing at the same riddle.

Bibliography

Paperback editions are indicated by * at the end of an entry

1 Old English Poetry

EDITIONS OF ORIGINAL TEXTS

The Wanderer, edited by R. F. Leslie (Manchester University Press, 1966)

The Wanderer, edited by T. P. Dunning and A. J. Bliss (Methuen, 1969)* These two editions are complementary to each other.

The Dream of the Rood, edited by Michael Swanton (Manchester University Press, 1970)*

TRANSLATIONS

The Earliest English Poems, translated by Michael Alexander (Penguin Classics, 2nd ed., 1977)*

Anglo-Saxon Poetry, selected and translated by R. K. Gordon (Dent, Everyman edition, 1954)*

Beowulf, a verse translation by Michael Alexander (Penguin Classics, 1973)*

FOR COMPARISON

The Penguin Book of Chinese Verse, translated by Robert Kotewall and Norman L. Smith, edited by A. R. Davis (Penguin, 1962)*

Arthur Waley, *Chinese Poems* (Allen & Unwin, 1946)*

Ezra Pound, 'Cathay', either in *Selected Poems* (Faber, 1975)* or in *Collected Shorter Poems* (Faber, 2nd ed., 1968)

SCHOLARLY COMMENTARY

T. A. Shippey, *Beowulf* (Edward Arnold, 1978)*

Ritchie Girvan, *Beowulf and the Seventh Century: Language and Content*, with a new chapter by Rupert Bruce-Mitford (Methuen, 1971)*

CULTURAL AND HISTORICAL BACKGROUND

Peter Hunter Blair, *An Introduction to Anglo-Saxon England* (Cambridge University Press, 2nd ed., 1977)*

LANGUAGE

Barbara Strang, *A History of English* (Methuen, 1970)* Chapters V to IX.

2 Early Middle English Poetry

Early Middle English Verse and Prose 1155–1300, edited by J. A. W. Bennett and G. V. Smithers, with a glossary by Norman Davis (Clarendon Press, Oxford, 1968)

Medieval English Lyrics: A Critical Anthology, edited with an introduction and notes by R. T. Davies (Faber, 1963)*

LANGUAGE

Barbara Strang, *A History of English* (Methuen, 1970)* Chapters IV and V.

3 The High Middle Ages: I

Fourteenth Century Verse and Prose, edited by Kenneth Sisam (Clarendon Press, Oxford, 1921. Last corrected edition, 1970)*

Selections from John Gower, edited by J. A. W. Bennett (Clarendon Press, Oxford 1968)*

John Gower: Confessio Amantis, translated by Terence Tiller (Penguin Classics, 1963)*

The Complete Works of Geoffrey Chaucer, edited by F. N. Robinson (Oxford University Press, 2nd edition, 1966)*

This is the best complete edition of Chaucer's works. Various parts of *The Canterbury Tales* are published by Cambridge University Press in the series 'Selected Tales from Chaucer', each edited by Maurice Hussey, A. C. Spearing or James Winny (published from 1965 onwards, available in paperback). There is an edition of *Troilus and Criseyde*, edited by John Warrington, revised by Maldwyn Mills, published in Everyman's Library (J. M. Dent, 1974)*

SCHOLARLY COMMENTARY

Maurice Hussey, A. C. Spearing and James Winny, *An Introduction to Chaucer* (Cambridge University Press, 1965)*

S. S. Hussey, *Chaucer: An Introduction* (Methuen, 1971)*

Companion to Chaucer Studies, edited by Beryl Rowland (Oxford University Press, revised edition, 1979)*

Chaucer Criticism, edited by Richard J. Schoeck and Jerome Taylor, 2 volumes: I. *The Canterbury Tales*, II. *Troilus and Criseyde and The Minor Poems* (Notre Dame, Indiana, 1960–1)*

D. Pearsall, *Gower and Lydgate* (British Council, Writers and their Work series, 1969)*

A. C. Spearing, *Criticism and Medieval Poetry* (Edward Arnold, 2nd ed., 1972)

C. S. Lewis, *The Allegory of Love* (Clarendon Press, Oxford, 1936)*

LANGUAGE

Barbara Strang, *A History of English* (Methuen, 1970) Chapter IV, and a glance at Chapter III.

4 The High Middle Ages: II

Medieval English Lyrics: A Critical Anthology, edited by R. T. Davies (Faber, 1963)*

Poetry of the Age of Chaucer, edited by A. C. and J. E. Spearing (Edward Arnold, 1974)*

Piers Plowman, selections edited by Elizabeth Salter and Derek Pearsall (Edward Arnold, 1967)*

Piers The Ploughman, translated by J. T. Goodridge (Penguin Classics, 1959)*

Pearl, Cleanness, Patience, Sir Gawain and the Green Knight, edited by A. C. Cawley and J. J. Anderson (J. M. Dent, Everyman's Libarary, 1962)*

John Barbour, *The Bruce*, edited by W. W. Skeat (Early English Text Society, 1870–89, reprinted with corrections, Scottish Text Society, 1894)

The Bruce: An Epic Poem, translated by Archibald A. H. Douglas (MacLennan, Glasgow, 1964)

SCHOLARLY COMMENTARY

A. C. Spearing, *Criticism and Medieval Poetry* (Edward Arnold, 2nd ed., 1972)

J. Speirs, *Medieval English Poetry: The Non-Chaucerian Tradition* (Faber, 1957) Notorious, however, for its unfounded assumptions of mythic origins.

Elizabeth Salter, *Piers Plowman: An Introduction* (Blackwell, Oxford, 1963)

A. M. Kinghorn, *Medieval Drama* (Evans, 1968)

LANGUAGE

Barbara Strang, *A History of English* (Methuen, 1970)* Chapters IV and III

5 The Fifteenth Century: Scotland Up, England Down

Poets of the English Language, Volume I: *Langland to Spenser* edited by W. H. Auden and Norman Holmes Pearson, with emendations of texts and glosses by E. Talbot Donaldson (The Viking Press, N.Y., 1950; Penguin Books, 1978)*

English Poetry, 1400–1580, edited by William Tydeman (Heinemann, 1970)*

Medieval English Lyrics: A Critical Anthology, edited by R. T. Davies (Faber, 1963)*

A Scots Anthology from the Thirteenth to the Twentieth Century, edited by J. W. Oliver and J. C. Smith (Oliver & Boyd, Edinburgh, 1949)

The Middle Scots Poets, compiled by A. M. Kinghorn (Edward Arnold, 1970)*

A Choice of Scottish Verse 1470–1570, selected by John and Winifred MacQueen (Faber, 1972)*

Selections from Gavin Douglas, edited by David F. C. Coldwell (Clarendon Press, Oxford, 1964)*

William Dunbar: Poems, edited by James Kinsley (Clarendon Press, Oxford, 1958)*

Robert Henryson: Poems, edited by Charles Elliott (Clarendon Press, Oxford, 1963)

John Lydgate: Poems, edited by John Norton-Smith (Clarendon Press, Oxford, 1966)*

John Skelton: Poems, edited by Robert K. Kinsman (Clarendon Press, Oxford, 1969)*

SCHOLARLY COMMENTARY

D. Pearsall, *Gower and Lydgate* (British Council, Writers and their Work series, 1969)*

Scottish Poetry: A Critical Survey, edited by James Kinsley (Cassell, 1955)

A. C. Spearing, *Criticism and Medieval Poetry* (Edward Arnold, 2nd ed., 1972)

LANGUAGE

Barbara Strang, *A History of English* (Methuen, 1970), Chapter III

6 The English Renaissance

Silver Poets of the Sixteenth Century, edited by G. Bullett (J. M. Dent, Everyman's Library, 1947)*
Elizabethan and Jacobean Poets, edited by W. H. Auden and Norman Holmes Pearson (Penguin, 1970)*
Poets of the Elizabethan Age, edited by Geoffrey Hiller (Methuen, 1977)*
Christopher Marlowe: The Complete Poems and Translations, edited by Stephen Orgel (Penguin, 1971)*
William Shakespeare: The Poems, edited by F. T. Prince (Methuen, 1969)*
William Shakespeare: The Sonnets, edited by Martin Seymour Smith (Heinemann, 1967)*
Edmund Spenser: Poetical Works, edited by J. P. Smith, J. Cruikshank and E. de Selincourt (Oxford University Press, 1970)*
Spenser: The Faerie Queene, edited by T. P. Roche, Jr, and C. P. O'Donnell (Penguin, 1978)*
Thomas Wyatt: Collected Poems, edited by Kenneth Muir (Routledge & Kegan Paul, 1949)

7 The Seventeenth Century

Elizabethan and Jacobean Poets, edited by W. H. Auden and Norman Holmes Pearson (Penguin, 1970)*
Silver Poets of the Seventeenth Century, edited by G. Parfitt (J. M. Dent, Everyman's Library, 1975)*
The Metaphysical Poets, edited by Helen Gardner (Penguin, 1969)*
Minor Poets of the Seventeenth Century, edited by R. G. Howarth (J. M. Dent, Everyman's Library, 1930)*
Cavalier Poets: Selected Poems, edited by T. Clayton (Oxford University Press, 1978)*
Penguin Book of Restoration Verse, edited by Harold Love (Penguin, 1968)*

John Donne: Complete English Poems, edited by A. J. Smith (Penguin, 1971)*

Dryden: Poems and Fables, edited by James Kinsley (Oxford University Press, 1970)*

George Herbert: English Poems, edited by C. A. Patrides (J. M. Dent, Everyman's Library, 1974)*

Ben Jonson: Complete Poems, edited by George A. E. Parfitt (Penguin, 1975)*

Andrew Marvell: Complete Poems, edited by E. S. Donno (Penguin, 1972)*

Milton: Poetical Works, edited by Douglas Bush (Oxford University Press, 1966)*

Milton: Complete Poems, edited by John Carey and Alastair Fowler, 2 volumes (Longman, 1968)

Rochester: Poems, edited by David Vieth (Yale University Press, 1962)

8 The Eighteenth Century: Reason, Sensibility, Imagination

English Poetry 1700–1780, edited by David W. Lindsay (J. M. Dent, 1974)

The Oxford Book of Eighteenth-Century Verse, edited by David Nichol Smith (Clarendon Press, Oxford, 1926)

The Penguin Book of Eighteenth-Century Verse, edited by Dennis Davison (Penguin, 1973)*

Silver Poets of the Eighteenth Century, edited by Arthur Pollard (J. M. Dent, Everyman's Library, 1976)

Minor Poets of the Eighteenth Century, edited by Philip Henderson (J. M. Dent, 1930)

Poetry of the Landscape and the Night, edited by Charles Peake (Edward Arnold, 1967)

The Penguin Book of Scottish Verse, edited by Tom Scott (Penguin, 1970)*

William Blake: The Complete Poems, edited by A. Ostriker (Penguin, 1977)*

Robert Burns: Selected Poems, edited by G. S. Fraser (Heinemann, 1968)

S. T. Coleridge: Poetical Works, edited by E. H. Coleridge (Oxford University Press, 1912)*

A Choice of Cowper's Verse, edited by N. Nicholson (Faber, 1975)

George Crabbe: Selection, edited by John Lucas (Longman, 1968)

Gray, Collins and Goldsmith, edited by R. Lonsdale (Longman, 1969)

Samuel Johnson: The Complete English Poems, edited by J. D. Fleeman (Penguin, 1971)*

The Poems of Alexander Pope, edited by John Butt (Methuen, 1963)*

Poems by Allan Ramsay and Robert Fergusson, edited by A. M. Kinghorn and A. Law (Scottish Academic Press, 1974)

Jonathan Swift: Poetical Works, edited by Herbert Davis (Oxford University Press, 1967)

James Thomson: The Seasons and The Castle of Indolence, edited by James Sambrook (Clarendon Press, Oxford, 1972)

William Wordsworth: Poetical Works, edited by T. Hutchinson, revised by E. de Selincourt (Oxford University Press, 1936)*

SCHOLARLY COMMENTARY

Ian Jack, *Augustan Satire*, 1660–1750 (Oxford University Press, 1952)

James Sutherland, *A Preface to Eighteenth-Century Poetry* (Oxford University Press, 1948)

9 The Nineteenth Century: Wordsworth to Hardy

The Penguin Book of Victorian Verse, edited by George Macbeth (Penguin, 1975)*

Victorian Poetry: City of Dreadful Night and other poems, edited by N. Messenger and J. R. Watson (J. M. Dent, 1974)

Poetry of the 'Nineties, edited by R. K. R. Thornton (Penguin, 1970)*

Writing of the 'Nineties, edited by Derek Stanford (J. M. Dent, 1971)

Pre-Raphaelites and Their Circle, edited by Cecil Y. Lang (University of Chicago Press, 1968)

Matthew Arnold: Selected Poems and Prose, edited by Miriam Allott (Dent, 1978)

Thomas Lovell Beddoes: Selected Poems, edited by Judith Higgins (Carcanet Press, 1976)

William Barnes: Poems, edited by Robert Nye (Carcanet Press, 1972)

William Blake: The Complete Poems, edited by A. Ostriker (Penguin, 1977)*

Poetry and Prose of William Blake, edited by G. Keynes (Nonesuch Press, 1927)

Robert Bloomfield; Poems (Gregg International, 1971)

Robert Browning: The Poems (2 volumes), edited by J. Pettigrew (Penguin, 1971)*

Robert Browning: The Ring and the Book, edited by R. Altick (Penguin, 1971)*

Byron: Poetical Works, edited by F. Page, revised by J. D. Jump (Oxford, 1971)*

John Clare: Collected Poems, edited by J. W. and Anne Tibble (J. M. Dent, 1965)

A. H. Clough: Poems, edited by F. L. Mulhauser (Oxford, 1974)

S. T. Coleridge: Poetical Works, edited by E. H. Coleridge (Oxford University Press, 1912)*

John Davidson: Poems (2 volumes), edited by A. Turnbull (Scottish Academic Press, 1973)

Poems of Thomas Hardy, selected by T. R. M. Creighton (Macmillan, 1974)

Selected Poems of Thomas Hood, edited by John Clubbe (Harvard University Press, 1970)

G. M. Hopkins: Poems, edited by W. H. Gardner and N. H. Mackenzie (Oxford University Press, 1967)*

John Keats: The Complete Poems, edited by John Barnard (Penguin, 1973)*

Walter Savage Landor: Poems, edited by Geoffrey Grigson (Centaur, 1971)

Edward Lear: The Complete Nonsense of Edward Lear, edited by J. Holbrook (Faber, 1947)

William Morris: A Choice of Verse, edited by Geoffrey Grigson (Faber, 1969)*

The Reminiscences of Lady Dorothy Nevill (Edward Arnold, 1906)

W. M. Praed: Selected Poems, edited by K. Allott (Routledge & Kegan Paul, 1953)

P. B. Shelley: Poetical Works, edited by T. Hutchinson, revised by G. M. Matthews (Oxford University Press, 1970)*

A Choice of Swinburne's Verse, edited by Robert Nye (Faber, 1973)

Tennyson: Poems and Plays, edited by T. Herbert Warren, revised by Frederick Page (Oxford University Press, 1971)

Wordsworth and Coleridge: Lyrical Ballads, edited by R. L. Brett and A. P. Jones (Methuen, 1963)*

Wordsworth: The Prelude (1805 and 1850 editions), edited by J. C. Maxwell (Penguin, 1971)*

Wordsworth: Poetical Works, edited by T. Hutchinson, revised by E. de Selincourt (Oxford University Press, 1936)*

W. B. Yeats: Collected Poems (Macmillan, 1950)

W. B. Yeats: Selected Poetry, edited by A. N. Jeffares (Pan, 1974)*

10 The Twentieth Century

The Oxford Book of Modern Verse, edited by Philip Larkin (Clarendon Press, Oxford, 1973)

The Faber Book of Modern Verse, edited by Michael Roberts, revised by Donald Hall (Faber, 1976)*

The Penguin Book of Contemporary Verse, edited by Kenneth Allott (Penguin, 1965)*

The Centuries' Poetry (5 volumes), edited by D. Kilham Roberts (Penguin, 1953)*

The Penguin Book of Irish Verse, edited by Brendan Kennelly (Penguin, 1971)*

Contemporary Scottish Verse, edited by Norman MacCaig and Alexander Scott (Calder & Boyars, 1970)*

Georgian Poetry, edited by James Reeves (Penguin, 1962)*

Poetry of the Thirties, edited by Robin Skelton (Penguin, 1964)*

Poetry of the Forties, edited by Robin Skelton (Penguin, 1968)*

An Anthology of Modern Verse 1940–1960, edited by Elizabeth Jennings (Methuen, 1967)

Penguin Poets: The Mid-Century: English Poetry 1940–60, edited by David Wright (Penguin, 1965)*

The New Poetry, edited by A. Alvarez (Penguin, 1974)*

Longer Contemporary Poems, edited by David Wright (Penguin, 1966)*

W. H. Auden: Collected Poems (Faber, 1976)

W. H. Auden: Collected Shorter Poems 1927–57 (Faber, 1969)*

W. H. Auden: Selected Poems, (Penguin, 1970)*

Samuel Beckett: Collected Poems in English and French (John Calder, 1978)*

Alan Bold: Auld Symie, Poems (Akros, 1971)

Ronald Bottrall: Poems 1955–73 (Anvil Poetry Paperbacks, 1975)*

Rupert Brooke: Poetical Works, edited by Sir Geoffrey Keynes (Faber, 1970)*

Basil Bunting: Collected Poems (Oxford University Press, 1978)*

Norman Cameron: Collected Poems 1905–53 (Hogarth Press, 1967)

Roy Campbell: Selected Poetry, edited by J. M. Lalley (Bodley Head, 1968)

Austin Clarke: Selected Poems, edited by Thomas Kinsella (Dolmen Press, 1976)

Stewart Conn: The Burning (Calder, 1978)*

Stewart Conn: Under the Ice (Faber, 1978)*

Keith Douglas: Complete Poems, edited by Desmond Graham (Oxford University Press, 1978)

Douglas Dunn: Terry Street (Faber, 1971)*

Douglas Dunn: Love or Nothing (Faber, 1974)*

Gavin Ewart: No Fool Like an Old Fool (Gollancz, 1976)*

T. S. Eliot: Collected Poems (Faber, 1963)*

T. S. Eliot: Selected Poems (Faber, 1954)*

T. S. Eliot: Selected Prose, edited by Frank Kermode (Faber, 1975)*

William Empson: Collected Poems (Chatto & Windus, 1962)

Robert Gairloch: Two Men and a Blanket, Memoirs of Captivity (Southside Publishers, 1975)

W. S. Graham: The Night-Fishing (Faber, 1955)
W. S. Graham: Malcolm Mooney's Land (Faber, 1970)
W. S. Graham: Implements in Their Places (Faber, 1977)*
Robert Graves: Collected Poems (Cassell, 1975)
Robert Graves: Selected Poems (Penguin, 1968)*
Thom Gunn: Fighting Terms (Faber, 1970)*
Thom Gunn: Jack Straw's Castle (Faber, 1976)
Thom Gunn: Poems 1950–66 (Faber, 1969)*
The Poems of Thomas Hardy, edited by T. R. M. Creighton (Macmillan, 1976)*
Seamus Heaney: Death of a Naturalist (Faber, 1969)*
Seamus Heaney: North (Faber, 1975)*
Seamus Heaney: Field Work (Faber, 1979)*
Ted Hughes: Hawk in the Rain (Faber, 1968)*
Ted Hughes: Selected Poems 1957–67 (Faber, 1972)*
Ted Hughes: Crow (Faber, 1974)*
James Joyce: Poems Penyeach (Faber, 1966)*
Patrick Kavanagh: Collected Poems (Martin, Brian and O'Keeffe, 1973)*
Philip Larkin: The Less Deceived (Marvell Press, 1974)*
Philip Larkin: North Ship (Faber, 1974)*
Philip Larkin: The Whitsun Weddings (Faber, 1971)*
D. H. Lawrence: Complete Poems (2 volumes), edited by V. de Sola Pinto and F. W. Roberts (Heinemann, 1957)
D. H. Lawrence: Selected Poems, edited by James Reeves (Heinemann, 1967)
D. H. Lawrence: Selected Poetry, edited by K. Sagar (Penguin, 1972)*
Alun Lewis: Selected Poetry and Prose (Allen & Unwin, 1966)
C. Day Lewis: Collected Poems (Cape, 1954)*
Michael Longley: Fishing in the Sky (Poet and Printer, 1975)*
Michael Longley: Lares (Poet and Printer, 1972)
Norman MacCaig: Old Maps and New (Selected Poems) (Hogarth Press, 1978)
Norman MacCaig: Tree of Strings (Chatto & Windus, 1977)
Louis MacNiece: Collected Poems (Faber, 1966)
Charlotte Mew: Collected Poems (Faber, 1966)
John Montague: Great Cloak (Dolmen Press, 1978)*
John Montague: Rough Field: Ulster 1961–71 (Dolmen Press, 1975)
Andrew Motion: Pleasure Steamers (Carcanet, 1978)
Edwin Muir: Collected Poems (Faber, 1964)
Edwin Muir: Selected Poems (Faber, 1965)*
Kathleen Raine: Collected Poems (Hamish Hamilton, 1973)
I. A. Richards: New and Selected Poems (Carcanet, 1978)*
Edgell Rickword: Collected Poems and Translations (Carcanet, 1976)

Isaac Rosenberg: Collected Poems, edited by Gordon and Harding Bottomly and Denys Wyatt (Chatto & Windus, 1974)

Siegfried Sassoon: Collected Poems 1908–56 (Faber, 1961)

Edith Sitwell: Collected Poems (Macmillan, 1957)

Edith Sitwell: Selected Poems, edited by John Lehmann (Macmillan, 1965)

Stevie Smith: Selected Poems, edited by James MacGibbon (Penguin, 1978)*

J. Burns Singer: Selected Poems, edited by Anne Cluysenaar (Carcanet, 1977)

C. H. Sisson: In the Trojan Ditch: Collected Poems and Selected Translations (Carcanet, 1974)

Stephen Spender: Collected Poems (Faber, 1966)

Charles Tomlinson: Selected Poems 1951–74 (Oxford University Press, 1978)*

Dylan Thomas: Collected Poems (J. M. Dent, 1977)*

R. S. Thomas: Selected Poems 1946–68 (Hart-Davis, 1968)

R. S. Thomas: Laboratories of the Spirit (Macmillan, 1977)*

Edward Thomas: Collected Poems (Faber, 1949)

Edward Thomas: Selected Poems (Faber, 1964)*

Vernon Watkins: Ballad of the Outer Dark and Other Poems (Enitharmon Press, 1979)*

Robert Wells: Winter's Task (Carcanet Press, 1977)

Sheila Wingfield: Her Storms 1938–77 (Dolmen Press, 1977)

Andrew Young: Complete Poems (Secker & Warburg, 1974)*

W. B. Yeats: Collected Poems (Macmillan, 1950)

W. B. Yeats: Selected Poetry, edited by A. N. Jeffares (Pan, 1974)*

Index

When appropriate, the main discussion(s) of a poet's work occur immediately after his or her name, with minor references following after a semi-colon.